Turbo Pascal® Advanced Techniques

Chris Ohlsen
Gary Stoker

CORPORATION

LEADING COMPUTER KNOWLEDGE

Turbo Pascal®
Advanced Techniques

Library of Congress Catalog Number: 89-50353

ISBN 0-88022-432-0

93 92 91 90 89   8 7 6 5 4 3 2 1

Interpretation of the printing code: the rightmost double-digit number is the year of the book's printing; the rightmost single-digit number, the number of the book's printing. For example, a printing code of 89-4 shows that the fourth printing of the book occurred in 1989.

Turbo Pascal Advanced Techniques is based on Version 5.5 of Turbo Pascal.

DEDICATION

To our wives,
Molly and Teresa,
for their patience and understanding.

Publishing Manager

Allen L. Wyatt, Sr.

Product Development Specialist

Bill Nolan

Project Coordinator

Gregory Croy

Editor

Midge Stoker

Editorial Assistant

Ann K. Taylor

Technical Editor

Chris Land

Indexed by

Sherry Massey

Illustrator

Susan Moore

Cover Design

Dan Armstrong

Book Design and Production

Dan Armstrong
Brad Chinn
David Kline
Lori Lyons
Jennifer Matthews
Jon Ogle
Joe Ramon
Dennis Sheehan

Composed in Garamond and OCRB
by Que Corporation and Precision Printing

ABOUT THE AUTHORS ▼

Chris Ohlsen

C hris Ohlsen received his Bachelor of Science
degree in Computer Science from California State
University, Stanislaus in 1987. Currently, he is a Turbo
Pascal support engineer at Borland International. He
has been using Turbo Pascal since 1983. He has written hundreds of programs in the various versions from
2.0 to 5.5. He has also done programming with Macintosh Turbo Pascal Versions 1.00 to 1.1. Chris has participated in prerelease testing of Versions 4.0, 5.0, and
5.5 of Turbo Pascal. He has also been a frequent user
of CompuServe in the Borland forums.

Gary Stoker

G ary Stoker received his Bachelor of Science
degree in Computer Science from California
State University, Stanislaus in 1987. He currently resides in Santa Cruz, California and is employed by Borland International as a technical support engineer in
the Turbo Pascal group. He has supported Turbo Pascal since Version 3.0 and has participated in prerelease
testing of Versions 4.0 through 5.5. He was also one of
two support engineers who gave primary support to
Turbo Pascal for the Macintosh. Part of his current
duties at Borland include serving as Sysop of the Borland Programming Forum A (BPROGA) on the CompuServe network and supporting Turbo Pascal for the
PC and Turbo Pascal for the Macintosh on this forum.

CONTENT OVERVIEW

Introduction 1

Part I   The Turbo Environment

Chapter 1   Integrated Development Environment   7
Chapter 2   Debugging Turbo Style 35

Part II   Low-Level Turbo Pascal

Chapter 3   Linking with Turbo Assembler 65
Chapter 4   Linking with Turbo C 91
Chapter 5   Inline Code 141
Chapter 6   Text File Device Drivers 173
Chapter 7   Interrupt Service Routines 197

Part III   The Kitchen Sink

Chapter 8   Overlays 231
Chapter 9   Window Management 261
Chapter 10   Graphics Routines 301
Chapter 11   Expanded Memory 343
Chapter 12   Networks 363
Chapter 13   Object-Oriented Programming 389
Chapter 14   Miscellaneous Tricks 417

Index 439

TABLE OF CONTENTS ▼

Introduction 1
    Why We Wrote This Book 1
    What This Book Covers............................. 2

I   The Turbo Environment   ▼

1   Integrated Development Environment.......... 7
    Tips for Installing Turbo Pascal 8
        Installing Turbo Pascal on a Floppy Diskette 8
        Installing Turbo Pascal on Your Hard Disk............. 8
    Keystroke Shortcuts 10
        Using Markers...................................... 10
        Changing Indentation of Blocks of Code.............. 10
        Finding Last Error Position........................... 10
        Working with Multiple Files.......................... 11
        Matching Braces.................................... 11
        Printing Program Listings 12
        Viewing Environment-Set Compiler Directives......... 12
        Enlarging the Cursor 12
    Project Management................................. 13
        Setting Directory Options............................ 13
        Setting Other Options............................... 14
        Establishing Compiler Directives...................... 16
    The Power of Pick Lists.............................. 18
        Understanding the TURBO.PCK File Format 19
    Editing the TURBO.PCK File.......................... 25
        Project Management Summary....................... 30
    Context-Sensitive Help.............................. 30
        IDE Menu Command Help........................... 31
        Editor Help.. 31
        Programming Help.................................. 31
        Error Help... 32
        THELP: Resident Help.............................. 33
    Review 34

2   Debugging Turbo Style 35
    Integrated Debugging............................... 35
        Debugger IDE Parameters........................... 36

Keystrokes for Debugging. 37
Simple Debugging Example 39
Memory Constraints. 41
    Debugging Small Programs 42
    Debugging Large Programs 43
Watches and Breakpoints 43
    Adding and Formatting Watches. 43
    Setting and Using Breakpoints. 46
Call Stack and Evaluate Windows 46
    Using the Call Stack 46
    Using the Evaluate Window. 48
Turbo Debugger 51
Additional Power with Complex Breakpoints. 53
    Watch Window and Inspect Window. 57
Remote Debugging. 59
386 Debugging 61

II   Low-Level Turbo Pascal

3   Linking with Turbo Assembler

3   Linking with Turbo Assembler 65
Restrictions for Linked Assembly Language 66
Entry and Exit Code. 67
Access to Variables. 67
    Using Global Variables. 67
    Using Value Parameters. 71
    Using Variable Parameters 72
    Accessing Parameters and Local Variables. 73
Function Results 75
Assembler and Objects. 76
    Static Objects 76
    Virtual Objects 77
    Virtual Method Tables. 78
    Calling Methods 80
    Writing a Method in Assembler. 81
Turbo Assembler. 81
    Using the ARG Directive. 81
    Using the RETURNS Keyword 82
    Using the LOCAL Directive 83
    Using the .MODEL Directive 84
    Using a Swap Procedure. 84
    Using a String Function. 87
Review 90

4 **Linking with Turbo C** **91**

Restrictions for Linked Object Files 92
Linking with Turbo C Runtime Library 103
Linking Utilities 105

5 **Inline Code** **141**

Assembly Language versus Inline Code 142
Creation of Inline Code 142
Inline Calls 145
Override Operators < and > 148
Jumps from Inline Code 149
Inline Procedure and Functions 151
Parameter Location 152
Returning Function Results 152
Accessing Parameters 153
Accessing Variable and Oversized Parameters 155
Using Variable Identifiers 156
Accessing Variables 157
Referencing Pointer Variables 157
Inline Macros 158
Parameters to Inline Macros 160
Functions as Inline Macros 164
Useful Inline Procedures, Functions, and Macros 166
Cursor Manipulation Routines 166
High and Low Word Returns 169
Flush File Buffer 170
Conclusion 172

6 **Text File Device Drivers** **173**

Simple Device Driver 176
Structure 178
Open Function 178
Close Function 179
Flush Function 179
InOut Function 180
Example Device Drivers 180

7 **Interrupt Service Routines** **197**

What Are Interrupts? 197
Logical Interrupts 198
Hardware Interrupts 198
Software Interrupts 199
Restrictions for Interrupt Service Routines 199

Using the Interrupt Keyword. 200
Setting Up the FAR Call 201
Saving the Old Interrupt Vector 202
Setting the New Interrupt Vector 202
Restoration Process 203
Sample Interrupt Service Routines. 204
Skeleton ISR 205
Print Screen Example 206
Break Handler. 212
Game Example 214
Timer Interrupt 224
Review 227

III The Kitchen Sink

8 Overlays 231

Overlay Buffer. 232
Requirements. 234
Simple Overlay Example 235
Structure and Implementation 239
.OVR File Layout 239
Program Layout 245
Overlay Stubs. 246
Pitfalls and Tricks 246
Common Errors 246
Overlaying Data 250
Keeping an Overlay in Memory. 254
Utilities. 255

9 Window Management 261

Requirements for Windows. 261
Storing Text Under Windows 262
Creating Window Borders 263
Adding Sound 264
Direct Video Access. 264
Determining Current Video Mode 264
Using Video Memory. 265
Window Stack 271
Defining Data Structure. 272
Using Window Stack Operations. 272
Window Frills 274
Drawing Window Borders 274

Putting Titles on Windows. 277
Adding Sound 277
Window Tools Unit 278
Editing Tools 285
Creating a Reverse Video Field 286
Creating the Input Field 287
Processing Characters 289
EditTool Unit 291

10   Graphics Routines. **301**
Device Independence. 306
Data Input in Graphics Mode 310
Printing Graphics Images. 317
BGI Tricks and Tips 326
Understanding Palettes 326
MCGA Palette. 327
EGA Palette 327
VGA Palette 329
Drawing Black on Color 329
SetRGBPalette Procedure 331
Saving and Restoring the BGI Image to Disk 333
BIOS Interface to the BGI. 337
Getting the Current Video Mode 338
GetRGBPalette Procedure. 339
Creating a Gray Scale 339
Using BIOS Interface 340

11   Expanded Memory **343**
Extended Memory 344
Expanded Memory 345
Using EMS 346
Logical and Physical Pages 347
EMS Access Unit 347
Sample EMS Program. 355
Special Considerations. 361

12   Networks **363**
Multiuser Difficulties 363
File Modes 364
Using Files as Semaphores 369
Network Tic-Tac-Toe 371
Record Locking. 379
Conclusion. 386

13   Object-Oriented Programming **389**

    Constructors 390
    The Fail Procedure 391
    Destructors 393
    Causes of Lockups 397
    Sample Object Program 399
    Object-Oriented Points To Ponder 411
    Saving Objects to Disk 412
    Glossary of Object-Oriented Programming Terms 412
    Summary 415

14   Miscellaneous Tricks **417**

    Self-Modifying Code 417
    Comparison of Complex Data Types 421
    Case Statements With Strings 424
    Math Functions 425
    Memory Locations 426
        Clock Ticks 426
        Inter Process Communication Area 426
        Extended Keyboard Address 427
        Keyboard Buffer 427
        PrintScreen 427
        Time-Out Length for Printers 428
    Files and Debugging 428
    Computing a Direct Address 429
    Absolute Disk Read/Write 429
    Patches 431
        Turbo Debugger Include Files Patches 432
            Patch for TPC.EXE 432
            Patch for TURBO.EXE 432
        VGA Mode Patch 433
        Interrupt 60h Overwritten Patch 433
        EGA Graphics Mode Patch 433
    Technical Support 434
        CompuServe Support 434
        Mail Support 435
        Phone Support 435
        Turbo Users Group 436
    Common Problems 436
    Conclusion 437

    Index **439**

Foreword

As professional Turbo Pascal programmers and veterans of our Turbo Pascal Technical Support group, Chris and Gary are uniquely qualified to guide you through the creation of sophisticated application programs. Between them, they have spoken or written to thousands of Turbo Pascal programmers. They have done technical reviews of all the Turbo Pascal documentation and software for the last several versions. And they have participated in design discussions and planning for future versions of Turbo Pascal.

From using Turbo Debugger and the Turbo Pascal integrated development environment (IDE), to writing text file device drivers, interrupt service routines, and mixing assembly language with Pascal, these guys know which tricks work and which don't. Follow them from beginning to end, as they take you from the special tricks of the IDE to a discussion of the object-oriented programming extensions available in Turbo Pascal Version 5.5.

David Intersimone
Director, Developer Relations
Borland International, Inc.

ACKNOWLEDGMENTS ▼

The authors would like to acknowledge Nan Borreson and Allen Wyatt for helping us get this book started. Special thanks to Keith, Jason, Anders, Neil, Rich, Kim, Brian, Michael, and of course everyone else who had their fingers in this mess (whether they know it or not).

TRADEMARK ACKNOWLEDGMENTS ▼

Que Corporation has made every effort to supply trademark information about company names, products, and services mentioned in this book. Trademarks indicated below were derived from various sources. Que Corporation cannot attest to the accuracy of this information.

BIBLIOGRAPHY

Turbo Pascal: Reference Guide, Turbo Pascal: User's Guide, Borland International, Inc. (1988)

Turbo Pascal: OOP Guide, Borland International, Inc. (1989)

Turbo C: Reference Guide, Turbo C: User's Guide, Turbo Debugger: User's Guide, Turbo Assembler: Reference Guide, Borland International, Inc. (1988)

IBM Personal Computer Technical Reference Manual, IBM, Revised Edition (April 1983)

Programmer's Guide to PC & PS/2 Video Systems, Microsoft Press, Richard Wilton (1987)

DOS Programmer's Reference, 2nd Edition, Que Corporation, Terry R. Dettmann, (1988)

Advanced MS DOS Programming, 2nd Edition, Microsoft Press, Ray Duncan, (1988)

Turbo Pascal Solutions, Scott, Foresman, and Company, Jeff Duntemann (1988)

The 8086 Book, Osborne/McGraw-Hill, Russell Rector — George Alexy (1980)

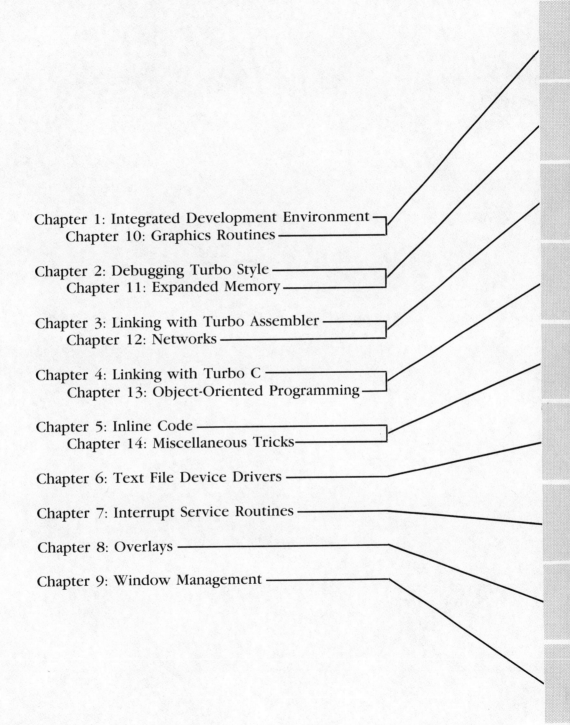

Chapter 1: Integrated Development Environment
    Chapter 10: Graphics Routines

Chapter 2: Debugging Turbo Style
    Chapter 11: Expanded Memory

Chapter 3: Linking with Turbo Assembler
    Chapter 12: Networks

Chapter 4: Linking with Turbo C
    Chapter 13: Object-Oriented Programming

Chapter 5: Inline Code
    Chapter 14: Miscellaneous Tricks

Chapter 6: Text File Device Drivers

Chapter 7: Interrupt Service Routines

Chapter 8: Overlays

Chapter 9: Window Management

Introduction

Turbo Pascal Advanced Techniques was written, as the title suggests, for intermediate and advanced users of Turbo Pascal. To benefit fully from this book, you should be familiar with the theory of computer programming and with the basics of Turbo Pascal. This book focuses on features of the language and the Turbo implementation, of which most people are not fully aware.

Topics discussed include a broad range of features. We not only discuss the many 5.0-specific features of Turbo Pascal—from getting the most out of the development environment, including the new debugging features, to the seldom-understood topics of text file device drivers and using expanded memory—but also we include information about Turbo Pascal Version 5.5. The importance of V5.5 can be summarized in one brief phrase: object-oriented programming. We show how to get the most out of the object-oriented extensions to the Turbo Pascal language.

Why We Wrote This Book

Why would two people who work for Borland International write a book about Turbo Pascal? After pondering the concepts of this book as well as listening to users of Turbo Pascal for a two-year period, we realized that we could provide a great service by tailoring the contents of a book around the questions asked most frequently by Turbo Pascal users. This book is the result of our research. Its topics are aimed at intermediate users—topics not fully understood by the majority of users.

1

One of the best ways to present the topics we discuss is by including many examples. We adhere to this philosophy, as a casual glance through these pages attests. Dozens of useful routines are included. Many of these examples are simple in nature but advanced in theory; such examples are presented in a step-by-step manner.

What This Book Covers

This book is divided into 14 chapter in 3 parts: The Turbo Environment, Low-Level Turbo Pascal, and The Kitchen Sink.

Part I, The Turbo Environment, covers all of the development environments the programmer can use while developing a Turbo Pascal program.

In Chapter 1, which covers the Integrated Development Environment (IDE) that is built around the Turbo Pascal compiler, we explain how to push the environment to its limits by showing you some little-known, but quite powerful, features of the IDE. We also present the context-sensitive help capability, the THelp utility, some Turbo Pascal editor shortcuts, and a utility program to edit the pick list.

Chapter 2 presents the two debugging environments available to Turbo Pascal programmers. Its first section is devoted to the debugger built into the IDE; its second section concentrates on Turbo Debugger. We show how to get the most out of Turbo Debugger by uncovering some powerful, but seldom-used features of the product.

Part II, Low-Level Turbo Pascal, presents links to assembly language, methods for interfacing to Turbo C, text file device drivers, and interrupt service routines. With the information provided, you will be well on your way to getting the most of these features.

Chapter 3 presents a thorough explanation of how to interface routines written with Turbo Assembler into programs written in Turbo Pascal. We explain what Turbo Pascal does before calling an external routine, how to pass parameters to an external routine, and how to write an external function. The examples in this chapter use Turbo Assembler.

Turbo C linking is the subject of Chapter 4. We present examples of linking C code into Turbo, some of the inherent difficulties of linking a module created with a high-level language, and a utility to help tailor the C module for the linking process.

Turbo Pascal provides another form of assembly-language interface: inline code. Inline code, covered in Chapter 5, is machine instruction coded inside one statement. This code can take several forms, all of which are presented in Chapter 5. Also included are many useful routines that can be easily adapted to your programs.

Chapter 6, Text File Device Drivers, explains text file device drivers from the most basic level, so that by the end of the chapter, almost anyone can take advantage of this powerful feature of Turbo Pascal. Included in this chapter is a replacement Crt unit that, when used, supports writes to the graphics screen on color adapters.

Interrupt service routines, known as ISRs, are the topic of Chapter 7. We explain the need for writing ISRs in certain applications as well as the concept behind interrupts. We also explain the restrictions of using some of Turbo Pascal's procedures and functions from within an ISR. We then present, in a step-by-step manner, the process of writing an interrupt service routine.

We entitled Part III The Kitchen Sink when, reviewing our outline, one of us remarked that the section contained "everything but the kitchen sink." This aptly named part includes an in-depth discussion of the overlay manager provided with Turbo Pascal.

For readers familiar with overlays from Turbo Pascal V3.0, we present in Chapter 8 a comparison of the two overlaying systems. We also present the setup requirements for creating an overlayed application and discuss common overlay manager errors. We provide a custom overlay initialization unit and several utility routines to help you better manage your overlays.

Chapter 9, Window Management, presents the background information necessary for developing a window management utility and methods for directly accessing display memory, including ways of avoiding snow on the IBM Color Graphic Adapters. Throughout the chapter, routines that can be combined into a window utility package are presented.

The Borland Graphics Interface (BGI) is discussed in Chapter 10. We show you the basics behind the BGI, as well as the concepts of writing device-independent programs, one of the BGI's strong points. We include a routine to transfer an image created with the BGI to an EPSON or EPSON-compatible printer.

Chapter 11 focuses on utilization of expanded memory from inside a Turbo Pascal program. We explain the concept of expanded memory (known as EMS), steps for accessing pages of EMS memory, and include a unit of EMS routines.

Networking is one of the most complicated programming environments—especially when using Turbo Pascal, because of the lack of built-in network support for the compiler. We do not let this hinder us, as we present in Chapter 12 a collection of utilities to help you create programs that will execute correctly in a networking environment.

Chapter 13 presents the object-oriented programming capabilities that have been added to Turbo Pascal in V5.5. We take the concepts presented in the Turbo Pascal Reference Manual several steps further, presenting the more advanced capabilities of object-oriented programming by including many examples of objects to demonstrate their power and flexibility.

The last chapter of the book includes several tricks and routines that did not quite fit in anywhere else. Chapter 14 presents a number of different programming tricks, from self-modifying code to standard mathematical functions not included in Turbo Pascal. We also discuss the pitfalls of writing code that remains resident—programs known as terminate-and-stay-resident programs (TSRs).

Part I

The Turbo Environment

CHAPTER
1

Integrated Development Environment

Turbo Pascal has made a big difference in the software development world. It made popular the Integrated Development Environment (IDE). Any serious programmer knows that along with programming come errors and bugs. By integrating the compiler with an editor and other useful tools in the IDE, Borland saves developers time.

No longer do you have to do the following:

1. Save the program.

2. Quit the editor.

3. Compile the code.

4. Link the code.

5. Run the program.

Nor, after you find an error in one of steps 3-5, do you have to go back to the editor to fix the problem and start over. If an error occurs while the computer is compiling, linking, or running a program in the IDE, Turbo Pascal highlights the error location in the editor.

To take full advantage of the Integrated Development Environment, you must install Turbo Pascal properly and establish the basic setup for the specific environment in which you want to work. This chapter provides information to help you install Turbo Pascal appropriately for your system,

7

work efficiently in the editor, set up directories and compiler directives for successful project management, and use and modify the pick list feature effectively.

Tips for Installing Turbo Pascal

Turbo Pascal V5.0 and 5.5 come with an excellent installation program that lets you install the program on a floppy diskette or on your hard disk.

Installing Turbo Pascal on a Floppy Diskette

To install Turbo Pascal on a floppy diskette, begin with a formatted, blank, double-sided, double-density diskette. The Turbo Pascal V5.5 installation program for a floppy diskette automatically copies either the Integrated Development Environment compiler or the command-line compiler (TURBO.EXE or TPC.EXE), the Turbo run-time library (TURBO.TPL). When you use the Install Turbo Pascal on a Floppy Drive option of the installation program, the archive files are not copied; this means that Turbo Pascal's graphics files will not be available to you. To access them, you must use the UNPACK.COM program on the TOUR/ONLINE HELP diskette to extract the compressed files from the BGI.ARC file that is on the OOP/DEMOS/BGI/DOC diskette. (Use UNPACK.COM to extract the information from any file that has a .ARC extension on your Turbo Pascal diskettes.)

Installing Turbo Pascal on Your Hard Disk

When you install Turbo Pascal V5.5 to a hard disk, you have two options: Install Turbo Pascal on a Hard Drive and Update Turbo Pascal 4.0 or 5.0 to Turbo Pascal 5.5 on a Hard Drive. After you choose the appropriate option, the installation program displays a window with options for you to indicate where specific Turbo Pascal files will be placed (see fig. 1.1). The default directory is \TP. If you change the Turbo Pascal directory, all of the subdirectory options will automatically reflect the change. We recommend keeping your graphics files in the current directory because the GRAPH.TPU file and .BGI/.CHR files are there. Turbo Pascal expects GRAPH.TPU to be in the current directory or one of the unit directories, but the .BGI/.CHR files are specified by the call to InitGraph if they are not in the current directory.

Fig. 1.1. Install Program.

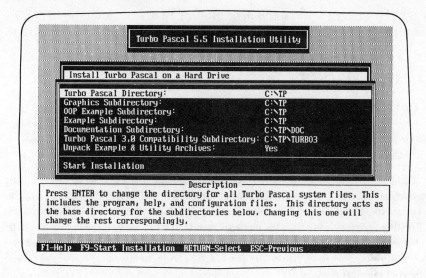

The last option in the hard disk window is Unpack Example & Utility Archives:. Unless you are desperate for disk space, select Yes. If you do not select Yes, you will need to use UNPACK.COM to extract the files you need from the .ARC files.

The installation program for a hard disk creates a TPC.CFG file—a configuration file for the command-line version of the compiler. Unfortunately, the installation program for Version 5.0 does not include an end-of-file marker at the end of the file. This causes problems when Turbo Pascal Compiler is called from programs like TABUILD (a program from the Turbo Pascal Database Toolbox). To fix this problem, load TPC.CFG into the Integrated Development Environment, add a carriage return to the end of the file, and save the modified file.

If you use the Update Turbo Pascal 4.0 to Turbo Pascal 5.0 on a Hard Drive option in Version 5.0's Install program, the installation copies new definitions of keystrokes over your old ones. Unfortunately, this overwrites the Ctrl-F7 keystroke. In Turbo Pascal V4.0, Ctrl-F7 inserts compiler directives into the code. Turbo Pascal V5.0 uses this keystroke to add an expression to the Watch window. To fix this discrepancy, run the TINST program. Select Editor Commands. Find the entry to Insert Options. It is probably set to Ctrl-F7. Move the cursor to this entry, press Enter, and enter Ctrl-O Ctrl-O. This will restore the correct keystroke sequence.

Keystroke Shortcuts

Turbo Pascal User's Guide describes the basics of using the IDE. This section deals with some of the lesser known but very powerful functions.

Using Markers

The Turbo Pascal editor is driven by WordStar-like commands and uses some other WordStar features also. One of these features are *place markers*. Using a place marker in a file is like leaving a book mark in a book; it holds your position in the file. You can use four place markers per file.

Suppose that you are working on a particular procedure in a large unit and you realize that you need to change the procedure's header in the interface section. You can leave a place marker where you are by pressing Ctrl-Kn (where *n* is a number from 0 to 3). Then press Ctrl-PgUp to go to the top of the file, find the procedure's header, and modify it. To return to where you were in the code, press Ctrl-Qn (where *n* is the number used in the set place marker).

Because you can use up to four place markers, you can position them at several important places in your unit/program. For example, you could set one marker at the begin statement of your unit initialization code and another at the implementation statement. Using these markers, you can quickly jump around within your code as you write or modify your unit. You cannot remove place markers, but you can reposition them to a different location in the file.

Changing Indentation of Blocks of Code

Formatted code is much easier to read than straight text. People commonly indent their code to show a block (for example, code between begin...end, after an if, etc). By using the commands to mark a block of text (Ctrl-KB for the starting position and Ctrl-KK for the end), you can change the amount of indentation for the entire marked block. Ctrl-KI will insert one space at the start of each line selected. Ctrl-KU will remove one space from the start of each line.

Finding Last Error Position

The find-last-error-position command, Ctrl-QW, helps you find your place as a place marker does. The only difference is that the compiler sets this place marker for you when an error has occurred. Additionally, the error message that occurred is displayed.

Working with Multiple Files

The pick list allows you to keep your markers active in each file. If you are developing a unit and another block of code (another unit or main program), you can use Alt-F6 to alternate between the two files. Alt-F6 pulls up the last file you were in; if no other files have been edited, Alt-F6 allows you to select a file to work with. We discuss project management, working with multiple files, and pick lists in more detail later in this chapter.

Matching Braces

When you are working with a complex math function, visual verification of a closing parenthesis ()), brace (}), or square bracket (]) is sometimes difficult. To simplify matters, you can use Ctrl-Q[or Ctrl-Q] to identify the matching element in a line of code. Move the cursor to the opening or closing brace in question and use Ctrl-Q[or Ctrl-Q] to find the bracket's partner. The cursor flashes to the matching bracket.

These commands can also help match comment braces. A common programming problem is unmatched comment braces. Consider the following code fragment:

```
1: { This is a comment
2: WriteLn ( 'Hello World!' );
3: { This is another comment }
```

When the compiler generates code for this fragment, the WriteLn statement on line 2 will not be generated. The compiler will read the opening brace on line 1 and then ignore all information until it reads the closing brace at the end of line 3. This can cause strange errors in code when the compiler ignores begin or end statements because they appear to be part of a comment. The most common error that results from this is Error 85 ";" expected on the end of the code. To help track the problem, use the Ctrl-Q commands. With the preceding code fragment, pressing Ctrl-Q[with the cursor resting on the { in line 1 does not move the cursor, which indicates the absence of a closing comment marker.

Printing Program Listings

To get a listing of your program to the printer, you have several choices, ranging from the easy to the roundabout.

The easiest method uses keyboard shortcuts. When you have marked no blocks in the editor (or after you clear them with Ctrl-KH), you can use Ctrl-KP to print the entire file. If you just want to print a section of the code, mark the start of the section with Ctrl-KB and the end with Ctrl-KK to highlight the block. Then when you use Ctrl-KP, only the highlighted block is printed.

A slightly more difficult method of printing the program listing involves saving the program and then pulling down the File menu (Alt-F) and selecting the OS shell option. Then, from the DOS prompt, type **Copy filename.pas prn**, where *filename.pas* is the source code you want printed. This copies the file to the PRN device via DOS.

Finally, the method that provides the best looking printout uses the LISTER.PAS program (provided on the examples diskette in the DEMOS.ARC file). This program does a lot for you. For example, it can expand include files for you so that you have only one program listing. Additionally, it will skip over page perforations. To use it, you must save your work, load LISTER.PAS into the compiler, and then run it.

Viewing Environment-Set Compiler Directives

Sometimes you will find it useful to see what compiler directives are set in the IDE. (We discuss compiler directives later in this chapter.) Use Ctrl-OO to insert the settings from the IDE at the top of your current file. Referring to this new listing of information can help you determine why something is or is not happening as you expect. For example, you can check to see whether you have enabled floating-point emulation.

Enlarging the Cursor

Some people find the cursor that automatically appears in the Turbo Pascal editor hard to see because it is too small. Listing 1.1 is a patch you can use only with Turbo Pascal Versions 5.0 and 5.5 to modify the compiler, changing the cursor from an underline cursor to a block cursor.

Listing 1.1. *Block cursor patch.*

```
Program EnvBlockCursor;
var
  F : file of byte;
  B : byte;
begin
  Assign(F,'TURBO.EXE');
  Reset(F);
  if FileSize(F) = 156321 then        {version 5.5}
  begin
    Seek(F,$E085);
    B := $EB;
    Write(F,B);
  end
  else
  if FileSize(F) = 149793 then
  begin
    Seek(F,$DB0A);
    B := $EB;
    Write(F,B);
  end
  else
    Writeln('Unknown version of Turbo');
  Close(F);
end.
```

This program seeks a location in the compiler and changes a value to modify the cursor size. Simply enter this program and run it. It will open the TURBO.EXE, verify that it is Version 5.0 or Version 5.5, and make the patch. Please make sure that you do this only to a backup copy of the software. Never modify your original copy.

Project Management

Turbo Pascal's directory options and pick lists allow easy project management. If you have a hard disk with sufficient space on it, you can have several different, independent projects available at one time.

Setting Directory Options

Turbo Pascal's configuration files contain many optional settings, including the following:

❑ Turbo directory

❑ EXE and TPU directory

❑ Include directories

❑ Unit directories

❑ Object directories

Setting directories is vital to project management. Several different directories can be set. The installation program will set the Turbo directory and Unit directories to the values you selected in the installation process. As you become more comfortable with Turbo and start making new directories, you can change these settings.

The Turbo directory is where Turbo Pascal looks for the TURBO.HLP file (the context-sensitive help file discussed in the following section). Also, if Turbo Pascal does not find a configuration file (TURBO.TP) in the current directory, it looks in the Turbo directory.

The EXE and TPU directory determines where the .EXE, .TPU, and .MAP files are to be placed. If this option is empty, the files will be placed where the source code is. The .MAP file will only be generated if the Options/Linker/Map file selection is set.

Include directories are where the compiler searches for include files. You can specify multiple directories by entering several names and separating them with semicolons (;). Turbo Pascal searches the current directory first and then the directories listed here.

Unit directories and object directories are where the compiler looks for unit files (.TPU) and object files (.OBJ). As you build tools, you will probably want to keep them in general directories. As with the include directories option, you can specify multiple unit directories and object directories by entering several names and separating them with semicolons (;).

Using these directory options, you can place your commonly used units, object code, and include files into specified directories. This way, you will not have to clutter your specific project directories with miscellaneous files.

Setting Other Options

The Turbo Pascal IDE lets you save your options in a file. This can be useful when you want set options for specific projects only.

Suppose, for example, that you are working on a package to manipulate matrices and do operations on those matrixes. To get the best possible values from that package, you would probably want to use the floating-point data type Extended. Therefore, you would want the numeric coprocessing compiler directive enabled. You would probably want to enable floating-point emulation also, for people who do not have a coprocessor. If the rest of the projects you are working on do not require the floating-point data type, it is wasteful to have the compiler directive enabled while you are working on them because the floating-point routines and the emulation may take up extra code space if they are not removed by the smart linker.

To work with different sets of compiler directives, first force the compiler directives into the code to satisfy any work you are doing with files in your current directory.

To change the files on a global level, change the environment's compiler settings:

1. Change to the directory of the project.

2. Load Turbo Pascal.

3. Change the environment settings to fit the project.

4. Pull down the Options window and specify Save Options. When specifying the name of the file, include the current directory. If the name of the file that you specify is TURBO.TP, Turbo Pascal automatically loads that file at start-up.

Turbo Pascal looks in the current directory for the TURBO.TP file. If this file is not found in the current directory, Turbo searches the directory in which it found the TURBO.EXE file. If the file is not found there, Turbo Pascal uses the default settings within TURBO.EXE.

You will probably want to set the following options in the TURBO.EXE file from the Options/Environment window of the TINST program:

☐ Enable Config auto save to automatically save any changes you make to the IDE. This way, if you change a compiler directive to reflect some new debugging you want to try, it will be saved to the configuration on disk.

☐ Enable Edit auto save to automatically save your text each time you quit the IDE or run a program. You may think that this is not important, but how many times have you lost changes made to a program by locking up the machine? This prevents you from having to input the changes again.

Establishing Compiler Directives

The following compiler directives are those you should set during development of a program. The directives should probably be set within your code so that they will not change any other projects that you are working on.

Debug Information: The {$D+} directive should always be on during the development of your program. This will allow you to step through the programs that you are writing with either the integrated debugger or Turbo Debugger. Additionally, with this compiler directive on, the compiler will position you at the error location if an error has occurred.

Emulation: Enabling emulation ({$E+}) is generally a good idea. The reason is that the code that the compiler generates can not always backtrack through pure 80x87 code to determine where an error occurred. So if you are getting errors that the compiler cannot find the position of in your code, use the emulation package. The error message that the compiler will display is typically Cannot find run-time error location. Just enabling emulation does not mean it will be used. If your machine has a coprocessor, you must quit Turbo (do not do an OS Shell) and set a DOS environment variable as follows:

```
SET 87=n
```

then reload Turbo Pascal and run the program. This will force the program to use the emulation package to determine the error location. The emulation package can sometimes locate an error that the 80x87 routines could not.

Force Far Calls: Using the Force Far Calls ({$F+/-}) compiler directive is tricky because it can cause problems in some contexts when it is enabled and in other contexts when it is not enabled. When you specify {$F+}, you will have problems if you are using assembly routines that are linked as near calls. For example, the BINED unit that comes with the Turbo Pascal Editor Toolbox provides the program with a great editor that uses only 15K of code; but if the BINED unit is compiled with Force Far Calls enabled, the routines will not work. On the other hand, if you are working with overlays, all blocks of code should be defined with Force Far Calls enabled due to unique conditions of the procedure stack.

Input/Output Checking: You should always have {$I+} set in your programs unless you are specifically checking the IOResult function for error codes. This is vital to your programs. The {$I+/-} compiler directive is set active by default and should remain that way unless you are absolutely positive that any error condition that can occur will be trapped by your program. This is extremely important due to the difficulty of finding I/O errors. Turbo Pascal resets the IOResult function to a zero value after calling it once, so the following roundabout method is needed to track I/O errors: after every I/O action, the IOResult function should be called and the function result assigned to another variable. That variable should be consulted to determine what error, if any, occurred.

Local Symbol Information: The Local Symbol Information compiler directive should be on ({$L+}) to complement the Debug Information compiler directive. This can be useful when you are tracing through a program and want to see what a procedure's local variables contain. Without Local Symbol Information on, the debugger will know nothing about any local procedure/function variables. If your program is getting large and you need to cut back on memory usage during compilation, you can disable this directive to save memory.

Range Checking: Of all the compiler directives to have enabled, the Range Checking directive is the most important. By default, range checking is not enabled ({$R-}), which can create all sorts of problems. Suppose that you have a variable defined as an array from 1 to 10. With range checking disabled, you can access that array with any index element you want (for example, MyVar [32000], MyVar [-1000], etc.). The locations that the compiler tries to access may not be within the data segment, and even if they were, they are definitely not within the bounds of a 10-element array. Even if you are not working with arrays, you should enable range checking because strings are arrays also. Turbo Pascal's default for range checking is off because of speed and size considerations. You can turn the directive off when your program is bug-free and ready to be optimized. Additionally, range checking enabled will flag an error if you make a call to a virtual object's method without first calling a constructor. This may not make sense until you understand what objects are and how they work. But until then, it is a good idea to keep this directive enabled.

Stack-Overflow Checking: Enable the {$S+} compiler directive. This will allow you to determine whether your program contains recursions to many levels and fills the stack. To fix the problem, you can step through the program and use the Call Stack feature of the debugger to find what procedures are active on the stack. If those procedures are behaving properly, your stack may need to be increased by using the Memory Allocation Size compiler directive parameter ({$M}).

Var-String Checking: Enabling the Var-String Checking directive ({$V+}) is important for the same reason the Range Checking directive is important. It allows you to overwrite memory without any complaint from the compiler. This directive ensures that strings of the correct length are passed to routines that expect a string of a specific length. For example, passing a string of length 5 to a routine expecting a string of length 50 would create a problem. The routine could try to set the string equal to some string length greater than 5, which would create the problem that the memory being assigned this larger string is not actually allocated to the string.

The Power of Pick Lists

One powerful feature for project management the IDE provides is the *pick list*, which is a list of the eight files you have edited most recently in the current editing session. In combination with the pick file, the pick list can be useful. The pick file is a file maintained by Turbo that contains information about the files in the pick list.

The pick list contains the following information about the nine files you were editing most recently: the last cursor position, the marked block, any place markers you used, your last global search/replace command, and the order in which the files were last used. With the pick list, you can switch from one file to another and retain all the information about where you were in each file (up to eight files). The Turbo Pascal editor builds the pick list as you continue through your editing session. Each time you open a new file, the current file position and other information is saved in the pick list. You can then reopen one of the files from the list by using the hot key (Alt-F3) or by pulling down the File menu and selecting Pick.

In addition to the editing information, the pick list keeps track of the files in the order in which you used them, with the most recently used files near the top, the older ones near the bottom. If you are working with more than nine files, the least recently used scrolls off the pick list, but the more recently used files remain available.

The Integrated Development Environment allows you to choose to save the pick list to disk (to the default file TURBO.PCK). When Turbo Pascal is being loaded, if the TURBO.PCK file is found in the current directory, the IDE loads the file at the top of the list into the editor and places the cursor at the last location. If the file is not in the current directory, the TURBO.EXE directory is searched next.

The TURBO.PCK file is a great help in project management. By having a TURBO.PCK file in each of your project directories, you can track where you were in each file, track your last search commands, keep your marked blocks, track what files you were using and what the last block read/write file was.

Understanding the TURBO.PCK File Format

Table 1.1 designates the format of the TURBO.PCK file. In this table, *location* refers to the absolute byte offset into the file (including two bytes for each carriage-return and line-feed combination).

Table 1.1. *Pick List Offsets*

Offset	Description
39 - 40	1
41 - 42	SizeOf (PickFiles) = 738 bytes
43 - 44	Location of the cursor (file #1)
45 - 124	Path and name of file #1
125 - 126	Location of the cursor (file #2)
127 - 206	Path and name of file #2
207 - 208	Location of the cursor (file #3)
209 - 288	Path and name of file #3
289 - 290	Location of the cursor (file #4)
291 - 370	Path and name of file #4
371 - 372	Location of the cursor (file #5)
373 - 452	Path and name of file #5
453 - 454	Location of the cursor (file #6)
455 - 534	Path and name of file #6
535 - 536	Location of the cursor (file #7)
537 - 616	Path and name of file #7
617 - 618	Location of the cursor (file #8)
619 - 698	Path and name of file #8
699 - 700	Location of the cursor (file #9)
701 - 780	Path and name of file #9
+ -- +	
781 - 782	2

Table 1.1 continues

Table 1.1 *continued*

Offset	Description
783 - 784	SizeOf (Linked PickList) = 18 bytes
785 - 786	Linked list of order of Pick List entries (file #1)
787 - 788	Linked list of order of Pick List entries (file #2)
789 - 790	Linked list of order of Pick List entries (file #3)
791 - 792	Linked list of order of Pick List entries (file #4)
793 - 794	Linked list of order of Pick List entries (file #5)
795 - 796	Linked list of order of Pick List entries (file #6)
797 - 798	Linked list of order of Pick List entries (file #7)
799 - 800	Linked list of order of Pick List entries (file #8)
801 - 802	Linked list of order of Pick List entries (file #9)

```
+ ------------------------------------------------------------------------------- +
```

Offset	Description
803 - 804	3
805 - 806	SizeOf Edit Options (1st block) = 153 bytes
807	X position of text file in window (file #1)
808 - 809	Location of window position (1,1) (file #1)
810 - 811	Location of cursor in X position (file #1)
812 - 813	Location of marker 0 (file #1)
814 - 815	Location of marker 1 (file #1)
816 - 817	Location of marker 2 (file #1)
818 - 819	Location of marker 3 (file #1)
820 - 821	Location of start marked block (file #1)
822 - 823	Location of end mark block (file #1)
824	X position of text file in window (file #2)
825 - 826	Location of window position (1,1) (file #2)
827 - 828	Location of cursor in X position (file #2)
829 - 830	Location of marker 0 (file #2)
831 - 832	Location of marker 1 (file #2)
833 - 834	Location of marker 2 (file #2)
835 - 836	Location of marker 3 (file #2)
837 - 838	Location of start marked block (file #2)
839 - 840	Location of end mark block (file #2)
841	X position of text file in window (file #3)
842 - 843	Location of window position (1,1) (file #3)
844 - 845	Location of cursor in X position (file #3)
846 - 847	Location of marker 0 (file #3)
848 - 849	Location of marker 1 (file #3)
850 - 851	Location of marker 2 (file #3)
852 - 853	Location of marker 3 (file #3)

Offset	Description	
854 - 855	Location of start marked block	(file #3)
856 - 857	Location of end mark block	(file #3)
858	X position of text file in window	(file #4)
859 - 860	Location of window position (1,1)	(file #4)
861 - 862	Location of cursor in X position	(file #4)
863 - 864	Location of marker 0	(file #4)
865 - 866	Location of marker 1	(file #4)
867 - 868	Location of marker 2	(file #4)
869 - 870	Location of marker 3	(file #4)
871 - 872	Location of start marked block	(file #4)
873 - 874	Location of end mark block	(file #4)
875	X position of text file in window	(file #5)
876 - 877	Location of window position (1,1)	(file #5)
878 - 879	Location of cursor in X position	(file #5)
880 - 881	Location of marker 0	(file #5)
882 - 883	Location of marker 1	(file #5)
884 - 885	Location of marker 2	(file #5)
886 - 887	Location of marker 3	(file #5)
888 - 889	Location of start marked block	(file #5)
890 - 891	Location of end mark block	(file #5)
892	X position of text file in window	(file #6)
893 - 894	Location of window position (1,1)	(file #6)
895 - 896	Location of cursor in X position	(file #6)
897 - 898	Location of marker 0	(file #6)
899 - 900	Location of marker 1	(file #6)
901 - 902	Location of marker 2	(file #6)
903 - 904	Location of marker 3	(file #6)
905 - 906	Location of start marked block	(file #6)
907 - 908	Location of end mark block	(file #6)
909	X position of text file in window	(file #7)
910 - 911	Location of window position (1,1)	(file #7)
912 - 913	Location of cursor in X position	(file #7)
914 - 915	Location of marker 0	(file #7)
916 - 917	Location of marker 1	(file #7)
918 - 919	Location of marker 2	(file #7)
920 - 921	Location of marker 3	(file #7)
922 - 923	Location of start marked block	(file #7)
924 - 925	Location of end mark block	(file #7)
926	X position of text file in window	(file #8)
927 - 928	Location of window position (1,1)	(file #8)
929 - 930	Location of cursor in X position	(file #8)

Table 1.1 continues

Table 1.1 *continued*

Offset	Description	
931 - 932	Location of marker 0	(file #8)
933 - 934	Location of marker 1	(file #8)
935 - 936	Location of marker 2	(file #8)
937 - 938	Location of marker 3	(file #8)
939 - 940	Location of start marked block	(file #8)
941 - 942	Location of end mark block	(file #8)
943	X position of text file in window	(file #9)
944 - 945	Location of window position (1,1)	(file #9)
946 - 947	Column of cursor position	(file #9)
948 - 949	Location of marker 0	(file #9)
950 - 951	Location of marker 1	(file #9)
952 - 953	Location of marker 2	(file #9)
954 - 955	Location of marker 3	(file #9)
956 - 957	Location of start marked block	(file #9)
958 - 959	Location of end mark block	(file #9)

```
+ ------------------------------------------------------------------------- +
```

Offset	Description	
960 - 961	4	
962 - 963	SizeOf Edit Options (2nd Block) = 54 bytes	
964 - 965	Block Status	(file #1)
966 - 969	Date/Time Stamp	(file #1)
970 - 971	Block Status	(file #2)
972 - 975	Date/Time Stamp	(file #2)
976 - 977	Block Status	(file #3)
978 - 981	Date/Time Stamp	(file #3)
982 - 983	Block Status	(file #4)
984 - 987	Date/Time Stamp	(file #4)
988 - 989	Block Status	(file #5)
990 - 993	Date/Time Stamp	(file #5)
994 - 995	Block Status	(file #6)
996 - 999	Date/Time Stamp	(file #6)
1000 - 1001	Block Status	(file #7)
1002 - 1005	Date/Time Stamp	(file #7)
1006 - 1007	Block Status	(file #8)
1008 - 1011	Date/Time Stamp	(file #8)
1012 - 1013	Block Status	(file #9)
1014 - 1017	Date/Time Stamp	(file #9)

Offset	Description

+ --- +

1018 - 1019	100
1020 - 1021	SizeOf (Search Options) = 12 bytes
1022	Number of Search Options = 10 bytes
1023	Number of selected Search/Replace options
1024 - 1033	Search/Replace options

+ --- +

1034 - 1035	101
1036 - 1037	SizeOf (Search Flags) = 1 byte
1038	Search Flags

+ --- +

1039 - 1040	102
1041 - 1042	SizeOf (Search String) = 32 bytes
1043	Length of Search String
1044 - 1074	Search String (Null terminated)

+ --- +

1075 - 1076	103
1077 - 1078	SizeOf (Replace String) = 32 bytes
1079	Length of Replace string
1080 - 1110	Replace String (Null terminated)

+ --- +

1111 - 1112	104
1113 - 1114	SizeOf (Block file name) = 80
1115 - 1194	Block file name

+ --- +

1195 - 1196	65535
1197 - 1198	SizeOf (End of file) = 2
1199 - 1200	End of file char (ASCII 26)

Within the TURBO.PCK file, there are several sections, separated by lines that look like this: +-------+. Each section begins with a unique number. Following this number is the size of the block that follows. The information that is stored for each file is stored as an array of records.

Section 1 contains the path and file name of each file on the pick list. Additionally, it contains the current cursor position as an offset into the file. When we mention offset into the file, or location, we refer to the byte count offset into the file. Each character counts as one byte; a carriage-return and line-feed combination counts as two bytes.

Section 2 stores the information that controls the order in which the files are displayed on the pick list. Each time you select a file, it moves to the top of the pick list.

Section 3 stores editor information for each of the files on the pick list. The first field in each record in section 3 contains the X position of the text file in the window. The second field contains the byte offset within the file at which the character in the window position (1,1) is stored. The column at which the cursor is currently located is indicated in the third field. The next four fields contain the byte offset within the file of the four place markers. The last two fields store the byte offset in the file of the begin block and end block markers, respectively.

Section 4 holds two pieces of information about each file: the status of the marked block and a date/time stamp.

Section 100 stores the search options. The first field indicates that up to 10 characters can be input. The next field indicates how many options the user has selected. The last field is an array of the characters that were actually selected.

Section 101 contains one byte that holds the search flags.

Section 102 stores the string for searching in a *search* (Ctrl-QF) or *search and replace* (Ctrl-QA). The length of the string and the actual null-terminated string are stored here.

Section 103 contains the *replace* string. The length and null-terminated string are stored together here.

Section 104 contains the name of the file specified by a *Block Read* (Ctrl-KR) or *Block Write* (Ctrl-KW). Any time a block has been marked using Ctrl-KB and Ctrl-KK, you can write the block to disk. You can also read a file from disk into the editor. This field holds the name of the last file accessed.

Section 65535 contains an end-of-file character, ASCII (26), to indicate the end of the TURBO.PCK file.

Editing the TURBO.PCK File

One flaw that many people have discovered in the IDE is the absence of a way to delete files from the TURBO.PCK files. If you are organized, it can be disconcerting to have a file NONAME.PAS in your project's pick list. The program developed in this section allows you to do some simple editing of the pick file. The program as presented here only lets you delete files from the pick file, but with the format of the file shown in the previous section, you could also modify the program to edit whatever you want.

The first thing to do in the program for editing the TURBO.PCK file is define some data structures (based on the information provided in table 1.2).

For section 1, first define the record to contain each file's information. Next, define an array of nine of these elements.

```
NameRecord = Record
                CursorPos : Word;
                PickName : Array [1..80] of Char;
             End;
NameArray  = Record
                num  : Word;
                size : Word;
                ar   : Array [1..9] of NameRecord
             End;
```

For section 2, simply define an array of nine words. Each of these words contains a particular entry position for the file.

```
FileOrder = Record
               num  : Word;
               size : Word;
               ar   : Array [1..9] of Word;
            End;
```

Section 3 is a record that contains more information than the others. It will have to contain all of the editor information about the position of the file, markers, and the marked block.

```
EditInfo  = Record
               ScreenOffset : Byte;
               UpLeftOffset : Word;
               CursorColumn : Word;
               PlaceMarkers : Array [1..4] of Word;
               StartOfBlock : Word;
               EndOfBlock   : Word;
            End;
```

```
EditArray = Record
               num  : Word
               size : Word;
               ar   : Array [1..9] of EditInfo;
            End;
```

The next section contains the status of the marked block and the date/time stamp. This is a simple record from which you make a nine-element array.

```
BlockInfo  = Record
                StatusOfBlock : Word;
                DateTimeStamp : LongInt;
             End;
BlockArray = Record
                num  : Word;
                size : Word;
                ar   : Array [1..9] of BlockInfo;
             End;
```

The remaining sections do not need to be modified to adding or deleting files from the pick list.

Listing 1.2 shows the PickEdit program.

Listing 1.2. PickEdit program.

```
Program PickEdit;

Uses
  Crt;

Type
  NameRecord  = Record
                   CursorPos : Word;
                   PickName  : Array [1..80] of Char;
                End;
  NameArray   = Record
                   num  : Word;
                   size : Word;
                   ar   : Array [1..9] of NameRecord
                End;
  FileOrder   = Record
                   num  : Word;
                   size : Word;
                   ar   :  Array [1..9] of Word;
                End;
  EditInfo    = Record
                   ScreenOffset : Byte;
                   UpLeftOffset : Word;
                   CursorColumn : Word;
```

```
                        PlaceMarkers : Array [1..4] of Word;
                        StartOfBlock : Word;
                        EndOfBlock   : Word;
                      End;
         EditArray    = Record
                        num  : Word;
                        size : Word;
                        ar   : Array [1..9] of EditInfo;
                      End;
         BlockInfo    = Record
                         StatusOfBlock : Word;
                         DateTimeStamp : LongInt;
                      End;
         BlockArray   = Record
                        num  : Word;
                        size : Word;
                        ar   : Array [1..9] of BlockInfo;
                      End;
         PickItems    = Record
                        one   : NameArray;
                        two   : FileOrder;
                        three : EditArray;
                        four  : BlockArray;
                      End;

Var
  pf : File;
  pl : PickItems;
  nm : Byte;

Function GetChoice : Byte;
{ This function will get the correct key press. It handles  }
{ 0..9 and Q to quit and ESC to abort. A byte value for the }
{ key is returned.                                          }
Var
  ch : char;
Begin
  Repeat
    ch := Upcase ( ReadKey );
  Until ( ch in ['1'..'9','Q',#27] ); { Check if key is ok }
  if ( ch = 'Q' ) Then                { If QUIT key is pressed }
    GetChoice := 0
  else
  if ( ch = #27 ) Then                { If ABORT key is pressed }
    GetChoice := $FF
  else
    GetChoice := Ord ( ch ) - Ord ( '1' ) + 1;
End;
```

Listing 1.2 continues

Listing 1.2 continued

```
Procedure ShowPick;
{ This procedure will display the names of the files in the pick }
{ list to the screen based on their order in the list.          }
Var
  loop,
  entry : Word;
  s : string;
Begin
  ClrScr;
  For loop := 1 To 9 Do
  Begin
    entry := pl.Two.Ar[loop] + 1;
    Write ( loop, '. [ ', entry, '[ ');
    s := pl.One.Ar[entry].PickName;
    s[0] := chr ( Pos ( #0,s ) - 1);
    WriteLn ( s );
  End;
End;


Procedure ReadPickFile;
{ This file opens the TURBO.PCK file and reads the pertinent }
{ information.                                               }
Begin
  Assign ( pf, 'TURBO.PCK' );
  Reset ( pf, 1 );
  Seek ( pf, 39 );                { Seek to start of information }
  BlockRead ( pf, pl, SizeOf ( pl ) );
End;


Procedure DeletePick ( b : Byte );
Var
  i,
  tmp : Word;
Begin
  tmp := pl.Two.Ar[b];            { Store array list info }
  for i := b + 1 to 9 do          { Delete item from array list }
    pl.Two.Ar[i-1] := pl.Two.Ar[i];
  pl.Two.Ar[9] := 9;
  b := tmp + 1;
  For i := 1 to 9 do              { Decrement elements in array list }
    If ( pl.Two.Ar[i] > tmp ) Then
      Dec ( pl.Two.Ar[i] );
  For i := b + 1 To 9 Do          { Reorganize the list to fill the }
  Begin                           { empty space in.                 }
    pl.One.Ar[i-1]   := pl.One.Ar[i];
    pl.Three.Ar[i-1] := pl.Three.Ar[i];
    pl.Four.Ar[i-1]  := pl.Four.Ar[i];
    FillChar ( pl.One.Ar[i], SizeOf ( pl.One.Ar[i] ), #0 );
```

```
      FillChar ( pl.Three.Ar[i], SizeOf ( pl.Three.Ar[i] ), #0 );
      FillChar (  pl.Four.Ar[i], SizeOf ( pl.Four.Ar[i] ), #0 );
    End;
    If ( b = 9 ) Then
    Begin
      FillChar ( pl.One.Ar[9], SizeOf ( pl.One.Ar[9] ), #0; )
      FillChar ( pl.Three.Ar[9], SizeOf ( pl.Three.Ar[9] ), #0 );
      FillChar ( pl.Four.Ar[9], SizeOf ( pl.Four.Ar[9] ), #0 );
    End;
End;

Procedure WritePickFile;
{ This procedure will update the TURBO.PCK file on the disk. }
Begin
  Seek ( pf, 39 );
  BlockWrite ( pf, pl, SizeOf ( pl ) );
End;

Begin
  ReadPickFile;
  Repeat
    ShowPick;
    Write ( 'Enter the number of file to delete, "Q" to quit
    or ESC to abort.' );
    nm := GetChoice;
    If ( nm > 0 ) AND ( nm < $FF ) Then
      DeletePick ( nm );
  Until ( nm = 0 ) OR ( nm = $FF );
  If ( nm < $FF ) Then
    WritePickFile;
  Close ( pf );
End.
```

The PickEdit program is quite simple. The data is read from the pick file at the start. A loop is entered where the file to delete is selected. From that loop, you can either quit or abort. If you quit, the changes you have made are written to disk. If you abort, the disk file is not updated.

Within the loop, several different routines are called. The first routine displays the names of the files stored in the pick list. The files are displayed based on the order in which they are displayed within the integrated environment. This is done by utilizing the FileOrder record. This record is set up as an array of words. The word values are the indexes of the files in that order. For example, if array element 1 in FileOrder is set to 4, the fourth file name in the NameArray variable is the first file displayed in the list.

Next in the loop, you get the file choice to delete. Valid keys are the pick list numbers, Q, and Esc. Pressing Q allows you to quit the program and save the changes. Pressing Esc aborts the program but does not save the changes.

The last routine in the loop is the routine to delete the selected file from the pick list. In this routine, the first thing that we do is store the selected value of the `FileOrder` array. Next, we delete the selected entry from the `FileOrder` array and remove the empty space. Then we go through the loop and decrement any of the `FileOrder` entries that are greater than the one selected, to make the `FileOrder` contiguous. Finally, the `NameArray`, `EditArray`, and `BlockArray` are all updated to reflect the deleted entry.

Project Management Summary

Project management with Turbo Pascal can be done with ease. Basic project management involves doing the following for each project:

❏ Define a directory.

❏ With the `Save options` command, create a TURBO.TP file in the IDE that specifies compiler directives, editor options, and directories.

❏ Create a TURBO.PCK file in the project directory to track the files you are working with and your editor information pertaining to each file.

Turbo Pascal can be in another directory entirely and be accessed through the DOS PATH command. When Turbo Pascal loads, it looks in the current directory for the TURBO.TP and TURBO.PCK files. If it does not find them there, it looks in the TURBO directory. The key to successful project management is using separate directories.

Context-Sensitive Help

Turbo Pascal's help capabilities are extraordinary. You can obtain help with the IDE menu commands, the editor, programming specifics—a particular procedure/function, a type, or a run-time library unit—or the last error message. The help available within the Integrated Development Environment is speedy enough, but Turbo Pascal enables you to look up a procedure definition with a simple hot-key combination from outside the IDE and even from outside Turbo Pascal.

IDE Menu Command Help

When you are within the IDE at a menu prompt, you have access to help at any time by pressing F1. When you press F1, help appears for the command you have highlighted on the screen. For example, you can get a description of what the OS shell is from within the Files menu. You can find out what is meant by setting Display swapping to Smart, Always, or Never. You can find out what Display swapping is.

Any time you are in doubt about what a particular command within the IDE will do, press F1 and read about the command before you try it.

Editor Help

While you are editing a file, you can again get help by pressing F1. Pressing F1 from within the editor pulls up help about the editor. Turbo Pascal realizes that you are in the editor; therefore, help pertaining to that appropriate subject appears on your screen.

The Turbo Pascal editor is based on a WordStar-like command set. If you are unfamiliar with WordStar, then these commands may be unfamiliar to you. The context-sensitive help displays a list of all the editor commands. Look for the command you need, press Esc to get back to the editing screen, and try the command. If you wanted help on another subject, press F1 a second time from the help screen to display the Help index, and select the topic with which you need help.

Programming Help

The programming help is the most useful of Turbo Pascal's help features. If you need to know something about a procedure, all you need to know is the name of the procedure or its unit. This help is easy to use. Simply position the cursor next to the library procedure, function, variable, type, or constant name, and press Ctrl-F1. The help screen is opened up to a page that discusses that particular topic. In fact, you can even get examples on most of the procedures/functions. If you want to know what the parameters to SetTextJustify are, move the cursor to SetTextJustify in your file, and press Ctrl-F1. You will see that SetTextJustify is a procedure that requires two word data type parameters: Horiz and Vert. Additionally, you get a brief description telling you that this procedure sets the text justification values for the OutText and OutTextXY routines, and is within the Graph unit (see fig. 1.2). You could get additional help about that entire unit. Finally, you see some choices to get help on other routines that are related to this routine.

Fig. 1.2. Context-sensitive help screen.

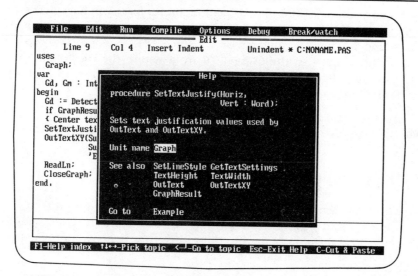

If you have a good understanding of the routines and what they do, you can use the help displays, rather than pulling out your bulky Turbo Pascal manuals each time you need to check a procedure's syntax. If you want to know the constants within the Crt unit for the various colors, you can get help on the Crt unit itself and page through the various constants and types defined within.

Error Help

Turbo Pascal also provides help on error conditions. When a compile-time or run-time error occurs, a bar appears at the top of the editor's screen with a message stating what the error condition is. While this bar is on the screen, pressing F1 displays a box that provides information about the error and some of its possible causes (see fig. 1.3). The error `Unexpected end of file` displays a message that you may have an unmatched `begin...end` pair, or you have an include file in the middle of a statement portion, or you did not close a comment. This kind of excellent error help is another reason you do not need a manual by your side at all times.

Fig. 1.3. Error Help Screen.

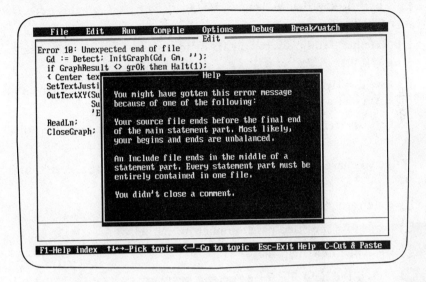

THELP: Resident Help

In addition to the help Turbo Pascal provides within the Integrated Development Environment, it also provides a program called THELP that gives you the power of the IDE help from outside the IDE. You can access THELP at any time—from your own editor, from Turbo debugger, and even from a word processor.

THELP provides the same power that the IDE help does. Place your cursor next to a procedure, function, type, constant, or variable, and press the hotkey to open THELP; it will display help about the selected topic. If it cannot find an entry for what you are looking for, it pulls up the Help index.

THELP works by reading in the special TURBO.HLP and TCHELP.TCH help files for Turbo Pascal and Turbo C, respectively. It will then produce the appropriate help that you are looking for based on those files.

You might think that this would consume large quantities of memory. With no swapping, THELP takes 41K of memory, but THELP can swap itself to disk or EMS, bringing its memory requirement down to 8K. You can change many settings within THELP:

❑ The display colors

❑ The hot key that activates THELP (default is 5 on the numeric keypad)

❑ Whether THELP swaps to EMS or to disk (as well as what disk to swap to)

❑ The display on which you want THELP to appear (if you have the luxury of a dual-monitor system)

You can also remove THELP from memory to free space for some other program.

While you have THELP loaded, you can do the following special things in it:

❑ Page through the various displays of help

❑ Jump to a specified page number in the help

❑ Display a new help file

❑ Search the help file for a specific keyword

❑ Paste a highlighted word, or any entire help-screen page, into your application

Review

In this chapter, we began by providing some tips for using the Turbo Pascal installation program and avoiding its pitfalls. Then we discussed useful, specific details of the Integrated Development Environment (IDE), including keystroke shortcuts for getting work done within the IDE.

The third section described ways to set up the Turbo Pascal IDE options for optimal project management, including maintaining separate project directories and utilizing Save options and the pick list. The fourth section noted the function and purpose of the Turbo Pascal pick list in detail, specifically listing and commenting on the format of the TURBO.PCK file and providing a program that will delete file entries from the pick list.

The final section in this chapter discusses the powerful help features of Turbo Pascal V5.0, including context-sensitive help and the THELP program.

Debugging Turbo Style

This chapter introduces the newest features of programming with Turbo Pascal: a source level debugger within the Turbo Pascal Integrated Development Environment and Turbo Debugger, one of Borland's newest language tools. We discuss each of these debugging environments fully in this chapter, from the simplest debugging needs to advanced use of each debugging tool. We also present ways you can get the most out of the debugging tools, including some advanced tips and tricks and information about features of each environment that are not widely used.

Integrated Debugging

The debugger built into Turbo Pascal V5.0 will be sufficient for most debugging needs. It lets you single-step through a program's code, executing either user-written procedures and functions as one command (step over) or executing each statement within a procedure or function (step into). It combines this with the capabilities to execute to an exact point in the program, set breakpoints, watch and change variables, evaluate expressions, view the call stack, and locate a procedure or function that might be in another file.

Debugger IDE Parameters

Several parameters must be set up in the Integrated Development Environment for the integrated debugger to work properly:

☐ Make sure Integrated debugging is switched On in the Debug menu (as shown in figure 2.1); otherwise, the integrated debugger will not operate.

Fig. 2.1. Turbo Pascal Debug menu.

```
    File    Edit    Run    Compile    Options    Debug    Break/watch
       Line 1    Col 1    Insert Indent
{$D+,L+,R+}                                 Evaluate       Ctrl-F4
{$V-}                                       Call stack     Ctrl-F3
Program DebuggingExampleOne;                Find procedure
{ Show the problems of using the $V- compiler  Integrated debugging   On
{ passing a typed string variable to a procedu  Standalone debugging  On
{ accepts a referance parameter of type STRING  Display swapping      Smart
                                            Refresh display
Const
  ArraySize = 5;          { Length of array in memory          }

Type
  Str20 = String[20];     { Type to be passed to demo proc     }

Var
  St1 : Str20;            { Variable to be passed to proc      }
  TrashedMemory : Array[1..ArraySize] Of Byte;
                          { Memory that will be over written }
  I : Integer;            { Loop control variable              }
  P : Pointer;

Procedure StringAssign( Var S : String );
{ This procedure will accept any length string parameter and }
Alt: F1-Last help  F3-Pick  F6-Swap  F9-Compile  X-Exit
```

☐ Use F5 to display the Watch window, toggling the Zoom state.

☐ Enable the Debug Information ({$D+}) and Local Symbol Information ({$L+}) compiler directives. If these directives are not properly set, you may be unable to debug certain areas within a program or within a unit. You can do this either through menu choices in the IDE or by placing the directives directly into the code. Directives placed in the source code module override settings made at the IDE menu. The {$D} and {$L} directives included in the source code are valid only within that particular module; they are not carried across unit boundaries. Keep this in mind when working on projects that include multiple files. Figure 2.2 shows the typical settings for the Options/Compiler menu.

Fig. 2.2. *Options/Compiler menu.*

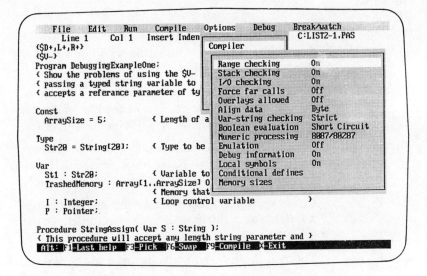

Keystrokes for Debugging

The IDE of Turbo Pascal has defined a large number of hot-key sequences for use with the integrated debugger. Table 2.1 outlines the keystrokes necessary to take full advantage of the integrated debugger contained in Turbo Pascal's IDE. Other items you will be using are contained in the Debug menu—specifically the Find procedure and Refresh display menu choices. The hot keys most used in the IDE are F4, F7, F8, Ctrl-F2, Ctrl-F7, Ctrl-F8, and Alt-F5.

Table 2.1. *Debugging Keystrokes in the IDE*

Keystroke	Function
F4	Executes current file (primary file) up to the current cursor position. Equivalent to the Run/Go to cursor menu choice.
F7	Executes the next program statement. The debugger will trace into the statement if it is a user-written procedure or function. Equivalent to the Run/Trace into menu choice.

Table 2.1 *continues*

***Table 2.1** continued*

Keystroke	Function
F8	Same as F7 except a user-written procedure or function is executed as one statement. Equivalent to the Run/Step over menu choice.
Ctrl-F2	Halts the execution of the program and the current debugging session. Resets state of any used memory. Equivalent to the Run/Program reset menu choice.
Ctrl-F3	Brings up the Call Stack window. Allows viewing of currently active procedures and functions. Equivalent to the Debug/Call stack menu choice.
Ctrl-F4	Brings up the Evaluate box. Allows user to change a variable or evaluate a statement. Equivalent to the Debug/Evaluate menu choice.
Ctrl-F7	The Add Watch window is brought to the screen. Whatever is at the current cursor position is placed into the window. Equivalent to the Break/Watch/Add watch menu choice.
Ctrl-F8	Toggles a breakpoint at the current cursor position. Equivalent to the Break/Toggle breakpoint menu choice.
Ctrl-F9	Runs the file currently in the editor (or primary file) after first doing a "Make." Equivalent to the Run/Run menu choice.
Alt-F5	Immediately toggles between the IDE display and the user's output screen. Equivalent to the Run/User screen menu choice.

F4 (Run/Go to cursor), F7 (Run/Trace into), F8 (Run/Step over), and Ctrl-F9 (Run/Run) keystrokes or menu choices begin executing the current file (or primary file if one is installed), thereby initiating a debugging session. Ctrl-F2 (Run/Program reset) ends a debugging session, returning any reserved memory to the Turbo Pascal Environment for future use.

Simple Debugging Example

Program listing 2.1 is an example of some of the basic debugging features in the integrated debugger. It shows how to add a watch variable, set a breakpoint, and switch to the output screen. Of course, it also demonstrates how to locate a logic error within the program presented. Line numbers are included for reference purposes only; do not enter them with the source code. Also be sure that the Integrated Debugging switch is set "ON" as explained earlier, or you will be unable to use this program.

Listing 2.1

```
1:  {$D+,L+,R+,A-}
2:  {$V-}
3:  Program DebuggingExampleOne;
4:  { Show the problems of using the $V- compiler directive   }
5:  { when passing a typed string variable to a procedure that }
6:  { accepts a reference parameter of type STRING.           }
7:
8:  Type
9:    Str20 = String[20];      { Type to be passed to demo proc }
10:
11: Const
12:   ArraySize = 5;
13:
14: Var
15:   St1 : Str20;             { Variable to be passed to proc  }
16:   TrashedMemory : Array[1..ArraySize] Of Byte;
17:                            { Memory that will be overwritten }
18:   I : Integer;            { Loop control variable          }
19:
20: Procedure StringAssign( Var S : String );
21: { This procedure will accept any length string parameter  }
22: { and assign a string constant to the parameter one       }
23: { character at a time.                                    }
24:
25: Const
26:   NewStr : String = '1234567890';
27:                            { String to be assigned to param }
28:
29: Var
30:   I : Integer;            { Loop control variable          }
31:
32: Begin
33:   S := '';                { Initialize Parameter           }
```

Listing 2.1 continues

Listing 2.1 *continued*

```
34:    For I := 1 to 23 Do      { Copy 23 characters into param   }
35:      S := S + NewStr[( I Mod 10 ) + 1];
36: End;
37:
38: Begin
39:   FillChar( TrashedMemory, SizeOf( TrashedMemory ), #0 );
40:                             { Init Memory to see corruption   }
41:   FillChar( St1, SizeOf( St1 ), #0 );
42:                             { Initialize var to be passed     }
43:   StringAssign( St1 );    { Call the procedure              }
44:   Writeln( St1 );         { Output the string to the screen }
45:   For I := 1 to ArraySize Do
46:     Write( TrashedMemory[I], ' ' );
47:                             { Output the corrupted memory     }
48: End.
```

After the example program has been entered into the Turbo Pascal 5.0 editor, initiate a debugging session by pressing F7. This keystroke compiles the program, and if no syntax errors are found, it begins running the program at line 39. This is noted by the highlight bar across the screen at the source line.

Continue this debugging process with the following steps:

1. Add a watch on the global variables St1, I, and TrashedMemory, and on the variable S that is local to procedure StringAssign. To add these watched variables, position the cursor under each variable definition, in turn, and press Ctrl-F7. This brings up the Add Watch window, with the highlighted variable in the window. Press Enter, and the highlighted variable is added to the Watch window at the bottom of the screen. (If the Watch window is not present, press F5 to bring it to the screen.)

2. Set a breakpoint in the program at the line where you want execution to stop temporarily. This can be done in one of several ways, but use the hot-key sequences outlined in table 2.1. Move the cursor to line 32, and press Ctrl-F8 to set the breakpoint. You can see the breakpoint by the highlighting of line 32 of the source file.

3. Press Ctrl-F9 to execute the program until the line with the breakpoint is encountered.

4. Examine the Watch window to see that three of the four variables contained therein have been initialized. The last variable, S, which is local to procedure StringAssign, will be initialized in the next statement.

5. Press F7 until the highlight bar is on line 35.

6. Each time you press F7 now, you can see the result on the variables in the Watch window. As the loop is executed the 21st through the 23rd times, as seen by the Watch on variable I, watch the effect on the variable TrashedMemory. Note that it has changed value, and this change holds even after the procedure terminates.

7. Press Ctrl-F9 to finish execution of the program.

8. After the End statement is executed, press Alt-F5 to view the output screen.

9. To fix this corruption, you need to ensure that you don't assign more characters to the parameter than the actual parameter can hold. With this assurance, it is safe to use the {$V-} compiler directive.

In this example, we have shown not only a major pitfall of using the {$V-} compiler directive but also how to use the Integrated Debugger to find the root of the problem.

The symptom was that variables were changing when they were not being accessed. The cause was easy to spot because this program was a "set up." But imagine a situation in which the offending procedure was contained in a different file. Then, without the debugger, we could have spent days searching for the cause.

Instead, we can look at what preceeds the area of memory that is changing and see where this is being accessed. In this case it is a string type variable, which is being passed to a procedure compiled with Var String Checking set to "relaxed" (same as {$V-}). Once this determination is made, we can watch the memory that is changing, single step the procedure, and find the exact cause of the corruption. This is what has been done in this example.

Memory Constraints

The following are simple things you can do to create more memory space for a debugging session. These suggestions apply to both small and large programs.

☐ Remove any unnecessary RAM-resident programs, like SideKick or SuperKey.

☐ Make sure your Compile and Link destinations are set to Disk. This frees additional RAM for the integrated debugger.

❑ If EMS is available, make sure that at least 64K is free and that you have the EMS switch in the Options for Editor menu choice in the TINST program set to On.

❑ If your machine has no EMS, try reducing the size of the Edit Buffer. It defaults to 64K and always reserves this much memory. However, if your source files are small, you can reduce the size of the buffer as far as possible, thereby making more memory available to the debugger.

❑ The size of the TURBO.TPL file can also have an effect on memory size. This is because the file will always be in memory every time the IDE is loaded. If you are working on a large application and have moved some of your units into this file with the TPUMover utility, then you are reducing memory for the compiler. It is suggested that you remove all units except PRINTER.TPU from the TURBO.TPL file and place them into a directory you have installed in the Units Directory option within the environment.

Debugging Small Programs

Small programs do not require as much memory to debug as large ones do. Nevertheless, you should think about the limited memory available when you start a debugging session. For instance, does your program use the Exec procedure? If so, you might need to limit the amount of memory used by the program you are debugging, to ensure enough free memory for the child process.

Instances in which you may need to conserve small amounts of memory for debugging purposes are when a program requires large amounts of heap space (for dynamic variables) and the overlay buffer if overlays are used. If either of these situations is the case, there are several things that can be done:

❑ You can turn Range Checking off {$R-} and perform this checking yourself by setting watch variables and viewing execution steps.

❑ You may need to turn off the Stack Checking directive {$S-} and the Input/Output checking directive {$I-} and instead perform the checking that these directives provide by setting a watch variable and monitoring its value through the program's execution.

Debugging Large Programs

Large programs are harder than small ones to debug in the integrated debugger. If the suggestions in this section do not provide enough memory for you to use the integrated debugger, or if you need more advanced debugging power, use Turbo Debugger. (Refer to the section of this chapter that details the use of the Turbo Debugger.)

Several things can increase the usability of the debugger for larger programs:

❏ If you are confident that a unit your program uses is bug-free, you can compile it with Debug Information off {$D-} and Local Symbol Generation off {$L-} (as well as the directives mentioned in the preceding section—{$R-}, {$S-}, and {$I-}).

❏ If your program or any used units do not use any dynamic variables, set the minimum heap size to zero. Then the compiler will not reserve memory for a heap that is never used. You can also adjust the stack size the program allocates to free memory for the debugger.

❏ Consider using overlays. By using overlays, you cause each overlayed unit to share the same memory space. This reduces the amount of code that is always kept in memory. The debugger built into Turbo Pascal 5.0 can debug a program that uses overlays. All the features of the debugger, all the keystrokes, and all the functions are fully supported while debugging an overlay—just as they are with any other program or unit. The only constraint is that such a program be compiled with the Destination set to Disk, and this is not a limitation of the debugger; it is the only way to generate the necessary overlay file. (The overlaying capabilities of Turbo Pascal 5.0 are examined in detail in Chapter 8.)

Watches and Breakpoints

Watch variables and breakpoints are valuable debugging tools.

Adding and Formatting Watches

The integrated debugger limits what can be placed in the Watch window, as outlined in table 2.2.

Table 2.2. *Valid Watch Items*

Watch Expression	Valid Values
Literal and constant types	All simple types, plus enumerated types
Operators	Any standard Pascal operators, plus the Turbo extensions
Typecasts	All typecasts supported by Turbo Pascal
Variables	All types supported from simple, predefined types to complex, user-defined data types and data structures
Built-in functions	`Abs`, `Addr`, `Chr`, `Hi`, `IOResult`, `Length`, `Lo`, `MaxAvail`, `Mem`, `MemAvail`, `MemL`, `MemW`, `Ofs`, `Ord`, `Pred`, `Ptr`, `Round`, `Seg`, `SizeOf`, `SPtr`, `SSeg`, `Succ`, `Swap`, and `Trunc`

For listing 2.1, we used Ctrl-F7 to add simple watch variables to the Watch window in the IDE. You can also use other methods to add a watch variable; each method adds the watched variable to the Watch window and accepts formatting parameters on the watched variables:

- [ ] Use the `Break/watch` menu. Within this menu are the options `Add watch`, `Delete watch`, and `Edit watch`. If you select `Add watch`, you are prompted to enter the name of the variable you want watched. The Watch window will then include the variable name and its current value.

- [ ] Press F6 to switch the active window to the Watch window. Place the cursor on an empty line in the Watch window, and press Enter to display the `Add Watch` window.

If `Unknown identifier` or `Symbol not found` appears next to the variable identifier in the Watch window, the identifier is misspelled, or the module in which it is defined does not contain the necessary debug information. (Refer to the Environment Parameters section of this chapter for ways to rectify the second condition.)

After entering the variable identifier, you may need or want to format the watch variable. The integrated debugger supports several formatting parameters (see table 2.3). To use a format parameter, append a comma and the specific parameter to the end of the variable identifier in the Add a Watch window. You can edit or add these parameters by editing the corresponding variable identifier in the Watch window.

Table 2.3. *Formatting Parameters for Watched Variables*

Format Specifier	Function
X, H, $	Displays the identifier in hexadecimal format with a preceding $. Valid for integer types only.
C	If a character variable's ASCII value is in the range 0 through 31, displays the special character associated with that ASCII value.
D	Displays all integer variables within the structure in decimal format.
F*n*	Displays a floating-point value with *n* significant digits. Valid values range from 2 to 18.
P	Used on `pointer` type variables only. Displays variable in `SEGMENT:OFFSET` notation.
R	Valid only on a `record` type variable. Displays the field name before its value in the record structure.
S	Displays a string with the # notation for elements in the ASCII range 0 through 31. Useful only with the `M` format specifier.
M	Dumps memory occupied by the variable. Additional format specifiers can be used to display the memory in certain formats.

You can edit a watch by beginning from the `Break/watch` menu or by pressing F6 to switch the active window to the Watch window (similar to the alternative way to add a watched variable). Then place the highlight bar on the variable you want to edit, and press Enter. When the `Edit watch` box appears, you can change the variable or add a format specifier to the variable.

The process for deleting a watch variable is similar to that for adding or editing a watch: use the `Delete watch` selection from the `Break/watch` menu; or use F6 to switch to the Watch window, highlight the desired item, and press Del.

Setting and Using Breakpoints

Breakpoints are useful when a program seems to be working correctly up to a certain area. You can set a breakpoint at the beginning of the trouble spot and single-step through the code until you find the problem. Breakpoints are also useful in testing new sections of code that have been added to an already debugged program. By setting a breakpoint at the beginning of a procedure or function, you can determine whether the new code is behaving properly.

Another reason for setting a breakpoint is to watch the modification of a variable. By toggling a breakpoint before a suspicious variable is modified and then single-stepping through the assignment statements in question, you can examine exactly what happens to a variable as your program executes.

The integrated debugger supports only simple breakpoints; it allows a break before executing a line of code. Turbo Debugger, on the other hand, supports many different types of breakpoints, as described later in this chapter.

There are two methods of setting a breakpoint in a source file. The most common method for adding or deleting a breakpoint is using Ctrl-F8. To toggle a breakpoint, view the next breakpoint, or remove all the breakpoints, you can go through the Break/watch menu.

Call Stack and Evaluate Windows

The Call Stack and Evaluate windows provide additional control in integrated debugging.

Using the Call Stack

The Call stack option lets you view the names and parameters of currently active procedures and functions. You can access the Call Stack window by pressing Ctrl-F3 or by choosing the Call stack selection from the Debug menu. The Call Stack window contains the names of all active procedures and functions, as well as the parameter's values that were passed to them. Because of size limitations, the window will not display large data types, such as arrays or records.

The Call Stack window is valuable for debugging a recursive routine, but its usefulness does not end there. Because the Call Stack window shows all active routines, you can set a breakpoint within a routine and then determine how control was passed to this routine by examining the call stack. The Call Stack window can display only 12 items on the stack at a time, but you can use the cursor keys to scroll through as many as 128 call stack items. Additionally, when the Call Stack window is active, you can place the cursor on any item in the window and press Enter to display the last active statement in the calling routine.

Listing 2.2 is a simple example of the use of call stack functions: viewing the call stack, scrolling through it, and viewing the last active line of code before the routine is called.

Listing 2.2

```
 1: {$N+,E+}
 2: Program Fibonacci;
 3: { This program will calculate the NumToCalc Fibonacci      }
 4: { number. It is intended as an example of using the call   }
 5: { stack to examine the currently active procedures         }
 6:
 7: Const
 8:   NumToCalc = 10;        { The specific Fib num to calc     }
 9:
10: Function Fib(Num : Integer) : Extended;
11: { Recursive function to calculate a Fibonacci number. This }
12: { function will be used to show how to use the call stack  }
13: { feature.                                                 }
14: Var
15:   Fib1, Fib2 : Extended; { Local vars for calculation      }
16:
17: Begin
18:   If Num = 0 Then
19:     Fib := 0.0
20:   Else
21:     If Num = 1 Then
22:       Fib := 1.0
23:     Else
24:     Begin
25:       Fib1 := Fib( Num - 1 );
26:       Fib2 := Fib( Num - 2 );
27:       Fib := Fib1 + Fib2;
28:     End;
29: End;
30:
31: Begin
32:   Writeln( NumToCalc,' Fibonacci Number is ',
33:           Fib( NumToCalc ):20:10 );
34: End.
```

After you enter this program, do the following:

1. Set a breakpoint on line 27 (by placing the cursor on that line and pressing Ctrl-F8).

2. Press Ctrl-F9 to begin executing the program.

3. When control is returned to the debugger, press Ctrl-F3 to display the Call Stack window. (Figure 2.3 shows what the call stack should look like at this point in the execution of the program.) There are 10 items on the call stack, 9 of which are active calls to the Fib function. The 10th item is the call to the main program, and this call occurs every time a program is run.

Fig. 2.3. *Call Stack from Listing 2.2*

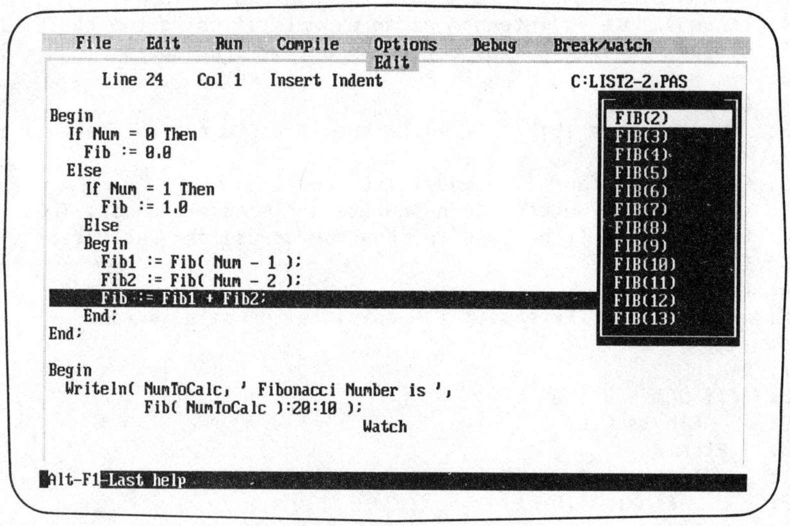

4. Place the cursor on the call to Fib (9), and press Enter. The cursor will be placed on the line of code that made this particular call (line 25).

5. Try different items on the stack, and see where the cursor is placed for each one.

Using the Evaluate Window

The Evaluate window, an extension of the Watch window, allows you to inspect or modify a data item and to evaluate some of the built-in functions in the run-time library. For restrictions on what can be evaluated, consult the Watch window presented in table 2.2.

The Evaluate window contains three separate sections:

❑ `Evaluate`, in which you enter the expression to be evaluated

❑ `Result`, in which the result of the evaluation appears

❑ `New value`, in which you can modify the value contained in the result area

Through the use of the `New value` box, you can modify the value of a variable, thereby seeing the effect of a change to the logic of the program without having to stop the debugging session, recompile the source code, and restart the debugging session. This is an excellent time-saving capability of Turbo Pascal 5.0.

Figure 2.4 shows the appearance of the Evaluate window. When you use Ctrl-F4 to bring up the Evaluate window, whatever word was at the current cursor location appears and is highlighted in the `Evaluate` section of the window. If the highlighted word appears as you desire, press Enter, and the `Result` section will show the result based on the value shown. Then you will have an opportunity to modify the value in the `New value` section.

Fig. 2.4. Evaluate window.

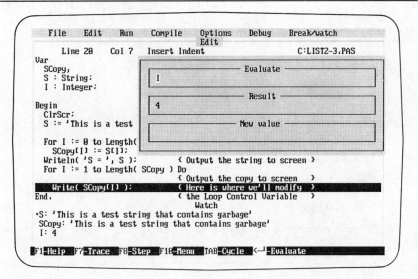

Listing 2.3 is a program that we will use as an example for the concepts presented here concerning the Watch window. We will periodically open an Evaluate window and change the value of one of the variables to see its effect on program execution.

Listing 2.3. *Evaluate Example*

```
 1: Program EvaluateDemo;
 2: { A simple example program that will show how to use the  }
 3: { evaluate option of the debugger to change the value of  }
 4: { a variable, and evaluate a function contained in the    }
 5: { System Unit.                                            }
 6: Uses Crt;                    { Link in the CRT unit       }
 7:
 8: Var
 9:    SCopy,                    { Define string vars for demo }
10:    S : String;
11:    I : Integer;             { Loop control variable       }
12:
13: Begin
14:    ClrScr;                   { Clear the output screen    }
15:    S := 'This is a test string that contains text.';
16:                              { Initialize string for demo }
17:    For I := 0 to Length( S ) Do
18:       SCopy[I] := S[I];      { Simple copy routine        }
19:    Writeln( 'S = ', S );     { Output the string to screen }
20:    For I := 1 to Length( SCopy ) Do
21:                              { Output the copy to screen   }
22:       Write( SCopy[I] );     { Here is where we'll modify  }
23: End.                 { the Loop Control Variable   }
```

After you enter the program in Listing 2.3, do the following:

1. Set a breakpoint on line 22.

2. Press Ctrl-F9 to begin execution of the program.

3. When control is returned to the debugger, set a watch on variables I, S, and SCopy.

4. Press F7 three times.

5. Press Ctrl-F4 to view the Evaluate window.

6. Enter **I** into the Evaluate section, and press Enter.

7. The Result section will show a value of four.

8. Use the cursor keys to move the cursor into the New value box, and enter a value of 10. This has the effect of causing the fifth through tenth characters of the string not to be printed to the screen.

9. Press F7 a few more times, and observe the behavior of the program. Play with this a while longer, trying different values and observe the results produced.

This example is presented to show one way to use the Evaluate window from within the IDE. The example shows that you can use this option not only to view an item but also to change an item's value. This has an advantage while debugging; for instance, imagine a situation when you realize that you forgot to give a variable a starting value or perhaps give it an incorrect value, and you do not want to recompile the program.

As we have shown in this section, the added capability the debugger provides in Version 5.0 of Turbo Pascal is valuable when attempting to locate problems in your programs. It gives you the ability to single-step your code, view and modify variables, as well as set breakpoints that will interrupt the program's flow. You also have the added capability of viewing what procedures and functions are currently active; this capability is valuable when tracking a problem, such as a stack overflow error. This, then, makes the IDE's debugger one of the most valuable additions to Turbo Pascal.

Turbo Debugger

The Turbo Debugger is one of Borland International's newest Professional Language development tools. It is similar to the debugger built into Turbo Pascal 5.0 but incorporates many additional, more powerful features, including support for specialized breakpoints (like I/O and changed memory breakpoints), the ability to debug a program in the 80386's virtual mode, and a facility to link two machines for the debugging process. These factors decrease required project development time.

Many of the functions of Turbo Debugger are similar to those of the IDE's debugger. You set watch variables and breakpoints, view the call stack, and evaluate an expression in the manner presented earlier in this chapter. You should not be intimidated by the seeming complexity of the stand-alone debugger. If you are comfortable with debugging in the IDE, using Turbo Debugger will be equally painless for you.

To debug a program within Turbo Debugger, you must follow most of the same rules as those outlined for the IDE:

❏ Turn on Debug Information {$D+}.

❏ Turn on Local Symbol Information {$L+}.

What is different? In the Debug menu, instead of switching on the Integrated debugging option, you switch on the Standalone debugging option. If you are using TPC.EXE (the command-line compiler), you must instruct TPC.EXE to include the debug information in the .EXE file that it generates. To do so, either include a /V option in the TPC.CFG file or include a /V on the command line whenever you are using TPC.EXE.

You can create an include file that contains the necessary command-line options for debugging purposes, as a way of making it easier to have the correct options set for using the Turbo Debugger. Then, if you are using TPC.EXE, create a batch file that calls TPC.EXE to generate the correct debugging information into the .EXE file it creates. Make sure, however, if you are using the integrated environment, that you define debug in the Options/Compiler/Conditional defines menu. Failing to do so will cause you to not get the correct information included in the code generated by the compiler. Listing 2.4, an include file, and listing 2.5, a batch file, are examples of such debugging setup files.

Listing 2.4. Debug Include File

```
{ Debugging include file that will be used in subsequent   }
{ programming examples.                                     }
{$IFDEF DEBUG}
  {$R+}
  {$S+}
  {$I+}
  {$D+}
  {$L+}
{$ELSE}
  {$R-}
  {$S-}
  {$I-}
  {$D-}
  {$L-}
{$ENDIF}
```

Listing 2.5. TPC Debugging Batch File

```
Echo Off
TPC /DDEBUG /V /L /M %1
Echo .
```

To use this batch file, (assuming that it is called TPCD.BAT), type **TPCD filename**, where **filename** is the program name you are attempting to compile. It might also be necessary to include your directory information into this batch file.

When you have set options as shown in listings 2.4 and 2.5, you are ready to debug a program. All the keystrokes with which you are familiar from using the IDE have the same functions in Turbo Debugger (see table 2.1).

Additional Power with Complex Breakpoints

It might seem that Turbo Debugger is just a stand-alone version of the IDE's debugger, but that is not the case. Turbo Debugger gives you the additional power of setting breakpoints on conditions other than an absolute statement, thus providing the possibility of using more advanced and complex breakpoint conditions than are available with the integrated debugger.

With Turbo Debugger, you can set breakpoints on several different conditions. For instance, you can set them on such global conditions as changed memory, global expression, or specific hardware conditions. Not only do you have control over what triggers the breakpoint, but you also control what will be done when the breakpoint is triggered. Additionally, you can set a pass count to instruct Turbo Debugger how many times the statement will be executed before triggering the breakpoint, thus causing the specified action to be executed.

Use Ctrl-F8 to set the breakpoint. Then, to customize exactly what you want to happen when the breakpoint occurs, do the following:

1. Press Alt-V B to bring up the Breakpoint window.

2. Press Alt-F10 to bring up the Breakpoint local menu. (See figure 2.5 for an example of the Breakpoint window and its local menu).

3. From here, you can set the action of what will happen when the breakpoint occurs. Some possible actions are these: break the program, send some information to the Log window, and execute an expression.

Fig. 2.5. *Breakpoint window.*

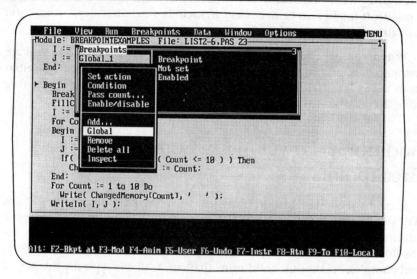

Several of the options on the Breakpoint local menu bring up submenus. For example, the Condition option summons a menu of choices on which the breakpoint can be controlled:

☐ Changed Memory Global breaks the program when anything in an area of memory changes its value; you can specify a data item and a size of the item to trigger the breakpoint by changed memory.

☐ Expression True sets the breakpoint to be triggered when a global expression becomes true; any time you choose this option, you will be prompted for the expression.

☐ Hardware sets a breakpoint on a hardware condition which is set by the 386 device driver or an add-on hardware debugger board.

☐ Always makes your breakpoints exactly like those found in the Turbo Pascal integrated debugger. These breakpoints are known as Global breakpoints.

Listing 2.6 is a program that demonstrates each of the types of breakpoints just listed; it does different things, depending on which breakpoint is triggered.

Listing 2.6. Breakpoint Program

```
Program BreakpointExamples;
{ This program is an example of several different types of  }
{ breakpoints that can be set within the Turbo Debugger.    }

{$I Debug.Inc}  { Include the debugging definition file       }

Uses Crt, Dos;  { Link in necessary standard units           }

Type
  ArrayType = Array[1..10] of Byte;

Var
  ChangedMemory : ArrayType;
  Count,
  I, J : Integer;

Procedure BreakpointEval;
Begin
  I := 0;
  J := 0;
End;

Begin
  BreakpointEval;
  FillChar( ChangedMemory, SizeOf( ChangedMemory ), #0 );
  I := 5;
  For Count := 1 to 20 Do
  Begin
    I := I + 1;
    J := J + 2;
    If( ( Count > 5 ) And ( Count <= 10 ) ) Then
      ChangedMemory[Count] := Count;
  End;
  For Count := 1 to 10 Do
    Write( ChangedMemory[Count], '   ' );
  Writeln( I, J );
End.
```

After you enter listing 2.6, do the following:

1. Compile to disk. (If you are using the IDE, make sure to enter DEBUG into the Options/Compiler/Conditional defines menu item.)

2. Load Turbo Debugger with the generated .EXE file.

3. Press Alt-V B to bring up the Breakpoints window.

4. Press Alt-F10 bring up the Breakpoints local menu.

5. Choose `Global` from the Breakpoints local menu (or use Ctrl-G).

6. Choose `Condition`.

7. To set this breakpoint on `Changed Memory Global`, press C.

8. Set the `Condition` to `Break`.

9. Press Ctrl-F9 to execute the program.

The first break should occur on the `FillChar` statement. Subsequent breaks should happen inside the `For` loop the next time the `ChangedMemory` array variable is accessed.

Now we will set up another type of global breakpoint—one on `Expression true`. Using listing 2.6 again, make sure the program is reset and all breakpoints are removed from the last example. Then do the following:

1. Bring up the Breakpoints window and its local menu.

2. Choose `Global` and then `Condition`.

3. From the Condition submenu, choose `Expression true`.

4. When prompted for the expression, enter: **I=6**.

5. Choose `Set action` from the Breakpoints local menu, and then choose `Log`.

6. When prompted for the expression to log, enter: **I**.

7. Press Ctrl-F9 to execute the program. No breaking of the program will occur because we are instructing the debugger to record some information to a different window.

8. Bring up the Log window so that we can view the results of the breakpoint. This is done with the Alt-V L keystroke combination.

Follow the next set of steps to set a specialized breakpoint and execute a statement when the breakpoint occurs. Begin by making sure the debugger has been reset and that all breakpoints have been cleared from the previous example.

1. Place the cursor on the second `For` loop, and press Ctrl-F8 to toggle a breakpoint.

2. Use Alt-V B and Alt-F10 to bring up the Breakpoints window and its local menu. You should see the breakpoint you just set in this window.

3. Choose Set action, and then choose Execute.

4. When prompted for what to execute, enter: **BreakPointEval**. This procedure will then be executed when this breakpoint occurs.

Watch Window and Inspect Window

Watches are added in TD exactly as they are in the Turbo Pascal integrated debugger—by pressing Ctrl-F7. When you have added an item to the Watch window, you access an Inspect window. The Inspect window is advantageous for viewing large data items because the Watch window can only display a limited amount of any data item.

To create an Inspect window, as shown in figure 2.6, do this:

1. Press F6 until the Watch window is highlighted.

2. Press Alt-F10 to bring up the Watch local menu.

3. Choose the Inspect option to enable the viewing of all of a data item.

Fig. 2.6. Inspect window.

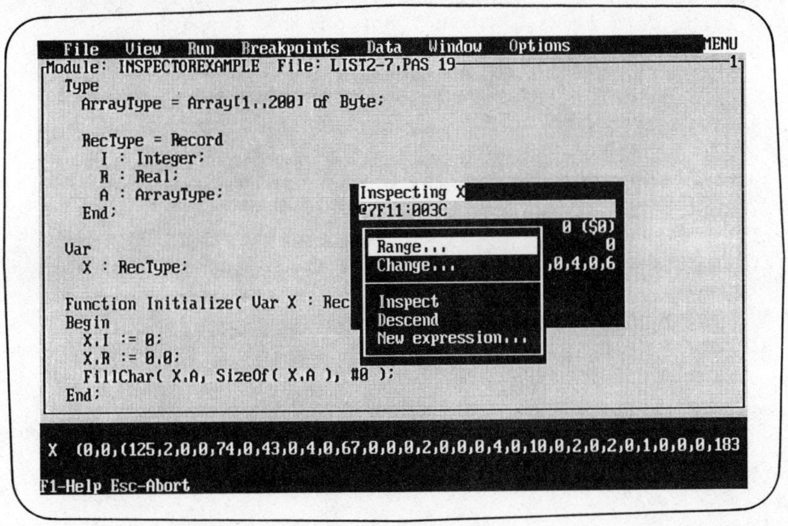

The Inspect window is not limited in displayable size as is the Watch window. One advantage of using the Inspect window is the ability to view any procedure or function's parameter list and return type. This lets you determine the types of parameters and return type on which a function or procedure depends and whether any problems exist at the current source line.

Like all other windows, the Inspect window has a local menu that controls several different features. Figure 2.6 shows the Inspector window and its local menus. If you do not want to view the entire structure, you can use the local menu's Range option to shrink the amount of data that is viewed. Additionally, you can change the current data item without having to go to an Evaluate box. By choosing the Inspect item option in the Inspect window's local menu, you can open another Inspect box on the current data item, thereby viewing a complex data item further. Opening such a window while viewing a function will show you the source for the function or procedure.

Listing 2.7. Inspect Window Example

```
Program InspectorExample;
{ This sample program is used to introduce the reader to the }
{ inspect window of the Turbo Debugger. We will use it to    }
{ view large data items, view a function, and inspect a      }
{ complex data item.                                         }

{$I DEBUG.INC}

Type
  ArrayType = Array[1..200] of Byte;

  RecType = Record
    I : Integer;
    R : Real;
    A : ArrayType;
  End;

Var
  X : RecType;

Function Initialize( Var X : RecType ) : Boolean;
Begin
  X.I := 0;
  X.R := 0.0;
  FillChar( X.A, SizeOf( X.A ), #0 );
End;
```

```
Begin
  If( Initialize( X ) ) Then
    Writeln( 'TRUE' )
  Else
    Writeln( 'False' );
End.
```

Listing 2.7 presents examples of the use of Inspect windows. After entering this listing, do the following:

1. Add the variable X to the Watch window by placing the cursor on an occurrence of X and pressing Ctrl-F7. X should then appear in the Watch window.

2. Press F6 until the Watch window is the active window (denoted by the title being highlighted).

3. Press Alt-F10 to bring up the Watch local menu.

4. To bring up the Inspect window, choose Inspect.

5. Examine all the structure of the variable X.

6. Continue tracing the program, and after entering the Initialize procedure, switch to the Inspect window (if not currently active).

7. Place the cursor on item A in the Inspect window, and bring up the Inspect local menu with Alt-F10.

8. Choose Inspect from the local menu, to see another Inspect window for the field *A* within the record.

9. Continue single-stepping through the code, watching what happens to the information within the Inspect windows.

Remote Debugging

The Turbo Debugger also supports what is known as *remote debugging*—the use of two machines, linked with a serial cable, one machine containing the debugger and the other machine containing the program to be debugged. By using the remote debugging facilities of the Turbo Debugger, it is possible to debug a large applications program because the machine that contains the applications program has only a small resident driver plus the program being debugged. This allows the applications program to have almost all available memory, instead of having the debugger *and* the program in memory.

The remote debugger requires the usage of a "null modem" cable, that is, a cable that links two serial ports and crosses at least the send and receive lines to link the two PCs. You will need to place all files (data, help, or support) relevant to the program being debugged onto the remote system. Note that it is not necessary to place the .EXE file to be debugged onto the remote system because Turbo Debugger will copy the .EXE file across the serial link if it is not available. The last file necessary on the remote machine is TDREMOTE.EXE. Next, have the debugger (TD) and its files on the main machine.

To initiate the remote portion, you will need to pass the necessary command line parameters to TDREMOTE. Table 2.4 shows the parameters supported by TDREMOTE. It will support three different speeds, 9600 Baud, 40,000 Baud, and 115,000 Baud, and two different comm ports, COM1 and COM2. Each of the parameters shown in table 2.4 must be preceded by a hyphen (-) or a forward slash (/).

Table 2.4. *Command-Line Parameters for TDREMOTE*

Option	Meaning
?	Display a help screen
h	Display a help screen
rp1	Use COM1 for the link (Port 1)
rp2	Use COM2 for the link (Port 2)
rs1	Set link to slow speed (9600 Baud)
rs2	Set link to medium speed (40,000 Baud)
rs3	Set link to fast speed (115,000 Baud)
w	Make options permanent by writing to TDREMOTE.EXE.

If no parameters are passed to TDREMOTE, then it will use the default speed of 115,000 Baud and the default port, COM1, or whatever was last written to the file with the w command-line parameter.

After loading TDREMOTE with the desired parameters on the remote system, you will need to load TD onto the main system. TD will use the same command-line parameters as TDREMOTE for setting the port and the communications speed (rs? for the speed and rp? for the specific port).

When the link is successfully established, the message `Turbo Debugger Online` will appear on the main system, and the message `TDREMOTE Online` will appear on the remote system. The controlling of the debugging session will be handled by the main system.

386 Debugging

One of the most unique features of the Turbo Debugger is the inclusion of a debugger that will work specifically on a 80386-based computer. This consists of a device driver and a specialized version of TD called TD386. This version of TD takes advantage of the special capabilities of the 80386 microprocessor.

The basis upon which the debugger works is by placing the program that is being debugged into the lower 640K of memory and placing the debugger into extended memory above the 1 megabyte range. Note that you must have a minimum of 700K of extended memory available to the debugger, or you won't be able to use the 80386 debugging capabilities of the Turbo Debugger.

After loading the user's program and the debugger into their portions of memory and starting the debugging session, TD386 will then flip between virtual mode to run the user program and protected mode to access the debugger. This is accomplished by making calls to the device driver TDH386.SYS, which must have been loaded into the machine at bootup time. By doing this, the program being debugged will be running in the same memory locations as it would if it were running as an .EXE file running under DOS. This aids in tracking down bugs in a program that occur only when run from DOS but disappear when run under the debugger.

The 386 version of the debugger (as well as TD when used on a 386 with the 386 device driver) behaves as the standard debugger. It does, however, give you the ability to set a hardware-based breakpoint—a breakpoint keyed on a hardware I/O port or memory location. For example, in listing 2.6, we set a breakpoint on `Changed Memory Global`. If you were using TD or TD386 on a 386-based system, it would have been using the hardware features of the debugger. This, or any other breakpoint set on the hardware, would have been indicated by the presence of an asterisk (*) next to the words `Global Breakpoint` in the left pane of the Breakpoint window.

One of the additional features of hardware breakpoints is the ability to set different criteria for the breakpoint's condition. You can set the bus cycle type, the range of addresses, and the range of data values to be matched by the breakpoint. Furthermore, you have three additional types of breakpoints that can be set. You can set a breakpoint on `instruction fetch, read from memory, and read or write a specific memory location.`

The capabilities of hardware debugging are not limited to just 386-based computers. Anyone can get some of the functionality of hardware debugging by simply installing a third-party hardware debugging board. One such board on the market, manufactured by Purart, is specifically for supporting the Turbo Debugger. It will allow you to set a breakpoint on `Changed Memory Global`, I/O port access, and memory reads and writes. The only requirement is that you load the device driver supplied with the board and that you pick an I/O port for communication between the board and the debugger. Using such a board will greatly speed up the debugging process.

As you can see, the new debugging environments provided to the professional programmer are advanced. They give you the ability to set many different types of breakpoints, view and modify variables as the program is executing, and substitute code that can be executed when a breakpoint occurs. You can also log parts of the program and data to a separate window, known as the Log window, and optionally dump this information to a file.

Both debugging environments are similar enough that migrating from the Integrated Debugger to the Turbo Debugger will be painless for most people. This way, all of the keystrokes that you are familiar with in one are applicable to the other. This power should be sufficient to debug almost any program that can be written for DOS.

Part II

Low-Level
Turbo Pascal

CHAPTER 3

Linking with Turbo Assembler

Turbo Pascal provides so much power and programming capability that there are few program features you cannot create with it. However, you may want to link into Turbo a procedure that was written in assembly language. Assembly language code can be smaller, faster, and better optimized than code written in Pascal. For example, in Chapter 9 we develop code to manipulate video memory. One routine moves information from one location to another. We do not use the Turbo Pascal Move procedure for this because it moves only one byte at a time; the assembly language routine used moves one word at a time, which increases the program's operating speed.

This chapter is not a tutorial on assembly language; it deals primarily with what is needed to link Turbo Pascal and assembly language programs. To benefit from this chapter, you need to begin with a basic understanding of 8086 assembler and assembly language. This chapter presents two topics: linking assembly language routines into Turbo Pascal and the ease of use of Turbo Assembler. The second section provides some sample programs specifically for use with Turbo Assembler and Turbo Pascal; in it, we develop a function that returns a string type. We will also develop a procedure.

Restrictions for Linked Assembly Language

Several restrictions follow that you must observe when writing code in assembly language to be linked to Turbo Pascal.

❏ Nested procedures and functions are special-case code and are not allowed to be declared external.

❏ Every PUBLIC defined in the assembly language must be resolved in the Pascal code. An .OBJ file may not rely on another .OBJ file to resolve any externals.

❏ You must determine whether the routine is to use the directive NEAR or FAR. If the procedure is defined after the {$F+} compiler directive or in the interface section of a unit, it will be a FAR call; otherwise, it is a NEAR call. Because a FAR call pushes two extra bytes on the stack for the return address, it is important to select the appropriate directive in the assembler code.

❏ The SS, SP, BP, and DS registers must be preserved and not modified by any procedure or function.

❏ The SP register must be restored at the end of the routine to remove any passed parameters. You can do this by specifying RET XX (where *XX* refers to the number of bytes of parameters to remove) or by using POP to remove each parameter. If you choose the latter of the two options, use care to save the return address. The return address (2 bytes for a NEAR call, 4 bytes for a FAR) is the last parameter pushed onto the stack and therefore the first to be removed by a POP.

❏ You cannot refer to an offset of an EXTRN procedure (i.e. CALL Proc1 + 10). You must refer just to the procedure itself (CALL Proc1). You can refer to offsets of your EXTRN variables.

❏ Dead-code removal is limited when working with .OBJ files. If no call is made to any routine in the .OBJ file, it will be linked out; if only one procedure within the object file is called, the entire .OBJ file is linked in.

❏ Turbo Pascal strips debug information from the assembler code.

Entry and Exit Code

Each procedure and function you write in Turbo Pascal has standard entry and exit code—code that is used to set up the procedure and code to restore it. The code is standard and does a few simple tasks.

Standard entry code saves the base pointer (BP), moves the stack pointer (SP) value into the base pointer, and allocates space on the stack for any local variables to be defined:

```
PUSH     BP
MOV      BP,SP
SUB      SP,local_variable_size
```

Standard exit code for all procedures and functions reverses what the entry code does. The standard exit code restores the stack pointer from BP and restores the base pointer from the stack. Finally, the code uses the RET instruction to return from this procedure, specifying how many parameters are to be removed from the stack:

```
MOV      SP,BP
POP      BP
RET      parameters
```

This code is generated by each procedure and function written in Turbo Pascal, but your assembly language routines need not follow this convention. Nevertheless, the entry and exit codes are good coding practice and allow you to manipulate the stack, access parameters, and add local variables easily. We strongly recommend that you use them. Turbo Assembler assumes that you are using this entry and exit code and even inserts it for you if you use a special .MODEL directive.

Access to Variables

From an assembly language routine, you can access variables and their values within a Pascal routine by using any of three methods: using global variables, passing variables to the routine as value parameters, and passing variables to the routine as variable parameters.

Using Global Variables

Accessing a global variable defined by Turbo Pascal from an assembly language program is a very straightforward procedure. When you define your data segment, you must also define the external variables you want to use. To add your global variables, determine the assembly language type that most closely matches your Turbo Pascal data type. Prefix the label of the variable with the reserved word external, and follow the label with the assembly language type. The following lines provide an example of defining a few Turbo Pascal global variables from within assembly language.

```
DATA      SEGMENT PUBLIC
          EXTRN myWord : Word
          EXTRN myByte : Byte
DATA      ENDS
```

Table 3.1 shows the Turbo Pascal data types and the associated assembly language definitions.

Table 3.1. *Global Variables as Assembly Language EXTRN*

Pascal	Assembly Language	Size
Byte	BYTE	1 byte
ShortInt	BYTE	1 byte
Integer	WORD	2 bytes
Word	WORD	2 bytes
LongInt	DWORD	4 bytes
Real	FWORD	6 bytes
Single	DWORD	4 bytes
Double	QWORD	8 bytes
Extended	TBYTE	10 bytes
Comp	QWORD	8 bytes
Pointer	DWORD	4 bytes

To access these global variables, you can refer to the label in your assembly language code. You can define your own variables in assembly language, but the variables you define in your assembly language code will be private to that code. If you need routines outside your assembly language code to refer to these variables, you must declare them EXTRN and have them defined by Turbo Pascal.

All variables declared in the assembly language as EXTRN or otherwise must be placed into a segment named DATA or DSEG. This segment can be BYTE-aligned or WORD-aligned in assembly language; when linked to Turbo, it will be word-aligned. The segment should not specify a class name. No variables in the data segment can be initialized; Turbo Pascal will ignore that request. When you define your variables, use ? to specify the value. The following code shows what is correct and what is incorrect.

```
myOne      DB 21h         ; wrong!
myTwo      DB ?           ; correct

myBuf1     DB 20 DUP (0)  ; wrong!
myBuf2     DB 20 DUP (?)  ; correct
```

Although Turbo Pascal allows you to refer to variables, constants, types, procedures, and functions by specifying the block (i.e. unit name or program name) and a period, this technique will not work in assembly language. For example, you can refer to CRT.TextAttr to access the word variable TextAttr in the Crt unit from Pascal, but you cannot specify the following:

```
EXTRN CRT.TextAttr : Word
```

If you need to do this because you have redefined a variable that is in another unit, you will have to do one of two things: do not redefine the variable name, or define another unique name and set that variable as absolute to the other variable's address. Listing 3.1 shows the assembly language and Turbo Pascal code to do the latter of the two solutions. The sample program returns the current text color and text background settings.

Listing 3.1. *Accessing a Global Variable*

```
;; The following is the Assembler code example
;;
.MODEL SMALL
DATA SEGMENT PUBLIC
   EXTRN TextAttr   : Byte
   EXTRN MyTextAttr : Byte
DATA ENDS

CODE SEGMENT PUBLIC
ASSUME CS:CODE,DS:DATA

Public MyFunc1,MyFunc2

MyFunc1 PROC FAR
   MOV AL,TextAttr      ; Move TextAttr to AL as function result
   RETF
MyFunc1 ENDP

MyFunc2 PROC FAR
   MOV AL,MyTextAttr  ; Move MyTextAttr to AL as function result
   RETF
MyFunc2 ENDP
```

Listing 3.1 *continues*

Listing 3.1 *continued*

```
ENDS
END
; End Assembler code example
{ Start Pascal code example }
Program Temp;

Uses
  Crt;

Var
  TextAttr    : Byte;    { Define TextAttr locally }
  MyTextAttr : Byte absolute CRT.TextAttr; { Point to CRT unit:TextAttr }
  Test       : Byte;     { Local garbage variable }

{$L TEMP.OBJ}

{$F+}
Function MyFunc1 : Word; external;
Function MyFunc2 : Word; external;
{$F-}

Begin
  test := MyFunc1;
  WriteLn ( test );
  test := MyFunc2;
  WriteLn ( test );
End.
```

Using Value Parameters

Both value parameters and variable parameters are pushed onto the stack in a left-to-right order. Therefore, the first parameter in the Pascal procedures definition will be placed onto the stack first, the next parameter will be pushed second, and so on.

A one-byte value parameter will be pushed onto the stack as two bytes; the high byte will be undefined. Two-byte parameters are also pushed onto the stack as two bytes. A four-byte parameter will be pushed onto the stack as two words. The most significant word will be pushed first, followed by the least significant word. A floating-point parameter is passed on the stack per its size. Finally, all other parameters (three-byte, five-byte, and greater) are passed on the stack as a pointer. It is then the responsibility of the procedure/function to define local storage and copy the value into that location.

Table 3.2 shows the different data types and how they are passed onto the stack.

Table 3.2. *Value Parameters on the Stack*

Type	Placed on Stack As
shortint, byte	word: value in low byte
integer, word	word
longint	double word
char	word: value in low byte
Boolean	word: 0 or 1 in low byte
enumerated	(values of 256 or less) word: value in low byte (greater than 256) Word
real	three words
single	double word
double	quad word
extended	five words
pointer	double word
string	double word pointer to value
set	double word pointer to a set that takes 32 bytes
array	(1 byte) word: value in low byte (2 byte) word (4 byte) double word (other) double word pointer to value
record	(see array)

When passing a string parameter from a procedure in one overlaid unit to a procedure in another overlaid unit, temporary storage is made on the stack. The string constant is placed in this location before the call, and the address on the stack is passed as a pointer to the second procedure in the other overlaid unit. This also holds true for sets.

Using Variable Parameters

Variable parameters are easy: they are always passed as a double-word pointer to the actual value. As with the double-word pointers passed as value parameters, you can use LDS or LES to retrieve them. (Read the first paragraph of the preceding ''Using Value Parameters'' section for information about the order of parameter placement on the stack.)

Accessing Parameters and Local Variables

Turbo Pascal entry and exit codes allow you to access your parameters and local variables by using BP relative addressing. This means that BP is pointing to the location of the stack on entry into the procedure. Because the parameters are pushed onto the stack before the procedure call, you can access them by manipulating BP.

To get an understanding of how the stack is set up, consider the sample Pascal procedure call and a diagram of the stack (shown in figure 3.1).

```
Procedure MyProc ( Var s : String; b : Byte; l : LongInt ); external

Begin
  st := 'This is a test string';
  MyProc ( st, 5, 1000 );
  ...
```

Fig. 3.1. *Stack during a procedure call.*

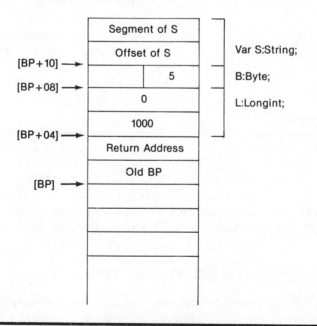

Because S is a variable parameter, it is pushed as the segment and offset of the actual string variable. B is a value parameter of size byte; therefore it is pushed as a word but occupies the low order of that word. L is a LongInt value parameter and therefore occupies four bytes of memory, two word values; the high order word is pushed first, followed by the low order word. Finally, the CALL itself pushes the return address. In a NEAR call such as this, only the offset of the return address is pushed. The last value on the stack comes from the entry code that stores the value in BP.

To access the various values in your assembly language code, you can define equates. An *equate* in assembly language is essentially like a constant in Pascal. The following shows equates that could be used in this example:

```
S    EQU DWORD PTR [BP+0A]
B    EQU BYTE  PTR [BP+08]
L    EQU DWORD PTR [BP+04]
```

To use these equates, set the string to an empty string and increment the byte, as follows:

```
LES  DI,S                ; Load ES:DI with the 4 bytes at BP+0A
MOV  ES:BYTE PTR [DI],0  ; Set the length byte to 0
INC  B                   ; Add 1 to B
```

Doing an increment B will have no effect outside of this procedure because B is a value parameter. Using the equate makes the code more readable. The equate will insert the information to the right of the EQU regardless of where the label to the left is. The following lines show how this will be translated to Assembler without using equates:

```
LES  DI,DWORD PTR [BP+0A]
MOV  ES:BYTE PTR [DI],0
INC  BYTE PTR [BP+08]
```

To access local variables, begin by allocating storage for them. If you look back at the standard entry code for the procedure, you will see an optional third line of code:

```
SUB  SP,local_variable_size
```

The BP has already been loaded with the current stack location, so the line above does not affect how passed parameters are accessed. You can access local variables in a similar fashion: instead of adding to the base pointer (BP), subtract. For example, let's keep the previous procedure definition and define two local parameters of type word. The stack will look like figure 3.2.

As with passed parameters, you can define an equate for each of the local variables. The equates for our sample stack would look like the following:

```
Temp1    EQU WORD PTR [BP-02]
Temp2    EQU WORD PTR [BP-04]
```

Fig. 3.2. Stack in a procedure with local variables.

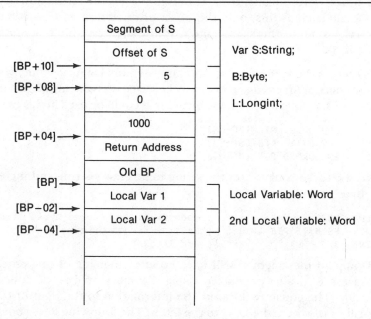

The one drawback to using the EQU to equate labels with parameters is that the label can only be used once in the entire module. The equate is global to the entire block of assembly language source code.

Function Results

Function results are returned through the registers, not the stack. Ordinal types are returned in AL, AX, or DX:AX. Real types are returned in DX:BX:AX (High order, middle word, low order). Floating-point types are returned through the math coprocessor's stack. Pointer types are returned in DX:AX. Strings are the exception to the rule; the caller pushes a pointer to a temporary storage location for the string before pushing any parameters, and the function returns the string value in that location and must not remove the pointer from the stack. Table 3.3 shows the registers of various function results.

Table 3.3. *Function Results*

Function Result	Registers
shortint, byte	AL
integer, word	AX
longint	DX:AX (most significant word: least significant word)
real	DX:BX:AX (most significant word: middle word: least significant word)
single, double, extended, comp	Math coprocessor top-of-stack register
pointer	DX:AX (segment: offset)
string	Pointer on stack to temporary storage

Assembler and Objects

Objects are stored in a format similar to a record, with a few differences. The object's fields are stored sequentially in the order that they are defined. Because objects can inherit from other objects, any inherited fields are listed first.

Static Objects

Let us define three simple inherited objects—static objects (we will discuss virtuals a little bit later). The three objects represent a location, a location with a character, and finally a location with a character and color attribute. The definition of the objects is described in the following chart and in figure 3.3.

```
Type
  Location    = Object
                    X, Y : Byte;
                    Procedure Init ( newX, newY : Byte );
                End;
  Character   = Object ( Location )
                    Ch : Char;
                    Procedure Init ( newX, newY : Byte; newCh :
                    Char );
                End;
```

```
Color__Char  =  Object ( Character )
                    Attr : Byte;
                    Procedure Init ( newX, newY, newAttr : Byte;
                        newCh : Char );
                End;
```

Fig. 3.3. *Definition of three inherited, static objects.*

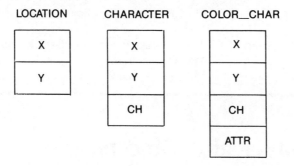

As you look at this figure, notice that even though CHARACTER and COLOR_CHAR do not actually define X and Y, they have them defined in their storage space. This is because they both inherit from LOCATION. In fact, as the figure shows, COLOR_CHAR inherits CH from CHARACTER.

Virtual Objects

Virtual objects differ from static objects in only one way, they have an additional field. This field is a 32-bit pointer to the object's Virtual Method Table (VMT). The VMT is a table in the Data Segment that contains the addresses of the object's virtual methods. Where is the VMT pointer placed within the object's structure? Well, it is placed after the fields of the first object in the inheritance structure that defines a virtual method or constructor. Again, let us look at a chart and a figure to demonstrate the layout of a virtual object in memory (see fig. 3.4).

```
Type
    Location      = Object
                        X, Y : Byte;
                        Procedure Init ( newX, newY : Byte );
                    End;
```

```
Character    = Object ( Location )
                 Ch : Char;
                 Constructor Init ( newX, newY : Byte; newCh :
                    Char );
                 Procedure ShowChar; Virtual;
                 Procedure HideChar; Virtual;
             End;
Color__Char = Object ( Character )
                 Attr : Byte;
                 Constructor Init ( newX, newY, newAttr : Byte;
                    newCh : Char );
                 Procedure ShowChar; Virtual;
             End;
```

Fig. 3.4. *Layout of a virtual object in memory.*

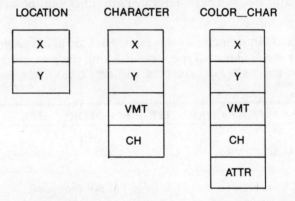

Notice how the layout of the virtual objects here are similar to the layout of the static objects in figure 3.3. Because the first virtual method and constructor is described in the object CHARACTER, both this object and any descendant objects (COLOR_CHAR) have a VMT entry as well. But notice that the descendant object has the VMT entry at the same offset in the structure as does the first object. This is done to allow for polymorphism.

Virtual Method Tables

For each virtual object type that is defined, there will be one Virtual Method Table (VMT) defined in the Data Segment. Even if you have 300 instances of this virtual object, each will reference the one VMT defined for that type.

The VMT is set up in memory as a table of pointers to the virtual methods of that particular object. The first two entries in the VMT are the size of the instance of the object and the negation of that size. These entries have dual purposes. The first purpose is to tell a call to New how much memory to allocate for the object. The second purpose is to help prevent your program from locking up. If you have Range Checking enabled {$R+}, any call to a virtual method prompts a check to see if the VMT address has been loaded into the instance of an object. If this has not been done (by calling a constructor), then the program can lock up the machine. Simply put, the program tries to get the address of a virtual method by looking it up at the location specified by the VMT pointer. If this pointer is not pointing to an actual VMT, then the program grabs a "garbage address" and jumps to that location of memory to run. What Range Checking does is subtract the second word value from the first word value. If the result is 0, then the VMT pointer is pointing to a valid VMT. Of course, the VMT pointer may be pointing to a location in memory that actually contains two values that negate each other, but the odds against that are steep.

The entries of virtual methods within the VMT are in the order that they were defined in the object's Type section. Using the preceding example, let us look at the VMT for CHARACTER and COLOR_CHAR (see fig. 3.5).

Fig. 3.5. The VMT for CHARACTER *and* COLOR__CHAR.

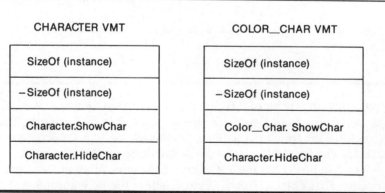

Notice in this figure how COLOR_CHAR has the VMT entry for ShowChar and HideChar at the same location as that of CHARACTER. This way, the object for COLOR_CHAR can be passed to a routine that is expecting an object of type Character. Also notice how the method ShowChar defined by COLOR_CHAR has replaced the original ShowChar method entry.

Calling Methods

Making a call to a method is similar to making a call to a normal procedure or function. The exception is that an additional parameter is passed as the last parameter to the method. This extra parameter is not something defined in Pascal, it is the Self parameter. This is a 32-bit pointer to the instance of the object itself.

A static method is called directly and can be described easily. First, any parameters need to be pushed onto the stack as for a normal procedure/ function call. Next, the 32-bit address of the instance of the object gets pushed on the stack in the same form that a pointer is (stack first, then offset). Finally, a call is made to the method.

Let us look at a fragment of code demonstrating how to call the static method LOCATION.INIT that we defined earlier. Let us say that we have a variable O defined as an object of (or a descendant of) LOCATION and that the new X and Y parameters are 10 and 20, respectively. The assembler code will look like the following:

```
mov  ax, 10
push ax
mov  ax, 20
push ax
les  di, O
push es
push di
call LOCATION
```

The steps for calling a virtual method are similar but a little more complicated. The parameters, including the Self parameter, are passed the same way. The actual call is what is different. The address must be pulled from the VMT. This is not too difficult because the VMT is stored in the instance of the object, and a pointer to this instance is already stored in ES:DI as the Self parameter. All you need do is get the offset of the VMT pointer within Self. You can do this by changing the value of DI. Then, you need to know the offset of the virtual method within the VMT. Finally, call that offset.

Using the preceding example, look at how you would call the virtual method ShowChar. Again, assume that O is an object. This time it will be an object of type CHARACTER or COLOR_CHAR or any descendant thereof.

```
les  di,O
push es                    ; Push Self parameter
push di
mov  di,es:[di+2]          ; Calculate offset of VMT pointer within Self
call DWORD PTR [di+4]      ; Calc offset of ShowChar within VMT and Call
```

Writing a Method in Assembler

The declaration of an external method is done by placing the External keyword at the implementation of the method. The type definition of the object does not reflect whether the method is or is not external.

An external method is not much different than an external procedure or function. The only difference is that an extra parameter is passed into the routine. This extra parameter is the last parameter pushed on the stack and is a 32-bit pointer. This is the Self parameter and is a pointer to the instance of the object that is being called. You can access this field simply as a pointer to a record. The record is the field within the object itself.

Turbo Assembler

Turbo Assembler provides several shortcuts to assembly language programming. Most of these extensions help take the difficulty out of programming in assembly language.

Using the ARG Directive

The ARG directive allows you not to have to use BP relative addressing as discussed in the previous section, ''Accessing Parameters and Local Variables.'' The ARG directive defines a label local to a procedure. Use of the ARG directive is straightforward and removes the restriction of having the label defined only once in the assembly language code. Turbo Assembler allows you to use the same symbol in another ARG for another procedure.

ARG automatically determines the offsets of the parameters relative to BP and computes the correct offset regardless of whether you use a FAR call or a NEAR call. In addition, it calculates the size of the parameter block for the RET instruction.

To use the ARG directive, list the parameters in reverse order to the order in which they are passed. The following line defines a procedure that takes a word parameter and a longint parameter:

```
Procedure MyProc ( w : Word; l : LongInt ); external;
```

The BP relative address would require the following assembler code for a NEAR procedure:

```
w    EQU WORD  PTR [BP+08]
l    EQU DWORD PTR [BP+04]
```

The following would be required for a FAR procedure:

```
l     EQU DWORD PTR [BP+06]
w     EQU WORD  PTR [BP+0A]
```

The ARG directive allows you to define the procedure and parameters as follows:

```
MyProc      PROC
            ARG l : DWORD, w : WORD = RetValue
```

The label w will automatically be equated to WORD PTR [BP+08] or WORD PTR [BP+0A] depending on whether the routine is NEAR or FAR. l will be equated to DWORD PTR [BP+04] or DWORD PTR [BP+06]. RetValue will be set to 6, the number of bytes of the parameter block (2 bytes for w plus 4 bytes for l). You can change the RET at the end of this procedure to look like this:

```
RET RetValue
```

instead of this:

```
RET 06
```

Turbo Pascal pushes BYTE size parameters as WORD size with the high-order byte undefined, so you must pass this information to the ARG directive. The following lines define a procedure that takes a byte and char parameter.

Pascal:

```
Procedure MyOtherProc ( b : Byte; c : Char );
```

Turbo Assembler:

```
MyOtherProc    PROC
               ARG c : BYTE : 2, b : BYTE : 2 = RetValue
```

The last line tells the ARG directive to define the variables b and c as an array of two bytes. By default, if you specify BYTE with no count, Turbo Assembler assumes a count of two (because the 8086 does not allow you to push an argument onto the stack as a byte).

Using the RETURNS Keyword

The RETURNS keyword is another useful enhancement provided by Turbo Assembler. The Turbo Assembler RETURNS keyword allows you to define an item on the stack that will not be removed from the stack on termination of the procedure.

All of Turbo Pascal's function results, except strings, are returned through the registers; the `string` function result is a pointer that is pushed onto the stack. Because Turbo Pascal returns only strings on the stack, you use RETURNS in a module to be linked to a Pascal program only if it is for a function returning a string. Additionally, RETURNS can be used only in combination with ARG.

The following example takes a `string` parameter and returns a `string` type function result:

Pascal:

```
Function MyFunc ( Var s : String ) : String; external;
```

Turbo Assembler:

```
MyFunc    PROC
          ARG s : DWORD = RetValue RETURNS res : DWORD
```

Using the LOCAL Directive

Turbo Assembler has shortcuts not only for passed parameters and string function results but also for local variables. With the LOCAL directive, you can do essentially the same thing that ARG did. LOCAL allows you to define your local variables and records their sizes in an optional label. The LOCAL directive does not set up the stack for the procedure, just the labels. The `size` parameter can be used to set up the stack.

The following lines show use of the LOCAL directive in the example described in the "Accessing Parameters and Local Variables" section:

Pascal:

```
Procedure MyProc ( Var s : String; b : Byte; l : LongInt ); external
```

Turbo Assembler:

```
MyProc    PROC
          ARG l : DWORD, b : BYTE : 2, s : DWORD = RetValue
          LOCAL Temp1 : WORD, Temp2 : WORD = LocalVarSize
    PUSH  BP
    MOV   BP,SP
    SUB   SP,LocalVarSize
```

Where ARG allows you to replace your equates to the base pointer (BP) plus an address, LOCAL allows you to replace equates to BP minus an address. To see how local parameters are allocated on the stack, refer to figure 3.2.

Using the .MODEL Directive

Since Turbo Assembler is designed to work with Turbo Pascal, a .MODEL directive has been defined to handle Turbo Pascal-specific code by doing the following things for you:

❏ It lets you list ARG parameters in the correct order (left to right) instead of reverse order; this makes your code more readable and matches your Pascal code.

❏ Standard entry and exit code is automatically inserted. No longer do you have to place the following at the start of your procedures

```
PUSH BP
MOV  BP,SP
```

or the following at the end.

```
MOV  SP,BP
POP  BP
```

❏ If you use the LOCAL directive, you do not have to specify

```
SUB  SP,Local_Var_Size
```

Turbo Assembler automatically computes the size based on the LOCAL directive and inserts this into the entry code.

❏ You do not have to specify the parameter block size in your RET instruction; Turbo Assembler automatically computes the size and inserts it.

Using a Swap Procedure

Listing 3.2 is an example of writing a Turbo Pascal procedure in Turbo Assembler. This procedure takes two untyped variable parameters and one word parameter. The purpose of the routine is to swap the two untyped parameter's values. The third word parameter specifies the number of bytes to be swapped. We need this third parameter because there is no way to determine the size of the untyped parameters. Listing 3.3 is the corresponding Turbo Pascal code.

Listing 3.2. *Swap Procedure—Turbo Assembler Code*

```
.MODEL TPASCAL
.CODE
Swap PROC FAR
     PUBLIC Swap
     ARG one : DWORD, two : DWORD, MoveSize : WORD

     push ds                ; Save DS
     mov  cx, MoveSize       ; Place the number of bytes to move into CX
     cmp  cx,0               ; If there are no bytes to move
     jz   Done               ;    then QUIT
     cld                     ; Clear the direction flag for LODSB/STOSB
     lds  si, one            ; Make DS:SI point to ONE
     les  di, two            ; Make ES:DI point to TWO
Looper:
     mov  al,BYTE PTR ds:si  ; Move one byte from ONE to AL
     mov  bl,BYTE PTR es:di  ; Move one byte from TWO to BL
     mov  BYTE PTR ds:si, bl ; Move AL to TWO
     mov  BYTE PTR es:di, al ; Move BL to ONE

     inc  si                 ; Add 1 to SI
     inc  di                 ; Add 1 to DI
     loop Looper             ; If there are still bytes to move, loop again

Done:
     pop  ds                 ; restore DS
     ret
Swap ENDP

ENDS
END
```

Listing 3.3. *Swap Procedure—Pascal Code*

```
Program XChange;

{$L SWAP.OBJ}

{$F+}
Procedure Swap ( var one, two; MoveSize : Word ); external;
{$F-}

Type
  recType = Record
              b : Byte;
              w : Word;
              r : Real;
              s : String;
            End;
```

```
Var
  r1,
  r2 : recType;

Begin
  r1.b := 163;              { Initialize record R1 }
  r1.w := 12345;
  r1.r := 3.14159;
  r1.s := 'This is a test. Number 1';

  r2.b := 136;              { Initialize record R2 }
  r2.w := 54321;
  r2.r := 123.321;
  r2.s := 'This is the second string. Number 2';

  Swap ( r1, r2, SizeOf ( r2 ) ); { Swap R1 and R2 }
End.
```

In listing 3.3 by stepping through the program from the debugger, you can set a watch on r1 and r2 and see that the values swap.

The first thing to notice in the Turbo Assembler code in listing 3.2 is the .MODEL TPASCAL, which relieves us of the entry and exit code, defining the equates for the parameters, and specifying how many bytes to remove from the stack with the RET command.

The DS register is saved because we are using two commands to load DS:SI and ES:DI with the parameters passed in. The untyped parameters have to be variable parameters (remember that all variable parameters are just pointers). We load DS:SI with the source variable (SI could be thought of as *Source Index*), and we load ES:DI with the destination variable (DI can also be thought of as *Destination Index*). Two Turbo Assembler commands are provided in 80 × 86 assembly language to move to and from the source and destination indexes: LODSB will move one byte from DS:SI into AL and increment the SI register; STOSB will copy AL into ES:DI and then increment DI. These commands are handy when dealing with pointers.

We use the CLD command to clear the direction flag because LODSB and STOSB will either increment SI and DI, respectively, or decrement them, based on the direction flag. By clearing the direction flag, we make them increment the registers.

The bare bones of the routine is simple:

❑ Load CX with the number of bytes to be moved.

❑ Move one byte from the source variable (One) into AL.

❏ Move one byte from the destination variable (Two) into BL.

❏ Put them back in the other variable.

❏ Increment the pointers to these variables to point to the next byte.

❏ Loop to do the next exchange.

To do the procedure just described looks easy in Pascal, but you have to define a local variable for temporary storage, like this:

```
Temp := One;
One := Two;
Two := Temp;
```

If you want to conserve your stack space, or you do not know what variables you want to swap ahead of time, use the Swap procedure.

Using a String Function

Listing 3.4 shows how to deal with a function in Turbo Assembler. It is a routine that strips all occurrences of a character from a string. This function requires two parameters: the string to be processed and the character to strip from the string. The modified string will be returned as a function result. Listing 3.5 is a program using the Assembler in listing 3.4.

Listing 3.4. *Strip Character—Turbo Assembler Code*

```
.MODEL TPASCAL
.CODE

StripChar PROC FAR
    PUBLIC StripChar
    ARG InpSt : DWORD, char : BYTE : 2 RETURNS OutSt : DWORD
    LOCAL counter : WORD

    push ds
    lds  si, InpSt      ; Load pointer to InpSt into DS:SI
    les  di, OutSt      ; Load pointer to OutSt into ES:DI
    mov  Counter,0      ; Zero out Counter
    lodsb               ; Load length byte into AL
    cmp  al, 0          ; If Length ( InpSt ) = 0
    je   Done           ;    then Quit
    mov  cl, al         ; Move length of InpSt into CX
    xor  ch, ch
    stosb               ; Move length of InpSt into OutSt
```

```
Looper:
    lodsb              ; Load a new Char from InpSt into AL
    cmp  al, char      ; Is this a char to strip?
    je   BottomOfLoop  ;   Yes: Don't add to function result
    stosb              ;   No: Add to OutSt and
    inc  Counter       ;        Increment Counter

BottomOfLoop:
    loop Looper        ; If not at end of InpSt, loop again

Done:
    mov  ax, Counter   ; Move length of OutSt into AL
    les  di, OutSt     ; Reload OutSt into ES:DI
    stosb              ; Save length of OutSt in OutSt

    pop  ds            ; Restore DS
    ret
StripChar ENDP

ENDS
END
```

Listing 3.5. Strip Character—Pascal Code

```
Program Strip;

{$L STRIP.OBJ}

{$F+}
Function StripChar ( s : String; ch : Char ) : String; external;
{$F-}

Var
  s : String;

Begin
  Write ( 'Enter a string to strip: ' );
  ReadLn ( s );
  s := StripChar ( s, ' ' );
  WriteLn ( s );
End.
```

Like the procedure example, this function example uses .MODEL TPASCAL. If you have the power to make your programming easy, use it! This example also uses the ARG and LOCAL directives. If you were to look at a diagram of the stack (see figure 3.3), you would see how all the parameters are laid out. In addition, you would see where the temporary storage is placed for the string function result.

Fig. 3.6. Strip character stack.

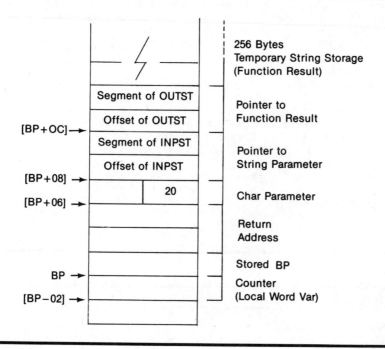

In this example, the local parameter `counter` determines how many actual characters are in the result string. Every time a character is added to the result string, the local variable is incremented. At the end of the routine, the local variable is copied into the start of the string. This is the location of the length byte of the string. The routine would run faster if a register (like DX) were used instead of a local parameter. Register operations are faster than BP relative addressing, but this is an example of how you could use a local variable within a Turbo Assembler program.

As with the swap procedure sample, the DS register is saved. The DS:SI and ES:DI pointers are used with LODSB and STOSB again. The length of the string is placed into CX. This value is checked to see whether the string is empty. If so, the program jumps to the end of the routine to quit; if not, the LODSB command is used to load a byte from DS:SI into AL. The AL register is then compared to the `char` parameter. If they are the same, the program skips and loops again; if not, then the character is stored into ES:DI with the STOSB command, and the counter is incremented.

Review

This chapter presents information about what is required to link assembly language code to Turbo Pascal, discussing the major restrictions. We provide details about passing parameters as either value or variable and show several diagrams of the stack and how parameters are placed on it. The features and advantages of using Turbo Assembler with Turbo Pascal are discussed. Finally, we provide several short, sample programs demonstrating the major concepts covered in the chapter.

Linking with Turbo C

Turbo Pascal's capability of linking object (.OBJ) files is not limited to files that are created in assembly language. It also gives you the limited capability of linking object files created with a higher-level language. Chapter 3 introduced the concepts of linking assembly language files with Turbo Pascal routines. This chapter focuses on creating Turbo C files that can be linked into Turbo Pascal; the concepts can be applied to other languages as well. We describe the required parameters for Turbo C and the calling conventions used by both Turbo Pascal and Turbo C, and we show what you can do to get around some of Turbo Pascal's linking limitations. This chapter also contains a support utility to automate some of the linking procedures. Through the use of this utility, you will be able to increase your use of Turbo Pascal's object file ''link-ability.''

Turbo Pascal is a powerful language that can accomplish many things, but you might encounter some situations in which it is not the ideal language to use. You may need to use the capabilities of another high-level language for some parts of some projects. In these situations, what you want to do is take advantage of the strong points of various languages by writing some sections in a different language and adding the resulting module into Turbo Pascal.

An advantage of using a C module in a Turbo Pascal program is the difference in execution speeds of the two languages. Routines that are coded similarly in Turbo Pascal and Turbo C show that the C routine is quicker. C routines are also more compact than Pascal routines, and compact routines execute faster.

Restrictions for Linked Object Files

Turbo Pascal places many restrictions on what can be contained in the object file to be linked into a program:

❏ To be able to link in an object file from a high-level language, you must be able to control the structure of the object file.

❏ You must be able to control the naming conventions used for the code segments and data segments: the code segment must be called CSEG or CODE; the data segment must be called DSEG or DATA.

❏ The object file cannot contain any initialized data. (In C this means no initialized statics.)

❏ All symbols must have legal Pascal identifier names.

❏ The object file cannot contain any groups or classes.

All these restrictions can be controlled when using Turbo C and Turbo Pascal. Other languages might not give you this control, thereby making the linking process that much more difficult.

Table 4.1 lists the command-line options that must be passed to the Turbo C compiler (TCC) when it is being used to create an object file for linking into a Turbo Pascal program. Failing to use any of these options will cause the linking process to fail. You can set these options through the Turbo C integrated environment by saving the options to a TCCONFIG.TC file and then converting this file to a configuration file that can be used by TCC. This configuration conversion utility TCCONFIG.EXE is included on the Turbo C distribution diskettes.

Table 4.1. *Parameters for TCC*

Option	Meaning
-wrvl	Enable all warnings
-p	Use Pascal calling conventions
-k-	Standard stack frame off
-r	Use the register variables
-u-	Underscore generation is off
-c	Compile to an .OBJ file—no .EXE file
-ms	Ensure small memory model
-zCCODE	Name the code segment CODE
-zP	Do not create the code group
-zA	Do not create the code class
-zRCONST	Name the static data segment CONST

-zS	Do not create the data group
-zT	Do not create the data class
-zDDATA	Name the data segment DATA
-zG	Do not create the BSS group
-zB	Do not create the BSS class
-Ipath	Path to the include files
-Lpath	Path to the library files

Another way of causing TCC to use these options is to enter the options *only* into the Turbo C editor (or any ASCII text editor) and then save it to disk in a file called TURBOC.CFG. After you create this configuration file and save it into your Turbo C directory, do the following things in Turbo Pascal to prepare to link in an object file:

1. Create a procedure header that matches the parameters of the routine in the object file. Be sure to include the correct parameter names and types in the header.

2. Make sure that the procedure is compiled with the correct call model. This can be controlled by its location in the Pascal code, placing it in the interface section of a unit rather than elsewhere in the code and using the {$F} compiler directive.

3. Use a {$L} compiler directive to instruct Turbo Pascal to link in the required object file.

Listing 4.1 is the C source code for our first example of linking a C routine into a Turbo Pascal program; listing 4.2 is the related Turbo Pascal program. This example is a C macro that converts a character to uppercase; incorporating the macro into a routine converts a Pascal string to all uppercase.

Listing 4.1. *Turbo C Character Conversion Module*

```
/* Sample module to be linked as an .OBJ file into Turbo    */
/* Pascal. Must be compiled with the TURBOC.CFG file in     */
/* Table 4.1.                                               */

#define UpCase(c) ((c) >= 'a' && (c) <= 'z' ? ((c) - 32) : (c))

/* Procedure UpString( Var S : String );                    */
/* Pascal procedure Header and parameters                   */
```

Listing 4.1 *continues*

Listing 4.1 *continued*

```
void pascal far UpString(char *s)
{
  register char *strPtr;

  for (strPtr = &s[1]; *strPtr != '\0'; strPtr++)
    *strPtr = upCase(*strPtr);
}
```

Listing 4.2. *Turbo Pascal Character Conversion Program*

```
Program CLinkDemo1;
{ This sample program is a simple example of how to create a   }
{ routine in Turbo C that can be linked into a Turbo Pascal    }
{ program.                                                     }
{ $A-, F- }

Uses Crt;

Var
  OldString,                 { Original String before conversion }
  NewString : String;        { Copy of string. This will be the  }
                             { string passed to the C routine.    }

{$L List4-1}                 { Link in the C OBJ file.            }

{$F+}                        { Enforce the Far Call requirement   }
Procedure UpString( Var S : String ); External;
{ Heading of the external procedure contained in the Turbo C    }
{ .OBJ file.                                                     }
{$F-}

Begin                        { Main program                      }
  ClrScr;                    { Clear the screen                  }
  GotoXY( 1,5 );             { Reposition the Cursor             }
  Write( 'Enter a lowercase string: ' );
  Readln( OldString );       { Prompt user and get the input     }
  NewString := OldString;    { Save copy of string for output    }
  UpString( NewString );     { Convert string to UpperCase       }
  Writeln( 'Lowercase = ', OldString );
  Writeln( 'Uppercase = ', NewString );
                             { Show the results to the user      }
  Write( 'Press any key to quit' );
  While( Not Keypressed ) Do
    { NOP };                 { Pause for a keypress              }
End.
```

To use listings 4.1 and 4.2, do this:

1. Enter the listings.

2. Compile the Turbo C file with TCC, making sure that the configuration file for TCC outlined in table 4.1 is available to the command-line compiler.

3. Use Turbo Pascal's IDE compiler or the command-line compiler. Make sure to have stack overflow checking and range checking turned off ({$S-} and {$R-}) within the compiling environment for this example.

Listings 4.3 and 4.4 show how a routine contained in the Turbo C object file can call a procedure in the Turbo Pascal code. This is possible by defining the Pascal procedure in the C code as external in the C code and having a result type void. Enter listings 4.3 and 4.4 using the steps just given for listings 4.1 and 4.2.

***Listing 4.3.** Turbo C Module (Call to Turbo Pascal)*

```
/* C module that will place a call to a procedure defined in */
/* the Turbo Pascal program that links in this module.       */

extern void PasProc (void);
/* External Pascal procedure that is called by this C module */

void pascal StartUpC (void)
{
  register int counter;
  for (counter = 1; counter <= 15; counter++ )
    PasProc();
}
```

***Listing 4.4.** Turbo Pascal Driving Program*

```
Program CCallsPascal;
{ This is a sample Pascal program that demonstrates a way of  }
{ interfacing a Turbo Pascal procedure to be called from the  }
{ Turbo C module that is linked in.                           }
{ $A-, F- }

Uses Crt;
```

***Listing 4.4** continues*

Listing 4.4 *continued*

```
Var
  Count : Integer;

{$L list4-3}

Procedure StartUpC; External;

Procedure PasProc;
{ This is the procedure that will be called from within the   }
{ Turbo C object module. All this will do is output a string  }
{ to the screen and increment a global variable. This         }
{ variable will keep track of the number of times the routine }
{ is called.                                                  }

Begin
  Inc( Count );             { Add 1 to global variable         }
  Write( Count, ' ' );      { Output the new value             }
End;

Begin
  Count := 0;               { Initialize the counter.          }
  ClrScr;                   { Clear the user screen            }
  StartUpC;                 { Call the external C routine       }
  Writeln;                  { Output a CR/LF to screen          }
  Writeln( 'The Pascal routine was called a total of ',
           Count, ' times.' );
                            { Report number of times called    }
  Write( 'Press any key to continue...' );
  While( Not Keypressed ) Do
    { NOP };                { Pause the program for keypress   }
End.
```

After executing the Turbo Pascal program, did you notice that the Pascal procedure was called only one time? That is because of one compatibility problem when calling a Turbo Pascal routine from inside the C module. If the C module is compiled with the −r switch, which instructs the C module to use the SI and DI registers as general purpose registers, this behavior will occur because Turbo Pascal does not save and restore the values contained in these registers. You must define a C macro that will save and restore these registers before and after the Pascal code is called. Listing 4.5 shows the header file that will be used to handle these registers; listing 4.6 is listing 4.3 after the necessary modifications have been made to allow it to work properly; listing 4.7 is the modified Turbo Pascal code from listing 4.4.

Listing 4.5. *SI and DI Save Routine*

```
/* SAVE THIS FILE AS SAVESIDI.H                              */
/*                                                           */
/* Header file to define a save and restore macro for the SI */
/* and DI registers. For use when a TC module is compiled    */
/* with the -r directive, and the module is to be linked to  */
/* a Turbo Pascal program.                                   */

typedef unsigned int WORD;

#define save_sidi {extern WORD far *_rsp; *_rsp++ = _SI; *_rsp++ = _DI;}
#define rest_sidi {extern WORD far *_rsp; _DI = *--_rsp; _SI = *--_rsp;}
```

Listing 4.6. *Modified C Module (from Listing 4.3)*

```
/* C module that will place a call to a Procedure defined in */
/* the Turbo Pascal program that links in this module.       */

#include "savesidi.h"   /* include macros to save si and di  */

extern void PasProc (void);
/* External Pascal procedure that is called by this C module */

void StartUpC (void)
{
  register int counter;
  for (counter = 1; counter <= 15; counter++ ) {
    save_sidi;
    PasProc();
    rest_sidi;
  }
}
```

Listing 4.7. *Modified Pascal Code (from Listing 4.4)*

```
Program CCallsPascal;
{ This is a sample Pascal program that demonstrates a way of  }
{ interfacing a Turbo Pascal procedure to be called from the  }
{ Turbo C module that is linked in.                           }
{ $A-, F- }

Uses Crt;
```

***Listing 4.7** continued*

```
Var
   Count : Integer;        { Counter var for # of calls to proc }
   _rsp : Pointer;         { Pointer to memory to save SI & DI  }
   SiDiStack : Array[0..10] of Word;
                           { Memory locations for SI and DI     }

{$L list4-6}

Procedure StartUpC; External;

Procedure PasProc;
{ This is the procedure that will be called from within the   }
{ Turbo C object module. All this will do is output a string  }
{ to the screen and increment a global variable. This         }
{ variable will keep track of the number of times the routine }
{ is called.                                                  }

Begin
   Inc( Count );           { Add 1 to global variable          }
   Write( Count, ' ' );    { Output the new value              }
End;

Begin
   Count := 0;             { Initialize the counter.           }
   _rsp := @SiDiStack;     { Initialize memory to save SI & DI }
   ClrScr;                 { Clear the user screen             }
   StartUpC;               { Call the external C routine        }
   Writeln;                { Output a CR/LF to screen           }
   Writeln( 'The Pascal routine was called a total of ',
            Count, ' times.' );
                           { Report number of times called     }
   Write( 'Press any key to continue...' );
   While( Not Keypressed ) Do
      { NOP };             { Pause the program for keypress     }
End.
```

Listings 4.8 and 4.9 demonstrate how a C module can make a simulated call to a Turbo Pascal run-time library routine. This is accomplished by first using C to define a Turbo Pascal procedure that has the same parameter list as the one we want to call from the Pascal run-time library. This Pascal routine will then be the one to actually call the Turbo Pascal run-time library routine.

Listing 4.8. Turbo C Module

```
/* This module will make a call to an external routine in the */
/* driving Turbo Pascal program that will make a call to a    */
/* routine in Turbo Pascal's run-time library.                */

#include "savesidi.h"

extern WORD PasDosVersion();
extern long PasDiskFree (WORD drive);
extern long PasDiskSize (WORD drive);

void startupc (long far *free, long far *size, WORD far *ver)
{
  save_sidi;
  *ver = PasDosVersion();
  rest_sidi;
  save_sidi;
  *free = PasDiskFree (0);
  rest_sidi;
  save_sidi;
  *size = PasDiskSize (0);
  rest_sidi;
}
```

Listing 4.9. Turbo Pascal Program

```
Program AnotherCExample;
{ This next example will interface several routines from Turbo }
{ Pascal's DOS unit so they are able to be called from the     }
{ external C module. This routine also defines the necessary   }
{ memory locations to store the SI and DI registers, as Turbo  }
{ Pascal trashes these values when C uses them as general      }
{ purpose registers.                                           }
{ $A-, F- }

Uses Crt, Dos;     { Link in these two standard units          }

Var
  Ver : Word;       { Location for result of DosVersion call   }
  Size : LongInt;   { Location for result of DiskSize call     }
  Free : LongInt;   { Location for result of DiskFree call     }
  _rsp : Pointer;   { Memory to store the SI and DI registers  }
  SiDiStack : Array[0..10] of Word;
```

Listing 4.9 continues

Listing 4.9 *continued*

```
{$L List4-8}        { Link in required C module                    }

Procedure StartupC( Var Free, Size : LongInt; Var Ver : Word ); External;
{ This is the header for the external C module that will be        }
{ called by this Turbo Pascal program.                             }

Function PasDosVersion : Word;
{ Local Function that will make the actual call to the routine }
{ in the DOS unit.                                             }

Begin
  PasDosVersion := DosVersion;
End;

Function PasDiskFree( Drive : Byte ) : LongInt;
{ Local Function that will make the actual call to the routine }
{ in the DOS unit.                                             }
Begin
  PasDiskFree := DiskFree( Drive );
End;

Function PasDiskSize( Drive : Byte ) : LongInt;
{ Local Function that will make the actual call to the routine }
{ in the DOS unit.                                             }
Begin
  PasDiskSize := DiskSize( Drive );
End;

Begin
  _rsp := @SiDiStack;         { Point to storage for SI and DI   }
  StartupC( Free, Size, Ver ); { Call the C module               }
  ClrScr;                     { Clear the User Screen            }
  GotoXY( 1,5 );              { Reposition the Cursor            }
  Writeln( 'Current DOS version is ', Lo( Ver ), '.', Hi( Ver ) );
  Writeln( 'Total disk capacity is  ', Size );
  Writeln( 'Total bytes free is     ', Free );
  Writeln;
  Writeln( 'Press any key to continue...' );
                             { Output the results and pause      }
  While( Not Keypressed ) Do
    { NOP };
End.
```

Listings 4.8 and 4.9 may not seem to be the most efficient way to make this call. That is indeed the case. We could have made the call directly from the C module to Turbo Pascal's run-time library through the use of a pointer variable that actually contains the address of the procedure we want to call. Instead, we leave this as an exercise for you.

Our last, simple example, in listings 4.10 and 4.11, is a demonstration of modifying a variable defined in the Pascal code and then passing the modified variable to another routine defined in the Pascal code. We accomplish this by defining the variable globally to the Pascal code and externally in the C module; the variable can then be passed to the Pascal code where it will be modified. You can even modify a variable defined in Turbo Pascal's System or Crt unit from within the C code.

Listing 4.10. *Turbo C Variable Modification Module*

```
/* This C Module has its main procedure StartUpC called from */
/* the Turbo Pascal program that links this in. This will     */
/* then make a call to a procedure within the Pascal code.    */
/* Additionally, this module modifies a variable in the       */
/* Pascal code. This variable is actually contained within    */
/* Turbo Pascal's Crt unit.                                   */

#include "savesidi.h" /* include header for reg save routine */

extern WORD TPTextAttr;
                      /* variable defined in pascal code.     */

extern int I;          /* second variable defined in pascal  */

extern void CallFromC (int I);
/* Pascal procedure we will call from this C module           */

void StartUpC (void)
{
  register int count;
  for (count = 1; count <= 10; count++) {
    save_sidi;
    CallFromC(I++);
    rest_sidi;
    TPTextAttr = count;
  }
}
```

Listing 4.11. *Turbo Pascal Variable Modification Program*

```
Program LastSampleProgram;
{ This sample program interfaces one of the variables defined }
{ in Turbo Pascal's Crt unit. This variable is then modified  }
{ within the C module. We also have a Pascal procedure that   }
```

Listing 4.11 *continues*

Listing 4.11 *continued*

```
{ is called from the C routine.                           }
{ $A-, F- }

Uses Crt;              { Link in the Crt unit              }

Var
  _rsp : Pointer;      { Memory for the SI and DI registers }
  SiDiStack : Array[0..10] of Word;
  OldI, I : Integer; { Variable that will be modified in C }
  TPTextAttr : Word Absolute TextAttr;
                       { Declared ABSOLUTE so C can see it }

{$L List4-11}          { Link the C Module                 }

Procedure StartUpC; External;
{ This procedure is the main routine contained within the C }
{ external routines.                                        }

Procedure CallFromC( I : Integer );
{ This is a procedure that will be called from the external }
{ module created with Turbo C.                              }

Begin
  Writeln( 'Old Value of I was ', OldI );
  Writeln( 'New value of I is ', I );
  OldI := I;
End;

Begin
  _rsp := @SiDiStack;    { Point to memory for SI and DI   }
  I := 1;                { Initialize value of I to 1.     }
  OldI := 0;             { Set old value of I for later use }
  StartUpC;              { Call the C module               }
  Writeln( 'Press any key to continue....' );
  While( Not Keypressed ) Do
    { NOP };             { Pause for viewing of screen     }
End.
```

Most of the examples we provide in this chapter are simple because of the heavy restrictions that Turbo Pascal places on an object file that it attempts to link. Linking a Turbo C module that makes a call to an external routine that is not contained within the Turbo Pascal code is difficult to accomplish. The object module cannot contain any initialized data and can have no identifiers that contain the a symbol. Turbo C will generate an identifier with the a symbol in it for any C-intrinsic function. The problem of external routines not within the Pascal code happens any time the C module calls a function within the Turbo C Runtime Library.

Some of these problems can be overcome if you have the Turbo C Runtime Library source code. With this code, you can extract the necessary routines, assemble them for Pascal calling conventions, and then link the resulting object file into the Turbo Pascal program. Even this does not solve all of the linking problems.

One problem that requires special handling is this: when Turbo C uses a constant string, it places the string into initialized data, which ultimately goes into the data segment. That makes the resulting object file "unlinkable" with Turbo Pascal. You can circumvent this incompatibility by defining the constant string as an external in the C module and then defining it as a constant in the Turbo Pascal source code. For example, suppose that you had the following in the Turbo C module:

```
parse_string ("some intermediate string\n");
```

You would have to substitute the above with the following two lines of C code:

```
extern char *string1;
parse_string (string1 + 1);
```

The parameter passed to parse_string is the string constant plus one. This is necessary because Turbo Pascal defines its string type so that the first byte the string occupies is a dynamic length, which limits this technique to strings of fewer than 256 characters. Additionally, you would need to make the following constant definition from within the Turbo Pascal source code:

```
Const
  string1 : String[30] = 'some intermediate string'#10#0;
```

Linking with Turbo C Runtime Library

If you need to link a C module that makes a call to the Turbo C Runtime Library (RTL), you must have the Turbo C RTL source code. For without the code, Turbo Pascal cannot resolve the external definition to the required Turbo C RTL function.

To accomplish the otherwise impossible task of linking a C module that calls the Turbo C RTL, do the following:

1. After the C module has been coded, compile the code to an object file with the parameters specified in table 4.1.

2. Recompile the module from the Turbo C Runtime Library with the correct parameters for an object file that will be linked into Turbo Pascal.

3. Create the driving Turbo Pascal program. This program will need to link both the object file for the C module created earlier as well as the object file that contains the routine from the Turbo C Runtime Library. Each will have the corresponding function header and parameter types.

4. Compile the Turbo Pascal program.

Listing 4.12 provides the C source code for a call to the Turbo C function pow. Listing 4.13 contains the driving Turbo Pascal program that links in the C module that calls pow; it also contains the necessary code to link the POW.OBJ file into Turbo Pascal, thereby successfully creating the program. If you do not have the Turbo C RTL source code, you will not be able to create the POW.OBJ file necessary for this example.

Listing 4.12. *Turbo C Calling C RTL*

```
/* Simple C Module that will make a call to the C RTL function */
/* pow. Note that this is just a simple exercise, but is also  */
/* a useless one unless you own the Turbo C RTL.               */

#include <math.h>

extern double result;

void power (double *x, double *y)
{
   result = pow (*x, *y);
}
```

Listing 4.13. *Turbo Pascal Driving Routine for Call to C RTL Function*

```
Program LinkCRTL;
{ This program is a simple driving program that shows how to   }
{ link a C module that contains a call to a C RTL function into }
{ a Turbo Pascal program. Note that the Pascal program must be  }
{ the one that links the C RTL function into the final          }
{ executable file.                                              }

{$N+,E+}

Uses Crt;

Var
  X,Y : Double;
  Result : Double;

{$L pow}
```

```
Function pow( x, y : double ) : double; External;
{ Header for the Turbo C RTL routine that will be linked into   }
{ sample program.                                               }

{$L list4-12}

procedure power( x,y : double ); External;
{ External C routine contained in the module TESTPOW.OBJ. This  }
{ function will make a call to the Pascal routine that links    }
{ the necessary C RTL function.                                 }

Begin
  Result := 0;
  X := 2.0;
  Y := 6.0;
  power( x,y );
  Writeln( Result );
End.
```

Linking Utilities

This section will present you with a utility that will facilitate the linking process of a module created with Turbo C into a Turbo Pascal program. This utility is contained in two separate programs. The first, called TC2TP, is really just a driving program that will execute, or spawn, each of the necessary pieces of the conversion utility. TC2TP performs the following steps:

1. Retrieve the file name from the command line via the ParamStr procedure from Turbo Pascal.

2. Spawn TCC with the appropriate command-line options, as outlined previously, and instruct it to generate an assembly listing rather than compiling to an .OBJ file.

3. If there were no errors reported by TCC, the second part of this utility, C2P, is spawned.

4. If C2P reports a successful conversion, we then spawn the assembler installed in the ASMPath constant and instruct it to assemble the massaged .ASM file that was generated by TCC into a Turbo Pascal compatible .OBJ file.

Listing 4.14 is this main, front-end program.

Listing 4.14. *Program TC2TP*

```
{$R-,S-,I-,D+,F-,V-,B-,N-,L+ }
{$M 4096,0,0}

Program TC2TP;
{ This is the front-end program that will drive all of the    }
{ necessary processes to create a usable .OBJ file from a     }
{ Turbo C routine.  It will first spawn TCC to compile the C  }
{ module with the correct options set.  It will then spawn    }
{ the second part of this module, C2P.  C2P will massage the  }
{ .ASM file that was generated by the call to TCC to be       }
{ compatible with Turbo Pascal.                               }

Uses
  DOS, Tools;              { Link in the necessary units       }

Type
  Path           = String[71];

Const
{ These constants must be changed to reflect the location of  }
{ these programs on your system.  Failure to do this will     }
{ cause the program to not execute correctly.                 }
  TCCPath        : Path = 'R:\Tcc.exe';
  IncPath        : Path = 'R:\include';
  AsmPath        : Path = 'M:\tasm.exe';
  C2PPath        : Path = 'C2P.EXE';
  DoAssembly     : Boolean = TRUE;
  Optimize       : Boolean = TRUE;
  LargeCode      : Boolean = FALSE;

Var
  FileName       : Path;

Procedure ProcessCmdLine;
{ This procedure will process the command line for any        }
{ options that have been passed.  They will set the           }
{ appropriate info inside the program.                        }

Type
  CommandLine    = String[127];

Var
  I              : Word;
  Opt            : Path;

Begin
  For I := 1 to ParamCount Do
  Begin
    Opt := ParamStr(I);
```

```
      Case Opt[1] Of
        '/','-' : Case UpCase( Opt[2] ) of
                    'N' : DoAssembly  := FALSE; {No Assembly}
                    'L' : LargeCode   := TRUE;  {Large Code}
                    'I' : IncPath     := RightStr(Opt,3);
                                             {Include path}
                    'S' : Optimize    := FALSE; {Slow}
                  End;
          Else
             FileName := Opt;
        End;
    End;
End;

Procedure MyExec(Prog,Cmd : String);
{ This program will execute the required utility program that }
{ is used by this program.                                    }

Begin
  SwapVectors;
  Exec(Prog,Cmd);
  SwapVectors;
End;


Function SpawnTCC(FName : Path) : Boolean;
{ This routine will spawn the Turbo C command line compiler  }
{ assuring that the correct options have been passed to it.  }

Var
  CommandLine       : String;
  Model             : String[4];
  Opto              : String[9];

Begin
  If LargeCode Then
    Model := '-ml '
  Else
    Model := '-mc ';
  If Optimize Then
    Opto := '-Z -G -O '
  Else
    Opto := '';

  CommandLine  := Model + Opto + '-S -c -p -u- -k -I'+
                  IncPath + ' ' + FName;
  MyExec( TCCPath,CommandLine );
  If DOSError <> 0 Then
```

Listing 4.14 continues

Listing 4.14 continued

```
  Begin
    Writeln( 'Error spawning ',TCCPath );
    Writeln( 'DosError = ',DosError );
    SpawnTCC := FALSE;
    Exit;
  End;
  If DosExitCode = 0 Then
  Begin
    Writeln( 'C code compiled successfully!' );
    SpawnTCC := TRUE;
  End
  Else
    SpawnTCC := FALSE;
End;

Function SpawnC2P( FName : Path ) : Boolean;
{ This routine will spawn the second utility program in our   }
{ conversion routines.                                        }
Var
  ExitCode          : Integer;
  Msg               : Str80;

Begin
  MyExec( C2PPath,FName );
  If DosError <> 0 Then
  Begin
    Writeln('Error spawning ',C2PPath);
    Writeln('DOSError = ',DOSError);
  End;
  ExitCode := DOSExitCode;
  If ExitCode <> 0 Then
  Begin
    Case ExitCode of
      99 : Msg := 'File Not Specified';
      Else
        Msg := 'C2P error';
    End;
    Writeln(Msg);
  End;
  SpawnC2P := ( DOSError = 0 ) and ( ExitCode = 0 );
End;

Function SpawnAsm(FName : Path) : Boolean;
{ This program will spawn the Assembler installed by the ASM }
{ path in the constant.  You must make sure to point the path }
{ so it can locate the assembler.                             }
```

```
Begin
  MyExec( AsmPath,FName + ';' );
  If DOSError <> 0 Then
  Begin
    Writeln( 'DosError = ',DosError );
    Writeln( 'Error spawning ',ASMPath );
    SpawnASM := FALSE;
    Exit;
  End;
  If DosExitCode = 0 Then
  Begin
    Writeln( 'ASP file successfully assembled!' );
    SpawnAsm := TRUE;
  End
  Else
    SpawnAsm := FALSE;
End;

Procedure Advance2Lines;
{ Simple procedure to advance the screen two lines.            }

Begin
  Writeln;
  Writeln;
End;

Var
  Success          : Boolean;        { Local variable to Main }

Begin
  Advance2Lines;
  If( ParamCount < 1 ) Then
  Begin
    Writeln( 'TC2TP FileName' );
    Halt(99);
  End;
  ProcessCmdLine;
  Success := SpawnTCC( FileName );
  If Success Then
  Begin
    Advance2Lines;
    Success := SpawnC2P( FileName );
    If( Success and DoAssembly ) Then
    Begin
      Advance2Lines;
      Success := SpawnAsm( FileExt( FileName,'ASP' ) );
    End;
  End;
End.
```

The next part of this utility is a separate program, called C2P, that will read in the TCC generated .ASM file and massage, or convert, this file to a new .ASM file. This file now contains all the correct segment directives and identifier names so that when it is assembled, the file will be a Turbo Pascal-compatible .OBJ file.

Simply stated, the C2P routine will replace any segment names that occur in the C-generated .ASM file with names that are compatible to Turbo Pascal. It will also remove any GROUP information and change any identifiers to be compatible with Pascal.

With this in mind, here is the listing for the Pascal code that makes up the C2P program (see listing 4.15).

Listing 4.15. *Program C2P*

```
{$R-,S-,I-,D+,F-,V-,B-,N-,L+ }
{$M 8192,0,0}
Program C2P;
{ This program will process the .ASM file that has been      }
{ generated by the TC2TP program.  It will construct the file }
{ in such a manner as to allow the Turbo Pascal program to    }
{ link in the appropriate .OBJ file.                          }

Uses
  Tools;

Const
  BUFFERSIZE          = 16384;

Type
  StrPtr              = ^String;
  Path                = String[70];
  Str20               = String[20];
  Str80               = String[80];
  Str4                = String[4];
  Str8                = String[8];
  TextBuffer          = Array[1..BUFFERSIZE] of Byte;

Var
  Line                : String;
  OutFileName         : Path;
  F,OutF              : Text;
  InBuffer,
  OutBuffer           : TextBuffer;
  Code_Seg_Name       : Str20;

Const
  NumLines            : Word = 0;
  Proc_Keyword        : Str4       = 'PROC';
```

```
   Endp_Keyword      : Str4       = 'ENDP';
   Public_Keyword    : String[6] = 'PUBLIC';
   Extrn_Keyword     : String[5] = 'EXTRN';
   EndS_Keyword      : Str4       = 'ENDS';
   Segment_Keyword   : String[7] = 'SEGMENT';
   Assume_Keyword    : String[6] = 'ASSUME';
   Group_Keyword     : String[5] = 'GROUP';
   DGROUP_Keyword    : String[6] = 'DGROUP:';
   TEXT_Seg_Def      : String[5] = '_TEXT';
   DATA_Seg_Def      : String[5] = '_DATA';
   BSS_Seg_Def       : Str4       = '_BSS';

   Cur_Seg_Name      : Str20 = 'CODE';
   InCodeSegment     : Boolean = TRUE;

Procedure HaltError( ErrorCode : Integer; S : String );
{ Error handler, display error number, display error   }
{ message, terminate and set DOS error level to        }
{ ErrorCode.        }

Begin
  Writeln( 'Error ',ErrorCode );
  Writeln( S );
  Halt( ErrorCode );
End;

Procedure OutputLine( Line : String );
{ Procedure to output a new line to our assembly file.        }

Var
  E : Word;

Begin
  Writeln( OutF,Line );
  E := IOResult;
  If E <> 0 Then
    HaltError( E, 'Error writing ' + OutFileName );
End;

Procedure EndS_Def;
{ Procedure to output an end of segment identifier to the new }
{ assembly file being generated.        }

Var
  E : Integer;
  S : Str80;
```

Listing 4.15 continues

Listing 4.15 *continued*

```
Begin
  S := Cur_Seg_Name + '         ' + 'ENDS';
  OutputLine( S );
  InCodeSegment := FALSE;
End;

Procedure BeginS_Def;
{ Procedure to output the beginning of a segment to the new   }
{ assembly file being generated.                              }
Var
  E : Integer;
  S : String;
  Allignment : Str4;

Begin
  If InCodeSegment Then
  Begin
    Allignment := 'BYTE';
    Cur_Seg_Name   := 'CODE';
  End
  Else
  Begin
    Allignment := 'WORD';
    Cur_Seg_Name := 'DATA';
  End;
  S := Cur_Seg_Name + '  SEGMENT ' + Allignment + ' PUBLIC';
  OutputLine( S );
End;

Procedure Assume_Def;
{ Procedure to output the correct ASSUMEs for the new        }
{ assembly file being generated.                             }

Var
  E : Integer;

Begin
  OutputLine( '          ASSUME CS:CODE,DS:DATA' );
End;

Function CompareString( Var S1,S2 : String ) : Boolean;
{ if the strings are equal (including length) returns true    }

Begin
  CompareString :=
      CompMem( S1,S2,Succ( Length( S1 ) ) ) = _EQUAL_;
End;
```

```
Procedure Examine( Var S,Orig_Line : String );
{ The main logic line processing routine!  This procedure  }
{ determines how to translate each line into an assembly   }
{ language suitable for a TP4 bound asm module.  Since      }
{ there are only two segments we'll be using in the TP4 bound }
{ ASP file (the output file), the logic engine toggles     }
{ between emitting code (and the associated statements) and }
{ data (and its statements).                                }
Var
  SS : String;
  FirstWord : Str80;
  E : Integer;
  _Data_,_BSS_,_TEXT_
                  : Boolean;
Begin
  SS := S; { make a copy of the string and work on  }
          { the copy }

  { if this is an end segment definition then end   }
  { the current segment and Exit }

  If WordOnLine( EndS_Keyword,SS ) Then
  Begin
    Ends_Def;
    Exit;
  End;

  { if this is an ASSUME statement, then translate it }
  { and Exit }

  If WordOnLine( Assume_Keyword,SS ) Then
  Begin
    Assume_Def;
    Exit;
  End;

  { We ignore all GROUP statements }

  If WordOnLine( Group_Keyword,SS ) Then
    Exit;

  { the following conditional checks for an inline asm}
  { reference to DGROUP. If found, it is changed to   }
  { DATA in the ASP file. }

  If Pos( Dgroup_Keyword,SS ) > 0 Then
    ReplaceString( 'DGROUP','DATA',Orig_Line );
```

Listing 4.15 continues

Listing 4.15 continued

```
{ now get the first word on the line.  At this point}
{ all we need to do is check the first word, because}
{ we've already looked for ASSUME, GROUP, and ENDS  }
{ statements.  We now decide whether this is a       }
{ segment definition; if so, it is translated        }
{ accordingly.  Otherwise it is either code or data }
{ and it is written out to the ASP output file.      }

If WordOnLine( Segment_Keyword,SS ) Then
Begin

  FirstWord := ParseWord( SS,' ' ); { parse the first word  }

  { reset some booleans }
  _Data_  := FALSE;
  _BSS_   := FALSE;
  _TEXT_  := FALSE;

  { check to see if this line is a segment definition }
  If CompareString( FirstWord,DATA_Seg_Def ) Then
    _Data_:= TRUE
  Else
    If CompareString(FirstWord,BSS_Seg_Def) Then
      _BSS_  := TRUE

  { in case we're in a large memory model, we don't look }
  { for the segment _TEXT explicitly, instead, we look    }
  { for a segment which includes the string _TEXT.        }

  Else
    If Pos( TEXT_Seg_Def,FirstWord ) > 0 Then
    Begin
      _TEXT_  := TRUE;
      Code_Seg_Name := FirstWord;
    End;

  { if this is a segment, we decide whether it's code }
  { or data, and deal with it.  Otherwise, the line is}
  { either code, comment, or data, and should be      }
  { passed to the ASP file }

  If _Data_ or _BSS_ or _TEXT_ Then
  Begin
    If _TEXT_ Then
      InCodeSegment := TRUE
    Else
      InCodeSegment := FALSE;
    BeginS_Def; { start a new segment }
  End
```

```
      Else
        OutputLine( Orig_Line );
   End
   Else
     OutputLine(Orig_Line); { code, data,or comment, so     }
                            { output }
 End;

 procedure Process_Line(S : String);

 Var
   E : Integer;
   Line : String;

 Begin
   { prepare Line for processing: }
   Line := Trim(Line);        { trim leading and trailing}
                              { white space }
   If Length( Line ) = 0 Then{ if the length of trimmed   }
                             { string is 0, then Exit.  }

     Exit;

   Line := ExpandTabs( S );   { replace tabs with spaces }
   Line := UpperCase( Line );  { uppercase chars only      }

   Examine( Line,S ); { Call main logic. NOTE: This        }
                      { routine takes as parameters both }
                      { the prepared var Line and a copy }
                      { of the original source line.     }

 End;

 procedure Process_Asm_File( FPath : Path );

 Var
   E,
   L : Integer;

 Begin
   OutFileName := FileExt( FPath,'ASP' );
   Assign( F,FPath );
   SetTextBuf( F,InBuffer );
   Reset( F );
   E := IOResult;
   If E <> 0 Then
     HaltError(E,FPath + ' not found.');
   Assign( OutF,OutFileName );
   SetTextBuf( OutF,OutBuffer );
```

Listing 4.15 continues

***Listing 4.15** continued*

```
    Rewrite( OutF );
    E := IOResult;
    If E <> 0 Then
      HaltError(E,'Error opening '+OutFileName);
    Writeln('Creating new file: ',OutFileName);
    Writeln('working...');
    While Not EOF( F ) Do
    Begin
      Inc( NumLines );
      Readln( F,Line );
      E := IOResult;
      If E <> 0 Then
        HaltError( E,'Error reading ' + FPath );
      Process_Line( Line );
    End;
    Close( F );
    E := IOResult;
    Close( OutF );
    E := IOResult;
    If E <> 0 Then
      HaltError( E,'Error closing '+OutFileName );

End;

Var
  FName : Path;

Begin
  If ParamCount < 1 Then
  Begin
    Writeln( 'C2P AsmFileName' );
    Halt(99);
  End;
  FName := ParamStr( 1 );

  If Pos( '.',FName ) = 0 Then
    FName := FName + '.ASM';

  Process_Asm_File( FName );
  Writeln( NumLines,' lines processed' );
  Writeln( 'Success!' );
End.
```

The remaining files make up the unit TOOLS.PAS. As you can see, this is a collection of many different assembler routines that are necessary for the C2P and TC2TP programs. Simply assemble them to an .OBJ file so that they can be linked into the TOOLS.PAS unit when it is compiled. Make sure to save them with the appropriate names; otherwise, the compilation of the TOOLS.PAS file will fail.

Listing 4.16. EXPTABS.ASM

```
CODE        SEGMENT BYTE PUBLIC
            ASSUME CS:CODE

            PUBLIC ExpandTabs

;function ExpandTabs(S : String) : String

ExpTabsRes          EQU     DWORD PTR [BP+0Ah]
ExpTabsStr          EQU     DWORD PTR [BP+06h]

ExpandTabs          PROC FAR
            PUSH    BP
            MOV     BP,SP
            PUSH    DS
            LDS     SI,ExpTabsStr
            LES     DI,ExpTabsRes
            CLD
            LODSB
            STOSB
            MOV     CL,AL
            XOR     CH,CH
            JCXZ    ExitCode
LookForTab:
            LODSB
            CMP     AL,9
            JNE     CopyChar
            MOV     AL,' ';
CopyChar:
            STOSB
            LOOP    LookForTab
ExitCode:
            POP     DS
            POP     BP
            RET     04h
ExpandTabs          ENDP

CODE        ENDS
            END
```

Listing 4.17. INKEY.ASM

```
;****************************************************************
; Inkey.ASM - A FAR PROC for use in TP4 unit to return
;             the character and scancode of a pressed key.
;
; function InKey(var ScanCode : Byte) : Char;
;
; This function uses BIOS keyboard function Oh to return the
; information about the key pressed.  You can compare this
; to the Turbo CRT's ReadKey, except Inkey always returns
; the charcaters ASCII value and the scancode.
;
; Instead of doing:
;
;   Ch := ReadKey;
;   if Ch = #0 then
;     ScanCode := Byte(ReadKey);
;
; you would:
;
;   Ch := Inkey(ScanCode);
;
; For keys where the ASCII code is irrelevant (or
; nonexistent) the #0 is returned (just like
; with ReadKey).  Note that the VAR parameter points to
; a byte, and the function returns a Char.  Turbo Pascal
; 4 completely ignores the value in the unused byte of
; a word.  That's why we need not zero out AH on exit.
; Also note we take care only to move a byte into
; ScanCode, since a Pascal type declared as a BYTE is
; exactly that!
;
; NOTE: To save stack usage and speed this function, nothing
; is pushed on the stack.  The stack frame is set up with
; BX, a register we may freely use within a TP4 unit.
; Since there is only one parameter and it is accessed
; just once we use a SS: segment override with the
; ScanCode parameter based on our BX stack frame.
; This saves us the trouble of saving and restoring BP
; (or anything for that matter).
;
; by Richard S. Sadowsky
;
;****************************************************************

CODE      SEGMENT BYTE PUBLIC
          ASSUME CS:CODE

          PUBLIC InKey
```

```
; function Inkey(var Scancode : Byte) : Char;

; note the SS: segment override in the following EQU and
; the use of BX as a stack frame.

ScanCode            EQU DWORD PTR SS:[BX+04h]


InKey               PROC FAR

        MOV         BX,SP               ; Set up BX based stack frame
        XOR         AX,AX               ; zero out AX
        INT         16h                 ; BIOS Keyboard service 0
        LES         DI,ScanCode         ; ES:[DI] points to var ScanCode
        MOV         ES:[DI],AH          ; copy in scancode returned by BIOS

;   NOTE: AL already contains the Character that was
;   returned by the BIOS keyboard function, so
;   we just leave it there (Turbo expects the Char
;   function result in it).

        RET         04h                 ; remove parameter and return
InKey               ENDP

CODE    ENDS

        END
```

Listing 4.18. MACROS.ASM

```
        IFNDEF      PRESERVE_REG
PRESERVE_REG        EQU 1
        ENDIF

lo                  EQU (WORD PTR 0)
hi                  EQU (WORD PTR 2)

DOS                 EQU 021h

FORWARD             EQU 0
BACKWARD            EQU 1

StringOps           MACRO SOURCEPTR,DESTPTR,DIRECTION
        LDS         SI,SOURCEPTR
        LES         DI,DESTPTR
        IF          DIRECTION
```

Listing 4.18 continues

Listing 4.18 *continued*

```
        STD
        ELSE
        CLD
        ENDIF
                ENDM

;
; Normalizes a pointer.  Pointer may not use AX,CX, or DX as
; either the segment or offset portions of the pointer.
; Preserves all registers (not the flags), unless either
; _SEGMENT_ or _OFFSET_ is a register, in which case the
; register specified is Normalized, as in
;    Normal    ES,DI
;
;
_Normal_            MACRO _SEGMENT_,_OFFSET_

        IF      PRESERVE_REG
        PUSH    AX
        PUSH    CX
        PUSH    DX
        ENDIF

        MOV     DX,_OFFSET_
        MOV     AX,DX
        MOV     CL,4
        SHR     DX,CL
        MOV     CX,_SEGMENT_
        ADD     CX,DX
        MOV     _SEGMENT_,CX
        AND     AX,0Fh
        MOV     _OFFSET_,AX
        IF      PRESERVE_REG
        POP     DX
        POP     CX
        POP     AX
        ENDIF
                ENDM

;
; Normalizes a pointer in memory.  If PRESERVE_REG = 0
; then NormalVar uses ES,DI,SI,AX, and BX. Note that
; regardless of the value of PRESERVE_REG BX is never
; used by _Normal_, therefore, we use it freely in
; NormalVar.
;
```

```
NormalVar       MACRO _POINTER_
        IF PRESERVE_REG
        PUSH    AX
        PUSH    DI
        PUSH    SI
        PUSH    DS
        PUSH    ES

        ELSE
        MOV     BX,DS
        ENDIF

        LES     DI,_POINTER_
        LES     DI,ES:[DI]

        _Normal_ ES,DI
        LDS     SI,_POINTER_
        MOV     [SI].lo,DI
        MOV     AX,ES
        MOV     [SI].hi,AX
        IF PRESERVE_REG
        POP     ES
        POP     DS
        POP     SI
        POP     DI
        POP     AX
        ELSE
        MOV     DS,BX
        ENDIF
                ENDM

StandEntry      MACRO
        PUSH    BP
        MOV     BP,SP
                ENDM

StandExit       MACRO PARAMSIZE
        POP     BP
        RET     PARAMSIZE
                ENDM

LocalVar        MACRO _SIZE_
        SUB     SP,_SIZE_
                ENDM

UnDoLocals      MACRO
        MOV     SP,BP
                ENDM
```

Listing 4.18 continues

Listing 4.18 continued

```
PushPtr         MACRO _PTR_
        LES     DI,_PTR_
        PUSH    ES
        PUSH    DI
                ENDM

PushSPtr        MACRO _SPTR_
        LEA     DI,_SPTR_
        PUSH    SS
        PUSH    DI
                ENDM
```

Listing 4.19. MEMCOMP.ASM

```
COMMENT %
**
**  CompMem - A routine to compare two areas of memory for equality
**  by Richard S. Sadowsky [74017,1670]
**  version 1.0  5/11/88
**  released to the public domain
**  assembled with MASM 5.1
**
%
CODE        SEGMENT BYTE PUBLIC
            ASSUME CS:CODE

            PUBLIC CompMem

; function CompMem(var Block1,Block2; Size : Word) : Word
; return 0 if Block1 and Block2 are equal for Size bytes
; if not equal, return the position of first non matching byte
; the first byte is considered to be 1

CompMem         PROC FAR

        MOV     BX,SP           ; stack frame with BX
        MOV     DX,DS           ; preserve DS in DX
        XOR     AX,AX           ; zero out AX

        MOV     CX,SS:[BX+04h]  ; get Size
        JCXZ    Fini            ; if zero then exit

        LDS     SI,SS:[BX+0Ah]  ; address of block1 in DS:SI
        LES     DI,SS:[BX+06h]  ; address of block2 in ES:DI

        CLD                     ; forward string operations
```

```
        REPE      CMPSB            ; look for first non match or CX = 0
        JE        Fini             ; equal so exit (o in AX)

        MOV       AX,SS:[BX+04h]   ; get size again
        SUB       AX,CX            ; return position of first non match

Fini:   MOV       DS,DX            ; restore DS
        RET       0Ah              ; remove params from the stack

CompMem           ENDP

CODE    ENDS

        END
```

Listing 4.20. PARSE.ASM

```
        INCLUDE MACROS.ASM


CODE    SEGMENT BYTE PUBLIC
        ASSUME CS:CODE

        PUBLIC ParseWord


R_N_FunctionRes  EQU DWORD PTR [BP+0Ah]
R_N_S            EQU DWORD PTR [BP+06h]
R_N_Number       EQU [BP+04h]

RightStr_N        PROC NEAR
        StandEntry
        MOV       DX,DS

        StringOps R_N_S,R_N_FunctionRes,FORWARD

        MOV       CX,R_N_Number    ; Number to
        XOR       CH,CH
        JCXZ      R_N_ReturnNullStr

        LODSB
        CMP       AL,CL
        JB        R_N_ReturnNullStr

        SUB       AL,CL                ; adjust CL accordingly
```

Listing 4.20 continues

Listing 4.20 continued

```
        XOR      AH,AH
        MOV      BX,CX
        DEC      BX

        ADD      SI,BX

        INC      AL

        MOV      CL,AL              ; copy length to CL

        STOSB                       ; store length of result

        REP      MOVSB              ; copy CL chars
        JMP      SHORT R_N_ExitCode
                                    ; all done

R_N_ReturnNullStr:
        XOR      AL,AL
        STOSB

R_N_ExitCode:
        MOV      DS,DX
        StandExit 06h
RightStr_N      ENDP


L_N_FunctionRes EQU DWORD PTR [BP+08h]
L_N_S           EQU DWORD PTR [BP+04h]
L_N_Number      EQU [BP+02h]


LeftStr_N       PROC NEAR
        MOV      DX,BP              ; save BP in DX
        MOV      BP,SP              ; stack frame with BP
        MOV      BX,DS

        StringOps L_N_S,L_N_FunctionRes,FORWARD

        MOV      CX,L_N_Number       ; Number to
        XOR      CH,CH

        LODSB                        ; length of _S in AL
        CMP      AL,CL               ; check to see if length of _S
        JAE      StrOK               ; >= length of number
        MOV      CL,AL               ; no, so adjust number

StrOK:

        MOV      AL,CL               ; put adjusted length in AL
```

```
        STOSB                         ; copy it to FunctionRes

        JCXZ        L_N_ExitCode      ; if length is 0 then all done

        REP         MOVSB             ; copy Number chars

L_N_ExitCode:
        MOV         DS,BX
        MOV         BP,DX
        RET         06h
LeftStr_N           ENDP

;function ParseWord(var _S : String; DelimChar : Char) : String;

FunctionRes         EQU DWORD PTR [BP+0Eh]
_S                  EQU DWORD PTR [BP+0Ah]
DelimChar           EQU [BP+08h]
TempStr             EQU [BP-100h]

ParseWord           PROC FAR
        PUSH        BP
        PUSH        DS
        MOV         BP,SP
        LocalVar    100h

        CLD

        LDS         SI,_S

        LODSB
        OR          AL,AL
        JZ          ReturnNullStr

        MOV         BL,AL

        MOV         CL,AL
        XOR         CH,CH


        LES         DI,_S
        MOV         AL,DelimChar
        INC         DI

        REPNE       SCASB
        JNZ         ReturnWholeStr

        XOR         BH,BH
        SUB         BL,CL
```

Listing 4.20 continues

Listing 4.20 continued

```
        PUSH       BX

        DEC        BX

        PushPtr    FunctionRes
        PushPtr    _S

        PUSH       BX

        CALL       LeftStr_N
        POP        AX
        POP        AX

        POP        BX
        INC        BX

        PushSPtr   TempStr
        PushPtr    _S

        PUSH       BX

        CALL       RightStr_N
        POP        AX
        POP        AX

        CLD
        MOV        AX,SS
        MOV        DS,AX
        LEA        SI,TempStr
        LES        DI,_S

        LODSB
        MOV        CL,AL
        XOR        CH,CH
        STOSB

        REP        MOVSB

        JMP        SHORT ExitCode

ReturnWholeStr:
        StringOps  _S,FunctionRes,FORWARD
        LODSB
        MOV        CL,AL
        XOR        CH,CH
        STOSB
        REP        MOVSB
```

```
        LES      DI,_S
        XOR      AL,AL
        STOSB
        JMP      SHORT ExitCode

ReturnNullStr:
        LES      DI,FunctionRes
        STOSB

ExitCode:
        UndoLocals
        POP      DS
        StandExit 06h
ParseWord        ENDP



CODE   ENDS

        END
```

Listing 4.21. RIGHTSTR.ASM

```
;**************************************************************
;
; RightStr.ASM - A FAR PROC for use in a TP4 unit as
;
; function RightStr(_S : String; Number : Word) : String;
;
; returns all the characters starting at Number to the
; end of string.  A NULL string is returned if Number is
; greater than the length of _S, or if _S = '', or if
; Number = 0.
; ex.
;   the pascal line
;
;   S := RightStr('hello world',7);
;   the variable S now contains the value
;   'world'
;
; Note: since this routine is written for use in a Turbo
; Pascal 4 program, it does not preserve AX,BX,CX,DX.ES,
; DI,SI.  Turbo Pascal does not require that we save these
; registers, so to speed things up, we don't!  As always,
; BP,DS are preserved.
;
;
;**************************************************************
```

Listing 4.21 continues

Listing 4.21 continued

```
              INCLUDE MACROS.ASM


CODE          SEGMENT BYTE PUBLIC
              ASSUME CS:CODE

              PUBLIC RightStr

; The parameters: TP4 always push the FunctionRes address first.
; Then comes the _S : String, followed by Number : Word.
; We declare this as far for use in a unit

FunctionRes       EQU DWORD PTR [BP+OCh]
_S                EQU DWORD PTR [BP+O8h]
Number            EQU [BP+06h]

; if this function is to be used in the interface section of a
; unit, then FAR is correct.  Otherwise, if you need or want
; to use this function differently, you must understand how
; TP4 decides what size pointer to call a routine with, as
; well as how to adjust the parameters on the stack to
; correspond to the proper PROC declaration.  This will be
; covered shortly in another upload.

RightStr          PROC FAR
      StandEntry
      MOV         DX,DS

      StringOps _S,FunctionRes,FORWARD

      MOV         CX,Number      ; starting position in str
      XOR         CH,CH          ; zero out high byte of CX

      JCXZ        ReturnNullStr  ; if CX = 0 then nothing to do

      LODSB                      ; get length of _S
      CMP         AL,CL          ; compare it to Number
      JB          ReturnNullStr  ; Number > Length(S) so ret ''

      SUB         AL,CL          ; sub Number from Length(_S)

      XOR         AH,AH          ; zero out high byte of AX
      MOV         BX,CX          ; copy Length(S) to BX
      DEC         BX             ; subtract 1

      ADD         SI,BX          ; add BX to offset of _S

      INC         AL
```

```
        MOV       CL,AL           ; copy length to CL

        STOSB                     ; store length of result

        REP       MOVSB           ; copy CL chars
        JMP       SHORT ExitCode  ; all done

ReturnNullStr:
        XOR       AL,AL
        STOSB

ExitCode:
        MOV       DS,DX
        StandExit 06h
RightStr          ENDP

CODE    ENDS

        END
```

Listing 4.22. *SEARCH.ASM*

```
        INCLUDE MACROS.ASM

CODE    SEGMENT BYTE PUBLIC
        ASSUME CS:CODE

        PUBLIC SearchBlock

;SearchBlock(var FindStr; FindSize : Word; var Block;
;            BlockSize : Word) : Word;

FindStr       EQU DWORD PTR [BP+0Eh]
FindSize      EQU WORD  PTR [BP+0Ch]
Block         EQU DWORD PTR [BP+08h]
BlockSize     EQU WORD  PTR [BP+06h]

SearchBlock       PROC FAR
        PUSH      BP
        MOV       BP,SP           ; stack frame with BP
        PUSH      DS
        XOR       AX,AX
        MOV       CX,BlockSize
        JCXZ      ExitCode        ; if BlockSize = 0 then all done
        MOV       BX,CX
```

Listing 4.22 continues

Listing 4.22 continued

```
          MOV      DX,FindSize
          OR       DX,DX
          JZ       ExitCode        ; if FindSize = 0 then all done

          CMP      DX,BX
          JA       ExitCode        ; FindStr is bigger than Block

          SUB      CX,DX           ; adjust CX for size of FindStr
          INC      CX

          CLD                      ; forward string ops

          LES      DI,Block        ; the block to search is dest
          _Normal_ ES,DI

FindFirstChar:
          LDS      SI,FindStr      ; the string to find is source

          LODSB                    ; load first byte into AL
          REPNE    SCASB           ; look for match of first byte
          JNZ      NotFound        ; if Z flag not set then exit

          MOV      AX,CX           ; save CX in AX
          MOV      CX,DX           ; get FindSize

          PUSH     DI              ; push posit in block in case
                                   ; we need to restart search

          DEC      CX              ; we already found first char
          JCXZ     Bingo           ; if FindSize was 1 then we
                                   ; found it!

FindRest:
          REPE     CMPSB           ; cmp source to dest while =
          JZ       Bingo           ; if Z is set then we found it

          POP      DI              ; restore index into dest
          MOV      CX,AX           ; restore loop counter
          JCXZ     NotFound        ; no more block to search
          INC      CX
          LOOP     FindFirstChar   ; restart the search

NotFound:
          XOR      AX,AX           ; if we make it here then the
          JMP      SHORT ExitCode  ; jump to exit code

Bingo:
          POP      DI              ; we must pop DI off the stack
```

```
        SUB     BX,DX           ; account for FindSize
        INC     BX
        SUB     BX,AX           ; calculate posit

        MOV     AX,BX           ; store as function result

ExitCode:
        POP     DS
        POP     BP
        RET     0Ch
SearchBlock     ENDP

CODE    ENDS

        END
```

Listing 4.23. TRIM.ASM

```
;******************************************************************
; function Trim(S : String) : String
;
; Returns string with leading and trailing white space removed
; from S.  White space is considered to be a space ' ' (ascii
; code 20h or 32 decimal), and all characters less than a
; space.  In other words characters with ascii codes 0..32 are
; white space.  If a line of all white space is passed as S,
; then an empty string '' will be returned.
;
; ex.
; Trim('  Hello there  ') would return 'Hello there'
; Trim(#9#9'if C > 0 then'#9) would return 'if C > 0 then'
;
; by Richard S. Sadowsky
; version .5   7/7/88
; Copyright (c) 1988, Richard S. Sadowsky
; Los Angeles, California
;
;******************************************************************


CODE    SEGMENT BYTE PUBLIC
        ASSUME CS:CODE

        PUBLIC Trim
```

Listing 4.23 continues

Listing 4.23 continued

```
;****************************************************************
; Some equates to refer to the function result, and the function's
; string parameter.
;****************************************************************

TrimResult      EQU    DWORD PTR [BP+0Ah]
TrimStr         EQU    DWORD PTR [BP+06h]

Trim            PROC FAR
        PUSH    BP                 ; save BP
        MOV     BP,SP              ; set up base pointer
        PUSH    DS                 ; save DS, we use it
        LDS     SI,TrimStr         ; source str is function param
        LES     DI,TrimResult      ; dest str is function result
        CLD                        ; foward string ops
        XOR     BX,BX              ; use BX as counter
        LODSB                      ; get the length byte
        STOSB                      ; copy it to dest str
        XOR     CH,CH              ; zero high byte of CX
        MOV     CL,AL              ; mov str length into CL
        JCXZ    ExitCode           ; all done is length is 0

;****************************************************************
; First we search forward for white space.  We continue looking
; until the first non white space character is found, or we
; have searched the whole string.  When a non white space
; character is found, we fall into the NotWhiteSpace loop
; below.
;****************************************************************

Leading:
        LODSB                      ; get next byte
        CMP     AL,' '             ; Is it white space?
        JG      NotWhiteSpace      ; if not jump to NotWhiteSpace
        LOOP    Leading            ; repeat for next char
        JMP     SHORT AdjLength    ; done with string

;****************************************************************
;  The following code simply copies however many characters
;  are left in the string to the destination.  BL is used
;  to count the characters copied.  As soon as the first
;  non-white-space character is encountered in the string
;  we fall into this Loop.
;****************************************************************
```

```
NotWhiteSpace:
      STOSB                           ; copy the byte to dest
      INC       BL                    ; inc our char count
      LODSB                           ; get next char in AL
      LOOP      NotWhiteSpace         ; loop while CX <> 0

;******************************************************************
; Now we adjust the length byte of the destination str to the
; number of characters we copied in the NotWhiteSpace loop.
;******************************************************************

AdjLength:
      LES       DI,TrimResult         ; point to length byte in dest
      MOV       ES:[DI],BL            ; mov in new length

;******************************************************************
; Now we point to the last byte of the destination string and
; set the direction flag (backward string ops).  We then see how
; many trailing white space characters there are, and subtract
; this number from the length byte.
;******************************************************************

Trailing:
      XOR       CH,CH                 ; zero high byte of CX
      MOV       CL,BL                 ; length of dest string
      JCXZ      ExitCode              ; if zero we're done

      XOR       DX,DX                 ; we use DX as a counter
      LDS       SI,TrimResult         ; Point to TrimRes
      ADD       SI,BX                 ; point to last char in TrimRes
      STD                             ; backward string ops

Trail: LODSB                          ; Get byte in AL
      CMP       AL,' '                ; is it whitespace?
      JA        AdjLength2            ; if not, then adjust length
      INC       DL                    ; otherwise inc our counter
      LOOP      Trail                 ; repeat for next char

;******************************************************************
; Now we adjust the length byte of the function result to the
; number of characters after trailing white space is removed.
; BL contains the length of the function result and DL contains
; the number of trailing white space characters to be removed.
;******************************************************************

AdjLength2:
      OR        DL,DL                 ; is DL zero?
      JZ        ExitCode              ; yes, so exit
      SUB       BL,DL                 ; subtract DL from BL
```

Listing 4.23 continues

Listing 4.23 *continued*

```
        LES     DI,TrimResult       ; point to length of TrimRes
        MOV     ES:[DI],BL          ; mov in new length

ExitCode:
        POP     DS                  ; restore DS (or else)
        POP     BP                  ; restore BP
        RET     04h                 ; pop parameters off stack
Trim    ENDP

CODE    ENDS
        END
```

Listing 4.24. *UCASE.ASM*

```
CODE    SEGMENT BYTE PUBLIC
        ASSUME CS:CODE

        PUBLIC UpperCase

;function UpperCase(S : String) : String

UpperRes        EQU     DWORD PTR [BP+0Ah]
UpperStr        EQU     DWORD PTR [BP+06h]

UpperCase       PROC FAR

        PUSH    BP
        MOV     BP,SP
        PUSH    DS
        LDS     SI,UpperStr
        LES     DI,UpperRes
        CLD
        LODSB
        STOSB
        MOV     CL,AL
        XOR     CH,CH
        JCXZ    ExitCode

LowerLoop:
        LODSB
        CMP     AL,'a'
        JB      CopyChar
        CMP     AL,'z'
        JA      CopyChar
        SUB     AL,'a'-'A'
```

```
CopyChar:
        STOSB
        LOOP        LowerLoop

ExitCode:
        POP         DS
        POP         BP
        RET         04h

UpperCase       ENDP

CODE    ENDS
        END
```

Listing 4.25. TOOLS.PAS

```
{$S-,R-,V-}
Unit Tools;

Interface

Uses
  DOS;

Const
  _EQUAL_          = 0;


Type
  Str3 = String[3];
  Str80 = String[80];
  Path = String[70];

Function UpperCase( S : String ) : String;

Function CompMem( Var Block1,Block2; Size : Word ) : Word;
{
 return 0 if Block1 and Block2 are equal for Size bytes
 if not equal, return the position of first non matching byte
 the first byte is considered to be 1
}

Function ExpandTabs( Var S : String ) : String;
{ expands each tab into a single space. Used before parsing }
```

Listing 4.25 continues

Listing 4.25 continued

```
Function Trim( Var S : String ) : String;
{ FAST assembly language Trim routine, trims leading and trailing }

Function SearchBlock( Var FindStr; FindSize : Word; Var Block;
            BlockSize : Word ) : Word;
{ generic Block search routine.  Takes untyped VAR parameters }

Procedure ReplaceString( StrToFind,StrToRep : Str80; Var S : String );
{ Finds StrToFind and replaces it with StrToRep in string S. }
{ ignores case when searching for the string to replace.     }

Function RightStr( S : String; Number : Word ) : String;
{ returns all characters to the right of character Number }

Function ParseWord( Var S : String; DelimChar : Char ) : String;
{ parses input string S up to the first occurrence of DelimChar.}
{ The parsed string is returned, and chopped out of the string S}
{ see WordOnLine implementation for sample use of ParseWord     }

Function WordOnLine( Var The_Word,The_Line : String ) : Boolean;
{ returns TRUE if The_Word appears on The_Line }

Function FileExt( PName : Path; Extension : Str3 ) : Path;
{ force a file extension }

Function InKey( Var ScanCode : Byte ) : Char;
{ return character and scancode with a single call }

Implementation

{ the external Assembly language routines: }

{$L UCASE.OBJ}
{$L MEMCOMP.OBJ}
{$L EXPTABS.OBJ}
{$L TRIM.OBJ}
{$L SEARCH.OBJ}
{$L PARSE.OBJ}
{$L INKEY.OBJ}
{$L RIGHTSTR.OBJ}

Function UpperCase( S : String ) : String; External;

Function CompMem( Var Block1,Block2; Size : Word ) : Word; External;

Function ExpandTabs( Var S : String ) : String; External;

Function Trim( Var S : String ) : String; External;
```

```
Function SearchBlock( Var FindStr; FindSize : Word; Var Block;
        BlockSize : Word ) : Word; External;

Function ParseWord( Var S : String; DelimChar : Char ) : String; External;

Function InKey( Var ScanCode : Byte ) : Char; External;

Function RightStr( S : String; Number : Word ) : String; External;

Procedure ReplaceString( StrToFind,StrToRep : Str80; Var S : String );

Var
  L,P : Word;
  SS : String; {scratch string }
  STF,STR : Str80;

Begin
  SS := UpperCase( S ); {use the scratch string }
  STF := UpperCase( StrToFind );
  STR  := UpperCase( StrToRep );
  L := Length( SS );
  P := SearchBlock( STF[1],Length(STF),SS[1],L );

  If P > 0 Then
  Begin
    Delete(S,P,Length(StrToFind));
    If Length( StrToRep ) > 0 Then
      Insert( StrToRep,S,P );
  End;

End;

Function WordOnLine( Var The_Word,The_Line : String ) : Boolean;
{ returns TRUE if The_Word appears on The_Line }

Var
  S : String; {scratch string }
  Wrd : Str80;  { the parsed word }

Begin
  S := Trim( The_Line );
  While( Length( S ) > 0 ) Do
  Begin
    Wrd := ParseWord( S,' ' );
    S := Trim( S );
    If CompMem( Wrd,The_Word,
            Succ( Length( Wrd ) ) ) = _EQUAL_ Then
```

Listing 4.25 continues

Listing 4.25 continued

```
    Begin
      WordOnLine := TRUE;
      Exit;
    End;
  End;
  WordOnLine := FALSE;
End;

Function FileExt( PName : Path; Extension : Str3 ) : Path;

Var
  Position,L       : Word;

  PathName         : Path;

Const
  Period           : String[1] = '.';

Begin
  PathName := PName;
  Position := Pos( Period,PathName );
  If Position > 0 Then
  Begin
    L := Length( PathName );
    PathName[0] := Char( L - Succ( L - Position ) );
  End;
  FileExt := PathName + '.' + Extension;
End;

End.
```

As a test of this routine, use any of the C code presented in this chapter, or even the CPASDEMO program that is part of the DEMOS.ARC file on the Turbo Pascal distribution diskettes. To use the utility, simple enter the following command at the DOS prompt:

```
TC2TP CPASDEMO
```

This will create a file called CPASDEMO.OBJ, which can then be linked into the CPASDEMO.PAS file by compiling this with TPC. When this is completed, you will have a fully functional Turbo Pascal program.

As you can see, the linking process for anything but an assembler-generated .OBJ file is difficult. We have presented ways in this chapter to link in a C module. By controlling many of the parameters used by the TCC compiler, we can successfully link C modules.

This chapter presents many of the things that are possible to accomplish with Turbo C and then link into your Turbo Pascal code. The linking process is not for the faint hearted because of the extreme difficulty of linking a C routine that contains calls to the Turbo C Runtime Library into Turbo Pascal.

5

Inline Code

This chapter presents a topic related to the use of assembly code and statements inside a Turbo Pascal program (concepts presented in Chapter 3). Creating an object file in assembly language is only one way to incorporate assembly language instructions into a Turbo Pascal program. Another way is to use the inline statement, which allows the inclusion of machine statements directly in the Turbo Pascal source code. You can include an inline statement in any of several places; the placement dictates what code the compiler will generate from an inline statement.

This chapter answers questions about the ways of using inline code within Turbo Pascal programs. It discusses creation of an inline statement; conversion of assembly language code into inline statements; and use of inline procedures, functions, and macros. It also presents some useful routines you can include in your own programs.

Inline code is nothing more than machine code placed directly into a Turbo Pascal program. The syntax of the inline statement is quite simple; it comprises the inline keyword and any number of hexadecimal values that correspond to machine instructions, separated by forward slashes (/), like this:

```
Inline( HexValue/HexValue/HexValue... );
```

The hexadecimal values that comprise inline statements are nothing more than the direct translation of the assembly language mnemonics into machine code. PC users can create these hexadecimal codes by using the DOS DEBUG utility to create almost any inline statement necessary.

141

Assembly Language versus Inline Code

Assembly language is the closest a programmer can come to writing in the native language of a computer; each assembly language statement translates into one machine instruction. In a high-level language like Turbo Pascal, by contrast, execution of each statement may require many machine instructions. Some high-level languages—Turbo C, for example—allow programmers to place assembly language code directly in the higher-level language's source code. As an alternative, Turbo Pascal provides the inline statement.

There is little difference between Turbo Pascal's inline statement and an assembly language mnemonic. An assembly language mnemonic is intelligible to the programmer and is what is fed to an assembly language program, like Turbo Assembler. A hexadecimal value that is passed to the inline statement is essentially the same thing; the difference is that the hex value is the assembly language mnemonic after translation from human-readable form to machine-readable form. The following is an assembly language mnemonic and its corresponding inline statement:

```
MOV AH,09h                Inline( $B4/$09 );
```

Anything that can be done in an assembly language routine can be done with Turbo Pascal's inline statement. You can reference parameters, global variables, and local variables. You can also call another procedure or function from within inline code.

Creation of Inline Code

A knowledge of assembly language mnemonics makes creating inline code easy. One way of creating the hexadecimal values necessary for an inline statement is to use DOS's DEBUG utility. Inside DEBUG, you can use the A command to assemble the mnemonics and U to unassemble what is in memory. When viewing the unassembled code, you can extract the information needed to create the hex values that comprise our inline code.

The steps that follow demonstrate how you can create inline statements for inclusion in a Turbo Pascal program using the Assemble and Unassemble options provided by DEBUG:

1. Make sure DEBUG is available on your system.

2. Type **DEBUG** at the DOS prompt.

3. You will be greeted with a hyphen prompt (-) on the next screen line.

4. Enter the command **A 0100**, and press Enter.

5. DEBUG responds with a segment and offset address and then places the cursor a few spaces to the right of this address.

6. Enter the code in listing 5.1.

Listing 5.1. *Assembly Mnemonics*

```
MOV   AH,30
INT   21
CMP   AL,03
JL    ????
CMP   AH,1E
JGE   ????
```

7. After you enter the last line of listing 5.1, press Enter on the first line that contains only a segment and offset address.

8. DEBUG responds with its hyphen prompt (-).

9. Enter **U** (for Unassemble).

10. DEBUG responds with 18 lines of information. Each line will begin with the segment and offset address of the code, followed by several hexadecimal digits. Following this is the assembly language mnemonics you entered. Each pair of hexadecimal digits are the values you will place into Turbo Pascal's inline statement. The display should resemble that shown in the following code fragment:

```
20FD:0100 B430        MOV   AH,30
20FD:0102 CD21        INT   21
20FD:0104 3C03        CMP   AL,03
20FD:0106 7C05        JL    010D
20FD:0108 80FC1E      CMP   AH,1E
20FD:010B 7D00        JGE   010D
20FD:010D 90          NOP
```

11. Save this information so that you can create inline statements to include into a test program later in this chapter. You can do this either by recording the information with a pencil and paper or by pressing Shift-PrtSc several times until all the information is recorded.

Now you are ready to write the `inline` code. Listing 5.2 shows the final `inline` statements from this sample assembly language program. Listing 5.3 is a Turbo Pascal program that incorporates this routine.

The placement of the `inline` code in listing 5.3 is within the main program. In such cases, the compiler places the machine instructions contained in the `inline` code at that point in the program's code. The `inline` code can also be placed as the sole code within a procedure, with or without a `Begin...End` pair (see the section, "Inline Macros," later in this chapter). In the latter case, without the `Begin...End` pair, it is known as an *inline macro*; with the pair of `Begin` and `End` statements, it is called an *inline procedure*. We discuss examples of each of these later in this chapter.

Listing 5.2. *Translated Inline Statement*

```
Inline( $B4/$30/         {   MOV     AH,30  }
        $CD/$21/         {   INT     21     }
        $3C/$03/         {   CMP     AL,03  }
        $7C/$05/         {   JL      5      }
        $80/$FC/$1E/     {   CMP     AH,1E  }
        $7D/$00/         {   JGE     0      }
        $90 );           {   NOP            }
```

Listing 5.3. *Final Turbo Pascal Program*

```
Program FirstInlineDemo;
{ This is the first demonstration program that shows how to   }
{ create an inline statement by using DOS's Debug utility.    }
{ This demo's only purpose is to show how easy it is to       }
{ create an Inline statement.  It serves no other purpose.    }

Procedure InlineDemo;
{ Procedure that contains the do-nothing inline statement.    }

Begin
  Inline( $B4/$30/         {   MOV     AH,30  }
          $CD/$21/         {   INT     21     }
          $3C/$03/         {   CMP     AL,03  }
          $7C/$05/         {   JL      5      }
          $80/$FC/$1E/     {   CMP     AH,1E  }
          $7D/$00/         {   JGE     0      }
          $90 );           {   NOP            }
End;
```

```
Begin
  Writeln( 'Calling InlineDemo' );
  InlineDemo;
  Writeln( 'Finished with InlineDemo' );
  Readln;
End.
```

Inline Calls

Inline code can have many different uses when it is found in the middle of Turbo Pascal code. For instance, if you were curious about the code the compiler generated, you could do this:

1. Place one marker within the code at the beginning of the code to be examined and another marker at the end. Such a marker usually consists of a sequence of several NOPs (which stands for *NO oPeration*) and can be coded easily with the inline directive. Following is a sequence of three NOPs coded into a single inline statement:

    Inline($90/$90/$90);

2. Search for the NOPs with DEBUG, and disassemble the code until the next marker.

Listing 5.4. *Example Using NOPs*

```
Program ViewCodeGeneration;
{ This is a sample program that shows how to use an Inline    }
{ statement to view the code generated by the compiler.  We   }
{ will also use DOS's debug utility to view the code that     }
{ the compiler has generated.                                 }

Uses
  Crt;

Var
  X,
  I : Word;

Begin
  ClrScr;
  Writeln( 'This is a sample to show usage of an inline statement' );
  I := 0;
```

Listing 5.4 continues

Listing 5.4 *continued*

```
  Randomize;
  X := Random( MaxInt );
  Inline( $90/$90/$90 );
  For I := 1 to 10 Do
    X := X * I;
  Inline( $90/$90/$90 );
  Writeln( 'X = ', X );
  Writeln( 'I = ', I );
  Readln;
End.
```

Listing 5.4 is a Turbo Pascal program that contains NOP markers. Compile this program to disk, and then load DOS's Debug utility. We will now proceed to examine the code that was produced by the compiler for this program.

1. First, you must determine what segment the program was loaded into. This is done by entering the U command at the Debug prompt. The output should resemble what is shown below in figure 5.1. The only difference should be that the first four digits will be slightly different because this is the segment address into which the sample program was loaded.

Fig. 5.1. *Output from Debug utility.*

```
D:\BORLAND\SPRINT\BOOK\WORK>  Thu  6-01-1989 16:18:26
-»debug list5-4.exe
-u
42E6:0040 9A00005A43      CALL      435A:0000
42E6:0045 9A0000F842      CALL      42F8:0000
42E6:004A 55              PUSH      BP
42E6:004B 89E5            MOV       BP,SP
42E6:004D 9AC201F842      CALL      42F8:01C2
42E6:0052 BF5601          MOV       DI,0156
42E6:0055 1E              PUSH      DS
42E6:0056 57              PUSH      DI
42E6:0057 BF0000          MOV       DI,0000
42E6:005A 0E              PUSH      CS
42E6:005B 57              PUSH      DI
42E6:005C 31C0            XOR       AX,AX
42E6:005E 50              PUSH      AX
42E6:005F 9ACC075A43      CALL      435A:07CC
```

---

2. Now, instruct Debug to search for the NOPs placed into the code in the inline statement. This is done by entering the following line at the Debug prompt:

```
S 42E6:0040 200 90
```

This instructs Debug to search, starting at segment 42E6, offset 0040 and proceeding for 200 bytes, for any occurrence of the Hex digit 90.

3. Debug should respond with the following information:

```
42E6:0084
42E6:0085
42E6:0086
42E6:00A4
42E6:00A5
42E6:00A6
```

This is where Debug was able to locate the NOP operations that were coded in the inline statement.

4. Now, to view the actual code that was generated by the compiler, you can unassemble starting at segment 42E6 offset 0086. To do this, enter the command:

```
U 42E6:0086
```

Your screen should look something like what is shown in figure 5.2. The only difference should be the segment address.

By using these tactics, it is possible to view the code that is generated by the compiler. In this way, you could determine if what was coded in Pascal produced the code that you expected. Additionally, you could place NOPs before and after a section of inline code and then use this same technique to verify that the inline statement generated the code you expected.

Another instance in which use of an `inline` directive is preferable to a sequence of Pascal statements in a Turbo Pascal program is when you want to invoke PrtSc from within a program. You can do it with a simple `inline` call; the following code fragment shows the two bytes of code necessary to simulate the pressing of PrtSc from within a Turbo Pascal program:

```
Inline( $CD/$05 );
```

Fig. 5.2. Actual code generated by compiler.

```
D:\BORLAND\SPRINT\BOOK\WORI
-»debug list5-4.exe
-u 42e6:86
42E6:0086 90              NOI
42E6:0087 C70640000100    MOI
42E6:008D EB04            JMI
42E6:008F FF064000        INC
42E6:0093 A13E00          MOI
42E6:0096 F7264000        MUI
42E6:009A A33E00          MOI
42E6:009D 833E40000A      CMI
42E6:00A2 75EB            JNZ
42E6:00A4 90              NOI
42E6:00A5 90              NOI
```

Override Operators < and >

Turbo Pascal supports two operators (< and >) that precede an argument to inline code and are used to change the size of an argument contained within a particular inline statement.

By default Turbo Pascal codes each value contained in an inline statement as one byte if it is within the range of 0 through 255 and as two bytes otherwise. As a programmer, you can control this by using the override operators < and >. If the value coded in the inline statement is less than 255, you can force it to be coded in two bytes by preceding the value with the > operator. This fills the second byte generated as part of the inline statement with a value of zero. The following lines show the use of the > override operator and the resulting code generated by the compiler:

```
Inline( $1122/>$33 );
```

generates:

```
$22 $11 $33 $00
```

The < operator, by contrast, instructs the code generator to generate only one byte of code for a value greater than 255. In such cases, the high byte of the value will not be part of the code generated. The following lines show the use of the < override operator and the resulting code generated by the compiler:

```
Inline( $1122/<$3344 );
```

generates:

```
$22 $11 $44
```

Jumps from Inline Code

You can execute any of the many jump instructions supported by the 80 × 86 series of processors from within inline code, as you can with all assembly language code. However, coding a jump instruction from within inline code is not made easy by the Turbo Pascal code generator. To generate a jump, you must figure the displacement necessary to get to the correct statement within the inline code. Things get especially tricky when you want to add new code to existing inline code that contains a jump. You must fully understand what the inline statement is doing and, if necessary, recode the displacement value for any jump instructions. This can be a tedious process, and if you miss the displacement by any amount, you will probably lock your machine and force a reboot.

The destination of the jump is best described in terms of its displacement value because the value in the jump instruction is relative to the current instruction pointer or IP (*not* the offset within the current code segment). A positive value indicates a forward jump; a negative value indicates a backward jump.

Coding a negative displacement involves more than inserting a negative value into the inline statement; it requires the twos complement of the required displacement. To calculate a number's twos complement, take the binary number plus its twos complement that yields a value of zero. The twos complement of −1 is $FF; the twos complement of −16 is $F0. Use table 5.1 to facilitate your calculation of twos complement numbers.

Table 5.1. *Twos Complement Table*

− 1 = $FF	− 17 = $EF	− 33 = $DF	− 49 = $CF
− 2 = $FE	− 18 = $EE	− 34 = $DE	− 50 = $CE
− 3 = $FD	− 19 = $ED	− 35 = $DD	− 51 = $CD

Table 5.1 continues

Table 5.1 *continued*

− 4 = $FC	− 20 = $EC	− 36 = $DC	− 52 = $CC
− 5 = $FB	− 21 = $EB	− 37 = $DB	− 53 = $CB
− 6 = $FA	− 22 = $EA	− 38 = $DA	− 54 = $CA
− 7 = $F9	− 23 = $E9	− 39 = $D9	− 55 = $C9
− 8 = $F8	− 24 = $E8	− 40 = $D8	− 56 = $C8
− 9 = $F7	− 25 = $E7	− 41 = $D7	− 57 = $C7
− 10 = $F6	− 26 = $E6	− 42 = $D6	− 58 = $C6
− 11 = $F5	− 27 = $E5	− 43 = $D5	− 59 = $C5
− 12 = $F4	− 28 = $E4	− 44 = $D4	− 60 = $C4
− 13 = $F3	− 29 = $E3	− 45 = $D3	− 61 = $C3
− 14 = $F2	− 30 = $E2	− 46 = $D2	− 62 = $C2
− 15 = $F1	− 31 = $E1	− 47 = $D1	− 63 = $C1
− 16 = $F0	− 32 = $E0	− 48 = $D0	− 64 = $C0

Listing 5.5 is an `inline` statement that contains both a forward jump and a backward jump. It is presented purely as a vehicle for demonstrating jump theory; it does nothing useful.

Listing 5.5. *Inline Jump Instructions*

```
Inline( $31/$C0/          { XOR AX,AX   }
        $B9/$FF/$00/      { MOV CX,00FF }
        $40/              { INC AX      }
        $3D/$10/$00/      { CMP AX,0010 }
        $74/$05/          { JZ  5       }
        $49/              { DEC CX      }
        $75/F7/           { JNZ -9      }
        $EB/$04/          { JMP 4       }
        $31/$C0/          { XOR AX,AX   }
        $EB/$F1 );        { JMP -15     }
```

The first line of the code in listing 5.5 sets to zero the AX register. It is coded as an `XOR AX,AX` because this is faster than the intuitive method of `MOV AX,0`. The second line moves the value FF hexadecimal into the CX register, which becomes the counter for the looping construct used in this example. The routine then increments the AX register and compares it with 10 hex. If it is equal, the routine does a forward jump with a displacement of 5. When the zero flag is set, this jump moves the routine to the second occurrence of the `XOR AX,AX` construct. If this first jump is not executed, the routine decrements the CX register. If CX has become zero, the routine executes a jump backward with a displacement of −9. According to table 5.1, the twos complement of −9 is $F7, so that is the value inserted into the JNZ instruction. This causes the routine to return control to the INC AX instruction when the jump is executed. The final JMP 4 instruction is executed when CX is finally decremented to a value of zero. When this statement is executed, control is passed to whatever follows the last line of the inline statement.

You must be careful when coding a jump backward; the jump instruction and the jump offset must be included in the calculation of the displacement value. Therefore, in the preceding example, to get back to the beginning of the INC AX instruction, you must count the two bytes of the jump instruction as part of the displacement value. Entering a value of $00 as a placeholder for the jump displacement is a useful trick for creating jumps within inline code.

One pitfall you must be aware of when modifying inline code is this: if the code contains jump instructions, it may be necessary to recalculate the jump's displacement value to ensure that the routine will still function as desired.

Inline Procedure and Functions

Inline code need not be relegated only to the stream of the main program. It can also be placed into procedures and functions, with or without surrounding Pascal code. In either case, it is possible to access both global and local variables from within inline code. Doing so is a simple matter of locating the parameters and any local variables on the stack and knowing how Turbo Pascal will pass a variable to a procedure. Having this information makes it easy to write procedures that contain inline code.

When accessing parameters and local procedures, you must be mindful of the appropriate calling conventions. A routine declared within the main program or listed only in the implementation portion of a nonoverlayed unit (overlays are discussed in Chapter 8) is a NEAR call. A routine defined in the interface section of a unit or surrounded by the Force Far Calls compiler directive {$F+} is a FAR call. Whether a routine is a NEAR call or a FAR call determines the size of the return address that is pushed onto the stack, which in turn affects the location of parameters on the stack.

Parameter Location

Calling conventions include not only the call model used for the call to the subroutine but also the order in which parameters are pushed onto the stack before control is officially transferred to the subroutine with the 80 × 86's CALL or CALL FAR functions. Regardless of whether the parameter is a value or reference parameter, when the parameter is passed to a routine, it is pushed onto the stack from left to right; the difference between the value or reference parameter is in what was pushed onto the stack, not when it was pushed there. Following the parameters to the procedure is the return address, where control will be returned when the called routine finishes.

Reference parameters are always passed to the stack with a full address that points to the actual location of the variable within the data segment. The size of this address is 32 bits, with the 16-bit segment address pushed first, followed by the 16-bit offset address.

Value parameters can be slightly trickier than reference parameters. If the parameter's size is one, two, or four bytes or a floating-point variable, the actual value is pushed onto the stack. If the parameter is a string type, record type, or array type, a 32-bit pointer to a temporary storage location is pushed onto the stack. (Note that the 8086 processor supports a POP instruction that transfers only a word from the stack; it does not support byte-sized POPs. This forces the compiler to push byte-sized parameters as a word where the first byte pushed is the unused filler, which is zero, followed by the actual parameter.)

> Turbo Pascal V5.0 passes 8087 floating-point types on the 8086 processor's stack—not the 8087 stack as Turbo Pascal V4.0 did. This change reduces the chance of creating an overflow situation for the 8087 coprocessor. Because of this difference, however, any *inline* code written in Turbo Pascal V4.0 that used the 8087 must be rewritten for Turbo Pascal V5.0.

Returning Function Results

Turbo Pascal returns function results in registers based on the data type the function returns. In each case, it is up to the programmer to place the required return value in the appropriate register when creating inline functions. The location of the function return types are shown in table 5.2.

Table 5.2. *Function Results Locations*

Function Result Type	Returned In
Byte-sized results	AL
Word-sized results	AX
Double-word-sized results	DX:AX
Six-byte real value	DX:BX:AX
8087 types	ST(0)
String type results	Temporary copy on stack

Accessing Parameters

The code generator automatically generates entry code to the procedure or function, as shown in the following code fragment:

```
PUSH BP
MOV  BP,SP
```

The entry code transfers the stack pointer into the base pointer, allowing you to reference the passed parameter relative to the base pointer (or BP register). If the procedure or function is a FAR call, the first parameter passed will be found at an offset of six bytes relative to the BP register; if the procedure or function is a NEAR call, the parameters will be found at an offset of four bytes relative to BP.

The following code fragment shows the location of two parameters that have been passed to a procedure. The procedure is a NEAR call, as reflected by the reference to the first parameter. The size of each parameter dictates the relative offset to BP for any other parameters that might also be on the stack. This is shown by the second MOV instruction, which is an addition of four bytes above the first parameter's location—because the first parameter is a long integer, four bytes in size.

```
Procedure Foo( L : LongInt; I : Integer );
Begin
    Inline( $8B/$46/$04/        { MOV   AX,[BP+04] }
            $8B/$5E/$08/        { MOV   BX,[BP+08] }
```

Listing 5.6 is an example of an inline function that takes two parameters of type byte, adds them together, and places the return value in the correct register for the function's return type. Listing 5.6 also illustrates accessing parameters that have been passed to the function.

Listing 5.6. *Inline Function*

```
Program TestOne;
{ This sample program illustrates calling a function that    }
{ contains an inline function. It will simply add two byte   }
{ sized parameters, and place the result into the temporary  }
{ memory location that the Turbo Pascal code generator  will  }
{ allocate on the stack. This is illustrated by the last MOV  }
{ instruction before the end of the function.                }
Var
  X, Y : Byte;     { Variables that will be passed to function }
  Result : Word;   { Result of the call to function AddBytes  }

Function AddBytes( X, Y : Byte ) : Word;
{ This function will simply transfer the two parameters passed }
{ into the AX and BX registers and add them. It will then     }
{ place the result of the function into the memory locations  }
{ That Turbo Pascal has allocated for the function result.    }
Begin
   Inline( $31/$CO/             { XOR AX,AX        }
           $8B/$46/$04/         { MOV AX,[BP+04]  }
           $8B/$5E/$06/         { MOV BX,[BP+06]  }
           $01/$D8/             { ADD AX,BX        }
           $89/$46/$FE );       { MOV [BP-02],AX  }
End;


Begin
   X := 20;          { First operand to be passed to the function }
   Y := 30;          { Second operand to be passed to function   }
   Result := AddBytes( X, Y ); { Call the function              }
   Writeln( Result ); { Echo result of function to the screen   }
   Readln;           { Pause till return is hit to view output  }
End.
```

To understand what is necessary to access any local variables and parameters that may exist on the stack, you may find it useful to know what the stack looks like when calling a procedure. Figure 5.3 illustrates the state of the stack when entering a simulated procedure named Foo, shown in the following code fragment. The figure also shows where BP is pointing and the relation of BP to the parameters and local variables that are on the stack.

```
Procedure Foo( Zig, Zag : Word );
Var
  Flip : Integer;
  Flop : Integer;
```

Fig. 5.3. The stack when Foo *is entered.*

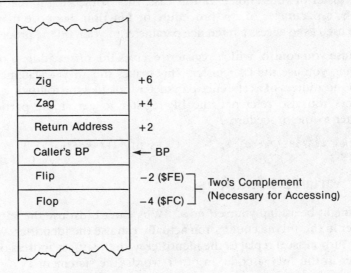

To access a local variable to a procedure requires a negative offset from BP; and to specify a negative offset, you must use the twos complement of the required offset (see table 5.1).

Figure 5.3 shows the positive offset required to access a procedure's parameters and the negative offset to access local variables and also demonstrates the location of any parameter passed to the procedure as well as the address to which the routine returns when the procedure terminates.

Accessing Variable and Oversized Parameters

Variable parameters are more difficult to access from inline code because when you pass a reference parameter to a procedure or function, you are really passing a 32-bit address of where the parameter exists. This is also true when you are passing an oversized parameter—those for records, arrays, and string variables—to a procedure or function.

Because these parameter types are passed with an address, before you can access the actual value of the parameter, you must retrieve the address of the parameter. You have to move the address off the stack and then use the address to access the value of the parameter. To make this process easier, you can use the 8086 instruction LES, which will load the segment address of something in memory into the ES register and the offset address into a register of your choice. In this case, the "something in memory" would be a parameter of any procedure or function. Suppose that you want to use LES to access a reference parameter to your inline procedure.

Because you control which register receives the offset address of the parameter, you use the DI register. This makes the inline statement to transfer the address of a reference parameter look like the following code fragment. You also reference the BP register to get at the particular parameter to the procedure.

```
Inline( $C4/$BE/Param1 );        { LES DI, [BP+<offset>] }
```

Using Variable Identifiers

You might be asking yourself now, "Why can't I just use the variable identifier in the inline code?" You actually can use the identifier. When you do, Turbo Pascal replaces the identifier with the offset address of the identifier in the inline code. In other words, the statement

```
Inline( $89/$86/Foo );    { MOV AX,Foo }
```

causes the compiler to replace the occurrence of Foo with the offset of Foo within the data segment. This has the net effect of loading the AX register with the value contained within the variable named Foo. If Foo had been a local variable within an inline procedure, instead of substituting the offset address of Foo within the data segment, the compiler would replace Foo with the offset address of Foo from the BP register.

Listing 5.7 applies this operation to a procedure to access a reference parameter. The procedure accesses a parameter, increments it by one, and translates the results to the calling program.

___

Listing 5.7. *Variable Parameter Access with Inline Code*

___

```
Program AccessVarParam;
{ This is an example program that demonstrates how to access a  }
{ var parameter from an inline code. It involves using the LES  }
{ operator to load into the extra segment the segment address   }
{ of the address passed for the variable parameter, and then    }
{ request the offset be placed into the DI register. We can      }
{ then use this as a pointer to where the parameter is actually }
{ stored. After all, that is what we receive-a pointer.          }
Var
   Result : Word;     { This is the variable that will be passed }
                      { as a var parameter to the procedure.     }
   IncValue : Byte;   { Value we will add to the var parameter   }
```

```
Procedure AddValue( Var X : Word; Y : Byte );
{ This inline procedure will accept a var parameter, and then   }
{ add to it the second parameter that has been passed to this   }
{ procedure. It serves no other purpose other than to show how  }
{ to access a var parameter.                                    }
Begin
    Inline( $8B/$46/$04/          { MOV  AX,[BP+04] }
            $C4/$7E/$06/          { LES  DI,[BP+06] }
            $26/$01/$05 );        { ADD  ES:[DI],AX }
End;
Begin
  Result := 10;        { Initialize the var parameter to 10        }
  IncValue := 40;      { Set the value to increment the var param }
  AddValue( Result, IncValue );
  Writeln( Result ); { Echo results to the screen                  }
  Readln;            { Pause for screen viewing                    }
End.
```

Accessing Variables

Accessing global variables from within inline code is easy. Turbo Pascal replaces a variable identifier that occurs within an inline statement with that identifier's offset relative to the data segment. To access a global variable, use the correct form of the MOV instruction to move the value contained in the symbol into the requested register.

Accessing a local variable is just as easy. Keep in mind that Turbo Pascal not only replaces an occurrence of a variable identifier with its offset relative to the data segment, but if that identifier happens to be a local variable, Turbo Pascal replaces the occurrence of the identifier with its offset relative to the base pointer. You can then access a local variable by using its identifier in the inline code.

Referencing Pointer Variables

To access the referent of a pointer variable that is passed from within inline code, remember that all that is passed to a procedure for a variable parameter is the address (not the value) of the variable. To access the value in that case, you used the LES instruction. Similarly, a pointer being passed to a procedure is really just an address; in fact, it is the same type of address—the only difference being that it is pointing into the heap stack, where a variable parameter is pointing into either the stack segment or the data segment. The difference results from the place from which the procedure in question is called. Therefore, the same instruction for accessing a variable parameter is used for accessing the referent of a pointer that is passed to a procedure as a value parameter, as shown in listing 5.8.

Listing 5.8. *Variable Versus Pointer Parameters*

```
Program VarParamTest;
{ This program is a demonstration of how Turbo Pascal will     }
{ replace the occurrence of a pointer that is passed to a      }
{ procedure with its address, the same way it will when passed }
{ a var parameter.                                             }
Type
  WordPtr = ^Word;
Var
  VarParam : Word;
  Ptr : WordPtr;
Procedure IncPtrReferent( Target : WordPtr );
{ This procedure will increment the referent of the pointer    }
{ that has been passed to the routine.                         }
Begin
  Inline( $C4/$BE/Target/..........{ LES  DI,[BP+offset]   }
          $26/$FE/$05 );...........{ INC  BYTE PTR ES:[DI] }
End;
Procedure IncVarParameter( Var Target : Word );
{ This is a procedure that will increment the var parameter    }
{ that has been passed to this routine.                        }
Begin
  Inline( $C4/$BE/Target/..........{ LES  DI,[BP+offset]   }
          $26/$FE/$05 );...........{ INC  BYTE PTR ES:[DI] }
End;
Begin
  New( Ptr );
  VarParam := 12;
  Ptr^ := 12;
  Writeln( 'VarParam = ', VarParam );
  Writeln( 'Ptr^     = ', Ptr^ );
  IncPtrReferent( Ptr );
  IncVarParameter( VarParam );
  Writeln( 'VarParam = ', VarParam );
  Writeln( 'Ptr^     = ', Ptr^ );
  Readln;
End.
```

Inline Macros

Many programmers do not know the difference between an inline macro and a procedure that contains inline code.

A procedure that contains `inline` code includes the procedure keyword followed by the procedure name and any parameters that must be passed to the procedure. This is followed by any definitions of local types, constants, variables, and local procedures or functions that are nested within the procedure. Any such definitions are followed by a `Begin` statement, which is followed by the procedure's code. A general format follows:

```
Procedure ProcName[( Parameter List : Type )] [ : ReturnType];
Const
    constant defs;
Type
   Type defs;
Var
   Variable defs;
Additional Procedure or Function Definitions;
Begin
   Body;
End;
```

An inline macro also contains a procedure (or function) keyword followed by a parameter list but no local variables, types, constants, nested procedures and functions, or `Begin` and `End` statement pairs. All an `inline` macro contains is the procedure (or function) keyword followed by an optional parameter list, followed by the keyword `inline`. The following lines show the general syntax used for an `inline` macro:

```
Procedure ProcName[( Parameter List : Type)] [ : Return Type];
Inline( opcode1/opcode2/......./opcodeN );
```

When the compiler encounters an `inline` macro, it temporarily stores the code and then inserts it directly and untranslated into the point in the compiled code at which the macro's name appears. The compiler does not generate a `CALL` statement, push parameters, or generate any entry code for the macro; it simply places the `inline` code into the output stream at the point at which the keyword occurs.

To clarify further, a procedure or function that contains `inline` code and a `Begin...End` pair will exist in the code segment in one place only. Any time the compiler encounters the procedure name within the code, a CALL instruction is generated to transfer control to the point in the code stream at which the instructions for the procedure reside. By contrast, when the compiler encounters an `inline` macro, the code for an `inline` macro is inserted into the code stream generated by the compiler each and every time it encounters an occurrence of the `inline` macro's name.

At the beginning of the chapter, we presented a single line of `inline` code that would call the same interrupt that is called when the PrtSc key is pressed. This could have been placed into an `inline` macro, thereby clarifying what that particular `inline` statement was actually supposed to do. Placing the code as a macro costs us nothing as far as the size of the compiled code is concerned and has the added benefit of clarifying what the code is attempting to accomplish. Here is the original `inline` statement to call the Print Screen interrupt:

```
Inline( $CD/$05 );
```

Here is an `inline` macro to accomplish the same task:

```
Procedure PrintScreen;
  Inline( $CD/$05 );
```

Parameters to Inline Macros

`Inline` macros can use parameters. These parameters are pushed onto the stack the same as parameters to regular procedures. The difference between the `inline` macro and a regular procedure is that the macro contains no entry or exit code apart from what is necessary to push the parameters onto the stack. It is up to the macro to access the parameters on the stack and then remove them from the stack before terminating the `inline` code. Failing to remove the parameters from the stack causes major problems in the execution of the code that follows the `inline` macro.

One major difference in accessing parameters that are passed to `inline` macros, as opposed to those passed to standard procedures, is that you cannot reference the parameter by name from within an `inline` macro. (Other identifiers, such as global variables, can be accessed by using their identifier directly within the `inline` code.) To access a parameter that has been passed to the `inline` macro, use POP to place the parameters into registers, and then use the contents of the registers within the rest of the `inline` code.

If the parameter happens to be a pointer or a variable parameter, you can POP these bytes off the stack into the ES and DI register. By doing so, you simplify the code necessary to access the given parameter or pointer.

Listing 5.9 contains a short routine that will access each different type of parameter that can be passed to an `inline` macro. Each of the routines does different things with the parameters passed. In some instances, they simply increment or decrement the value passed. In others, they add a passed value to the reference parameter that was also passed. Both value parameters and reference parameters are used. If the parameter is an oversized parameter, the conventions explained in the "Accessing Variable and Oversized Parameters" section of this chapter are applicable.

Listing 5.9. *Inline Macro and Parameter Types*

```
Program TestInlineParameters;
{ This program will define several different inline routines }
{ and pass different types of parameters to them. We will    }
{ pass each of the predefined types within Turbo Pascal as   }
{ parameters to these routines, assign them to an identical  }
{ global variable, and then terminate. This routine is meant }
{ to be an example of parameter passing to inline macros.    }
Var
  B  : Byte;
  Si : ShortInt;
  Ch : Char;
  I  : Integer;
  W  : Word;
  L  : LongInt;
  S  : String;
Procedure IncByte( Var B1 : Byte; B2 : Byte );
{ This macro will increment a byte sized parameter passed as }
{ the second parameter, and place the result into the first  }
{ parameter, which happens to be a reference parameter.      }
Inline( $58/              { POP AX           }
        $5F/              { POP DI           }
        $07/              { POP ES           }
        $40/              { INC AX           }
        $26/$89/$05 );    { MOV ES:[DI],AX   }
Procedure DecShortInt( Var S1 : ShortInt; S2 : ShortInt );
{ This macro will decrement a shortint parameter that has    }
{ been passed as the second parameter, and then transfer the }
{ result into the memory location occupied by the reference  }
{ parameter.                                                 }
Inline( $58/              { POP AX           }
        $5F/              { POP DI           }
        $07/              { POP ES           }
        $48/              { DEC AX           }
        $26/$89/$05 );    { MOV ES:[DI],AX   }
Procedure UpperCase( Ch1 : Char; Var Ch2 : Char );
{ This inline macro will receive a character variable as the }
{ first parameter, and a reference parameter as the second.  }
{ All this will do is convert the character passed as the    }
{ first parameter into uppercase, and then return this new   }
{ character as a new value stored in the second parameter.   }
Inline( $5F/              { POP DI           }
        $07/              { POP ES           }
        $58/              { POP AX           }
        $3D/$61/$00/      { CMP AX,$61       }
        $7C/$08/          { JL  08           }
        $3D/$7A/$00/      { CMP AX,$7A       }
        $7F/$03/          { JG  03           }
```

Listing 5.9 continues

Listing 5.9 continued

```
        $2D/$20/$00/      { SUB AX,$20      }
        $26/$89/$05 );    { MOV ES:[DI],AX }
Procedure AddInteger( Var I1 : Integer; I2 : Integer );
{ This inline macro will add the value passed as the second   }
{ parameter to the value passed in the first parameter, and   }
{ store the result in the first parameter. This works much    }
{ the same way that the INC operator works in Turbo Pascal.   }
Inline( $58/             { POP AX        }
        $5F/             { POP DI        }
        $07/             { POP ES        }
        $26/$01/$05 );   { ADD ES:[DI],AX }
Procedure SubWord( Var W1 : Word; W2 : Word );
{ This routine will subtract the value of the second         }
{ parameter, and store the result of the subtraction into the }
{ contents of the first parameter. This behaves like the DEC  }
{ function in the Turbo Pascal System unit.                   }
Inline( $58/             { POP AX        }
        $5F/             { POP DI        }
        $07/             { POP ES        }
        $26/$29/$05 );   { SUB ES:[DI],AX }
Procedure AddLongInt( Var L1 : LongInt; L2 : LongInt );
{ This is a more complicated routine that will add the second }
{ parameter to the first. Since this is a LongInt value, we   }
{ must handle overflow of the low order word by incrementing  }
{ the high-order word.                                        }
Inline( $58/             { POP AX             }
        $5A/             { POP DX             }
        $5F/             { POP DI             }
        $07/             { POP ES             }
        $26/$01/$05/     { ADD ES:[DI],AX     }
        $73/$04/         { JB  04             }
        $47/$47/         { INC DI [2]         }
        $FF/$05 );       { INC WORD PTR ES:[DI] }
Function UpString( S : String ) : String;
{ This is the most complicated of the routines as it must be  }
{ able to pass the result of the function back to the Turbo   }
{ program in the area of memory that it expects.  All this    }
{ function will do is convert an entire string to uppercase   }
{ characters.                                                 }
Inline( $5E/             { POP  SI            }
        $59/             { POP  CX            }
        $5F/             { POP  DI            }
        $07/             { POP  ES            }
        $06/             { PUSH ES            }
        $57/             { PUSH DI            }
        $1E/             { PUSH DS            }
        $8E/$D9/         { MOV  DS,CX         }
        $FC/             { CLD                }
        $AC/             { LODSB              }
```

```
              $AA/                { STOSB            }
              $8A/$C8/            { MOV   CL,AL      }
              $30/$ED/            { XOR   CH,CH      }
              $E3/$0E/            { JCXZ  0E         }
              $AC/                { LODSB            }
              $3C/$61/            { CMP   AL,61      }
              $72/$06/            { JB    06         }
              $3C/$7A/            { CMP   AL,7A      }
              $77/$02/            { JA    02         }
              $2C/$20/            { SUB   AL,20      }
              $AA/                { STOSB            }
              $E2/$F2/            { LOOP  -0E        }
              $1E );             { POP   DS         }
Begin
  IncByte( B, 12 );              { Inc B by 1 and return the value   }
  Writeln( B );                  { Echo the result to the screen     }
  DecShortInt( Si, -13 );        { Dec Si by 1 and return the value  }
  Writeln( Si );                 { Echo the result to the screen     }
  UpperCase( 'h', Ch );          { Convert h to uppercase and return }
  Writeln( Ch );                 { Echo results to the screen        }
  I := 1234;
  AddInteger( I, 3210 );         { Add 3210 to integer variable I    }
  Writeln( I );                  { Echo results to the screen        }
  W := 150;
  SubWord( W, 100 );             { Decrement W by a value of 100     }
  Writeln( W );                  { Echo the result to the screen     }
  L := $1FFFF;
  AddLongInt( L, $10 );          { Add value to LongInt variable L   }
  Writeln( L );                  { Echo the result to the screen     }
  S := ''this is a test{';
  S := UpString( S );            { Convert the string S to uppercase }
  Writeln( S );                  { Echo the result to the screen     }
  Readln;                        { Pause for user viewing            }
End.
```

Of the routines in listing 5.9, the most interesting is the UpString function. The way Turbo Pascal returns a string from a function causes some back-bending routines to be included to the inline macro. Turbo Pascal expects to find the result of a string function in the temporary location allocated—in this case, in the stack segment. We have to place this return location's address back onto the stack because Turbo Pascal will generate code to transfer the string result from this location into the memory occupied by the variable that is being assigned the function's result.

In the UpString function in listing 5.9, this was handled with the following steps:

1. Load the SI and CX registers with the offset and segment addresses of the actual parameters that have been passed to the routine. POP

the segment address into CX because you will be using LODSB, which uses the DS register for its segment address. Since you must preserve the DS by pushing DS onto the stack, and you must also be able to replace the address of the function's return location, you temporarily hold this segment address in CX. This allows you to safely PUSH DS and then transfer the value in CX into DS.

2. Load the DI and ES register with the location for the function result. Since Turbo expects this to still be on the stack when the function terminates, follow the POP instructions with corresponding PUSH instructions to restore this address onto the stack.

3. PUSH DS and transfer the segment value saved in CX into DS for usage by the LODSB instruction.

4. Single-step through each byte of the string variable. Each time a byte is loaded into AL with the LODSB instruction, it is compared to the ASCII value of the lowercase *a* and the lowercase *z*. If it falls into this range, the ASCII value is decreased by 20 (hex), and the result stored into the memory location pointed to by ES:DI with the STOSB instruction. If the ASCII value does not fall within this range, the value is copied into the correct memory location.

5. Use the POP DS instruction to restore DS.

6. Return control to the next line of code.

Functions as Inline Macros

Because of the way Turbo Pascal returns function results, it is especially useful and easy to code functions as inline macros. Table 5.2 outlines the locations where Turbo Pascal expects to find function results. Listing 5.10 is a simple inline macro that returns the uppercase letter of the parameter that was passed to the function.

***Listing 5.10.** Inline Macro Returning Function Result*

```
Program FirstInlineMacro;
{ This is a sample program that demonstrates the coding of an }
{ inline macro that will return the uppercase of a character. }
{ It simply compares the value of the character passed to the }
{ routine, and determines if it is in the range a to z. If    }
{ so, it will subtract $20 from the value of the character    }
{ passed. This has the effect of changing the character to    }
{ its uppercase representation.                               }
```

```
Var
  S : String;               { Test string used in this example  }
  I : Byte;                 { Loop control variable             }
Function UpperCase( Ch : Char ) : Char;
{ This inline macro will convert the character passed as a      }
{ parameter to its uppercase representation.                    }
Inline( $58/               { POP AX          }
        $3D/$61/$00/        { CMP AX,$0061    }
        $7C/$08/            { JL   08         }
        $3D/$7A/$00/        { CMP AX,$007A    }
        $7F/$03/            { JG   03         }
        $2D/$20/$00 );      { SUB AX,0020     }
Begin
  S := '?@this is a testz[\'; { Initialize string to boundary }
                              { values.                        }
  Writeln( 'Before translation S = ', S ); { Echo to screen   }
  For I := 1 to Length( S ) Do{ Convert each character         }
    S[I] := UpperCase( S[I] );
  Writeln( 'After translation  S = ', S );{ Echo to screen    }
  Readln;                     { Pause for viewing               }
End.
```

The code in listing 5.10 POPs the parameter into the AX register. It then does its calculations and comparison on the value in AX. Because Turbo Pascal expects to find function results of type byte, char, integer, or word in the AX register, the function can be terminated without ever placing anything into this register.

You might be asking yourself at this point, "Why code in inline when the compiler gives me this same function?" This question can be answered in one word: *speed*. Because the compiler does not need to generate the CALL and RET instructions or any entry or exit code as it would if this were a standard function, you save machine cycles by using an inline macro.

For accessing global variables from within an inline macro, the guidelines for regular inline code apply. Since the compiler replaces the occurrence of an identifier with its offset within the data segment, you can use the identifier and the correct form of the assembly language mnemonic to operate on the global symbol. (See the code presented earlier in this chapter for examples of accessing global variables from within inline code.)

Local variables, on the other hand, are not applicable to an inline macro. This is because an inline macro is really not a procedure or function in the true sense of the word. Inline macros do not exist at a single place in the code segment; they are inserted into the code stream at each point at which their identifiers appear in the source code. Because `inline` macros do not exist as true procedures, they cannot have local variables. If you attempt to define local variables, the compiler will flag the occurrence of the `inline` keyword as an error and give you the message `Begin Expected`.

Useful Inline Procedures, Functions, and Macros

This section is a collection of examples of some kinds of problems that can be solved with the concepts discussed in this chapter—`inline` procedures, functions, and macros. Each example is followed by a short explanation of the concept behind it.

Cursor Manipulation Routines

Listing 5.11 is a collection of cursor manipulation routines. Included are routines to turn the cursor on and off, define a block cursor, and return the cursor state to the default.

There are two ways of turning the cursor off:

- Place the cursor into a nondisplayable location on the screen.

- Redefine the cursor's start scan line to $20 and the end scan line also to $20.

The problem with the first method is that screen output cannot be done, because it would occur at the nondisplayable locations. However, the first method is included here because the routine to define a block cursor can be easily modified to turn the cursor off based on this second method. In fact, you can see how easy it is by comparing the notes inside the comments to the procedure.

Listing 5.11. *Cursor Manipulation Routines*

```
Program CursorControl;
{ This program will use several different inline procedures  }
{ to do different types of cursor manipulations. Included    }
{ here are routines to hide the cursor, restore the cursor,  }
{ define a block cursor, and to restore the cursor to its    }
{ default underline state.                                   }
Uses Crt;          { Included here so we can do a ClrScr     }
Var
   Row, Column : Byte;     { Position to replace cursor       }
```

```
        Mode : Byte Absolute $40:$49;{ To determine video mode      }
        Ch : Char;                   { Used for user input           }
Procedure CursorOn;
{ This procedure will turn the cursor on by returning it to a }
{ displayable position. The position is determined by the      }
{ global variables Row and Column. This is necessary because  }
{ of the way in which we hide the cursor. Note that we also    }
{ define a local variable into the Bios Data Area so we can    }
{ determine the current active video page.                     }
Var
   ActivePage : Byte Absolute $40:$62;
                          { Bios Data Area for the current page      }
Begin
   Inline( $B8/$00/$02/        {   MOV AX,0200        }
           $8A/$BE/ActivePage/{   MOV BH,ACTIVEPAGE  }
           $8A/$36/Row/         {   MOV DH,ROW          }
           $8A/$16/Column/      {   MOV DL,COLUMN       }
           $CD/$10 );           {   INT 10              }
End;
Procedure CursorOff;
{ This procedure turns the cursor off by placing it into a     }
{ position that is not normally displayable. That is, we       }
{ reposition the cursor to screen position 255,255. This is    }
{ one of two documented ways to hide the cursor. Again we      }
{ define a local variable to determine the current video page  }
Var
   ActivePage : Byte Absolute $40:$62;
                          { BIOS data area for the active page        }
Begin
   Inline( $B8/$00/$02/        {   MOV AX,0200        }
           $8A/$BE/ActivePage/{   MOV BH,ACTIVEPAGE  }
           $B6/$FF/             {   MOV DH,$FF          }
           $B2/$FF/             {   MOV DL,$FF          }
           $CD/$10 );           {   INT 10              }
End;
Procedure NormalCursor;
{ This procedure will return the cursor to its normal state.   }
{ Since the definition of the cursor is dependant upon the     }
{ current video mode (mono versus color), we declare a         }
{ variable into the BIOS data area where the current video     }
{ mode value is kept. We can then use this inside the inline    }
{ code.                                                         }
Begin
   Inline( $B8/$00/$01/        {   MOV AX,0100        }
           $8A/$0E/Mode/        {   MOV CL,MODE         }
           $B1/$07/             {   CMP CL,07           }
           $75/$06/             {   JNZ 06              }
           $B5/$0B/             {   MOV CH,0B           }
           $B1/$0C/             {   MOV CL,0C           }
```

Listing 5.11 continues

Listing 5.11 continued

```
            $EB/$04/            { JMP 04                }
            $B5/$06/            { MOV CH,06             }
            $B1/$07/            { MOV CL,07             }
            $CD/$10 );          { INT 10                }
End;
Procedure BlockCursor;
{ We can redefine the cursor to be any size by changing the   }
{ beginning and ending scan lines. This procedure will set    }
{ the beginning value at 0 regardless of monitor type. It     }
{ will then set the ending scan line based on the type of     }
{ monitor on the system.                                      }
{ To modify this routine to turn the cursor off, simply       }
{ follow the comments next to the assembly mnemonics inside   }
{ the inline code.                                            }
Begin                         {                  Cursor Off }
   Inline( $B8/$00/$01/       { MOV AX,0100                 }
            $B5/$00/          { MOV CH,00     MOV CH,20 }
            $8A/$0E/Mode/      { MOV CL,MODE                 }
            $38/$C8/           { CMP AL,CL                   }
            $75/$06/           { JNZ 04                      }
            $B1/$0C/          { MOV CL,0C     MOV CL,20 }
            $EB/$02/           { JMP 02                      }
            $B1/$07/          { MOV CL,07     MOV CL,20 }
            $CD/$10 );         { INT 10                      }
End;
Begin
   ClrScr;                      { Clear the output screen        }
   Row := 10;                   { Set the cursor restore Y Coord }
   Column := 20;                { Set the cursor restore X Coord }
   Write( 'Ready to kill the Cursor?' );
   Ch := Readkey;
   Writeln;
   Writeln( 'I''m Gone!' );
   CursorOff;                   { Turn off the cursor            }
   Readln;                      { Pause for viewing              }
   CursorOn;                    { Turn the cursor back on        }
   Writeln( 'I''m Back!' );
   Readln;                      { Pause for screen viewing       }
   BlockCursor;                 { Redefine to a block cursor     }
   Writeln( 'Now I''m a Block Cursor!' );
   Readln;                      { Pause for screen viewing       }
   NormalCursor;                { Restore to original state      }
   Writeln( 'I''m an underline again... :(' );
   Readln;                      { Pause for screen viewing       }
End.
```

High and Low Word Returns

The routines in listing 5.12 return the high and low words of a LongInt type variable. They are written as inline macros because this type of routine is perfectly suited to such an implementation.

Inline macros that are functions expect to find their results in certain registers, depending on the result type of the function. The two functions in listing 5.12 return a word value, which Turbo Pascal expects to find in the AX register. Because the functions are inline macros, the parameters to the macro are pushed onto the stack. There is no entry or exit code, and you can use this to your advantage. When a long integer variable is pushed onto the stack (when it is a value parameter), the low word is pushed first, followed by the high word. This means that to return the high word of a long integer variable, all that is necessary is to place this value into the AX register and terminate the function. You only have to POP the low word first into some other register and then POP the high word into AX. Two bytes of code are all it takes.

The same holds true for returning the low word of the variable. All you have to do is POP the first word off the stack (this is the low word of the parameter), POP the high word into an unused register, and terminate the function. That leaves the proper result waiting in the AX register, just where you want it.

Listing 5.12. *LoWord and HiWord Functions*

```
Program HiLoWordDemo;
{ This is a very simple example of the power of an inline    }
{ macro. All that the two routines will do is return the low }
{ and high words of the long integer value parameter that was }
{ passed.                                                     }
Var
  L : LongInt;        { Variable to be passed to the function }
  W : Word;           { Variable for function result          }
Function HiWord( L : LongInt ) : Word;
{ This function will return the high word of the longint      }
{ variable that was passed.                                   }
Inline( $5B/        {  POP BX  }
        $58 );      {  POP AX  }
Function LoWord( L : LongInt ) : Word;
{ This function will return the low word of the longint value }
{ that was passed to this function.                           }
Inline( $58/        {  POP AX  }
        $5B );      {  POP BX  }
```

Listing 5.12 continues

Listing 5.12 continued

```
Begin
  Writeln( 'HiWord = ', HiWord( $FFFF0000 ) );
                      { Call the routine with a value          }
  Writeln( 'LoWord = ', LoWord( $FFFF0000 ) );
                      { Call the routine with a value          }
  L := $0000FFFF;
  W := HiWord( L );   { Call the function with a variable      }
  Writeln( 'HiWord = ', W );{ Echo result to screen            }
  L := $0000FFFF;
  W := LoWord( L );   { Call the function with a variable      }
  Writeln( 'LoWord = ', W );{ Echo results to the screen       }
  Readln;                   { Pause for screen viewing          }
End.
```

Flush File Buffer

Listing 5.13 makes some DOS calls to force DOS to write any buffered information for a file directly to a diskette. This ensures that all data a program has written to a file is actually on the physical disk and not held in memory.

The conventional way to accomplish this is to make a DOS call to duplicate the file's handle. Then the handle is passed to another DOS function to close the handle. This has the effect of writing all buffered information to the diskette. The code in listing 5.13 does the same thing and checks the version of DOS in use. The code is written to do that because DOS V3.3 provides a routine to flush the file's buffers. This routine first determines the version of DOS. If it is V3.3 or greater, the routine makes a call to subfunction 68h to flush the buffers; otherwise, it duplicates the handle and closes the handle. Any error codes are returned by the function as its result.

Listing 5.13. Flush File Buffer

```
Program TestFlushFileBuffers;
{ This program will demonstrate the usage of the inline macro }
{ FlushFileBuffers. This is used to guarantee that all info   }
{ has actually been written to the disk, and is not held in   }
{ memory.                                                     }
Type
  Str4 = String[4];        { Component type for output file   }
  FileType = File of Str4; { File type definition              }
```

```
Var
  S : Str4;                    { Variable to be written to file }
  F : FileType;                { Output file variable           }
  I : Integer;                 { Loop control variable          }
  W : Word;                    { Result of call to function     }
Function FlushFileBuffers( Var F ) : Word;
{ This inline macro will do several things on its way to       }
{ flush DOS's file buffers. It first determines if the DOS     }
{ version is 3.3 or greater. If so, it will make a call to     }
{ a special sub function of Int21 that will do the updating    }
{ for us. Otherwise, it will force a duplicate of the file     }
{ handle. It then goes on to close this duplicate handle.      }
{ If any errors are encountered by the routine, the error      }
{ value is returned in the AX register as the result type of   }
{ the function.                                                }
Inline( $5F/          { POP  DI }
        $07/          { POP  ES }
        $B4/$30/      { MOV  AH,30 }
        $CD/$21/      { INT  21    }      { Check DOS Version        }
        $3C/$03/      { CMP  AL,03 }      { is Version 3.3 or later  }
        $7C/$18/      { JL   OTHER }
        $80/$FC/$1E/  { CMP  AH,1E }
        $7D/$13/      { JGE  OTHER }
        $B4/$45/      { MOV  AH,45 }
        $26/$8B/$1D/  { MOV  BX,ES:[DI] }
        $CD/$21/      { INT  21    }      { Force duplicate handle   }
        $72/$14/      { JB   ERROR }
        $8B/$D8/      { MOV  BX,AX }
        $B4/$3E/      { MOV  AH,3E }
        $CD/$21/      { INT  21    }      { Close duplicate          }
        $72/$0C/      { JB   ERROR }
        $EB/$07/      { JMP  END   }
{ OTHER: }
        $B4/$68/      { MOV  AH,68   }    { DOS 3.3 has a function      }
        $26/$8B/$1D/  { MOV  BX,ES:[DI] } { to flush buffers. Call it.  }
        $CD/$21/      { INT  21   }
{ END:   }
        $B8/$00/$00 ); { MOV  AX,0       }
Begin
  Assign( F, 'test514.dat' );  { Associate Name with file Var }
  Rewrite( F );                { Open the file for Output     }
  For I := 1 to 10 Do          { Place 10 values into file    }
  Begin
    Str( I, S );               { Convert counter to string    }
    Write( F, S );             { Write counter to the file    }
  End;                         {                              }
  W := FlushFileBuffers( F );  { Call the function            }
  Writeln( 'Call to FlushFileBuffers yields a ', W );
                               { Echo results to the screen   }
  Readln;                      { Pause for viewing of screen  }
End.
```

Conclusion

As you can see, for some operations the usage of inline procedures and macros can be a powerful feature of Turbo Pascal. It is possible to create quick and powerful routines without linking an external .OBJ file.

Text File Device Drivers

Turbo Pascal Version 5.5 includes a powerful capability for Pascal programmers—the power of text file device drivers. This capability is not widely understood even though device drivers have been part of the language specification since Version 4.0. This chapter presents a step-by-step approach to understanding and using text file device drivers and ultimately putting their power to work for you. It introduces the concepts behind a text file device driver, how it operates, and how you can write one.

A *text file device driver* (TFDD) is a collection of input and output routines that can be linked directly into Turbo Pascal text-file-handling routines. They will be called any time an I/O statement of any kind is called by your program. This gives you the ability to write a driver that will interface a specific device with Turbo Pascal.

To implement a TFDD within Turbo Pascal, you have to write five routines to enable the driver to handle its various tasks:

❏ Initializing the device

❏ Input from the device

❏ Output to the device

❏ Opening the device

❏ Closing the device

All of these routines are then linked directly into the text-file-management routines of Turbo Pascal, which allows you to think of the device as a text file (hence the name *text file device driver*). They are included in Turbo's I/O routines when the initializing procedure and open procedures are executed.

Some uses for TFDDs include talking to a serial device, writing information to the printer, writing to the screen, and writing to printer and screen at the same time. Additionally, you could write a device driver that will allow you to write to the graphics screen. The *Turbo Pascal Reference Guide* describes use of TFDDs for talking to a serial device; this chapter presents other uses.

The setup of a TFDD includes a routine to associate the device with each of the driving routines. This can be thought of as what is called by the Assign procedure because your initialization routine will perform this same function. You also need a routine to handle input and a routine to handle output. Depending on the TFDD's purpose, you may want to write the setup to handle input and output from the same function.

Listing 6.1 is an example of an initialization procedure. The function of this particular routine is to initialize each field of the file variable that was passed to it. This is essential for all TFDDs to function properly.

Listing 6.1. *Generic Initialization Procedure*

```
{$F+}
Procedure AssignDev( Var F : Text );
{ Simple example procedure that shows the structure of an      }
{ initialization procedure. It sets up each field of the file  }
{ variable F.                                                  }
Begin
  With TextRec( F ) Do
  Begin
    Handle := $FFFF;
    Mode := fmClosed;
    BufSize := SizeOf( ABuffer );
    BufPtr := @ABuffer;
    OpenFunc := @AnOpenFunc;
    CloseFunc := @ACloseFunc;
    InOutFunc := @AnInOutFunc;
    FlushFunc := @AFlushFunc;
    BufPos := 0;
    Name[0] := #0;
  End;
End;
```

Examining listing 6.1, you can probably tell what other routines must be defined.

The next necessary routine after initialization is an `Open` function to handle the opening of the device. In our example, it is a function named `AnOpenFunc`. This is where the driver becomes dependent on the device with which it is communicating. A BIOS device, like the screen or printer, does not need to be opened; in such cases, the `Open` function returns a value of zero and does nothing else. On the other hand, a true I/O device (one that has an I/O port within the CPU's address space) requires an opening routine.

The `Open` function must be a FAR call because the function has become part of Turbo's I/O routines. As such, the function can be called from any point in a program that uses the driver. Failure to make the `Open` function a FAR call can have disastrous results, often forcing a system reboot.

If an error occurs during this function (or any other function that is part of the driver), it is expected that the function will return a specific value to indicate what error has occurred. This is important because Turbo will generate an I/O error, with the error number being what was returned by the function's result value. This error, like all I/O errors, can be trapped by your program; the difference with this one is that you can control the value reported by the I/O error.

The same things hold true for the `Close` function. If the device you are writing a driver for does not need a `Close` function, you can create a function that returns a value of 0 and does nothing else. Otherwise, it is necessary to send the device the correct closing operations.

It might be easiest to include a single "ignore-type" function that you can associate to any routine that is not necessary. The `Ignore` function will simply assign a value of zero to its name, which indicates that the function was successful. This reduces the code necessary for the TFDD and makes it easier to understand.

If you are handling `Input` from a routine, then your function would need to get the information from the device and place it into the `BufPtr^` field of the `TextRec`. You would then place the number of characters read into the `BufEnd` field of the `TextRec`. You must also place a value of 0 into `BufPos`.

If, on the other hand, you were handling `Output` from a routine, then it would be necessary for your routine to output from `BufPtr^` the number of characters specified by `BufPos` and then set `BufPos` to 0 indicating the buffer is again empty.

Simple Device Driver

Listing 6.2, a simple example of a device driver, and listing 6.3, a program to test the driver, demonstrate how simple it is to link the component parts to create a powerful set of input or output routines.

Listing 6.2. Example TFDD

```
Unit TFDD;
{ This is the first sample text file device driver. Its task   }
{ is to send output from a Write or a Writeln statement into a }
{ string variable somewhere in memory. It will also introduce  }
{ you to the structure of a text file device driver, and what  }
{ is necessary to implement one.                               }
Interface
Uses
  Dos;
Type
  BufferType = String;
Var
  theBuffer : BufferType;
  BufferPtr : ^BufferType;
Procedure AssignDev( Var F : Text );
{ This procedure will set up the file variable F to point to   }
{ each of the necessary support routines. It also will         }
{ initialize each of the separate data fields within the text  }
{ file variable that was passed to this routine.               }
Implementation
{$F+}                       { FAR calls are REQUIRED in a TFDD. }
Function NulRoutine( Var F : TextRec ) : Integer;
{ This routine will be assigned to any of the functions        }
{ within the file routines that are not necessary. It will     }
{ return a result of 0, which is reported for IOResult. This   }
{ way any function that calls this is guaranteed to return     }
{ with no errors.                                              }
Begin
  NulRoutine := 0;      { Set function result to 0 = No Error  }
End;
Function InOutRoutine( Var F : TextRec ) : Integer;
{ This is the routine that will handle the output of the       }
{ information to the memory location used for the buffer. It   }
{ is called anytime the program calls a Write or a Writeln     }
{ statement.                                                   }
Var
  I : Integer;           { Loop counter used to write buffer   }
Begin
  With F Do
  Begin
    If Mode = fmOutput Then
```

```
      Begin
        If BufPos > BufEnd Then
        Begin
          For I := BufEnd To ( BufPos - 1 ) Do
            If( ( BufferType( BufferPtr^ )[0] ) < #255 )Then
              BufferType( BufferPtr^ ) :=
                    BufferType( BufferPtr^ ) + BufPtr^[I];
        End
        BufPos := BufEnd;
    InOutRoutine := 0;
      End
      Else
        InOutRoutine := los;          { File not open for output }
    End;
End;
Procedure AssignDev( Var F : Text );
{ This procedure will set up the file variable F to point to  }
{ each of the necessary support routines. It also will        }
{ initialize each of the separate data fields within the text }
{ file variable that was passed to this routine.              }
Begin
  With TextRec( F ) Do
  Begin
    Handle := $FFFF;
    Mode := fmClosed;
    BufSize := SizeOf( Buffer );
    BufPtr := @Buffer;
    OpenFunc := @NulRoutine;
    FlushFunc := @NulRoutine;
    CloseFunc := @NulRoutine;
    InOutFunc := @InOutRoutine;
    Name[0] := #0;
  End;
End;
Begin
  BufferPtr := @theBuffer;
  FillChar( BufferPtr^, SizeOf( BufferPtr^ ), #0 );
End.
```

Listing 6.3. *Driving Program*

```
Program TestTFDD;
{ This program will test the unit in listing 6.2. It will     }
{ open the device, and then place information into it with a  }
{ write and a writeln statement.                              }
```

Listing 6.3 continues

Listing 6.3 continued

```
Uses
  Crt, TFDD;            { Link in the necessary units      }
Type
  Str5 = String[5];     { Just to define a sub string type }
Var
  RAM : Text;           { Text file to be passed to TFDD   }
  R : Real;             { One of the values placed in buffer }
  I : Integer;          { Another of the variables in buffer }
  Ch : Char;            { Another type of variable         }
  S : Str5;             { Last of the different types      }
Begin
  AssignDev( Ram );     { Call the Initialization routine  }
  Rewrite( Ram );       { Open the file for output         }
  R := 999.324;         { One value to be written          }
  I := -123;            { Another value for the buffer     }
  Ch := 'Y';            { A character value for the buffer }
  S := 'Test';          { A substring type for the buffer  }
  Writeln( Ram, 'This is a ', S, ' of ', R:4:2, ' ', Ch, I );
                        { Place all of these in buffer     }
  Close( Ram );         { Close the device                 }
  Writeln( theBuffer ); { Send buffer to screen for viewing }
  Readln;               { Pause for Screen Viewing         }
End.
```

Structure

The structure of a text file device driver can be simple, yet it enables the performance of powerful routines. Later in this chapter, we present several device drivers. The most elaborate of these implements is a BIOS Crt unit that can easily be used to perform Write or Writeln statements from graphics mode.

Each of the separate routines that comprise a TFDD has a specific task and is called by several of the internal routines to the Turbo Pascal run-time system. This section provides more detail about each of the functions installed in the TextRec type, where the functions can be called from the run-time library, and their purposes.

Open Function

The Open function is called whenever a user program calls the Reset, Rewrite, or Append standard procedures. Any user routine is expected to prepare the file variable for input or output, depending on the Mode field of the TextRec type, which is set by the appropriate system routine *before* control is passed to the open function. If the Mode is set to fmInput, a Reset has been called, and you must set the device for input. On the other hand, if the Mode is set to fmOutput, you know that Rewrite was called, and you must set up the driver to handle output. This is the flexibility of the TFDD at work. All you have to do is recognize what mode is being accessed and set the routine to handle that mode.

Some problems may arise when the Mode is set to fmInOut. In this case, intuition indicates that text files are either input or output—never both. The capability to be both input and output is generally given to random access files only. With text files, you will get this Mode when calling the Append standard procedure. When you get this Mode inside an Open function, you must reset the Mode to fmOutput and allow the function to terminate. Failing to do this will have catastrophic results.

Close Function

The Close function is the simplest of the TFDD routines. Its only purpose is to communicate to the device that its job is done. It also sets the Mode field of the TextRec to fmClosed to restrict future access to the device. If the device were to be accessed again in the future, a run-time error would result.

Flush Function

The Flush function can be called by a number of different routines within the Turbo Pascal file system. For instance, it is called on every input or output statement—i.e., every read, readln, write, and writeln statement. This is to ensure that all information is either read from or written to the buffer.

This part of your routine should begin by determining what the Mode is set to. If it is set to fmOutput, the routine should make sure any information still in the buffer is written to the device. If the mode is set to fmInput, you can either leave the buffer untouched or flush it by setting the BufPos field equal to the BufEnd position; doing so will cause you to lose any unread information that might still be in the buffer.

InOut Function

Of all the procedures and functions that comprise a TFDD, the InOut function is the one that does most of the device's work. It drives both inputting and outputting routines. Since it is called to handle either of these, the first thing this routine must do is check the Mode field to determine what its current job is.

If the Mode is set to fmInput, the routine does this:

1. Reads information from the input device

2. Places the information into the BufPtr area of memory

3. Sets the BufEnd field of the TextRec equal to the number of characters read from the input device

4. Sets the BufPos field to zero. If you set BufPos equal to BufEnd, the EOF standard function returns a value of true.

If the Mode is set to fmOutput, on the other hand, this routine responds to a request to send data to the device by taking information from BufPtr and writing it to the device. You can determine the number of characters to be written by examining the BufPos field. The information in the buffer will start at position zero and proceed for BufPos items. The routine sends all this information, or some of it will be lost.

When the InOut routine terminates, and the Mode is set to fmOutput, you must reset BufPos to a value of zero. This indicates that all the information has been written to the device.

Example Device Drivers

This section contains several useful examples of text file device drivers, including the following:

❏ Printer output routine

❏ Routine to echo a single writeln statement to the screen and to the printer

❏ BIOS Crt unit that allows you to execute write statements while in graphics mode. (This is something the BGI does not support; see Chapter 10 for more information.)

Listing 6.4. Replacement Printer Unit

```pascal
Unit Printer2;
{ This unit is a replacement for the Printer unit that came   }
{ with Turbo Pascal V5.0. Its purpose is two-fold. It will    }
{ allow a user to change the printer port that the .LST file  }
{ is writing to on-the-fly. This takes the place of           }
{ LstOutPtr and the routine on page 369 of the Turbo Pascal   }
{ V3.02A manual. The second purpose of this unit is to        }
{ circumvent DOS's stripping of a Ctrl-Z ($1A, the End Of     }
{ File character) when writing to the printer as an ASCII     }
{ device. Ctrl-Z was usually sent as part of a graphics       }
{ string to a printer. In Turbo Pascal V3.0, an ASCII device  }
{ was opened in binary mode, and in V5.0 an ASCII device is   }
{ opened in ASCII mode and DOS thus strips a Ctrl-Z.          }
Interface
Uses
  DOS;                                   { for using INTR() }
Var
  LST : Text;                      { Public LST file variable }
Procedure SetPrinter( Port:Byte );
{       SetPrinter sets the printer number to Port where Port }
{ is 'n' in 'LPTn'. i.e. To write to LPT1: SetPrinter(1),     }
{ for LPT2: SetPrinter(2). SetPrinter changes the Port that   }
{ subsequent Write operations will write to. This lets you    }
{ change the printer that you are printing to on-the-fly.     }
Implementation
{       The following routines MUST be FAR calls because they }
{ are called by the Read and Write routines. (They are not    }
{ Public (in the implementation section) because they should  }
{ only be accessed by the Read and Write routines.            }
{$F+}
{       LSTNoFunction performs a NUL operation for a Reset or }
{ Rewrite on LST (Just in case)                               }
Function LSTNoFunction( Var F: TextRec ): integer;
Begin
  LSTNoFunction := 0;                         { No error      }
end;
{       LSTOutputToPrinter sends the output to the Printer    }
{ port number stored in the first byte or the UserData area   }
{ of the Text Record.                                         }
Function LSTOutputToPrinter( Var F: TextRec ): integer;
var
  Regs: Registers;
  P : word;
begin
  With F do
```

Listing 6.4 continues

Listing 6.4 *continued*

```
Begin
  P := 0;
  Regs.AH := 16;
  While (P < BufPos) and ((regs.ah and 16) = 16) do
  Begin
    Regs.AL := Ord(BufPtr^[P]);
    Regs.AH := 0;
    Regs.DX := UserData[1];
    Intr($17,Regs);
    Inc(P);
  end;
  BufPos := 0;
End;
if (Regs.AH and 16) = 16 then
  LSTOutputToPrinter := 0              { No error            }
  else
    if (Regs.AH and 32 ) = 32 then
      LSTOutputToPrinter := 159        { Out of Paper        }
  else
      LSTOutputToPrinter := 160;       { Device write Fault }
End;
{$F-}
{      AssignLST both sets up the LST text file record as    }
{ would ASSIGN, and initializes it as would a RESET. It also }
{ stores the Port number in the first Byte of the UserData   }
{ area.                                                      }
Procedure AssignLST( Port:Byte );
Begin
  With TextRec(LST) do
    begin
      Handle       := $FFF0;
      Mode         := fmOutput;
      BufSize      := SizeOf(Buffer);
      BufPtr       := @Buffer;
      BufPos       := 0;
      OpenFunc     := @LSTNoFunction;
      InOutFunc    := @LSTOutputToPrinter;
      FlushFunc    := @LSTOutputToPrinter;
      CloseFunc    := @LSTOutputToPrinter;
      UserData[1] := Port - 1;  { We subtract one because }
  end;                          { Dos Counts from zero.   }
end;

Procedure SetPrinter( Port:Byte ); { Documented above      }
Begin
  With TextRec(LST) do
    UserData[1] := Port - 1;{ We subtract one because DOS }
End;                        { Counts from zero.           }
```

```
Begin  { Initialization }
  AssignLST( 1 );           { Call assignLST so it works  }
End.                         { like Turbo's Printer unit   }
```

The primary purpose of listing 6.4 is to replace the standard Printer unit that is supplied with Turbo Pascal V5.0 because Turbo Pascal opens its Printer unit and the LST device in a cooked Mode. Cooked Mode indicates to DOS that it is a text device; any text device cannot receive an EOF marker, therefore, it is stripped from the output stream. The driver in listing 6.4 chooses a Mode that will pass any character to the printer. An EOF marker, or ASCII character 26, is essential to sending graphics output to the printer.

Listings 6.5 and 6.6 allow a single write statement to be directed to both the printer and the screen. In its current form, the screen output does not take into account any attributes that may be set. You can modify this easily by changing the WriteChar procedure to use Interrupt $10, service 9. The only drawback is that the routine will have to be modified to update the cursor position so that the next call does not overwrite the character written by the previous call.

Listing 6.5. *Unit to Echo to Screen and Printer*

```
Unit EchoDev;
{ This routine implements a text file device driver that will }
{ echo a single write or writeln statement to the screen and }
{ to the printer. It does this by outputting each character   }
{ in the buffer to the screen with a BIOS interrupt, and to   }
{ the printer. It can easily be expanded to include a Boolean }
{ variable that will determine whether the echoing is to take }
{ place or not.                                               }
Interface
Uses
  Dos;                       { This unit is necessary for a TFDD }
Var
  Echo : Text;               { This is the Echo device           }
  LptPort : Byte;            { LPT Port number for output        }
Implementation
{$F+}
Function NulRoutine( Var F : TextRec ) : Integer;
{ This routine will be called for any routine that is not      }
{ necessary for use by the text file device driver.            }
```

Listing 6.5 *continues*

Listing 6.5 continued

```
Begin
  NulRoutine := 0;           { Return an I/O result of 0          }
End;
Procedure WriteChar( Ch : Char );
{ This routine will output the character passed with a BIOS   }
{ routine. This handles the screen part of the echoing TFDD   }
Var
  DisplayPage : Byte Absolute $40:$62;
                              { BIOS Data Area of Active Page }
  Regs : Registers;          { Used in the INTR call         }
Begin
  Regs.AH := $0E;            { Write character in teletype Mode }
  Regs.AL := Ord( Ch );
  Regs.BH := DisplayPage;
  Regs.BL := 0;
  Intr( $10, Regs );
End;
Function EchoOutput( Var F: TextRec ): integer;
{ This is the Output driving routine. It is called for each   }
{ write or writeln statement. When this routine is invoked,   }
{ each character in the buffer will be written to the printer }
{ and written to the screen.                                  }
Var
  Regs: Registers;        { Used in the INTR Call            }
  P : word;               { Position within the Text Buffer  }
Begin
  With F do
  Begin
    P := 0;
    Regs.AH := 16;
    While (P < BufPos) and ((Regs.ah and 16) = 16) do
    Begin
      WriteChar( BufPtr^[P] );
      Regs.AL := Ord(BufPtr^[P]);
      Regs.AH := 0;
      Regs.DX := UserData[1];
      Intr($17,Regs);
      Inc(P);
    end;
    BufPos := 0;
  End;
  if (Regs.AH and 16) = 16 then
    EchoOutput := 0                { No error              }
  else
    if (Regs.AH and 32 ) = 32 then
      EchoOutput := 159            { Out of Paper          }
  else
    EchoOutput := 160;             { Device write Fault }
```

```
End;
{$F-}
Procedure AssignEcho( Var F : Text );
{ This is the procedure that will set up the Text Record to    }
{ allow output to both the printer and the screen. It sets     }
{ up all of the fields in the TextRec, to support the          }
{ Input and Output routines in Turbo Pascal.                   }
Begin
  With TextRec( F ) Do
    begin
      Handle      := $FFFF;
      Mode        := fmOutput;
      BufSize     := SizeOf(Buffer);
      BufPtr      := @Buffer;
      BufPos      := 0;
      OpenFunc    := @NulRoutine;
      InOutFunc   := @EchoOutput;
      FlushFunc   := @EchoOutput;
      CloseFunc   := @EchoOutput;
      UserData[1] := LptPort - 1;  { We subtract one because }
    end;                           { Dos Counts from zero.   }
end;
Begin  { Initialization }
  LptPort := 1;                { Default LPT port. Change this to }
                              { output to a different LPT port.  }
  AssignEcho( Echo );         { Set up the Echo device.          }
End.
```

Listing 6.6. *Driving Program for EchoDev Unit*

```
Program TestEchoDev;
{ This is a sample program that is used to test the Echo      }
{ device set up in the EchoDev unit. The EchoDev unit          }
{ interfaces a file variable called Echo. Any writes to this }
{ device will be written to both the screen and the printer. }
{ The device is opened automatically; therefore, we don't      }
{ need to call Assign or Rewrite.                              }
Uses
    Crt, EchoDev, Printer;
Begin
  ClrScr;
  GotoXY( 10,10 );
  Writeln( 'This is written to the Screen' );
  GotoXY( 10,5 );
  Writeln( Echo, 'This line is written to Screen and Printer' );
  Writeln( LST, 'This is on the printer only.' );
  Readln;
End.
```

Listing 6.7. *BIOS Crt Unit*

```
{  BIOSCRT--A unit to allow text output through the standard  }
{ BIOS calls. This unit will work in both text and graphics   }
{ modes. It was primarily written to allow use of the MS-DOS  }
{ system font in graphics mode to compensate for the current  }
{ lack of a BGI system font. Note: This method will *NOT* work }
{ with most Hercules boards because they don't properly       }
{ support the BIOS calls in graphics mode.                    }
{ Notes: If you are using this unit on a CGA in the graphics  }
{ mode, you should run the GRAFTABL program from your DOS     }
{ supplemental program disk (this loads the extended CGA      }
{ character set into memory).                                 }
Unit  BiosCrt;
interface
uses Dos;
var BiosWriteMode  : byte;  { Bios write mode to use for TFDD }
    BiosTextAttr   : byte;  { Bios text attribute byte        }
    BiosStartAttr  : byte;  { Original startup attr           }
    LastBiosMode   : byte;  { last Bios screen mode in use    }
    LastBiosWidth  : byte;  { last Bios screen width used     }
    LastBiosPage   : byte;  { last Bios screen page used      }
{-----------------------------------------------------------}
{ Below are listed the important Bios variables for the video }
{ display. These are set by the Bios and are provided for     }
{ reading only. Do not change any of these values or erratic  }
{ display operation will result.                              }
    BiosMode      : byte absolute $0040:$0049;
    BiosMaxX      : word absolute $0040:$004A;
    BiosCrtLength : word absolute $0040:$004C;
    BiosCursorPos : array [0..7] of word absolute $0040:0050;
    BiosCursorMode: word absolute $0040:$0060;
    BiosActivePage: byte absolute $0040:$0062;
    BiosAddr6845  : word absolute $0040:$0063;
    Bios6845Mode  : byte absolute $0040:$0065;
    BiosPalette   : byte absolute $0040:$0066;
    BiosMaxY      : byte absolute $0040:$0084;
    BiosCharSize  : word absolute $0040:$0085;
    BiosInfo      : byte absolute $0040:$0087;
    BiosInfo3     : byte absolute $0040:$0087;
    BiosFlags     : byte absolute $0040:$0087;
    BiosDCC       : byte absolute $0040:$008A;
    BiosSavePtr   : pointer absolute $0040:$00A8;
    BiosFontTable : byte absolute $F000:$FA6E;
{ The following are the inline macros used to access the BIOS }
{ routines                                                    }
function BiosWhereX:integer;
{ get current cursor X pos }
inline(
  $B7/$00        { mov BH,0}
 /$B4/$03        { mov AH,3}
```

```
   /$55          { push BP}
   /$CD/$10      { int $10}
   /$5D          { pop BP}
   /$30/$E4      { xor AH,AH}
   /$88/$D0);    { mov AL,DL}
function BiosWhereY:integer;
{ get current cursor Y pos }
inline(
   $B7/$00       { mov BH,0}
   /$B4/$03      { mov AH,3}
   /$55          { push BP}
   /$CD/$10      { int $10}
   /$5D          { pop BP}
   /$30/$E4      { xor AH,AH}
   /$88/$F0);    { mov AL,DH}
procedure BiosWhereXY(var X,Y:integer);
{ get current cursor X,Y pos }
inline(
   $B7/$00       { mov BH,0}
   /$B4/$03      { mov AH,3}
   /$55          { push BP}
   /$CD/$10      { int $10}
   /$5D          { pop BP}
   /$07          { pop ES}
   /$5B          { pop BX}
   /$26/$88/$37  { mov ES:[BX],DH}
   /$07          { pop ES}
   /$5B          { pop BX}
   /$26/$88/$17); { mov ES:[BX],DL}
procedure BiosGotoXY(X,Y:integer);
{ move cursor to indicated X,Y }
inline(
   $58           { pop AX}
   /$5A          { pop DX}
   /$88/$C6      { mov DH,AL}
   /$B7/$00      { mov BH,0}
   /$B4/$02      { mov AH,2}
   /$55          { push BP}
   /$CD/$10      { int $10}
   /$5D);        { pop BP}
procedure BiosTextColor(FColor:integer);
{ Set text foreground color }
inline(
   $58                 { pop AX}
   /$24/$0f            { and AL,$0F}
```

Listing 6.7 continues

Listing 6.7 continued

```
      /$8A/$26/>BiosTextAttr { mov AH,[>BiosTextAttr]}
      /$80/$E4/$F0          { and AH,$F0}
      /$08/$E0              { or AL,AH}
      /$A2/>BiosTextAttr);  { mov [>BiosTextAttr],AL}
procedure BiosTextBackGround(BColor:integer);
{ Set text background color }
inline(
   $58                      { pop AX}
   /$B1/$04                 { mov CL,4}
   /$D2/$E0                 { shl AL,CL}
   /$8A/$26/>BiosTextAttr { mov AH,[>BiosTextAttr]}
   /$80/$E4/$0F             { and AH,$0F}
   /$08/$E0                 { or AL,AH}
   /$A2/>BiosTextAttr);     { mov [>BiosTextAttr],AL}
function GetBiosTextAttr:integer;
{ Get the current Bios text Attribute }
Inline(
   $B7/$00       { mov BH,0}
   /$B4/$08      { mov AH,8}
   /$55          { push BP}
   /$CD/$10      { int $10}
   /$5D          { pop BP}
   /$88/$E0      { mov AL,AH}
   /$30/$E4);    { xor AH,AH}
procedure SetBiosWriteMode(Mode:integer);
{ Set Bios write mode to use }
inline(
   $58                      { pop AX}
   /$A2/>BiosWriteMode);  { mov [>BiosWriteMode],AL}
procedure SetBiosPage(Page:integer);
{ Set active bios video page }
inline(
   $58          { pop AX}
   /$B4/$05     { mov AH,5}
   /$55         { push BP}
   /$CD/$10     { int $10}
   /$5D);       { pop BP}
procedure BiosCursorOFF;
{ Turn the cursor off }
inline(
   $B4/$03        { mov AH,3}
   /$55           { push BP}
   /$CD/$10       { int $10}
   /$5D           { pop BP}
   /$80/$CD/$20 { or ch,$20}
   /$B4/$01       { mov AH,1}
   /$55           { push BP}
   /$CD/$10       { int $10}
   /$5D);         { pop BP}
```

```
procedure BiosCursorON;
{ Turn the cursor on }
inline(
    $B4/$03        { mov AH,3}
    /$55           { push BP}
    /$CD/$10       { int $10}
    /$5D           { pop BP}
    /$80/$E5/$1F   { and CH,$1F}
    /$B4/$01       { mov AH,1}
    /$55           { push BP}
    /$CD/$10       { int $10}
    /$5D);         { pop BP}
{ The following are the string procedures to access the BIOS   }
{ routines                                                     }
procedure BiosWrite(S:String);
{ Bios based text write }
procedure BiosWriteLn(S:String);
{ Bios based text writeln }
procedure BiosClrEol;
{ Clear to end of line}
procedure BiosClrScr;
{ clear the screen }
procedure BiosLowVideo;
{ Turns off high intensity attr bit }
procedure BiosHighVideo;
{ Turns on high intensity attr bit }
procedure BiosNormalVideo;
{ Restores video attr to start up value }
procedure AssignBiosCrt(var F:Text);
{ Assigns text output to BiosCrt }
procedure BiosTextMode(Mode:byte);
{ Sets new Bios video display mode }
procedure BiosPixGoto(X,Y:integer);
{ goto character at pixel location }
implementation
{ The following are the inline macros used to access the BIOS  }
{ routines                                                     }
{ Write Bios character via TTY write }
procedure TtyWrite(Ch:Char; Color:integer);
Inline(
    $5B            { pop BX}
    /$58           { pop AX}
    /$B4/$0E       { mov AH,14}
    /$55           { push BP}
    /$CD/$10       { int $10}
    /$5D);         { pop BP}
{ Write Bios character via Char/Attribute write }
procedure OutChar(Ch:Char; Color:integer);
```

Listing 6.7 continues

Listing 6.7 continued

```
Inline(
    $5B               { pop BX}
   /$58               { pop AX}
   /$B9/$01/$00   { mov CX,1}
   /$B4/$09       { mov AH,9}
   /$55               { push BP}
   /$CD/$10           { int $10}
   /$5D);             { pop BP}
{ This does a Bios based screen scroll }
procedure BiosScrollUp(StartXY,EndXY,Lines:word);
inline(
    $58                   { pop AX}
   /$5A                   { pop DX}
   /$59                   { pop CX}
   /$8A/$3E/>BiosTextAttr { mov BH,[>BiosTextAttr]}
   /$B4/$06               { mov AH,6}
   /$55                   { push BP}
   /$CD/$10               { int $10}
   /$5D);                 { pop BP}
{ This does a Bios based screen scroll }
procedure BiosScrollDown(StartXY,EndXY,Lines:word);
inline(
    $58                   { pop AX}
   /$5A                   { pop DX}
   /$59                   { pop CX}
   /$8A/$3E/>BiosTextAttr { mov BH,[>BiosTextAttr]}
   /$B4/$07               { mov AH,7}
   /$55                   { push BP}
   /$CD/$10               { int $10}
   /$5D);                 { pop BP}
{ This updates the LastBios registers prior to a call that   }
{ changes them                                               }
procedure SaveLastBiosMode;
inline(
    $B4/$0F                   { mov AH,15}
   /$55                       { push BP}
   /$CD/$10                   { int $10}
   /$5D                       { pop BP}
   /$A2/>LastBiosMode         { mov [>LastBiosMode],AL}
   /$88/$26/>LastBiosWidth    { mov [>LastBiosWidth],AH}
   /$88/$3E/>LastBiosPage);   { mov [>LastBiosPage],BH}
{ Sets the display mode to the values given }
procedure ForceBiosMode(Mode:byte);
inline(
    $58           { pop AX}
   /$B4/$00       { mov AH,0}
   /$55           { push BP}
   /$CD/$10       { int $10}
   /$5D);         { pop BP}
```

```
{ This saves the current Bios display mode in the LastMode      }
{ registers                                                     }
{ Then updates the display to the new mode value given          }
procedure BiosTextMode(Mode:byte);
begin
  SaveLastBiosMode;
  ForceBiosMode(Mode);
end;
procedure BiosLowVideo;
{ Turns off high intensity attr bit }
begin
   BiosTextAttr := BiosTextAttr and $08;
end;
procedure BiosHighVideo;
{ Turns on high intensity attr bit }
begin
   BiosTextAttr := BiosTextAttr or $08;
end;
procedure BiosNormalVideo;
{ Restores video attr to start up value }
begin
   BiosTextAttr := BiosStartAttr;
end;
{ Clear to the end of the text line starting from the current  }
{ X position                                                    }
procedure BiosClrEol;
var i,x,y : integer;
begin
   BiosWhereXY(x,y);
   for i := BiosWhereX to (BiosMaxX - 2) do
   begin
     TtyWrite(#$20,BiosTextAttr);
   end;
   OutChar(#$20,BiosTextAttr);
   BiosGotoXY(x,y);
end;
{ Clear the entire screen }
{ Warning: in Graphics mode you must set both foreground and    }
{ background to the desired color to be used or strange things  }
{ will happen                                                   }
procedure BiosClrScr;
begin
   if BiosMaxY = 0 then
     BiosScrollUp(0,(24 shl 8) or pred(BiosMaxX),0)
   else
     BiosScrollUp(0,(BiosMaxY shl 8) or pred(BiosMaxX),0);
end;
```

Listing 6.7 continues

Listing 6.7 continued

```
{ Delete a line from the screen }
{ Warning: in Graphics mode you must set both foreground and  }
{ background to the desired color to be used or strange things }
{ will happen                                                 }
procedure BiosDelLine;
begin
   if BiosMaxY = 0 then
     BiosScrollUp(BiosWhereY shl 8,(24 shl 8)
       or pred(BiosMaxX),0)
   else
     BiosScrollUp(BiosWhereY shl 8,(BiosMaxY shl 8)
       or pred(BiosMaxX),0);
end;
{ Insert a line on the screen }
{ Warning: in Graphics mode you must set both foreground and  }
{ background to the desired color to be used or strange things }
{ will happen                                                 }
procedure BiosInsLine;
begin
   if BiosMaxY = 0 then
     BiosScrollDown(BiosWhereY shl 8,(24 shl 8)
       or pred(BiosMaxX),0)
   else
     BiosScrollDown(BiosWhereY shl 8,(BiosMaxY shl 8)
       or pred(BiosMaxX),0);
end;
{ goto to the closest character X,Y point based on the Pixel  }
{ X,Y coordinate                                              }
procedure BiosPixGoto(X,Y:integer);
var CxSize,CySize : integer;
begin
   CySize := BiosCharSize;
   if CySize = 0 then CySize := 8;
   CxSize := 8;
   BiosGotoXY(X div CxSize,Y div CySize);
end;
procedure BWrite(Attr,Count:integer; Buf:Pointer);
type BufArray = array[0..65521] of char;
     BufPtr = ^BufArray;
var  P : BufPtr;
     i : integer;
begin
   P := Buf;
   i := 0;
   While i < Count do
   begin
     TtyWrite(P^[i],Attr);
     inc(i);
   end;
```

```
end;
procedure BkWrite(FColor,BColor,Count:integer; Buf:Pointer);
type BufArray = array[0..65521] of char;
     BufPtr = ^BufArray;
var  P : BufPtr;
     i : integer;
begin
  P := Buf;
  i := 0;
  While i < Count do
  begin
    OutChar(#10,BColor);                  { Output a block character}
    OutChar(#9,BColor or $80);         { Fill in the hole        }
    TtyWrite(P^[i],(BColor xor FColor) or $80);
                                       { Then write char         }

    inc(i);
  end;
end;
procedure FastBkWrite(FColor,BColor,Count:integer; Buf:Pointer);
type BufArray = array[0..65521] of char;
     BufPtr = ^BufArray;
var  P : BufPtr;
     i : integer;
begin
  P := Buf;  { this works just like BkWrite, but assumes that }
  i := 0;    { the #219 character is available in the system  }
  While i < Count do
            { for CGA systems this means that you must run  }
  begin     { the GRAFTABL program from your DOS disk first }
    OutChar(#219,BColor);              { Output a block character }
    TtyWrite(P^[i],(BColor xor FColor) or $80);
                                       { Then write char          }

    inc(i);
  end;
end;
{ Write a string via the Bios TTY write function             }
procedure BiosWrite(S:String);
begin
  case BiosWriteMode of
    1 : BWrite((BiosTextAttr and $0f)
          or $80,Length(S),Addr(S[1]));
    2 : BkWrite(BiosTextAttr and $0f,(BiosTextAttr shr 4)
          and $0f, Length(S),Addr(S[1]));
    3 : FastBkWrite(BiosTextAttr and $0f,(BiosTextAttr shr 4)
          and $0f, Length(S),Addr(S[1]));
    else
      BWrite(BiosTextAttr and $0f,Length(S),Addr(S[1]));
  end;
end;
```

Listing 6.7 continues

Listing 6.7 continued

```
{ Same thing as BiosWrite, but with CRLF added              }
procedure BiosWriteLn(S:String);
begin
   BiosWrite(S);
   TtyWrite(#10,BiosTextAttr);
   TtyWrite(#13,BiosTextAttr);
end;
{ The following are the procedures which allow BiosWrite to }
{ use the TFDD                                              }
{$F+}    { force fall calls for TFDD }
{-- Ignore this function call --}
function TfddBiosIgnore(var F:TextRec):integer;
begin
   TfddBiosIgnore := 0;
end;
{------------------------------------------------------------------}
{-- Write a string via the Bios TTY write function --}
{-- background is palette(0) - (usually black) --}
function TfddBiosWrite(var F:TextRec):integer;
begin
   with F do
   begin
     case BiosWriteMode of
       1 : BWrite((BiosTextAttr and $0f) or $80,BufPos,BufPtr);
       2 : BkWrite(BiosTextAttr and $0f,(BiosTextAttr shr 4) and
             $0f, BufPos,BufPtr);
       3 : FastBkWrite(BiosTextAttr and $0f,(BiosTextAttr shr 4)
             and $0f, BufPos,BufPtr);
     else
       BWrite(BiosTextAttr and $0f,BufPos,BufPtr);
     end;
     BufPos := 0;
   end;
   TfddBiosWrite := 0;
end;
{$F-}  { finished with the local TFDD so return world to normal }
procedure AssignBiosCrt(var F:Text);
begin
   with TextRec(F) do
   begin
     Handle := $FFFF;
     Mode := fmClosed;
     BufSize := SizeOf(Buffer);
     BufPtr := @Buffer;
     OpenFunc := @TfddBiosIgnore;
     CloseFunc := @TfddBiosIgnore;
     FlushFunc := @TfddBiosWrite;
```

```
        InOutFunc := @TfddBiosWrite;
        Name[0] := #0;
      end;
  end;
{ init with current known attribute by reading the screen }
begin
    BiosStartAttr := GetBiosTextAttr;
    BiosTextAttr := BiosStartAttr;
    BiosWriteMode := 0;
    SaveLastBiosMode;
end.
```

Mixing the use of BiosCrt and other Crt-type routines may cause confusion of background/foreground colors. The BiosCrt will always use its own foreground (from BiosTextAttr) and the existing BIOS background. In Xor write the background is unchanged, and the characters are Xored into the foreground. The special BiosBkWrite procedure allows you to write your own background in the graphics mode attribute while in text mode. In graphics mode the background is generated by writing a solid block in the foreground and then writing the desired character on top with a preXored color.

For this to work properly, the BIOS background should be black (Palette(0) = black) because the #219 block character is not normally available in CGA, so two characters that are available are used to simulate a block character. BiosWriteMode(3) is the same as BiosWriteMode(2) except that it assumes that the #219 character is available. To make the character available on a CGA display, run GRAFTABL. On EGA/VGA displays the #219 character is normally available, so you can use the mode 3 write without problems. Be careful about user-loaded fonts, however; they may have redefined the appearance of character #219.

7

Interrupt Service Routines

In this chapter, we talk about what interrupts are and how they work. We discuss the steps and many restrictions that must be observed in setting up and removing routines that are called by interrupts. Finally, we provide examples of interrupt service routines (ISRs). One example outputs a graphics screen to the printer. Another example develops a "quick-and-dirty" timing unit that times routines based on the clock tick.

What Are Interrupts?

The CPU needs a way to communicate with the devices that are attached to it—the keyboard, floppy disk drive, hard disk drive, video display adapter, printer, and others. The CPU could constantly monitor whether each device needs to be serviced, but that would take a considerable amount of time away from the processor's main task of executing code. Instead, the way these devices indicate that they need service is with interrupts. A device that needs service sends an interrupt signal that tells the CPU to stop what it is doing and process the interrupt.

At the start of the CPU's low memory is a table that stores a segment and offset of code to be executed when a specific interrupt occurs. When an interrupt occurs, this is what happens:

1. The CPU flags, CS, and IP registers are saved.

2. The location within the table is computed based on the interrupt number that occurred.

3. The CS and IP registers are loaded with the value stored in the table.

The values in the table are referred to as vectors, so it is called the *interrupt vector table*.

Logical Interrupts

There are three types of interrupts: logical, hardware, and software. Table 7.1 shows the uses of logical interrupts.

Table 7.1. *Logical Interrupts*

INT $00:	Denotes that a division by zero has occurred
INT $01:	Commonly used for single-stepping through code
INT $03:	Similar to INT 1; commonly used for a breakpoint
INT $04:	Denotes that an overflow has occurred

Hardware Interrupts

The hardware interrupts are how the hardware devices get the attention of the CPU. Table 7.2 shows the uses of hardware interrupts.

Table 7.2. *Hardware Interrupts*

INT $02:	Nonmaskable; used when a memory parity error or some other fatal error has occurred
INT $06:	Reserved
INT $07:	Reserved
INT $08:	Called by the timer 18 times a second
INT $09:	Used by the keyboard
INT $0A:	Reserved

INT $0B and $0C: Used by the asynchronous communications port (COM2 and COM1, respectively)

INT $0D: Used by the fixed disk controller

INT $0E: Used by the floppy disk drive controller

INT $0F: Used by the printer (LPT1)

Software Interrupts

Software interrupts allow a program to call another block of code. The calling program does not need to know the address of this block of code. DOS and BIOS routines are good examples of this. To access the routines of DOS and BIOS, a program needs to use interrupts. The main DOS interrupt is hex 21.

If there is only one main DOS interrupt, how is more than one service of DOS called? The register AH (the high byte of register AX) is used to indicate which service of DOS is being called. For example, INT $21 with $2A in AH will call the DOS service to get the system date.

The next question is how are the results of the interrupts returned to the program? The registers will contain the results of almost all interrupts. The exceptions of the rules are the absolute disk read and write interrupts, INT $25 and $26. These special case interrupts are discussed in Chapter 13. In the case of the DOS interrupt to get the system date, register CX will contain the year, DH will contain the month, and DL will contain the day.

For a complete listing of all available interrupts and their services, consult a DOS or PC technical reference manual. *DOS Programmer's Reference* by Que Corporation is a good book that discusses both the documented and undocumented interrupts.

Restrictions for Interrupt Service Routines

Interrupt Service Routines (ISRs) are routines that are called when an interrupt occurs. Because interrupts can occur at any time, they can cause problems. DOS is not *reentrant*, which means it cannot have two functions being used at the same time. If you have an ISR load while DOS is in the middle of something, the ISR cannot make a call to DOS. There are some exceptions; some DOS services can be interrupted by other DOS services, but that is a tricky subject. The best bet is to use the INDOS flag.

The INDOS flag is an undocumented DOS service—$34. This will return a pointer in ES:BX to a location in memory. This location will be either 0 or 1. If the location is set to 0, DOS is not busy; if the location is 1, DOS is being used. Because this is an undocumented service, Microsoft does not have to support it in future versions of DOS; but if Microsoft does not support the service, many programs on the market will not work properly.

In addition to DOS not being reentrant, some of Turbo Pascal's code is not reentrant. *Turbo Pascal V5.0 Reference Guide* states that input/output operations and dynamic memory allocation routines are not reentrant. Turbo Pascal's nonreentrant features include any routines that use DOS calls, so most of the DOS unit is included as well. Some of the Graph, Graph3, and Crt units' code is also not reentrant. The six-byte, floating-point library is fully reentrant, but the floating-point emulator and code for the 8087 chip is not.

Four steps are required to safely set up an interrupt service routine:

1. Declare the procedure an interrupt procedure.

2. Set it up as a FAR call.

3. Save the old interrupt vector.

4. Set the new interrupt vector.

If you fail to do any of these things, you will probably encounter serious problems with your programs. The following sections describe the steps in detail.

Using the Interrupt Keyword

To declare a procedure an interrupt procedure, place the keyword interrupt after the definition of the procedure header, similar to the use of the external keyword. You can access some or all of the registers by defining them as parameters to your interrupt procedure. The order of the parameters is as follows:

```
Flags, CS, IP, AX, BX, CX, DX, SI, DI, DS, ES, BP
```

All of the parameters should be defined as type word. If you need only a few of the parameters, you only have to define a few, but you must include all parameters that appear in the list to the right of the ones you need. For example, if you want to access the CX register, you must place DX, SI, DI, DS, ES, and BP in the parameter list as well.

In addition to allowing the procedure to access registers as pseudo-variables, the `interrupt` keyword does a few other things: it causes all of the registers to be pushed onto the stack at the start of the call and the stack and data segment registers to be set up for you. This allows you to define your own local variables to this procedure or to access global variables. Upon termination of this special procedure, all of the registers are popped off the stack and restored. Finally, an IRET is used instead of a RET (IRET denotes an Interrupt Return instead of a simple return).

Following is an example of defining an interrupt procedure that allows you to access the AX register:

```
Procedure MyISR ( AX, BX, CX, DX, SI, DI, DS, ES, BP : Word ); Interrupt;
Begin
  ...
End;
```

Setting Up the FAR Call

A FAR call is required when the code to be executed may be called from outside the current code segment. Because Turbo Pascal Versions 4.0, 5.0, and 5.5 allow multiple code segments, this is important. An interrupt can occur at any time; there is no guarantee that you will be in the same segment of code as your interrupt service routine. In fact, all of the system run-time library code is placed into its own segment. Set up an interrupt service routine as a FAR call by placing the {$F+} compiler directive before the procedure statement.

Using the sample interrupt procedure from the preceding section, consider how you can use the {$F+} compiler directive:

```
{$F+}
Procedure MyISR ( AX, BX, CX, DX, SI, DI, DS, ES, BP : Word ); Interrupt;
{$F-}
Begin
  ...
End;
```

The {$F-} is used after the procedure header. This is not required, but if it is not done, all of the procedures and functions following this in the code will be FAR calls, which is usually not desired. If it is desired, the {$F+} compiler directive is set in the integrated development environment or earlier in the code. Using conditional compilation statements, you can change the code to reflect the state of the {$F+} compiler directive:

```
{$IFOPT F+}
Procedure MyISR ( AX, BX, CX, DX, SI, DI, DS, ES, BP : Word ); Interrupt;
{$ELSE}
{$F+}
Procedure MyISR ( AX, BX, CX, DX, SI, DI, DS, ES, BP : Word ); Interrupt;
{$F-}
{$ENDIF}
Begin
  ...
End;
```

This code says: if the {$F+} compiler directive is already set, do not set again and remove; if the directive is not already set, set it for this procedure and deactivate it afterward.

Saving the Old Interrupt Vector

The next step after making a procedure an interrupt procedure that is defined FAR is to save the old interrupt vector. When your program is ready to terminate, you will want to restore the original interrupt vector; your code will no longer be loaded in the machine, so having the vector point to your code makes no sense and can lock up the machine. You may want to call the original interrupt from within your interrupt handler. (For examples of why you may want to do that, look at the sample programs in the final section of this chapter.)

To store the old interrupt vector, DOS provides an interrupt that will look up the interrupt number you specify in the interrupt vector table and return the vector currently set. This is much safer than looking directly into the interrupt vector table.

To make things even simpler, Turbo Pascal provides a procedure that handles calling this DOS interrupt. All you need to do is call the GetIntVec procedure. It takes two parameters: a byte that represents the interrupt number you want to query and a pointer. The pointer is the parameter that is returned by the routine and contains the vector of the interrupt.

Setting the New Interrupt Vector

To set the entry in the vector table to point to your ISR, DOS provides an interrupt, and Turbo Pascal has a procedure to help you. The SetIntVec procedure requires two parameters: the interrupt for which you want to modify the vector and a pointer to your procedure. You can place an "at" symbol (@) in front of the procedure name you want to install. Using the example we mentioned earlier, you would do this as follows:

```
GetIntVec ( $09, MyOldISR );
SetIntVec ( $09, @MyISR );
```

The first procedure call saves the old interrupt vector into a variable defined as a pointer called MyOldISR. The next routine points the interrupt 9 vector to the procedure MyISR. The SetIntVec procedure will take any procedure as a parameter; it is up to you to make sure that the procedure is an interrupt procedure and is defined FAR.

Restoration Process

The restoration process is just as important to your interrupt service routine as the steps for setting it up. When your program finishes running, all the memory for where your code and data resides is released to DOS. DOS can next do whatever it wants with that memory. If you leave an interrupt vectored to your procedure, what will happen is uncertain; your procedure is no longer loaded, and the memory at that location may contain garbage.

Turbo Pascal provides an exit procedure that simplifies the task. An *exit procedure* is a block of code that will be executed before control is returned to DOS. Regardless of whether the program is terminated through Ctrl-Break, an error, or normal termination, the exit procedure will be executed. About the only time an exit procedure will not be executed is if the machine is turned off.

Within the exit procedure, we will again use the SetIntVec procedure to set the interrupt vector that we modified back to the value we saved. If the code to save the interrupt vector is as follows:

```
GetIntVec ( $09, MyOldISR );
SetIntVec ( $09, @MyISR );
```

then the exit procedure looks like this:

```
{$F+}
Procedure MyExitProc;
{$F-}
Begin
  ExitProc := oldExitProc
  SetIntVec ( $09, MyOldISR );
End;
```

Looking at this code, you will notice that the {$F+}/{$F-} is used again. Because we have no idea from what segment of code this routine may be called, we have to make it a FAR call.

The first job of the exit procedure is to restore the old ExitProc value. This value was saved when the initialization for this block of code was executed; it is important to save the old ExitProc because these values can be chained to have many different exit procedures running, one after another. We can set up our initialization for the exit procedure as follows:

```
Var
  oldExitProc : Pointer

Begin
  oldExitProc := ExitProc;
  ExitProc := @MyExitProc;
```

This is the same idea as installing an interrupt vector. You store the old value in a pointer variable. Next, you set the ExitProc to the @ and the procedure name.

Now, think about the exit procedure example again. The reason we restore the ExitProc value first is that the code in the exit procedure may cause another error. If this happens, we want any other exit procedures that exist later to be executed.

Next, the procedure uses SetIntVec to restore the interrupt vector to the original vector value. After this is done, the interrupt is restored.

Sample Interrupt Service Routines

The balance of this chapter consists of examples of ISR programs, and most of the routines are useful as more than examples. The examples are provided in the order of the interrupt they are hooking.

The first example gives a bare-bones unit of the minimum code required to write an interrupt service routine. This will be modified and used in each of the following examples.

The second example uses interrupt 05 and allows you to toggle between a text print screen and a graphics print screen.

The third example is a Ctrl-Break handler that will let you break a program at any time. (Turbo Pascal lets you break only during I/O.) This unit uses interrupt 09.

The fourth example is a game that uses the keyboard interrupt 09 and provides an example of trapping the keyboard interrupt and passing information on to a program.

The fifth and final example is connected to interrupt 1C—the timer tick interrupt—and the routine is a performance timer. It lets you time how long execution of a block of code takes.

Skeleton ISR

Listing 7.1 is a generic unit to implement an interrupt service routine. The unit does nothing but install an interrupt vector and restore it at the end of the program. To use this unit, go through and replace the characters XX with the interrupt for which you want to install a service routine. When you see <XX>, replace it with the interrupt number; the <XX> denotes that an actual number is expected here.

This unit follows everything mentioned in the previous "Setting the New Interrupt Vector" and "Restoration Process" sections. The procedure to which you will want to add your code to is procedure ISR. You can optionally call JumpOldISR if your specific case requires it.

The procedure ISR is defined by the unit to access all the registers; this is optional. If you have no need to access all the registers, you can ignore the fact that they are defined or remove them from the definition.

***Listing* 7.1.** *Skeleton.Pas*

```
Unit IntXX;

INTERFACE

Uses
  DOS;

IMPLEMENTATION

Var
  OldExitProc,
  SaveIntXX : pointer;

Procedure JmpOldISR(OldISR: Pointer);
{ An inline macro procedure. The code for this will be inserted at the }
{ point that it is called. The purpose of this macro is to jump to the }
{ interrupt service routine at the address passed in.                  }
  Inline($5B/$58/$87/$5E/$0E/$87/$46/$10/$89/
         $EC/$5D/$07/$1F/$5F/$5E/$5A/$59/$CB);
```

***Listing* 7.1** *continues*

Listing *7.1 continued*

```
{$F+}
Procedure ISR( Flags,CS,IP,AX,BX,CX,DX,SI,DI,DS,ES,BP:word ); Interrupt;
{ This interrupt procedure is the new ISR for Interrupt XX. }
Begin
  JmpOldISR( SaveIntXX );
End;

Procedure IntXXExitProc;
{ This procedure will be called upon exit of the program. Its purpose }
{ is to restore the interrupt that was stolen at startup.             }
Begin
  ExitProc := OldExitProc;
  SetIntVec( <XX>, SaveIntXX );  { Restore the old ISR }
end;
{$F-}

Begin
  OldExitProc := ExitProc;          { Set up exit procedure }
  ExitProc := @IntXXExitProc;       { " }
  GetIntVec( <XX>, SaveIntXX );   { Save old ISR value }
  SetIntVec( <XX>, @ISR );    { Set up new ISR }
end.
```

Print Screen Example

The print screen example that follows (and all other examples in this chapter) uses the skeleton ISR unit described in the preceding section.

Interrupt 05 is used for printing the screen. When the key combination Shift-PrtSc is used, the keyboard interrupt handler calls this interrupt. Additionally, if you want your program to do a print screen at any time, you can issue a INTR ($05, r), where *r* is a variable defined as type registers. This interrupt does not expect the registers to be loaded with any specific value.

The drawback of the print-screen interrupt is that it prints only a text screen. The GPrint unit (described in Chapter 10) allows you to print a graphics screen to an EPSON or EPSON-compatible printer. Listings 7.2, 7.3, and 7.4 use that unit to enable the print-screen interrupt to print a graphics screen.

A global Boolean variable, GraphPrn, is defined in listing 7.2. Based on the value of this variable, the GPrint unit is called or the original interrupt vector is jumped to. If GraphPrn is true, the graphics printing is performed.

Listing *7.2. Int05.Pas*

```
Unit Int05;

INTERFACE

Uses
  DOS,
  GPrint;

Var
  GraphPrn : Boolean;

IMPLEMENTATION

Var
  OldExitProc,
  SaveInt05 : pointer;

Procedure JmpOldISR(OldISR: Pointer);
{ An inline macro procedure. The code for this will be inserted at the }
{ point that it is called. The purpose of this macro is to jump to the }
{ Interrupt Service Routine at the address passed in.                  }
  Inline($5B/$58/$87/$5E/$0E/$87/$46/$10/$89/
         $EC/$5D/$07/$1F/$5F/$5E/$5A/$59/$CB);

{$F+}
Procedure Key_ISR; Interrupt;
{ This interrupt procedure is the new ISR for Interrupt 05. Based  }
{ on the value of the global boolean variable GraphPrn, either the }
{ graphics print screen is called ( TRUE ), or the old ISR print-  }
{ screen is called ( FALSE ).                                      }
Begin
  If GraphPrn Then
  Begin
    HardCopy ( 1 );     { This value may differ for non-Epson printers. }
  End
  Else
    JmpOldISR( SaveInt05 );
End;

Procedure Int05ExitProc;
{ This procedure will be called upon exit of the program. Its purpose }
{ is to restore the interrupt that was stolen at startup.             }
Begin
  ExitProc := OldExitProc;
  SetIntVec( 5, SaveInt05 );  { Restore the old ISR }
end;
{$F-}
```

Listing *7.2 continues*

Listing 7.2 continued

```
Begin
   OldExitProc := ExitProc;      { Set up exit procedure }
   ExitProc := @Int05ExitProc;
   GetIntVec( 5, SaveInt05 );    { Save old ISR value }
   SetIntVec( 5, @Key_ISR );     { Set up new ISR }

   GraphPrn := FALSE;            { Default to normal print screen }
end.
```

Listing 7.3. GPrint.Pas

```
Unit GPrint;
{----------------------------------------------------------------}
{ This unit is designed to send graphics images to EPSON-        }
{ compatible and late model IBM ProPrinter dot matrix printers.  }
{ It takes the image from the currently active view port,        }
{ determined by a call to GetViewSettings, and transfers that    }
{ image to the printer.                                          }
{----------------------------------------------------------------}

Interface

Uses Dos, Graph;       { Link in the necessary standard units    }

Var
   LST : Text;          { New printer file variable               }

Procedure HardCopy (Gmode: Integer);
{ Procedure HardCopy prints the current ViewPort to an IBM or    }
{ EPSON-compatible graphics printer.                             }
{                                                                }
{ Valid Gmode numbers are :                                      }
{      -4 to -1 for EPSON and IBM Graphic Printers               }
{       0 to 7  for EPSON Printers                               }

Implementation

Procedure HardCopy {Gmode: Integer};

Const
   Bits : Array [0..7] of Byte = (128,64,32,16,8,4,2,1);
                    { Values of each bit within byte variable  }

Var
   X,Y,YOfs       : Integer;    { Screen  location variables   }
   BitData,MaxBits : Byte;       { Number of bits to transfer   }
   Vport          : ViewPortType;{ Used to get view settings    }
```

```
    Height, Width   : Word;        { Size of image  to transfer  }
    HiBit, LoBit    : Char;        {     Char size of image       }
    LineSpacing,                   { Additional  Info for  dump   }
    GraphixPrefix   : String[10];  {     "      "  "    "         }
    BKColor         : Byte;        { Value of current bk color    }

Begin
  LineSpacing   := #27+'3'+#24;  { 24/216 inch line spacing     }
  Case Gmode Of
    -1:   GraphixPrefix := #27+'K';  { Standard Density          }
    -2:   GraphixPrefix := #27+'L';  { Double Density            }
    -3:   GraphixPrefix := #27+'Y';  { Dbl. Density Dbl. Speed   }
    -4:   GraphixPrefix := #27+'Z';  { Quad. Density             }
    0..7: GraphixPrefix := #27+'*'+Chr( Gmode );{ 8-Pin Bit Img  }
    Else
      Exit;                          { Invalid Mode Selection    }
  End;
  BKColor := GetBKColor;
  GetViewSettings( Vport );        { Get size of image to be     }
  Height := Vport.Y2 - Vport.Y1;   { printed                     }
  Width  := ( Vport.X2 + 1 ) - Vport.X1;
  HiBit := Chr( Hi( Width ) );     { Translate sizes to char     }
  LoBit := Chr( Lo( Width ) );     { for  output to printer      }
  Write( LST, LineSpacing );
  Y := 0;                          { First Y coordinate          }
  While Y < Height Do              { Do not go beyond viewport    }
  Begin
    Write( LST,GraphixPrefix,LoBit,HiBit );
                                   { Tell printer graphics info }
    For X := 0 to Width-1 Do       { Go across screen lt to rt. }
    Begin
      BitData := 0;                { Initialize to all off (0)  }
      If y + 7 <= Height Then      { Make sure there are 8      }
        MaxBits := 7               { lines of info and set it   }
      Else                         { accordingly                }
        MaxBits := Height - Y;
      For YOfs := 0 to MaxBits do  { Go top to bottom on line   }
        If( GetPixel( X, YOfs+Y ) <> BKColor ) Then
            BitData := BitData or Bits[YOfs];
                                   { If pixel on, add to output }
      Write( LST, Chr( BitData ) );{ Byte is created, output it }
    End;
    WriteLn ( LST );
    Inc( Y,8 );                    { Inc by 8 as each line is 8 }
                                   { actual scan line in height }
  End;
  Writeln ( LST, #12 + #27 + 64 );
```

Listing 7.3 continues

Listing *7.3 continued*

```
End;
{---------------------------------------------------------------}
{ What follows is the code for the Text File Device Driver for  }
{ the LST file variable defined above.  This is necessary as    }
{ Turbo opens the LST device defined in the printer unit in a   }
{ "Cooked" mode.                                                }
{---------------------------------------------------------------}

{$F+}

Function LSTNoFunction( Var F: TextRec ): Integer;
{ This function performs a NUL operation on LST in case a Reset }
{ or a Rewrite is called.                                      }
Begin
  LSTNoFunction := 0;
End;

Function LSTOutputToPrinter( Var F: TextRec ): Integer;
{ This function sends the output to the printer port number    }
{ stored in the first byte of the UserData area of the Text    }
{ Record.                                                      }
Var
  Regs: Registers;
  P : word;
Begin
  With F do
  Begin
    P := 0;
    Regs.AH := 16;
    While( ( P < BufPos ) And ( ( Regs.AH and 16 ) = 16 ) ) Do
    Begin
      Regs.AL := Ord( BufPtr^[P] );
      Regs.AH := 0;
      Regs.DX := UserData[1];
      Intr( $17,Regs );
      Inc( P );
    end;
    BufPos := 0;
  End;
  If( Regs.AH and 16 ) = 16 Then
    LSTOutputToPrinter := 0                  { No error             }
  Else
    If( Regs.AH and 32 ) = 32 Then
      LSTOutputToPrinter := 159              { Out of Paper         }
    Else
      LSTOutputToPrinter := 160;             { Device write Fault }
End;

{$F-}
```

```
Procedure AssignLST( Port:Byte );
{ This procedure sets up the LST text file record as would the  }
{ Assign procedure, and initializes it as would a call to the   }
{ Reset procedure.  It then stores the LPT port number in the   }
{ first byte of the UserData Area of the TextRec type.          }

Begin
  With TextRec( LST ) do
  Begin
    Handle       := $FFF0;
    Mode         := fmOutput;
    BufSize      := SizeOf( Buffer );
    BufPtr       := @Buffer;
    BufPos       := 0;
    OpenFunc     := @LSTNoFunction;
    InOutFunc    := @LSTOutputToPrinter;
    FlushFunc    := @LSTOutputToPrinter;
    CloseFunc    := @LSTOutputToPrinter;
    UserData[1] := Port - 1;  { Sub 1 as DOS counts from zero   }
  End;
End;

Begin
  AssignLST( 1 );             { Sets output printer to LPT1 by }
                             { default.  Change this value to }
                             { select other LPT ports.        }
End.
```

The MyGraph program (listing 7.4) demonstrates how you can use the Int05 unit (listing 7.2). First, a sample graphics image is printed on the screen. At any point in graphics mode, you can use the PrtSc key to print the graphics image. To continue, you must press Enter to go through the ReadLn. Next, 25 lines of a test string are printed on the screen. When you use the PrtSc key in text mode, the text on the screen is printed. If you note where the GraphPrn variable is set to true and where it is set to false, you will see how to structure a program to use the Int05 unit. At any point while you are working with graphics, you should be able to do a print screen. If you are not in a graphics mode, you will only be able to print text.

Listing 7.4. MyGraph.Pas

```
Program MyGraph;

Uses
  CRT,
  Graph,
  Int05;

Var
  gDriver,
  gMode,
  x,
  y : Integer;

Begin
  gDriver := Detect;
  InitGraph (gDriver,gMode,'');
  If ( GraphResult <> grOk ) Then
    Halt ( GraphResult );
  GraphPrn := TRUE;
  x := 0;
  While ( x < 100 ) Do
  Begin
    y := 0;
    Inc ( x, 4 );
    While ( y < 100 ) Do
    Begin
      Inc ( y, 4 );
      Line (x,y,100-x,100-y);
    End;
  End;
  ReadLn;
  CloseGraph;
  GraphPrn := FALSE;
  TextMode ( co80 );
  ClrScr;
  For x := 1 To 25 Do
    WriteLn ( 'This is a test.' );
  ReadLn;
End.
```

Break Handler

Turbo Pascal provides the facilities to break a program with Ctrl-Break when any I/O operations are being performed. This feature can be toggled on or off based on the CheckBreak Boolean variable, which is defined in the Crt unit.

The unit in listing 7.5, BreakOut, allows you to expand on the break capabilities of the compiler. This code will install an interrupt service routine off the keyboard handler. When the signal comes through the port indicating that Ctrl-Break was pressed, interrupt $23 is called. This activates the Turbo Pascal exit procedure, providing a safe exit from the program.

Why would you want to break at any time? There are plenty of good reasons. The best answer is if you go into an infinite loop in your program. If the loop does no I/O, standard Turbo Pascal will not let you break out; this unit allows you to do so.

The main work done in this unit is in the Procedure Key_ISR. This routine checks the keyboard port location ($60). If CheckBreak is true, and the port returns the code for the Break key, and the memory location $0000:$0417 contains the bits for the Ctrl key being pressed, then the interrupt $23 is called. If any of these conditions are not met, the old interrupt vector is called.

Listing 7.5. BreakOut.Pas

```
Unit BreakOut;
{ This unit will intercept hardware interrupt $9 and check for a Ctrl-Break.  }
{ If the interrupt does not contain a Ctrl-Break the preceding Int9 is called.}
{ If Ctrl-Break was pressed we call Turbo's int23 handler to stop execution   }
{ of the program, while still executing the ExitProcs.                        }

INTERFACE

Uses DOS,CRT;

IMPLEMENTATION

Var
  Int23,
  OldExit,
  OldKBD : pointer;

Procedure JmpOldISR ( OldISR: pointer );
  Inline ( $5B/$58/$87/$5E/$0E/$87/$46/$10/$89/
           $EC/$5D/$07/$1F/$5F/$5E/$5A/$59/$CB );

{$F+}
Procedure Key_ISR; Interrupt;
```

Listing 7.5 continues

Listing 7.5 *continued*

```
Begin
  If CheckBreak AND ( ( Mem [0000:$0417] AND 4 ) = 4 ) AND
                    ( Port[$60] = 70 ) Then
    Begin
      Inline ( $E4/$61/$8A/$E0/$0C/$80/$E6/$61/    { Clean up as the  }
               $86/$E0/$E6/$61/$B0/$20/$E6/$20 ); { Bios would       }
      JmpOldISR( Int23 );    {Jump to current Int23 handler (turbo's) }
    End;
  JmpOldISR( OldKBD );        {Jump to Old Keyboard handler }
End;

Procedure Exitit;
Begin
  ExitProc := OldExit;        { Restore Old ExitProc pointer }
  SetIntVec ( 9, OldKBD );    { Restore Old Int9 Handler     }
End;
{$F-}

Begin
  OldExit := ExitProc;        { Save old ExitProc pointer }
  ExitProc := @Exitit;        { Set new ExitProc pointer  }
  GetIntVec ( $23, Int23 );   { Get Turbo's Int23 Vector  }
  GetIntVec ( 9, OldKBD );    { Get Current Int9  Vector  }
  SetIntVec ( 9, @Key_ISR );  { Set Int9 to our routine   }
End.
```

Game Example

This sample program is a fun, simplistic game with much room for improvement. The basic idea of the game is to move a ship on the bottom of the screen back and forth and shoot at aliens near the top of the screen. The driving force behind this program is an interrupt service routine. This ISR is set from the same interrupt as the previous example, interrupt 09 (the keyboard interrupt).

The major difference between this ISR and the preceding example is that based on the values coming in the port from the keyboard, specific Boolean variables are set to true. This means we can create an event-driven program to control the keyboard actions. Using a keyboard interrupt service routine is much faster than reading the keyboard using ReadKey.

In this game, the left- and right-arrow keys control the movement of your ship at the bottom of the screen. The space bar will fire a shot from your ship towards the aliens at the top of the screen. The object of the game is to shoot all of the aliens.

Examine the code in listings 7.6 and 7.7 to see how things are set up. Notice all of the constants at the start of the main program and the conditional compilation statements. After you finish looking at the code, continue reading this discussion.

Listing *7.6.* *GameInt9.Pas*

```
Unit GameInt9;

INTERFACE

Uses
  DOS,CRT;

Var
  Left,
  Right,
  Space,
  Escape : Boolean;
  P : Byte;

IMPLEMENTATION

Var
  OldExitProc,
  SaveInt09 : pointer;

procedure JmpOldISR(OldISR: pointer);
  inline($5B/$58/$87/$5E/$0E/$87/$46/$10/$89/
         $EC/$5D/$07/$1F/$5F/$5E/$5A/$59/$CB);

{$F+}
procedure Key_ISR( Flags,CS,IP,AX,BX,CX,DX,SI,DI,DS,ES,BP:word ); Interrupt;
Begin
  P := Port [$60];
  If ( P = 75 ) Then
    Left := TRUE
  Else
  If ( P = 77 ) Then
    Right := TRUE
  Else
  If ( P = 57 ) Then
    Space := TRUE
  Else
  If ( P = 1 ) Then
    Escape := TRUE
  Else
    JmpOldISR( SaveInt09 );
```

Listing *7.6 continues*

Listing 7.6 continued

```
   Inline($E4/$61/$8A/$EO/$OC/$80/$E6/$61/   { Clean up as the    }
          $86/$EO/$E6/$61/$BO/$20/$E6/$20);  { Bios would         }
End;

Procedure Int09ExitProc;
Begin
  ExitProc := OldExitProc;
  SetIntVec( 9, SaveInt09 );
end;
{$F-}

Begin
  OldExitProc := ExitProc;
  ExitProc := @Int09ExitProc;
  GetIntVec( 9, SaveInt09 );
  SetIntVec( 9, @Key_ISR );

  Left := FALSE;
  Right := FALSE;
  Space := FALSE;
  Escape := FALSE;
end.
```

Listing 7.7. Game.Pas

```
Program Game;

Uses
  CRT,
  DOS
{$IFDEF DEBUG}
  ;
{$ELSE}
  ,
  GameInt9;
{$ENDIF}

Const
  ShotChar     = #24; { Define the shot character as an arrow }
  ShotWaitTime = 500; { Number of times to call UpdateShot before doing so }
  MaxShots     = 2;   { 2 shots on the screen at a time }

  ShipChar     = '^';
  Ship         = ShipChar + ShipChar + ShipChar;

  AlienChar    = ' ';
  Alien        = AlienChar + AlienChar + AlienChar;
```

```
      AlienWaitTime = 500;
      MaxAliens    = 5;
      AlienY       = 5;
      AlienPts     = 50;

{$IFDEF DEBUG}
  left   : boolean = false;
  right  : boolean = true;
  space  : boolean = false;
  escape : boolean = false;
{$ENDIF}


Type
  ShotRec  = Record
                 Shooting : Boolean;
                 ShotX,
                 ShotY    : Byte;
             End;
  ShotArr  = Array [1..MaxShots] of ShotRec;
  AlienRec = Record
                 Alive : Boolean;
                 X     : Byte;
                 Delta : ShortInt;
             End;
  AlienArr = Array [1..MaxAliens] of AlienRec;


Var
  Score      : Word;
  Shot       : ShotArr;
  Aliens     : AlienArr;
  ShotDelay  : Word;
  AlienDelay : Word;
  ScrSeg     : Word;
  ScrWidth   : Byte;
  ShipX,
  ShipY      : Byte;
  i          : Byte;

Function ScrChar ( x, y : Byte ) : Char;
{ This procedure will calculate the offset into video memory based   }
{ on the [X,Y] coordinates passed in. The character at this location }
{ in memory will be returned as the function result.                 }
Begin
  If ( y > 0 ) Then
    ScrChar := Chr ( Mem [ ScrSeg : (( x - 1 ) * 2 ) +
                                    (( y - 1 ) * ScrWidth * 2)]);
End;


Procedure MoveLeft;
{ This procedure is called if a key event occurs indicating that }
```

Listing 7.7 *continues*

Listing 7.7 continued

```pascal
{ the ship is to be moved left one space.                     }
Begin
  If ( ShipX > 1 ) Then
  Begin
    Dec ( ShipX );
    GotoXY ( ShipX, ShipY );
    Write ( Ship + ' ' );
  End;
  Left := FALSE;
End;

Procedure MoveRight;
{ This procedure is called if a key event occurs indicating that }
{ the ship is to be moved right one space.                     }
Begin
  If ( ShipX < ( ScrWidth - Length ( Ship ) ) ) Then
  Begin
    GotoXY ( ShipX, ShipY );
    Write ( ' ' + Ship );
    Inc ( ShipX );
  End;
  Right := FALSE;
End;

Procedure Fire;
{ This procedure is called if a key event occurs indicating that }
{ the ship has fired a shot at the aliens.                     }
Var
  i : Byte;
Begin
  Space := FALSE;
  i := 1;
  While ( Shot [i].Shooting ) AND ( i < MaxShots ) Do { Find an open }
    Inc ( i );                                    { shot record. }
  If ( Not Shot [i].Shooting ) AND ( i <= MaxShots ) Then
  Begin
    Shot [i].Shooting := TRUE;                       { Set the shot }
    Shot [i].ShotX := ShipX + ( Length ( Ship ) div 2 ); { record.   }
    Shot [i].ShotY := ShipY - 1;
  End;
End;

Function RemoveAlien ( x, y : Byte ) : Byte;
{ This function is called to remove an Alien from the screen.  }
{ The first Alien discovered at the [X,Y] coordinates passed   }
{ in will be removed from the screen. The function will return }
{ array offset of the Alien removed ( for scoring purposes ).  }
```

```
Var
   i    : Byte;
   done : Boolean;
Begin
   i := 0;
   done := FALSE;
   While ( i < MaxAliens ) AND ( Not done ) Do
   Begin
     Inc ( i );
     If ( AlienY = y ) AND ( Aliens [i].Alive ) AND
        ( x in [(Aliens [i].X)..(Aliens [i].X+Length (Alien))] ) Then
     Begin
       done := TRUE;
       Aliens [i].Alive := FALSE;
       GotoXY ( Aliens [i].X, AlienY );
       Write ( '   ' );
     End;
   End;
   RemoveAlien := i;
End;

Procedure IncScore ( i : Byte );
{ This procedure will increment the score using the base }
{ score value multiplied by the speed of the Alien.      }
Begin
   Score := Score + ( AlienPts * Abs ( Aliens [i].Delta ) );
   GotoXY ( ( ScrWidth - 10 ), 1 );
   Write ( Score : 5 );
   Sound ( 500 );
   Delay ( 100 );
   NoSound;
End;

Procedure UpdateAliens;
{ This routine will update the Aliens on the video screen. }
Begin
   Inc ( AlienDelay );                     { Add one to the global counter }
   If ( ( AlienDelay Mod AlienWaitTime ) = 0 ) Then { Check delay factor }
     For i := 1 to MaxAliens Do
       If ( Aliens [i].Alive ) Then       { If the Alien is active }
         If ( Aliens [i].X >= ScrWidth - ( Length ( Alien ) + 1 ) ) OR
            ( Aliens [i].X <= 1 ) Then
         Begin
           GotoXY ( Aliens [i].X, AlienY );
           Write ( '    ' );
```

Listing 7.7 continues

Listing 7.7 *continued*

```
                Aliens [i].Delta := -Aliens [i].Delta;
                Inc ( Aliens [i].X, Aliens [i].Delta );
                GotoXY ( Aliens [i].X, AlienY );
                Write ( Alien );
             End
             Else
             Begin
                GotoXY ( Aliens [i].X, AlienY );
                Write ( '     ' );
                Inc ( Aliens [i].X, Aliens [i].Delta );
                GotoXY ( Aliens [i].X, AlienY );
                Write ( Alien );
             End;
End;

Procedure UpdateShot;
{ This procedure will update any shots that are active on the screen. }
Var
  i : Integer;
Begin
  Inc ( ShotDelay );                            { Add one to the global counter }
  If ( ( ShotDelay mod ShotWaitTime ) = 0 ) Then       { Check delay factor }
    For i := 1 to MaxShots Do
    Begin
      If ( Shot [i].Shooting ) Then                    { If the shot is active }
      Begin
        If ( ScrChar ( Shot [i].ShotX, Shot [i].ShotY ) = AlienChar ) Then
        Begin
                { An Alien moved on top of the bullet }
          IncScore ( RemoveAlien ( Shot [i].ShotX, Shot [i].ShotY ) );
          Shot [i].Shooting := FALSE;
        End
        Else
        If ( ScrChar ( Shot [i].ShotX, Shot [i].ShotY - 1 ) = AlienChar ) Then
        Begin
                { The bullet will move into an Alien }
          GotoXY ( Shot [i].ShotX, Shot [i].ShotY );
          Write ( ' ' );
          IncScore (RemoveAlien ( Shot [i].ShotX, Shot [i].ShotY - 1 ) );
          Shot [i].Shooting := FALSE;
        End
        Else
        Begin
                { The shot will not hit anything yet }
          GotoXY ( Shot [i].ShotX, Shot [i].ShotY );
          Write ( ' ' );
          Dec ( Shot [i].ShotY );
          If ( Shot [i].ShotY <= AlienY - 1 ) Then
            Shot [i].Shooting := FALSE
```

```
            Else
            Begin
              GotoXY ( Shot [i].ShotX, Shot [i].ShotY );
              Write ( ShotChar );
            End
          End
        End
      End
End;

Procedure EventLoop;
{ Main event loop of the program. }
var
  ch : char;
Begin
  Repeat
    If ( Left ) Then          { Key Event }
      MoveLeft;
    If ( Right ) Then         { Key Event }
      MoveRight;
    If ( Space ) Then         { Key Event }
      Fire;
    UpdateAliens;             { Update Event }
    UpdateShot;               { Update Event }
    While ( KeyPressed ) Do
      ch := ReadKey;
  Until ( Escape );           { Key Event signalling Exit }
End;

Procedure SetUpScrInfo;
{ Get the screen width and base video address for the ScrChar routine. }
Var
  r : Registers;
Begin
  r.ah := $0F;
  Intr ( $10, r );    { Call BIOS Interrupt 10h Service 0Fh }
  ScrWidth := r.ah;
  Case ( r.al ) Of
    0,1,2,3 : ScrSeg := $B800;
    7 : ScrSeg := $B000;
  End;
End;

Procedure OffCursor;
{ Deactivate the cursor on the screen }
Var
  r : Registers;
Begin
  r.ah := $01;
```

Listing 7.7 continues

Listing *7.7 continued*

```
    r.cx := $2020;      { Start and end scan lines for the cursor      }
    Intr ( $10, r );    { Interrupt 10h, service 01h - Set cursor size }
End;

Procedure OnCursor;
{ Reactivate the cursor on the screen }
Var
  r : Registers;
Begin
  r.ah := $01;
  If ( ScrSeg = $B000 ) Then
    r.cx := $0C0D       { Start and end scan lines for Monochrome cursor }
  Else
    r.cx := $0607;    { Start and end scan lines for Color cursor }
  Intr ( $10, r );    { Interrupt 10h, service 01h - Set cursor size }
End;

Procedure InitVars;
{ Initialize the global variables }
Var
  i : Integer;
Begin
  Score := 0;
  ShotDelay := 0;
  GotoXY ( ( ScrWidth - 17 ), 1 );
  Write ( 'Score: ', Score : 5 );
  For i := 1 to MaxShots do
    Shot [i].Shooting := FALSE;
  Randomize;
  For i := 1 to MaxAliens do
  Begin
    Aliens [i].X := Random ( ScrWidth - 5 ) + 2;
    Aliens [i].Alive := TRUE;
    Aliens [i].Delta := Random (3) + 1;
  End;
  ShipX := 1;
  ShipY := 25;
End;


Begin
  OffCursor;              { Turn off the cursor              }
  ClrScr;                 { Clear the video screen           }
  SetUpScrInfo;           { Get current video information     }
  InitVars;               { Initialize the global variables   }
  GotoXY ( ShipX, ShipY ); { Draw the initial ship location on }
  Write ( Ship );         {    the screen.                    }
  EventLoop;              { Main event loop                  }
  OnCursor;               { Turn on the cursor               }
ClrScr;
End.
```

Much of the program's characteristics is controlled by the constants in the main program. We set how many shots can be fired at once, how many aliens there are, the shape of each alien, the shape of the ship, the shape of the shots, the base point value for each alien shot, and the delay factor for the shots and aliens. The program tries to utilize these constants and not rely on set values within the code. The program was tested with the following screen modes: Mono 80x25 and Color 40x25, 80x25, 80x60 (Analog VGA), and 80x132 (Analog VGA).

The concept of event-driven programming may not be familiar to you, but it is an excellent method of programming. It says, ''If an event has occurred, process it; otherwise, do your normal tasks.'' The only events in this program relevant to this chapter's discussion are specific keystrokes and updates. In this program, an update event occurs all the time. We need to update the aliens or a shot on the screen.

Within the event loop, we process three specific routines: the update event procedures UpdateAliens and UpdateShot, and the stripping of any keys in the keyboard buffer. The interrupt service routine passes any keystrokes to the old keyboard interrupt vector. We need to check whether any keys were pressed and, if so, to clear them from the buffer.

Since the aliens and shots move so fast on the screen, they need to be slowed. We do this by using an increment of the global counter variable each time the update procedure is called. Then we do a MOD of that variable with a predefined constant. If the result of this operation is zero, we can enter the procedure and do our update. This effectively slows the rate at which the aliens and shots move. The delay factor that is set in the example is for a 10MHz AT. If you are working on a slower or faster machine, you may want to modify the delay variables AlienWaitTime and ShotWaitTime.

If you noticed the conditional defines in the code, you may wonder what they are used for. Because the program traps the keyboard handler, it might be a good idea to debug the program without the interrupt service routine loaded. Of course, the keyboard events will never happen, but we can debug other areas of code instead. If DEBUG is defined (by using {$DEFINE DEBUG}), the GameInt9 unit is not placed into the uses statement, and the variables defined in that unit are defined within the scope of this program.

The cursor is turned off at the start of the program and back on at the end. This is done to prevent the cursor from getting in the way during the run of the program. Professional looking programs do not have a cursor flying all over the screen.

Most of the hard work in developing a good game program is already done here. You should be able to modify the program to do things like have the aliens drop one level after each iteration, have the aliens drop bombs at the ship, provide shields for the ship, and many other variations.

Timer Interrupt

Interrupt 08 is called to do routine things like update the system clock 18.2 times every second. This interrupt should not be modified. If you need to have a routine that is called this often, you should install it off interrupt 1C to allow interrupt 08 to go through its duties of changing the system time and whatever else is required. Then the last routine processed by the interrupt 08 calls interrupt 1C.

The unit that follows this discussion (listings 7.8 and 7.9) sets up an interrupt service routine off the user timer interrupt (1C). All that this routine does is increment a global variable and call the old interrupt vector. This allows you to do some primitive timing of the length of time required to process routines.

If you are trying to make your program as fast as possible, you will want to trim code that is slow. The easy way to do this is to use a profiler. A *profiler* is a program that tracks the amount of time various portions of your program take to execute. This unit gives you a primitive method of doing this.

To use this unit, all you have to do is place it in your uses statement. To start the timing, set the global variable TimeCt to zero. When you want to stop and see the number of clock ticks that have occurred, assign TimeCt to another variable. The value in your variable will be the number of clock ticks it took to get from the point where you started.

Of course, you are not actually starting and stopping the timer. The timer is always being updated 18.2 times per second. All you are doing is resetting the counter variable and then reading its value.

For an example of how this unit is used, examine listing 7.9. This program asks how many lines of text you want to display and then displays an 80-character screen using direct video writes for the specified number of lines. Next, the program displays one character at a time, 80 times the number of lines designated. Then DirectVideo is set to false, which makes the Write and WriteLn procedures default to writing through BIOS routines. Next, the displaying of strings and characters is repeated. Between each set of displaying, the number of ticks passed is saved. At the end of the program, the statistics are displayed on the screen. You will see what a dramatic difference direct video writing can make.

Listing 7.8. Int1C.Pas

```
Unit Int1C;

INTERFACE

Uses
  DOS,CRT;

Var
  TimerCt : LongInt;

IMPLEMENTATION

Var
  OldExitProc,
  SaveInt1C : pointer;

Procedure JmpOldISR(OldISR: Pointer);
  Inline($5B/$58/$87/$5E/$0E/$87/$46/$10/$89/
         $EC/$5D/$07/$1F/$5F/$5E/$5A/$59/$CB);

{$F+}
Procedure Timer_ISR( Flags,CS,IP,AX,BX,CX,DX,SI,DI,DS,ES,BP:word ); Interrupt;
Begin
  Inline ( $FA );    { CLI }
  Inc ( TimerCt );   { increment the counter }
  Inline ( $FB );    { STI }
  JmpOldISR( SaveInt1C );
End;

Procedure Int1CExitProc;
Begin
  ExitProc := OldExitProc;
  SetIntVec( $1C, SaveInt1C );
end;
{$F-}

Begin
  OldExitProc := ExitProc;
  ExitProc := @Int1CExitProc;
  GetIntVec( $1C, SaveInt1C );
  SetIntVec( $1C, @Timer_ISR );
end.
```

Listing 7.9. *TimeIt.Pas*

```pascal
Program Timer;

Uses
  Crt,
  Int1C;

Var
  w : LongInt;
  loopct : LongInt;
  result1,
  result2,
  result3,
  result4 : LongInt;

Begin
  Write ( 'Loop how many times? ' );
  ReadLn ( loopct );

(******************************************************)
(***** Write String/Char directly to video memory *****)
(******************************************************)

  DirectVideo := TRUE;
  timerct := 0;
  For w := 1 To loopct Do
    Write (
'12345678901234567890123456789012345678901234567890123456789012345678901234567890');
  result1 := timerct;

  timerct := 0;
  For w := 1 To ( loopct * 80 ) Do
    Write ( '1');
  result2 := timerct;

(******************************************************)
(********** Write String/Char via BIOS calls **********)
(******************************************************)

  DirectVideo := FALSE;
  timerct := 0;
  For w := 1 To loopct Do
    Write (
'12345678901234567890123456789012345678901234567890123456789012345678901234567890');
  result3 := timerct;

  timerct := 0;
  For w := 1 To ( loopct * 80 ) Do
    Write ( '1');
  result4 := timerct;
```

```
WriteLn ( 'Direct Video : String = ', result1 : 5, ' Char = ', result2 : 5 );
WriteLn ( 'Bios Writes  : String = ', result3 : 5, ' Char = ', result4 : 5 );

  ReadLn;
End.
```

Review

In this chapter, we reveal that interrupt service routines are tricky but not difficult to write. You have to follow strict guidelines for setting up and removing ISRs; additionally, you have to make sure that your ISR code itself follows some guidelines, specifically that the code is reentrant.

The best way to learn is by example, and this chapter provides many examples. We hope that each sample program will be of some use to you.

Part III

The Kitchen Sink

CHAPTER 8

Overlays

Turbo Pascal Version 3.0 had a facility known as overlays that allowed different sections of code to reside in the same areas of memory. This area of memory was called the *overlay buffer*, and each procedure was swapped to and from this buffer from the overlay file on the disk. This allowed programmers who were using Turbo Pascal V3.0 to create large application programs.

Borland removed the overlay capability from Turbo Pascal V4.0, instead giving programmers the ability to use multiple code segments in their programs. This precluded the need to use overlays to write large programs; however, it limited programmers to memory recognized by DOS. The result was that programmers could actually write larger programs with Turbo Pascal V3.0 than they could with V4.0.

In Turbo Pascal V5.0, Borland restored overlay capability to Turbo Pascal. The theory of overlays in Turbo Pascal V5.0 is different from that implemented in V3.0. In V3.0, overlays were done on the procedural basis; an overlay consisted of a collection of procedures. If a nonoverlayed procedure occurred between overlayed procedures, then the compiler generated separate overlay files. The overlay files had the same name as the program but with a numerical extension. The first overlay file had a .000 extension, and each subsequent overlay file incremented this extension.

Turbo Pascal V5.0 overlays items on a unit basis and creates a single overlay file that contains all the code for all the units that have been overlayed. The programmer no longer has to worry about what procedures

231

are placed into what file. The overlay manager in Turbo Pascal V5.0 handles this and many other implementation questions and problems.

Another problem that the V5.0 overlay manager overcomes is that you no longer bear the burden of grouping the overlays in such a way as to keep one overlay procedure from calling another overlay procedure in a different overlay group. The Turbo Pascal V5.0 overlay manager resolves such problems for you.

One other difference that should be pointed out at this time is the grouping of overlays. In Turbo Pascal V3.0, it was possible to have an overlay group within an overlay group. In other words, procedures that were nested within procedures could be overlayed, and doing so would create a sub-overlay group. Turbo Pascal V5.0 does not support the same concept from within units. For further discussion of this topic, see the "Common Errors" section later in this chapter.

> Throughout this chapter, the user must be careful of the name used for the main program when it is saved. This is because the overlay manager receives the name of the overlay file in the call to OvrInit. This name *must* match the program's name when the program is saved to disk. For instance, if you save the first example as EX1.PAS, then you must change the file name passed to OverInit to EX1.OVR.

Overlay Buffer

The overlay buffer is allocated between Turbo Pascal's stack segment and the heap area, and the allocated overlay buffer defaults to a size large enough to hold the largest unit that has been overlayed. Since Turbo Pascal V5.0 overlays code on a unit basis, the buffer size is equal to the largest of the units that are being overlayed by the program. This allows the compiler to maximize the size of the heap space by minimizing the space for the overlay.

When a unit resides in the overlay buffer, all of the procedures and functions within the overlay fall into the same order as they are defined in the source for the unit, as illustrated in figure 8.1.

Fig. 8.1. *Layout of an overlay in the overlay buffer.*

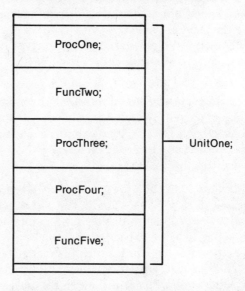

Since the overlay buffer is large enough to hold only the largest of the overlayed units, it is entirely possible that there will be more than one overlay in the buffer at any point in time. If there is not sufficient room for another overlay to be loaded into the buffer, the program needs to swap something from the buffer for the new overlay. This is one of the things the overlay manager does for you.

When it becomes necessary to swap an overlay out of the buffer, the overlay manager first attempts to swap out an overlay that has no active calls. An *active call* is a routine that has yet to execute to its completion. If the overlay manager determines that all routines in the buffer have an active call, it attempts to dispose of the overlay that has the oldest active call. This optimizes the performance of the overlay manager. (You can alter the swapping procedure if necessary; a few pointers are presented in the "Pitfalls and Tricks" section later in this chapter.)

Version 5.0 of Turbo Pascal implemented its overlay buffer as a circular queue. Units entered the front of the queue and were pushed to the end as each new unit was added. Eventually, a unit would be pushed out of the buffer in favor of a new unit that was called by the program.

Turbo Pascal Version 5.5 has given the programmer the opportunity to change the way the swapping algorithm for overlayed units is implemented. By default, the overlay manager in V5.5 behaves exactly as V5.0's overlay manager. The difference is in two procedures that have been added to V5.5, called `OvrSetRetry` and `OvrGetRetry`.

By passing a value to the `OvrSetRetry` procedure, the overlay manager will flag the value's amount of the overlay buffer as a "probation area." Therefore, whenever a unit is accessed and it resides in this area, it will be moved to the head of the overlay buffer. If, on the other hand, no call is made to a routine in the unit while it is in the probation area, it is free to be replaced by some other unit when it is needed by the program.

Requirements

The overlay manager in Turbo Pascal V5.0 is much smarter than the one provided with V3.0. You do not have to change your coding style just because you are using overlays. The only requirement is that all calls, direct or indirect, to routines within an overlayed application be FAR calls. This includes not only the routines within the overlayed unit, but also any routine that may call an overlayed procedure.

You can easily satisfy the FAR call requirement by placing the compiler directive {$F+} at the top of each module the program uses, as well as the main program itself. The FAR call requirement could affect external assembly language code as well as any `inline` code that may exist in or be linked in with a unit. If you are attempting to compile a unit for possible overlaying in the future, being aware of the FAR requirements can save you debugging time later.

The only other directive necessary is the Overlay Code Generation directive {$O}, which has two meanings:

❏ When a plus (+) or minus (−) follows it, the unit can (+) or cannot (−) be overlayed. To use the directive this way, place {$O+} at the top of any unit you may want to overlay. It instructs the compiler to create the code for the unit in such a way as to make it overlayable. This directive does not tell the compiler to overlay the unit; it instructs the compiler only to take special precautions when compiling, so that the code *could* become an overlay.

☐ When the {$O} directive occurs in the main program, it is followed by a unit name to instruct the compiler to actually overlay that unit file.

Simple Overlay Example

Listings 8.1 through 8.4 are all part of the same program. Listings 8.1 through 8.3 are the units that will be included in the main program, which is found in listing 8.4.

Listing 8.1. *Overlay Unit 1*

```
Unit OvrOne;
{ This is actually the last unit in the overly chain. It is    }
{ called from overlay number two. This routine is simply a     }
{ demo of how to create an overlayed program.                  }
{$O+,F+}              { Instruct compiler this can be overlayed }
Interface
Uses Crt;             { Link in the CRT unit for ClrScr call    }
Procedure Proc1;
Procedure Proc2;
Implementation
Procedure IncWord( Var W : Word );
{ A simple support routine that will increment a word value    }
{ passed. If the value is equal to MaxWord, then we will       }
{ wrap the value back to zero.                                 }
Begin
  If( W = 65535 ) Then  { Determine if value needs wrapped     }
    W := 0
  Else
    Inc( W );
End;
Procedure Proc1;
{ This procedure will prompt the user for a value and then     }
{ increment this value by one.                                 }
Var
  W1 : Word;              { Local variable to be entered        }
```

Listing 8.1 continues

Listing 8.1 *continued*

```
Begin
  Write( 'Enter a value (0-65535) : ' );
  Readln( W1 );
  IncWord( W1 );
  Writeln( 'After calling IncWord, value has become ', W1 );
End;
Procedure Proc2;
{ This routine is simply an interface to the procedure listed }
{ above. It is included here as a demo of overlaying of       }
{ procedures.                                                 }
Begin
  ClrScr;
  Writeln( 'About to call Proc1.....' );
  Delay( 2500 );
  Proc1;
End;
End.
```

Listing 8.2. *Overlay Unit 2*

```
Unit OvrTwo;
{ This is simply an interface unit to unit OvrOne. It is       }
{ called from the driver procedure in OvrThre, and will call   }
{ the interfaced procedure Proc1. It is included as an         }
{ example of an overlayed application.                         }
{$O+,F+}            { Instruct compiler this can be overlayed }
Interface
Uses OvrOne;
Procedure OvrTwo1;
Implementation
Procedure OvrTwo1;
{ This procedure will simply make a call to the procedure      }
{ interfaced in unit OvrOne.                                   }
Begin
  Proc1;          { Call the procedure...                     }
End;
End.
```

Listing 8.3. *Overlay Unit 3*

```
Unit OvrThre;
{ This is the last unit in the string of several demos. It    }
{ simply interfaces a single procedure, which is called from   }
{ the main program. When called, it will make a call to the    }
```

```
{ procedure in unit OvrTwo. It serves no useful purpose     }
{ except to introduce the user to an overlayed application. }
{$O+,F+} { Instruct the compiler this unit can be overlayed. }
Interface
Uses Crt, OvrOne, OvrTwo; { Link in the necessary units.     }
Procedure Driver;
Implementation
Procedure Driver;
{ This is the driving procedure for this demo program. It is }
{ called from the main program, and will call each of the   }
{ routines in turn.                                          }
Var
  Ch : Char;
Begin
  OvrTwo1;                 { Call the first overlay          }
  Writeln( 'Returned back to OvrThre.' );
  Writeln( 'Now calling OvrOne directly....' );
  Proc1;                   { Now call it directly instead.   }
  Writeln( 'Back in OvrThre.' );
  Writeln( 'Press a key to return to main program.....' );
  Ch := Readkey;
End;
End.
```

Listing 8.4. *Overlay Program*

```
Program OverlayDemoOne;
{ This simple do-nothing demo program is designed as an     }
{ introduction to adding overlays to a program. Note that   }
{ the only requirement in the main program is that the      }
{ standard unit Overlay must be used in the main program    }
{ before any other unit. Also note the directives in the    }
{ main program to actually overlay the units.               }
{$F+}
Uses Crt, Overlay, OvrOne, OvrTwo, OvrThre;
{ Instruct the compiler to overlay these units.             }
{$O OvrOne}
{$O OvrTwo}
{$O OvrThre}
Var
  Ch : Char;               { Used to pause the output screen }
Begin
  ClrScr;                  { Clear the output screen.        }
  OvrInit( 'Mainprog.ovr' );{ Initialize the Overlay Manager }
  If( OvrResult <> 0 ) Then { Check for any error            }
```

Listing 8.4 continues

Listing 8.4 continued

```
Begin                          { If one is there report and quit }
  Writeln( 'Overlay Error#', OvrResult );
  Writeln( 'Program Halted.' );
  Halt( OvrResult );
End;
Writeln( 'This is a demo program that implements overlays.' );
Write( 'Press a key to call first Overlay.' );
Ch := Readkey;
Writeln( Ch );
Writeln( 'Calling first Overlay Procedure....' );
Delay( 2500 );
Driver;                        { Call the driving routine        }
Proc2;
Writeln( 'Now back in main program. Terminating...' );
Delay( 1000 );
End.
```

In the example program and units in listings 8.1 through 8.4, the largest of the overlays is unit OvrOne. Therefore, this unit determines the size Turbo Pascal reserves for the overlay buffer. Its size is such that OvrTwo and OvrThre can reside in the buffer at the same time. If OvrOne had called OvrTwo, and then OvrThre, OvrTwo, and OvrThre would reside in the buffer simultaneously. When they terminated and returned to OvrOne, OvrOne would need to be recalled from the .OVR file on the disk.

This can be verified by single stepping the CPU view in the Turbo Debugger and examining what happens upon a call to any of these procedures, as explained later in the section entitled "Overlay Stubs."

Note the locations of the {$O} and {$F} directives in the listings. Further, note that $O has two separate meanings. In the first case (that is, when $O is followed by a + or −), the meaning is that this unit can (+) or cannot (−) be overlayed. In the second case (that is, when $O falls in the main program), it is expected to be followed by a unit name to instruct the compiler to actually overlay that unit file.

The next point demonstrated by this example is the effectiveness of making a call from one procedure in an overlayed unit to a procedure in another overlay. Turbo Pascal V3.0 did not support this construct; it is an example of the complex nature of the overlay manager in Turbo Pascal V5.0.

Finally, this routine enforces the rule that all active calls must be FAR calls. This requirement exists because of the way the overlay manager is implemented. One thing the overlay manager is required to do is swap information to and from the stack. This occurs when it is necessary to swap out an overlay that contains an active call. If the requirement for FAR calls were not enforced, when it came time to bring back the routine with an active call, the overlay manager would not know the exact location of each item. If there were some NEAR routines sitting in the stack, the positions of active calls could not be predicted. When attempting to return control to a NEAR routine, you might not make it back to your original location, or worse you could lock you machine, forcing a reboot of your system.

Structure and Implementation

This section describes the way Turbo Pascal structures the .OVR file. It details the order used for placing information into the .OVR file. Additionally, we discuss the layout of the program file once loaded into memory from disk. These concepts are identical regardless of whether the overlay file is loaded into EMS memory and read from there or is being read from the physical disk.

.OVR File Layout

Each overlay file produced by the Turbo Pascal compiler has a specific format.

❏ A four-byte header

❏ Code for each of the routines in the first unit added to the overlay file

❏ A small fix-up table (discussed later in this section)

Each unit that is being overlayed by the main program has its code in the same .OVR file. This process (unit code followed by fix-up table) is repeated for each unit that is to be overlayed.

The order of each routine (that is, procedure and function) within an overlayed unit is exactly the same as the order within the specified unit's implementation section. Listing 8.5 shows a sample unit, and figure 8.2 shows the order of this unit's code within the .OVR file.

Listing 8.5. *Sample Unit for Procedure Order in .OVR File*

```
Unit FileOrd;
{ This do-nothing unit is for demonstration purposes only.   }
{ It is presented here to show how the procedures are ordered }
{ in the .OVR file.                                          }

Interface

Procedure PublicOne;

Procedure PublicTwo;

Procedure PublicThree;

Implementation

Procedure PublicOne;
Begin
End;

Procedure PrivateTwo;
Begin
End;

Procedure PrivateOne;
Begin
End;

Procedure PublicTwo;
Begin
End;

Procedure PublicThree;
Begin
End;

Procedure PrivateThree;
Begin
End;

End.
```

The compiler will not shift or shuffle the order of the procedures within each overlay in any manner. A unit is compiled from top to bottom, and then the compiled code is placed untranslated into the .OVR file. The only thing the compiler will do is add a table of information to the OVR file at the end of a unit's code.

Fig. 8.2. Order of unit's procedures in .OVR file.

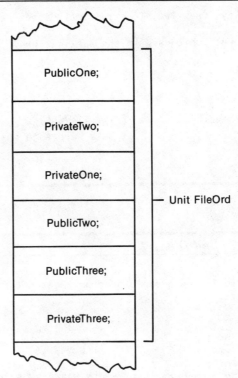

The order for the units within the .OVR file is determined by each of the uses statements within the application. Generally, the order of the units within the .OVR file is exactly the opposite of what is in the main program's uses statement. This is not the case in all instances, however. If the main program's uses statement does not list all units actually needed in the application (not a good idea!), a unit's uses statement also influences this order. Consider listings 8.6 through 8.10 as an example. When the .OVR file is created, it will look like what is shown in figure 8.3.

Listing 8.6. Main Program

```
Program MainProg;
{ Sample program to demonstrate the order of units within the  }
{ OVR file that is produced by Turbo Pascal.                    }
```

Listing 8.6 continues

Listing 8.6 *continued*

```
Uses Overlay, One, Two, Three; { Include the necessary units  }
{$F+}
{ Overlay each unit used in the application }
{$O A}
{$O Three}
{$O Two}
{$O One}
Begin
  OvrInit( 'Main.ovr' );   { Initialize the overlay manager  }
  One1;                    { Make sure each unit is linked.   }
  Two1;
  Three1;
End.
```

Listing 8.7. *Unit One*

```
Unit One;
{ First unit in the example program. Does not depend on any   }
{ other unit.                                                 }
{$O+,F+}
Interface
Procedure One1;
Implementation
Procedure One1;
{ Do-nothing procedure that should NEVER BE EXECUTED!  Its    }
{ only purpose is to determine the order of the units within  }
{ the OVR file produced by Turbo Pascal.                      }
Begin
  Inline( $90/$01/$90 );   { NOPs surrounded by unit number   }
End;
End.
```

Listing 8.8. *Unit Two*

```
Unit Two;
{ Second unit in example program. This unit will make a       }
{ "call" to the procedure in unit one. This establishes a     }
{ dependency by unit two upon unit one.                       }
{$O+,F+}
Interface
Uses One;
Procedure Two1;
Implementation
Procedure Two1;
```

```
{ This routine MUST NEVER BE CALLED!  It is a useless    }
{ procedure, whose only purpose is to determine the order of }
{ units within an OVR file.                              }
Begin
  Inline( $90/$02/$90 );
  One1;
End;
End.
```

Listing 8.9. *Unit Three*

```
Unit Three;
{ This is the third unit in this test program. Like the  }
{ units preceding this, its sole purpose is to determine the }
{ order of units within an OVR file. The routines in this }
{ unit must never be called, as unpredictable results will }
{ occur.                                                 }
{$O+,F+}
Interface
Uses One, A;
Procedure Three1;
Implementation
Procedure Three1;
{ This procedure is an example used to determine the order of }
{ units within an OVR file. This routine MUST NEVER BE   }
{ CALLED, as it could lock the machine. It establishes a }
{ dependency upon unit A.                                }
Begin
  Inline( $90/$03/$90 );
  A1;
End;
End.
```

Listing 8.10. *Unit A*

```
Unit A;
{ This unit is another in the example to determine the order }
{ of units within an OVR file. It interfaces a single   }
{ procedure that is called from unit three. This procedure, }
{ like the others, should NEVER BE CALLED.              }
{$O+,F+}
Interface
Procedure A1;
Implementation
```

Listing 8.10 continues

Listing 8.10 *continued*

```
Procedure A1;
{ This procedure MUST NEVER BE CALLED. It is here only to      }
{ determine the order of the units within the OVR file         }
{ produced when this unit is compiled as part of another       }
{ program.                                                     }
Begin
  Inline( $90/$41/$90 );
End;
End.
```

Fig. 8.3. Layout of .OVR file.

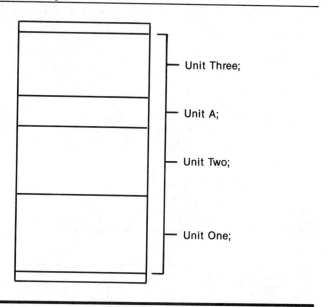

Not listing Unit A in the main program's uses statement caused this unit to follow the first unit that listed it in a uses statement. If the main program's uses statement were

    Uses A, One, Two, Three;

the order of the units in the .OVR file would look like what is shown in figure 8.4.

Fig. 8.4. Modified layout of .OVR file.

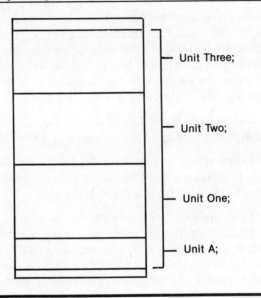

The .OVR file contains not only code but also what is called a *fix-up table*. This table follows the code for each overlay in the .OVR file and contains information used by the overlay manager to correct intersegment references in the overlay's code, based on the starting address of the program. This table is actually transient because it is read in with the overlay's code, applied to the code, and then disposed of. It does not remain in the buffer—hence the name *transient*.

This table must also be taken into consideration in the calculation of the optimum size for the overlay buffer. Though it does not remain in the buffer, it inflates the necessary size of the buffer.

Program Layout

We have discussed the overlay manager from the .OVR file's point of view; now we will discuss what happens during the execution of an overlayed program. For instance, we will show what the overlay manager does when an overlayed procedure is referenced. In a later section, we will combine this information with other facts about the overlay manager to allow you to overlay data files that have been converted into .OBJ files with the BINOBJ utility.

Overlay Stubs

Not every overlay procedure resides in the code segment. The overlay procedure might not even reside in the overlay buffer. Normally, when you access the address of a variable or procedure, you get the location in the code or data segment where the identifier starts. If the identifier is a procedure or function in an overlayed unit, what is at the address of the procedure or function is what is known as an *overlay stub*.

The overlay stub is just five bytes in size and can be one of two different things, depending on the current location of the overlayed routine:

1. If the overlay currently resides in the overlay buffer, the overlay stub contains a FAR JMP instruction to the location in the overlay buffer where the routine exists.

2. If the routine does not reside in the overlay buffer and needs to be loaded in from disk (or EMS—if the overlay file has been loaded there), the overlay stub consists of an INT 3F call, plus a two-byte value that is an offset within the overlay buffer of where to load the routine. The INT 3F call is really just a call to the overlay manager, which handles the interrupt by loading the requested unit into the buffer and then transferring control to the new routine in the buffer.

The overlay stub is the stumbling block that has been placed on overlaying of data within an application. In order to get over this block, the routine must recognize when the data is or is not available. Beyond that, it must also be able to bring the data into the overlay buffer if it is not currently there. This is covered in a following section called "Overlaying Data."

Pitfalls and Tricks

In this section, we discuss some common errors programmers make when using the overlay manager from within their applications, especially the first time they use overlays from within a program. We also describe some tricks to maximize your use of overlays.

Common Errors

Some of the most common errors are easy to overcome when you know what things can cause them. For instance, one of the most common errors is attempting to overlay a unit with initialization code before the overlay manager has been initialized. When this occurs, you get the generic overlay error, Run-time Error 208. When you receive this error, the first thing to check for are units with initialization code; even an empty Begin...End pair is considered initialization code. To help you get around this problem, we include a unit, in listing 8.11, that initializes the overlay manager. You can use this unit if you are using other units that have initialization code within them. This unit must precede any unit in the program's uses statement that will be overlayed.

Listing 8.11. *Overlay Initializing Unit*

```
Unit InitOvly;
{ This unit will initialize the Overlay Manager.  It can be   }
{ used in the situation where some of the units that a        }
{ program uses have initialization code.  It is especially    }
{ useful when no source code is available to a unit, or you   }
{ cannot remove a unit's initialization code.                 }
{$O+,F+}
Interface

Uses OverLay;

Const
  FileModeforOverlay = 0;  { Change this value for other mode }
  OverlayFileName : String = ''; { Change to correct name     }

Implementation

Uses
  Crt, Dos;                        { Link in library Units     }

Var
  OvrBufSize : LongInt;
{$IFDEF VER55}
  OldOvrReadFunc : OvrReadFunc;
{$ENDIF}

Function Exists( FName : String ) : Boolean;
{ This function returns either True or False, depending upon }
{ whether the file FName was in the current directory.  It   }
{ uses a new way of determining the existence of the file.   }
{ It is no longer necessary to turn off I/O checking and then }
{ attempt to reset the file in order to determine if the file }
{ exists.                                                     }
```

Listing 8.11 continues

Listing 8.11 continued

```
Var
   Result : String;        { Result of calling the FSearch Func  }

Begin
   Result := FSearch( FName, " );
   Exists := Result <> ";
End;

{$IFDEF VER55}

Procedure WriteMessageAt( X, Y : Byte; Message : String );
{ Output the Message parameter at screen locations X and Y    }

Begin
   GotoXY( X, Y );
   Write( Message );
End;

Procedure HandleOvrErr( Error : Integer );
{ This procedure will handle any error that happens when the  }
{ program attempts to read from the .OVR file.  This way, we  }
{ have the capability to recover from the error.              }
Var
   ErrorString : String;

Begin
   Str( Error, ErrorString );
   WriteMessageAt( 10,10, ErrorString );
End;

Function MyOvrRead( OvrSeg : Word ) : Integer;
{ This function will be called by the Overlay Manager before  }
{ any attempt is made to read from the file.  We must call    }
{ the original read function, which will return an error code }
{ to this function if it is not successful in reading the     }
{ required overlay from the .OVR file.                        }
Var
   Err : Integer;

Begin
   Repeat
     Err := OldOvrReadFunc( OvrSeg );
     If( Err <> 0 ) Then
       HandleOvrErr( Err );
   Until Err = 0;
   MyOvrRead := 0;
End;
```

```
{$ENDIF}

Begin
{$IFDEF VER55}

  OvrFileMode := FileModeforOverlay;

{$ENDIF}

  OvrInit( OverlayFileName );

{$IFDEF VER55}

  OldOvrReadFunc := OvrReadBuf;
  OvrReadBuf := MyOvrRead;

{$ENDIF}

  While( OvrResult = OvrNotFound ) Do
  Begin
    Writeln( 'File not found: ", OverlayFileName, "." );
    Write( 'Enter new name: ' );
    Readln( OverlayFileName );
    OvrInit( OverlayFileName );
  End;
  If( OvrResult <> OvrOK ) Then
  Begin
    ClrScr;
    Writeln( 'Unrecoverable Overlay Manager error.  Program Terminated.' );
    Halt;
  End;
  OvrInitEMS;                     { Will load the .OVR file into EMS }

{$IFDEF VER55}

  If( OvrResult = OvrOK ) Then
  Begin
    OldOvrReadFunc := OvrReadBuf;
    OvrReadBuf := MyOvrRead;
  End;
  OvrSetRetry( OvrGetBuf Div 3 );

{$ENDIF}

End.
```

The next most common error is the absence of the correct compiler directives. Remember that all units that you want to overlay must be compiled with the {$O+} and {$F+} compiler directives. The absence of either of these causes problems in the running of your overlayed application. The symptom of this problem can be as simple as a compiler error (This unit cannot be overlayed) or as complicated as procedures returning to random spots or a complete system lockup.

Another error involving overlays is the placement of the directive to overlay a unit. The {$O+} directive indicates only that the unit can be overlayed: it does not actually overlay the unit. If you want to overlay a unit, use the $O directive with a slightly different syntax. The correct syntax is as follows:

```
{$O unitname}
```

This directive instructs the compiler to overlay the unit named. However—and this is where most errors occur—this directive is valid in the main program only. It can never be placed within a unit. The compiler does not flag it as an error if you place the directive in a unit. This means that you actually can do it, but to do so is detrimental to the performance of the program.

If you were to place the {$O unitname} directive within a unit, it would inflate the size of the .OVR file. This is caused by the way the compiler compiles a program that uses overlays. When compiling a unit, the compiler starts with the unit listed last in the uses statement and places this code in the .OVR file. It proceeds through the uses statement, until it reaches the first unit listed. Then it looks at what uses this unit and proceeds through its uses statement. This will cause this unit and any unit it uses to be placed in the .OVR file another time.

If you have any units that contain this form of the {$O} compiler directive, remove the directive from them immediately. This will speed the execution of the program as well as conserve size in the .EXE and .OVR files.

Overlaying Data

Using what we have discussed to this point about the overlay manager, you may think that it would be easy to retrieve data from an overlayed unit. That is close to the case. Remember that overlays are swapped to and from the overlay buffer on a unit basis. Also recall that we can determine whether a unit is actually in the buffer or resides on the disk. By combining these facts, we can successfully overlay data.

First, we must determine whether the unit that contains the data is actually overlayed by looking at what is contained at the address of a do-nothing procedure. If that address contains a CALL FAR instruction, we know it is overlayed. (INT 3F is not a possibility because Turbo Pascal

V5.0 overlays on a unit basis. If we look at the address of a routine from within the same unit, we do not have to worry about finding an INT 3F call.) If the unit is overlayed, calling another routine in the same unit will guarantee that that routine resides not on the disk but in the overlay buffer.

After we determine whether a unit is overlayed, the next hurdle to overcome is finding the data from the overlay stub (if the unit actually was overlayed). Because we know that if the procedure is in an overlayed unit, the overlay stub contains a CALL FAR to the actual location of the procedure within the overlay buffer. We can gain access to this location and then reference this data.

Listing 8.12 is the unit that contains the data, and listing 8.13 is a main program that indirectly accesses the overlayed data.

Listing 8.12. *Unit to Access OBJ Data*

```
Unit DataAcc;
{ This unit will interface the Type declaration for the        }
{ information that is stored in the OBJ file. It has also       }
{ interfaced a routine to access the data. This is done        }
{ because as soon as we make a call to the accessing routine, }
{ we have guaranteed that the data also resides in the         }
{ overlay buffer.                                              }
{$O+,F+}              { Set the necessary compiler directives. }
Interface
Type
  DataType = Array[1..100] of Word;  { Data Type in OBJ file }
  DataTypePtr = ^DataType;            { Pointer to data type }
Function ReturnWord( Index : Word ) : Word;
Implementation
Procedure DummyProc;
{ This is a dummy procedure that exists only to determine      }
{ whether this unit has been overlayed. If it is, then        }
{ the address of this procedure should contain a JMP          }
{ instruction. Otherwise, it will contain the first byte of   }
{ the entry code to the procedure.                            }
Begin
End;
Procedure DataProc; External;
{$L Data.obj}                      { This is the actual data file }
Function UnitIsOverlayed : Boolean;
{ This function will determine if this unit has been          }
{ overlayed by any program that uses this unit.               }
Var
  P : ^Byte;                       { Used in overlay determination }
```

Listing 8.12 continues

Listing 8.12 continued

```
Begin
  P := @DummyProc;           { Look at First Byte of Proc.      }
  If( P^ = 234 ) Then         { Is it a JMP instruction?         }
    UnitIsOverlayed := True  { If so, this is overlayed         }
  Else
    UnitIsOverlayed := False;{ Otherwise it is not overlayed   }
End;
Function GetDataAddr : Pointer;
{ This function will return the address of where the data      }
{ actually begins in memory. If the unit is overlayed, then    }
{ referring to @DataProc will point to the actual data within }
{ the code segment. Otherwise, it will point return the        }
{ location of the data within the overlay buffer.              }
Var
  P : Pointer;           { Pointer to look at DataProc          }
  Offset, Segment : Word;{ Address words of location           }
Begin
  P := @DataProc;        { Get address of Stub or actual data  }
  If UnitIsOverlayed Then
  Begin { Calculate the location of the data within Buffer     }
    Offset := ( Mem[Seg( P^ ):( Ofs( P^ ) + 2 )] * 256 ) +
              ( Mem[Seg( P^ ):( Ofs( P^ ) + 1 )] );
    Segment := ( Mem[Seg( P^ ):( Ofs( P^ ) + 4 )] * 256 ) +
               ( Mem[Seg( P^ ):( Ofs( P^ ) + 3 )] );
    GetDataAddr := Ptr( Segment, Offset ); { Calc the address }
  End;
  Else
    GetDataAddr := @DataProc { We have actual memory location }
End;
Function ReturnWord( Index : Word ) : Word;
{ This function will return the Indexed data item from the     }
{ data procedure.                                               }
Var
  P : DataTypePtr;  { Pointer type to exact data type          }
Begin
  P := DataTypePtr( GetDataAddr );{ Find the address of data  }
  ReturnWord := P^[Index];        { Return the requested item }
End;
End.
```

Listing 8.13. Main Driving Program

```
Program AccessData;
{ This program will demonstrate how to access data that has   }
{ been converted to an OBJect file with the BINOBJ utility.   }
{ All that is necessary to access data in an overlayed unit,  }
```

```
{ is to first determine if the unit has been overlayed by the }
{ main program. If this is the case, then what resides at      }
{ the address of the procedure is a JMP instruction to the     }
{ location of the procedure within the overlay buffer.         }
{ Therefore, all that is necessary is to create a pointer to   }
{ where the data actually resides in the overlay buffer. All   }
{ of this is handled in the DataAcc unit.                      }
Uses
   Overlay, DataAcc;   { Link in the Overlay And Data Units    }
{$O DataAcc}           { Actually overlay the unit             }
Var
   W : Word;           { Variable to retrieve from the data    }
Begin
   OvrInit( 'List8-13.ovr' ); { Initialize the Overlay Manager }
   DummyProc;                  { Must call routine; otherwise, it is }
                              { smart-linked out of code        }
   For W := 100 DownTo 1 Do   { Read data from end to front     }
     Write( ReturnWord( W ), '   ' );{ Echo the data to screen  }
   Readln;                     { Pause for screen viewing        }
End.
```

Listing 8.14. *Program To Create Data File*

```
Program CreateData;
{ This program will create the data file used in the example }
{ program in listing 8.13. It simply creates a binary file   }
{ of type word, and then places the values 1 to 100 into     }
{ that new data file.                                        }
Var
   F : File of Word;      { Output File Type - Word             }
   W : Word;              { Variable type for the output file   }
Begin
   Assign( F, 'Data.Dat' );{ Associate the file name with F    }
   Rewrite( F );           { Open the file for Output only      }
   For W := 1 to 100 Do    { Loop 100 times for file output     }
     Write( F,W );         { Write the info to the file         }
   Close( F );             { Update the file properly           }
End.
```

The program in listing 8.14 creates the necessary output file that will be used by the program in listing 8.13. Simply run the file generation program, and then run the BINOBJ utility. Use the following command-line instruction to execute BINOBJ:

```
BINOBJ DATA.DAT DATA.OBJ DATAPROC
```

This will correctly configure the data file for use in the program in listing 8.13. Having successfully generated the data file, you can make the routine work.

254 Part III: The Kitchen Sink

Here is what the routine does:

1. It determines whether the unit that contains the data was actually overlayed by declaring an empty dummy procedure. It looks at the first byte occupied by this procedure to see whether it is a `JMP` instruction. If so, it considers this unit an overlayed unit. Otherwise, the unit is not overlayed, and simply accessing the `DataProc` variable yields the data from the static code segment.

2. If the unit is overlayed, the routine accesses the first byte occupied by the routine that yields the `JMP` instruction. The four bytes that follow this instruction are the actual location of the data within the overlay buffer.

3. The routine calculates the actual address by referencing the four bytes that follow the `JMP` instruction.

4. It makes a call to the data-accessing routine, which will get the information from wherever the data may reside. The same routine is capable of either task because we have successfully returned the address of where the information actually resides.

Keeping an Overlay in Memory

You may be wondering how you can control which units are in the overlay buffer at any given moment and how can you guarantee that a particular overlay will be there. It is possible on a limited basis.

Normally. this is a difficult process. Suppose that you have a program that uses nine different units, each the same size and each of which was overlayed. You have made a call to `OvrSetBuf` to increase the size of the overlay buffer to be large enough to hold three of these units. You can figure that you will have in the overlay buffer the currently active unit plus the unit that made a call to the active one. The third unit in the buffer is anyone's guess. If you knew that as soon as the active unit terminated you would then call, say, unit five, you could make a call to a dummy procedure inside unit five to guarantee that it would be placed into the overlay buffer. Such a dummy procedure should probably be empty (so that you do not inflate the size of the unit).

When a call is made to this procedure, the overlay manager brings it into memory and returns control to the appropriate unit. It then terminates, returning control to the unit that had the active call, and your next unit is waiting in the overlay buffer.

Utilities

This section presents a utility program that determines the order of the units in the overlay file. It consists of a short procedure that is placed inside each unit to be overlayed plus a routine to search for the signature that has been included by the short special procedure. The signature procedure itself must be kept as small as possible, and we must be sure to call the signature procedure somewhere inside the unit. Failing to call the routine will cause it to not be included inside the .OVR file when it is generated by the compiler, because the smart linker will remove it.

The routine in listing 8.15 consists of a JMP instruction to the end of the routine and a two-byte signature code. This code is searched for by another program that examines the contents of the .OVR file.

Listing 8.15. *Signature Routine and Surrounding Unit*

```
Unit List815;
{ This is a simple example of a unit that has the signature    }
{ procedure inside the implementation section. The only        }
{ purpose of this unit is to demonstrate usage of the          }
{ signature idea for determining the order of units in the OVR }
{ file.                                                        }
{$O+,F+}
Interface
Procedure One;
Implementation
Procedure Signature;
{ This is the signature procedure. It is important to keep in  }
{ mind that this procedure MUST be called, and that each unit  }
{ MUST have a UNIQUE identifier. To change the signature, all  }
{ that is necessary is to change the last two bytes of the     }
{ inline code to the new signature. You must also then create  }
{ a text file that contains the unit's name and its unique     }
{ signature. An example follows.                               }
Begin
   Inline( $EB/$03/          { JMP 03 }
           $90/$00/$00 );    { Signature }
End;
Procedure One;
{ Simple example procedure that calls the signature procedure  }
{ and then writes a message.                                   }
Begin
  Signature;
  Writeln( 'One...' );
End;
End.
```

Listing 8.16. *Driving Program for 8.15*

```
Program Test;
{ This is a simple test program that links in the unit listed  }
{ above. Its sole purpose in life is to link in the            }
{ signature unit.                                              }
Uses
   Overlay, List815;
{$O List815}                     { Overlay the unit            }
Begin
   OvrInit( 'List8-16.ovr' ); { Initialize the Overlay Manager }
   One;                          { Call the interfaced procedure }
End.
```

Listing 8.17. *Determining Unit Order in OVR file*

```
Program DetermineOVROrder;
{ This program is used to display the order of the units in    }
{ a program as they were placed into the OVR file. Since       }
{ each unit contains a call to a signature procedure, we will  }
{ read from a file that contains a unit name and it's unique   }
{ signature. Then, when we find a signature within the OVR     }
{ file, we can output the unit name that has that signature.   }
{ It should be saved with a file name of OVRORDER.PAS.         }
Uses
   Crt, Dos;                  { Necessary Support units         }
Const
   MaxSigs = 100;             { Maximum number of signatures    }
Type
   SigType = Array[1..2] of Byte;{ Signature is 2 bytes long    }
   SigRec = Record            { Type to hold name and signature }
     UnitName : String;
     Signature : SigType;
   End;
Var
   F : File of Byte;    { Open the OVR file as a file of BYTE   }
   TotalSigs,           { Total number read for sig file        }
   B : Byte;            { Value read from the file              }
   Signatures : Array[1..MaxSigs] of SigRec;
   SigRead : SigType;   { Signature read from the OVR file      }
   SigFileName,         { Name of the Signature file            }
   OvrFileName : String;{ Name of the OVR file used as input    }
Function Exists( FName : String ) : Boolean;
{ This function uses a new technique to determine if a file    }
{ exists. It uses the FExpand function, and passes it the      }
{ name of the file we are looking for. If FExpand returns a    }
{ NUL string, then the file does not exist in the current      }
{ directory. Note that this can be changed to accept a         }
{ second parameter, which would be a list of directories to    }
{ search.                                                      }
```

```
Var
  S : String;              { Result of call to FSearch function   }
Begin
  FName := FExpand( FName );{ Expand the name to a full name      }
  S := FSearch( FName, '' ); { Check for existence of file        }
  Exists := S <> '';         { Return result in function name     }
End;
Function GetFileNames( Var S, O : String ) : Boolean;
{ This function will read the command line for the two files      }
{ that will be searched. If either of them is not found, or       }
{ if there are not two arguments on the command line, the         }
{ function will return FALSE. It also returns FALSE if            }
{ either of the two files do not exist. Otherwise, it will        }
{ return TRUE, and the program will continue.                     }
Begin
  GetFileNames := True;     { Assume success                      }
  If( ParamCount < 2 ) Then { See how many parameters passed      }
  Begin                     { If fewer than two, quit             }
    Writeln( 'Usage:  OVRORDER signaturefile ovrfile' );
    Writeln;
    GetFileNames := False;  { Set Result to Failure               }
    Exit;
  End;
  S := ParamStr( 1 );       { Get first command line argument     }
  If( Not ( Exists( S ) ) ) Then
  Begin                     { If file not there fail              }
    Writeln( 'Signature File NOT FOUND.' );
    WRiteln;
    GetFileNames := False;
  End;
  O := ParamStr( 2 );       { Get second command line argument    }
  If( Not( Exists( O ) ) ) Then
  Begin                     { if file not there, fail             }
    Writeln( 'Overlay File NOT FOUND.' );
    Writeln;
    GetFileNames := False;
  End;
End;
Procedure Readsigfile( FName : String );
{ This procedure will read from the signature file, the unit      }
{ name and its corresponding signature.                           }
Var
  Temp,
  S : String;              { Temporary working strings            }
  Err,                     { Result of calling the VAL procedure  }
  Index,                   { Index into the SigRec Array          }
  P : Integer;             { Result of Pos function call          }
  F : Text;                { Input file Variable                  }
```

Listing 8.17 continues

Listing 8.17 continued

```
Begin
  FillChar( Signatures, SizeOf( Signatures ), #0 );
  Assign( F, FName );
  Reset( F );            { Open the Input File                }
  Index := 1;            { Set Starting position              }
  While( ( Not EOF( F ) ) And ( Index <= MaxSigs ) ) Do
  Begin                  { Read until End of File encountered }
    Readln( F, S );      { Read a data item                   }
    P := Pos( ' ', S ); { Parse the information              }
    Signatures[Index].UnitName := Copy( S, 1, P - 1 );
    Delete( S, 1, P );
    P := Pos( ' ', S );
    Temp := Copy( S, 1, P-1 );
    Val( Temp, Signatures[Index].Signature[1], Err );
    Delete( S, 1, P );
    Val( S, Signatures[Index].Signature[2], Err );
  End;
  TotalSigs := Index;
  Close( F );                 { Close the input file and terminate }
End;
Procedure ShowIt( S : SigType );
{ This procedure will step through the array of signatures,   }
{ and write out the unit name that has the signature passed.  }
{ If no signature is found, the procedure will terminate.     }
Var
  Index : Byte;              { Index into Signature Array          }
Begin
  Index := 1;                { Initialize Index                    }
  While( Index <= TotalSigs ) Do
  Begin                      { Step through the Array              }
    If( ( Signatures[Index].Signature[1] = S[1] ) And
        ( Signatures[Index].Signature[2] = S[2] ) ) Then
    Begin
      GotoXY( 10, WhereY ); { Position the cursor for output }
      Writeln( Signatures[Index].UnitName );
      Exit;                 { It's found so exit the procedure }
    End;
    Inc( Index );           { Not found, so check next item  }
  End;
End;
Begin
  If( Not( GetFileNames( SigFileName, OvrFileName ) ) ) Then
    Halt;                   { If files not found, exit program   }
  ClrScr;
  GotoXY( 5,2 );
  Writeln( 'Unit order in ',OvrFileName,':' );
  Writeln;
  Readsigfile( SigFileName ); { Read the signature file        }
```

```
Assign( F, OvrFileName );{ Associate the OVR file with F      }
Reset( F );              { Open the file.                     }
While Not EOF( F ) Do    { Read the entire file               }
Begin
  Read( F, B );              { Read a Byte from the file.      }
  If( B = 144 ) Then         { Compare to NOP Opcode Value     }
  Begin
    Read( F, SigRead[1] );{ Found a Possible signature.        }
    Read( F, SigRead[2] );{ Get next two bytes from file       }
    ShowIt( SigRead );     { Now see if valid signature        }
  End;
End;
Close( F );                 { Close the Input file             }
End.
```

The signature file is an ASCII text file that can be created with the Turbo
Pascal editor. Its format, shown below, is the unit's namc followed by the
two-byte code in the inline statement within the listed unit. You cannot
have two units with the same signature because the program shown in
listing 8.16 above cannot handle such a situation.

```
UnitOne; 00 00
UnitTwo; 00 01
UnitThree; 00 02
UnitFour; 00 03
```

CHAPTER 9

Window Management

Windows give a program user-friendliness and a finished touch. Almost all successful programs on the market incorporate windows in one form or another. All of Borland's products use windows, as do WordPerfect, Lotus 1-2-3, and OS/2. Windows allow the programmer to present users with a package of information. Instead of forcing users to search for instructions, the instructions can be placed in the middle of the screen bordered in bright colors.

Unfortunately, creating a program with windows that function properly is difficult. You have to make the program determine the type of display on which it is running, enable the program to save the information underneath the window (to be restored after the window is closed), and write formulas to draw lines for the window borders.

This chapter develops the low- and high-level tools required for an easy-to-use window management system. We develop a unit that uses external assembly language code linked with Turbo Pascal code to meet these goals. Additionally, we create a stack structure to control the windows and create a second unit to facilitate the development of data entry screens. The second unit provides tools to allow users to edit input fields.

Requirements for Windows

Turbo Pascal provides the most important tool for creating a program that uses windows, the window procedure.

```
Procedure Window ( X1, Y1, X2, Y2 : Byte );
```

261

This routine takes the X and Y values passed in and defines a rectangular region for textual output based on them. X1 and Y1 refer to the upper left corner ([1,1] being the upper left corner of the screen); X2 and Y2 define the bottom right corner of the window. There are limitations to this procedure: the information under the new window is not saved, no border is created, you cannot switch between active windows (only the current window is recognized), and there are no titles.

Two routines control the opening and closing of windows. The first routine, OpenWindow, creates the window, adds any borders and/or titles, and makes the sound to indicate a window being opened; to do this, it calls the MovWindow, DoBorder, and WindowSound routines:

```
Procedure OpenWindow ( X1, Y1, X2, Y2 : Byte; Border :
BorderType; BorderColor : Word; Title : String );
```

The other controlling routine is CloseWindow. This routine closes the active window, restores the information beneath, and makes the sound indicative of closing a window; CloseWindow calls the MovWindow and WindowSound routines:

```
Procedure CloseWindow;
```

Storing Text Under Windows

Two methods are available for storing the text where the window is to be placed:

❑ Access the video hardware memory directly.

❑ Go through the BIOS.

The advantage to using direct memory accessing rather than the BIOS is speed. By accessing the video memory directly, you avoid the speed cost of making a call to another routine. The disadvantages of this method depend on the user's computer hardware. If the user's machine is non-standard (rare for text display modes), going directly to the hardware will not get the correct information. Old IBM CGA adapters cause snow on the screen if video memory is being accessed at the same time the adapter is updating the screen's information; periodically, the video board scans through the video memory and sends signals to the display to show the information.

If you want your program to run under multitasking operating systems as well as DOS, you should probably use the BIOS. A multitasking system may have several different programs sharing the screen at the same time. To enable programs to share the screen, the operating system controls which program gets access to which part of the screen. If you go directly to the hardware, you may bypass the operating system; if you use the BIOS, the operating system can grab the information and direct it to the correct place.

This chapter develops tools that go directly to the hardware because most programmers write for DOS and want speed in their output.

The actual routine to save the text information under the window requires six parameters; the routine is defined in listing 9.7 as procedure MovWindow. Because you will need to restore the video memory, as well as store it, the first parameter specifies the direction of the move: from video memory to a buffer or from the buffer to video memory. The next four parameters are the same as the window procedure. The last parameter is a pointer to where the video memory will be stored. The actual code required for this routine is described in the section "Window Tools Unit." The procedure header is declared as follows:

```
Procedure MovWindow ( ToScreen : Boolean; X1, Y1, X2, Y2 : Word;
Buff : Pointer );
```

Creating Window Borders

Another desirable window management tool is borders (in different colors) and titles. Borders and titles allow you to draw attention to the windows by making them stand out. The routine to create borders and windows requires quite a few parameters:

```
Procedure DoBorder ( X1, Y1, X2, Y2 : Byte; Border : BorderType;
BorderColor : Word; Title : String );
```

As with previously described procedures, X1, Y1, X2, and Y2 define the area of the window. Border is for BorderType, which can be one of four settings: no border, straight line, double line, user-defined border (using the DefineBorder procedure). The BorderColor parameter represents the color in which the border is to be drawn. Title specifies the string to be placed at the top of the window; a zero-length string denotes no title.

Procedure DefineBorder allows you to define your own type of border. By default, it replaces any existing user-defined border, but you can fix this by modifying the code to handle multiple user-defined borders. The DefineBorder procedure requires several parameters that define how the borders are to be drawn: a parameter for each corner, horizontal lines, vertical lines, beginning and ending of titles. Each parameter is the ASCII value of the character to be drawn in the border at that position.

```
Procedure DefineBorder ( Num : Byte; UpLeft, UpRight, BtmLeft,
BtmRight, HorizLine, VertLine, BegTitle, EndTitle : Char );
```

Adding Sound

Sound is a nice frill to add to a program; some users like literal bells and whistles. Later in this chapter, we develop a routine that makes one sound for opening a window and a different sound for closing a window; the routine requires one parameter to denote the window being opened or closed:

```
Procedure WindowSound ( Open : Boolean );
```

Direct Video Access

Writing directly to the video memory gives your program the advantage of speed. When you are writing to the video memory, you need to determine the address of the display adapter being used. There are two families of display adapters: monochrome and color. Color display adapters come in a variety of standards: CGA, EGA, VGA, and MCGA, for example. The difference between these adapters is their graphics capabilities; each treats video memory in a different way for graphics, but they all treat video memory the same when in a text mode. Video memory is treated the same on a monochrome display adapter as on a color display adapter; what differs between the two are the segment address and the way colors are treated.

Determining Current Video Mode

To determine the correct address of the video display, based on the following:

	$Segment	*Offset*
Color Display	$B800	$0000
Monochrome Display	$B000	$0000

you can make a call to the system BIOS and request the current display mode. These display modes correspond to the different display adapters: monochrome or color. Listing 9.1 is a procedure we use in the Window Management unit to determine the active display mode.

***Listing 9.1.** Get Video Address*

```
Procedure GetVideoAddress;
{ Based on the current video mode, set the width of the screen and }
{ the base address of the video screen.                           }
```

```
Var
  reg : Registers;
Begin
  reg.AH := $0F;
  Intr ( $10, reg );  { BIOS interrupt to get current video mode }
  VidWidth := reg.AH;
  Case ( reg.AL ) Of
      0..3 : BaseAddr := $B800;  { Color display }
      7    : BaseAddr := $B000;  { Monochrome display }
      Else
      Begin              { Must be in a graphics mode, halt program }
        ReportError ( 'Not in a text mode!' );
      End;
  End;
End;
```

Looking at listing 9.1, you can see that we call interrupt $10, the BIOS interrupt for video services. When we load `reg.AH` with the hexadecimal value 0F, we are requesting BIOS interrupt $10, service $0f which returns the current video mode. Then, based on the values returned, we assign the appropriate segment of the video adapter.

`VidWidth` and `BaseAddr` are global variables to the unit being developed in this chapter. They will be defined as follows in the `interface` section of the unit:

```
Var
  { The width of the screen in the current video mode }
  VidWidth : Byte;
  { The base offset of display memory of the current display }
  BaseAddr : Word;
```

Using Video Memory

Now that you have a routine that tells you the base address of the current video display, you need a routine to determine the size of the video memory buffer. For this, use the `GetWindowSize` function, which takes the standard four parameters of the window.

Listing 9.2. *GetWindowSize*

```
Function GetWindowSize ( X1, Y1, X2, Y2 : Word ) : Word;
{ Calculate the total amount of memory needed to store the window, }
{ character and attribute.                                         }
Begin
  GetWindowSize := ( X2 - X1 + 1 ) * ( Y2 - Y1 + 1 ) * 2;
End;
```

Graphics modes treat video memory on the various display adapters differently, but text modes treat it the same. The layout for text mode video memory is simple. Two bytes are reserved for each character location: the first byte contains the ASCII representation of the character, and the second byte contains the attribute of the character. The bits in the attribute byte are set up in a special way to represent the various colors.

Figure 9.1 shows how the bits of the attribute byte are split to represent the foreground color, background color, and a blink bit. The blink bit determines whether the character blinks on and off. Since only 3 bits represent the background color, you can set it to only 8 different colors. On the other hand, you have a choice of 16 colors for the foreground.

Fig. 9.1. Video attribute byte.

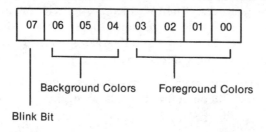

Each row of video memory is contiguous. If you are working on a screen 80 characters wide, each row takes 160 bytes (80 columns times 2 bytes per character). Therefore, the first row on the screen starts at offset 0 and goes to 159; the next row follows that, starting at 160 and going to 319; the third row follows that location; and so on. The following formula can be quickly derived to determine any location on the screen:

```
Offset := (( ScreenWidth * 2 ) * ( YLocation - 1 )) +
(( XLocation - 1) * 2);
```

In the formula, ScreenWidth is the current width of the screen, and YLocation and XLocation are values based on the desired character location, with [1,1] as the upper left corner of the screen. Based on this information, you could write one routine in Pascal that grabs video memory and stores it and another routine that restores the video memory to the screen. Unfortunately, this routine would probably cause snow to appear on old CGA displays. To get around this problem, use the assembly language code in listing 9.3.

Listing 9.3. *WindTool Assembler Code*

```
DATA    SEGMENT    WORD PUBLIC
        EXTRN      VidWidth:WORD,BaseAddr:WORD,CheckSnow:BYTE
DATA    ENDS

CODE    SEGMENT    BYTE PUBLIC
        ASSUME     CS:CODE, DS:DATA
        PUBLIC     MoveNoSnow
        PUBLIC     MoveFast
        PUBLIC     MovWindow

ToAddr    EQU      DWORD PTR [BP+6]  ; Target parameter
FromAddr  EQU      DWORD PTR [BP+10] ; Source parameter
Count     EQU      WORD  PTR [BP+14] ; Number of words to move

;MoveNoSnow ( Count : Word;FromAddr, ToAddr : Pointer );
MoveNoSnow        PROC FAR
    push    bp                ; Standard Turbo Pascal entry code
    mov     bp,sp             ; "

    push    ds                ; Save DS
    les     di,FromAddr       ; Move source address into ES:DI
    lds     si,ToAddr         ; Move target address into DS:SI
    cld                       ; Clear direction flag
    mov     cx,Count          ; Put number of words to be moved into CX
    jcxz    MoveNSDone        ; If no words to move, then exit now

    mov     dx,3DAh           ; Put CGA status port value in DX

AnotherChar:
    cli                       ; Stop interrupts, timing critical

VerticalSync:
    in      al,dx             ;*   Get CGA status byte
    test    al,8              ;**  Test vertical sync bit
    jnz     DisplayChar       ;**  If bit not set: jump to display the char
    rcr     al,1              ;*   Else: rotate bit 0 to the carry flag
    jc      VerticalSync      ;*   If carry flag set, loop again

DisplayEnable:
    in      al,dx             ; Get CGA status byte
    rcr     al,1              ; Rotate bit 0 to the carry flag
    jnc     DisplayEnable     ; Loop until carry flag not set

DisplayChar:
    lodsw                     ; Get word from string into AX
    sti                       ; Okay to do interrupts again
```

Listing 9.3 continues

Listing 9.3 continued

```
    stosw                   ; Move word from AX to destination address
    loop    AnotherChar     ; Loop until no more words to display

MoveNSDone:
    pop     ds              ; Restore DS
    pop     bp              ; Restore BP
    retf    10              ; Far return, 10 bytes of parameters
MoveNoSnow      ENDP


;Procedure MoveFast ( Count : Word; FromAddr, ToAddr : Pointer );
MoveFast        PROC FAR
    push    bp              ; Standard Turbo Pascal entry code
    mov     bp,sp           ; "
    les     di,FromAddr     ; Move source address into ES:DI

    mov     cx,Count        ; Move number of words to be moved to CX
    push    ds              ; Save DS
    lds     si,ToAddr       ; Move target address into DS:SI
    rep     movsw           ; Move CX words from ES:DI to DS:SI

    pop     ds              ; Restore DS
    pop     bp              ; Restore BP
    retf    10              ; Far return, 10 bytes of parameters
MoveFast        ENDP


;Procedure MovWindow ( ToScreen : Boolean; X1, Y1, X2, Y2 : Word;
;Buff : Pointer );
MovWindow       PROC FAR    ; Begin Procedure MovWindow
    push    bp              ; Standard Turbo Pascal Entry code
    mov     bp,sp           ;

                            ; Calculate number of word to move per line
    mov     ax,[bp+12]      ; move X2 to AX
    sub     ax,[bp+16]      ; AX = X2 - X1
    inc     ax              ; AX = X2 - X1 + 1
    push    ax              ; [BP-2] = X2 - X1 + 1

                            ; Calculate number of lines to move
    mov     ax,[bp+10]      ; move Y2 to AX
    sub     ax,[bp+14]      ; AX = Y2 - Y1
    inc     ax              ; AX = Y2 - Y1 + 1
    push    ax              ; [BP-4] = Y2 - Y1 + 1

                            ; Calculate number of bytes per line on screen
    mov     ax,VidWidth     ;
    shl     ax,1            ; AX = VidWidth * 2
    push    ax              ; [BP-6] = VidWidth * 2
```

```
                          ; Calculate Offset of window
        mov     ax,[bp+14]      ; AX = Y1
        dec     ax              ; AX = Y1 - 1
        mul     WORD PTR [BP-06]; AX = (Y1 - 1) * (VidWidth * 2)
        mov     dx,[bp+16]      ; DX = X1
        dec     dx              ; DX = X1 - 1
        shl     dx,1            ; DX = (X1 - 1) * 2
        add     ax,dx           ; AX = ((Y1 - 1) * (VidWidth * 2)) + ((X1 - 1) * 2)
        push    ax              ; [BP-8] = above formula

AnotherLine:
        mov     al,[bp+18]      ;
        cmp     al,0            ; See if we copy to screen
        jne     CopyFromScr     ;

        push    [bp-2]          ; Put number of words to move onto stack
        push    [bp+8]          ; Move buffer to stack
        push    [bp+6]          ; Move buffer to stack
        push    BaseAddr        ; Move video segment to stack
        push    [bp-8]          ; Move video offset to stack
        jmp     Check4SnowCheck ;

CopyFromScr:
        push    [bp-2]          ; Put number of words to move onto stack
        push    BaseAddr        ; Move video segment to stack
        push    [bp-8]          ; Move video offset to stack
        push    [bp+8]          ; Move buffer to stack
        push    [bp+6]          ; Move buffer to stack

Check4SnowCheck:
        mov     al,CheckSnow    ;
        cmp     al,0            ; Check the boolean variable CheckSnow
        jne     SnowChecking    ;
        call    MoveFast        ; If CheckSnow = FALSE then use MoveFast
        jmp     SkipSnow        ;
SnowChecking:
        call    MoveNoSnow      ; If CheckSnow = TRUE then use MoveNoSnow

SkipSnow:
        mov     ax,[bp-8]       ; AX := Video Offset
        add     ax,[bp-6]       ; AX := Video Offset + ScreenWidth
        mov     [bp-8],ax       ; Video Offset := Video Offset + ScreenWidth

        mov     ax,[bp-2]       ; AX := Words to move
        shl     ax,1            ; AX := AX * 2
        add     ax,[bp+6]       ; AX := AX + Buffer Offset
        mov     [bp+6],ax       ; Buffer Offset := Buffer Offset + bytes to move
```

Listing 9.3 continues

Listing 9.3 continued

```
     mov    ax,[bp-4]     ;
     dec    ax            ;
     mov    [bp-4],ax     ; Lines := Lines - 1
     cmp    ax,0          ; If Lines <> 0 then
     jnz    AnotherLine   ;   Goto display another line

     mov    sp,bp         ; Standard Turbo Pascal Exit Code
     pop    bp            ;
     retf   14            ;
MovWindow        ENDP     ; End of Procedure MovWindow

CODE   ENDS
END
```

Listing 9.3 contains three procedures: MoveNoSnow, MoveFast, and MovWindow. The parameter lists for MoveNoSnow and MoveFast are identical. Both have the same goal: move information from one place to another. MoveNoSnow has an additional goal of moving the information only when the status port on the CGA board indicates that it is appropriate to do so.

After the standard Turbo Pascal entry code, the first thing the MoveFast procedure does is load an address from the stack into ES:DI. Next, it loads the number of words to be moved from the stack into CX. Then DS:SI is loaded with another address. The actual moving of information is done in this line:

```
REP    MOVSW
```

This assembly language mnemonic instructs the computer to repeat the following command for the number of times stored in CX. The command to repeat moves one word from DS:SI to ES:DI and increments SI and DI. We use this routine instead of Turbo Pascal's built-in move procedure because the move procedure is written to use the MOVSB call instead of MOVSW. MOVSB moves one byte at a time; we will always be moving words, so the choice to use MOVSW makes sense.

The MoveNoSnow routine has the same task but needs to make sure that no snow is generated on the screen during the move. Snow is generated when a horizontal or vertical retrace is occurring at the same time something else is accessing video memory. The time between the retraces is short. Therefore, we can move only a couple of bytes at a time. This routine is structured around two loops: one loop checks the horizontal retrace; the other the vertical retrace. This checking is performed by looking at the port address $03DA and testing the bits. If the bit we are checking is set, the retrace is occurring, and we need to loop until it is done. The commands used for testing and looping are time critical. We turn off hardware interrupts when we are in the loops. Additionally, we need to use the fastest assembly language commands to do the test. If we are just slightly off, snow will occur. This is why we use RCR instead of TEST. TEST can take twice as long as RCR does. RCR takes the byte passed to it and rotates the bits one to the right; the bit rotated off is placed in the carry flag. Then, we jump based on the carry flag's status. This is the fastest way to test bit zero.

The MoveNoSnow routine can be sped up quite a bit at the cost of only a small amount of video snow. Tests on an IBM PC (4.77MHz) with an IBM CGA (which is prone to snow) showed that modifying the MoveNoSnow procedure to remove a couple of lines of code from the snow-checking loops almost doubles the output at the cost of a little snow on the left column of the screen.

```
VerticalSync:
    in      al,dx           ;*    Get CGA status byte
;   test    al,8            ;**   Test vertical sync bit
;   jnz     DisplayChar     ;**   If bit not set: jump to display the char
    rcr     al,1            ;*    Else: rotate bit 0 to the carry flag
    jc      VerticalSync    ;*    If carry flag set, loop again
```

The last procedure in listing 9.3 is MovWindow, which we mentioned briefly earlier in this chapter. MovWindow takes six parameters. The first parameter determines whether the routine is to put information on the screen or take it from the screen. The next four parameters are the familiar coordinates of the window. The last parameter is where the information is taken from, or put to, depending on the first parameter. This routine depends on several external variables. CheckSnow determines whether the program uses MoveNoSnow (if true) or MoveFast (if false), VidWidth is the value for the width of the screen in the current mode, and VidSeg is the segment address for the current video display.

Window Stack

To allow multiple pop-up windows, we will need to store the information about each window as it is opened. To do this, we will be implementing a stack structure for the windows. This stack storage technique will be built into the call to open the window and will be transparent to the programmer.

Defining Data Structure

A data structure needs to be defined to hold the window's information, containing the X,Y coordinates of the window's location on the screen and the buffer for the display information under the window. Because this structure occupies only eight bytes of memory for each element, we use an array to emulate a stack. Following is the element structure and the array:

```
Const
  MaxStack = 1000;  { Largest size for window stack }

Type
  StackElement = Record
                   sX1, sY1,
                   sX2, sY2 : Byte;
                   sBuff : Pointer;
                 End;
  StackType    = Array [0..MaxStack] of StackElement;

Var
  Stack : StackType;
  StackPtr : Byte;
```

The stack variable will be defined in the implementation section of the WindTool unit, to prevent access from outside the unit. In addition, only two routines will directly access this stack: OpenWindow and CloseWindow. OpenWindow adds an element to the stack for the new window being created. CloseWindow closes the current window, restoring the information beneath it, and then it reactivates the next window in the stack. CloseWindow takes no parameters. If there are no more entries on the stack, it activates the default Turbo Pascal window.

Figure 9.2 shows that for each window opened we need to track where the stack is. The global variable StackPtr is defined as a Word and serves this purpose. It will be incremented and decremented as the stack grows and shrinks to indicate the current stack position in the array. If the variable contains zero, the Turbo Pascal default window is the active window.

Using Window Stack Operations

Two routines manipulate the stack: PushWindow and PopWindow. PushWindow will be called whenever a window is to be opened. It allocates space for storage of a new window and increments the StackPtr. PushWindow takes the X,Y coordinates of the window area to be saved; PopWindow restores the last item on the stack. Item i in figure 9.2 shows

Fig. 9.2. *Window stack.*

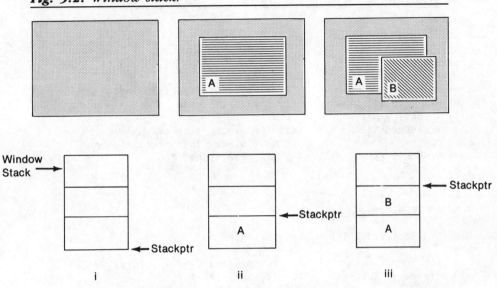

the empty stack and window. Item ii shows the stack after the call to
PushWindow one time. Item iii shows window and stack after a second call.
After one call to PopWindow, we return to the state of Item ii. After the last
call to PopWindow, we are back at Item i.

Listing 9.4. *PushWindow and PopWindow*

```
Procedure PushWindow ( pX1,pY1,pX2,pY2 : Byte );
{ Allocate memory on the internal window stack for the window, then }
{ save the memory in that area.                                     }
Begin
  If ( StackPtr = 0 ) Then       { Special case. If it is the first window    }
  Begin                          { opened, get the current window coordinates.}
    With Stack [ StackPtr ] Do
    Begin
      sX1 := Lo ( WindMin ) + 1;
      sY1 := Hi ( WindMin ) + 1;
      sX2 := Lo ( WindMax ) + 1;
      sY2 := Hi ( WindMax ) + 1;
    End;
  End;
  Inc ( StackPtr );                { Increment the stack pointer }
  With Stack [ StackPtr ] Do       { Store the X,Y coordinates }
```

Listing 9.4 continues

Listing 9.4 continued

```
  Begin
    sX1 := pX1;
    sY1 := pY1;
    sX2 := pX2;
    sY2 := pY2;
                              { Allocate storage for window }
    GetMem ( sBuff, GetWindowSize ( sX1, sY1, sX2, sY2 ) );
    If ( sBuff = NIL ) Then
      ReportError ( 'No heap left for window allocation.' );
                              { Move window into storage area }
    MovWindow ( FALSE, sX1, sY1, sX2, sY2, sBuff );
  End;
End;

Procedure PopWindow;
Begin
  With WindTool.Stack [ WindTool.StackPtr ] Do
  Begin
                              { Restore the window information }
    MovWindow ( TRUE, sX1, sY1, sX2, sY2, sBuff );
                              { Release heap storage }
    FreeMem ( sBuff, GetWindowSize ( sX1, sY1, sX2, sY2 ) );
  End;
  Dec ( StackPtr );           { Decrement the stack pointer }
End;
```

Window Frills

Now that have established the basics for the program's windows, we will develop trimmings for the windows. The kind of trimmings people prefer varies. This example uses colored borders, window titles, and sound. You can add other features as well, if you prefer; the code we are creating is open to extension.

Drawing Window Borders

You are limited to four border types: three predefined and one user-definable. You can easily expand the number of borders defined by changing the constant MaxBorders (defined in the implementation section of this unit). The calls to define the first three border types are in the initialization section of the unit.

```
DefineBorder ( 1, ' ',' ',' ',' ',' ',' ',' ',' ' );

DefineBorder ( 2, ' ',' ',' ',' ','-',' ',' ',' ' );

DefineBorder ( 3, ' ',' ',' ',' ','-',' ',' ',' ' );

DefineBorder ( 4, ' ',' ',' ',' ',' ',' ',' ',' ' );
```

The DefineBorder procedure takes several parameters. The first determines the number of the border type to set. The rest set the various corners, lines, and titles. To add additional border types, change MaxBorders, and add the call to DefineBorder to set your own border type.

When we have established the border types, we work with DoBorder to set the border and colors and to define the title of the window and add it to the window.

The first duty of DoBorder is to save the current screen-drawing color attributes. This needs to be done because we will be changing the screen colors to draw the border and create the title string. We will have to restore the original drawing color to what it was before we changed it. After we save the color attribute, the routine sets the text color and text background to the parameter that was passed in.

Next, the routine defines a full-screen window. If a previously defined window exists, GotoXY will conform to that window's definitions. GotoXY (1,1); goes not to the top left corner of the screen but to the current window's (1,1) position, so we redefine the entire screen to be a valid Turbo Pascal window. A check determines whether the BorderType passed into the procedure is within the valid range, and if the parameter does not fall in the range, it is set to BorderType 1.

The border drawing routine in listing 9.5 is next. It places the upper left corner of the window border into a string. Then a FOR loop adds the appropriate number of horizontal lines to the string. Finally, the upper right corner of the window is appended to the string. Building a string and writing it is faster than writing individual characters.

Listing 9.5. *DoBorder*

```
Procedure DoBorder ( X1, Y1, X2, Y2 : Byte; Border : BorderType;
                     BorderColor : Word; Title : String );
Var
  i : Integer;
  s : String;
  tmp : Word;
```

Listing 9.5 continues

Listing 9.5 continued

```
Begin
  tmp := TextAttr;                        { Save the current screen colors }
  TextColor ( Lo ( BorderColor ) );       { Set color for border }
  TextBackground ( Hi ( BorderColor ) );  { " }
  Window ( 1, 1, 80, 25 );                { Set window to entire screen }
  If ( Border > MaxBorders ) OR ( Border < 0 ) Then
    Border := 1;
  s := BArr [ Border ].UL;                { Build top line of window border }
  For i := 1 to ( X2 - X1 - 1 ) Do        { " }
    s := s + BArr [ Border ].HL;          { " }
  s := s + BArr [ Border ].UR;            { " }
  GotoXY ( X1, Y1 );                      { Print top line of window border }
  Write ( s );
  i := Length ( s );
  s [ 1 ] := BArr [ Border ].BL;          { Build bottom line of window border }
  s [ i ] := BArr [ Border ].BR;          { " }
  GotoXY ( X1, Y2 );                      { Print bottom line of border }
  Write ( s );
  FillChar ( s, i, ' ' );                 { Build center of window }
  s [ 0 ] := Chr ( i );                   { " }
  s [ 1 ] := BArr [ Border ].VL;          { " }
  s [ Length ( s ) ] := BArr [ Border ].VL; { " }
For i := ( Y1 + 1 ) to ( Y2 - 1 ) Do
Begin
  GotoXY ( X1, i );                       { Loop and print center of window }
  Write ( s );
End;

{ Build Title string }
If ( Length ( Title ) > 0 ) Then          { If title string is not zero, }
Begin                                     { don't draw a title string.    }
  If ( Length ( Title ) > ( X2 - X1 - 3 ) ) Then  { If string larger than }
    Title [0] := Chr ( X2 - X1 - 3 );             { window, shorten it.    }
  Insert ( BArr [ Border ].BT, Title, 1 ); { Add start Title character }
  Title := Title + BArr [ Border ].ET;    { Add end Title character   }
  GotoXY ( X1 + ( ( X2 - X1 + 1 ) Div 2 ) - ( Length ( Title ) Div 2 ), Y1 );
  Write ( Title );                        { Write the title to the window }
End;

  Window ( X1 + 1, Y1 + 1, X2 - 1, Y2 - 1 ); { Make Turbo aware of window  }
  TextAttr := tmp;                        { Restore orig. screen colors }
  ClrScr;
End;
```

Because the correct length of the string has already been generated, the routine modifies only the first and last characters of the string to contain the bottom border of the window. Then the middle elements for the vertical border are generated and written out in a FOR loop.

Putting Titles on Windows

The second half of the DoBorder procedure in listing 9.5 adds the title to the window. The first check is to see whether a title is to be drawn. If so, the routine has to determine whether the title fits inside the window. If the title string is too large, it will be truncated to fit in the bounds of the window. By modifying Title [0], we modify the length byte of the string. A *string* is actually an array from zero to the length specified within the square brackets. The number of good characters in the array is stored in element zero of the string, as in the following example:

```
Var
  s : String[10];
Begin
  s := 'Dog';
End;
```

In the preceding lines of code, s is an array [0..10] of characters. After the assignment of s := 'Dog';, s[0] contains a three (3), for 3 good characters in the array.

After we have determined the correct size of the string to be placed in the window title area, the special characters for beginning and ending the title need to be added. Finally, we calculate the position of the string within the window and output it.

The last bit of work in listing 9.5 is the clean-up. Turbo Pascal has to know about the new window, so we call the Window procedure, insetting the window by one position so that the border cannot be changed by simple Write and WriteLn calls. Next, the screen attributes that were saved at the start of the procedure are restored, and the new window is cleared.

Adding Sound

Adding sound to the window tools we are creating is a relatively simple task. Turbo Pascal provides two procedures for working with sound: Sound and NoSound. Sound takes a parameter of what frequency to send through the speaker, and the sound continues until the NoSound procedure is called.

The first thing listing 9.6 does is check the SoundOn variable. If SoundOn is false, the code to generate noise is skipped. If SoundOn is true, the Open parameter passed to the routine determines whether an open window or a close window sound is to be made. The procedure is set up with the sound as 3 different frequencies lasting 50 milliseconds each. The open window sound has a incrementing frequency; the close window sound decrements. (Of course, you can change these sounds to any you like.)

Listing 9.6. *Sound*

```
Procedure WindowSound ( Open : Boolean );
{ Based on value of the SoundOn boolean variable, make a sound for }
{ opening or closing a window.                                     }
Begin
  If ( SoundOn ) Then
  Begin
    If Open Then
    Begin
      Sound ( 100 );   { Open a window sound }
      Delay ( 50 );
      Sound ( 200 );
      Delay ( 50 );
      Sound ( 300 );
      Delay ( 50 );
      NoSound;
    End
    Else
    Begin
      Sound ( 300 );   { Close a window sound }
      Delay ( 50 );
      Sound ( 200 );
      Delay ( 50 );
      Sound ( 100 );
      Delay ( 50 );
      NoSound;
    End;
  End;
End;
```

Window Tools Unit

We have created many useful routines so far in this chapter: a procedure to move to video memory with and without snow checking, a routine to draw borders on windows, and procedures to manipulate a window stack.

You can use the unit we have developed to generate windows in your programs with little effort. All you will have to do is include the unit in your Uses statement and call the OpenWindow routine to do the work for you.

You might think that the routines in this unit are good only for creating pop-up windows, but they can be used for pull-down menus as well. A pull-down menu is really a window with menu choices in it.

Listing 9.7 links in the assembly language code from listing 9.3; you need to compile that assembly language code to an object file WINDTOOL.OBJ to be able to compile and link listing 9.7.

Listing 9.7. WindTool Unit Code

```pascal
Unit WindTool;

Interface

Uses
  CRT,
  DOS;

Type
  BorderType = Byte;

Var
  { The width of the screen in the current video mode }
  VidWidth : Word;

  { The base offset of display memory of the current display }
  BaseAddr : Word;

  { To control the sound on or off based on TRUE or FALSE }
  SoundOn  : Boolean;

Procedure OpenWindow ( X1, Y1, X2, Y2 : Byte; Border : BorderType;
                       BorderColor : Word; Title : String );

Procedure CloseWindow;

Procedure MoveNoSnow (  Count : Word; FromAddr, ToAddr : Pointer );

Procedure MoveFast ( Count : Word; FromAddr, ToAddr : Pointer );

Procedure MovWindow ( ToScreen : Boolean; X1, Y1, X2, Y2 : Word;
                      Buff : Pointer );

Procedure DoBorder ( X1, Y1, X2, Y2 : Byte; Border : BorderType;
                     BorderColor : Word; Title : String );

Procedure DefineBorder ( Num : Byte; UpLeft, UpRight, BtmLeft, BtmRight,
                         HorizLine, VertLine, BegTitle, EndTitle : Char );

Procedure WindowSound ( Open : Boolean );

Procedure GetVideoAddress;

Function GetWindowSize ( X1, Y1, X2, Y2 : Word ) : Word;

Implementation
```

Listing 9.7 continues

Listing 9.7 continued

```
Const
  MaxStack = 1000;   { Largest size for window stack }
  MaxBorders = 4;

Type
  BorderRec    = Record
                   UL, UR, BL, BR,
                   HL, VL,
                   BT, ET : Char;
                 End;
  BorderArray  = Array [ 1..MaxBorders ] of BorderRec;
  StackElement = Record
                   sX1, sY1,
                   sX2, sY2 : Byte;
                   sBuff : Pointer;
                 End;
  StackType    = Array [0..MaxStack] of StackElement;

Var
  BArr      : BorderArray;
  Stack     : StackType;
  StackPtr  : Word;

{$L WindTool.obj}

{$F+}
Procedure MoveNoSnow; External;

Procedure MoveFast; External;

Procedure MovWindow; External;
{$F-}

Procedure ReportError ( s : String );
{ Brute force error checking. If an error occurs, clear the screen and }
{ report problem, then terminate program. This is more for development }
{ error reporting then a shipping error generator.                     }
Begin
  ClrScr;
  WriteLn ( s );
  Halt ( 1 );
End;

Function GetWindowSize;
{ Calculate the total amount of memory needed to store the window, }
{ character and attribute.                                         }
Begin
  GetWindowSize := ( X2 - X1 + 1 ) * ( Y2 - Y1 + 1 ) * 2;
End;
```

```
Procedure PushWindow ( pX1,pY1,pX2,pY2 : Byte );
{ Allocate memory on the internal window stack for the window, then }
{ save the memory in that area.                                     }
Begin
   If ( StackPtr = 0 ) Then        { Special case. If it is the first window    }
   Begin                           { opened, get the current window coordinates.}
     With Stack [ StackPtr ] Do
     Begin
       sX1 := Lo ( WindMin ) + 1;
       sY1 := Hi ( WindMin ) + 1;
       sX2 := Lo ( WindMax ) + 1;
       sY2 := Hi ( WindMax ) + 1;
     End;
   End;
   Inc ( StackPtr );               { Increment the stack pointer }
   With Stack [ StackPtr ] Do      { Store the X,Y coordinates }
   Begin
     sX1 := pX1;
     sY1 := pY1;
     sX2 := pX2;
     sY2 := pY2;
                                 { Allocate storage for window }
     GetMem ( sBuff, GetWindowSize ( sX1, sY1, sX2, sY2 ) );
     If ( sBuff = NIL ) Then
       ReportError ( 'No heap left for window allocation.' );
                                 { Move window into storage area }
     MovWindow ( FALSE, sX1, sY1, sX2, sY2, sBuff );
   End;
End;


Procedure PopWindow;
Begin
  With WindTool.Stack [ WindTool.StackPtr ] Do
  Begin
                                { Restore the window information }
    MovWindow ( TRUE, sX1, sY1, sX2, sY2, sBuff );
                                { Release heap storage }
    FreeMem ( sBuff, GetWindowSize ( sX1, sY1, sX2, sY2 ) );
  End;
  Dec ( StackPtr );             { Decrement the stack pointer }
End;


Procedure DoBorder;
Var
  i : Integer;
  s : String;
  tmp : Word;
```

Listing 9.7 continues

Listing 9.7 *continued*

```
Begin
  tmp := TextAttr;                         { Save the current screen colors }
  TextColor ( Lo ( BorderColor ) );        { Set color for border }
  TextBackground ( Hi ( BorderColor ) );   { " }
  Window ( 1, 1, 80, 25 );                 { Set window to entire screen }
  If ( Border > MaxBorders ) OR ( Border < 0 ) Then
    Border := 1;
  s := BArr [ Border ].UL;                 { Build top line of window border }
  For i := 1 to ( X2 - X1 - 1 ) Do         { " }
    s := s + BArr [ Border ].HL;           { " }
  s := s + BArr [ Border ].UR;             { " }
  GotoXY ( X1, Y1 );                       { Print top line of window border }
  Write ( s );
  i := Length ( s );
  s [ 1 ] := BArr [ Border ].BL;           { Build bottom line of window border }
  s [ i ] := BArr [ Border ].BR;           { " }
  GotoXY ( X1, Y2 );                       { Print bottom line of border }
  Write ( s );
  FillChar ( s, i, ' ' );                  { Build center of window }
  s [ 0 ] := Chr ( i );                    { " }
  s [ 1 ] := BArr [ Border ].VL;           { " }
  s [ Length ( s ) ] := BArr [ Border ].VL; { " }
  For i := ( Y1 + 1 ) to ( Y2 - 1 ) Do
  Begin
    GotoXY ( X1, i );                      { Loop and print center of window }
    Write ( s );
  End;

  { Build Title string }
  If ( Length ( Title ) > 0 ) Then         { If title string is not zero, }
  Begin                                    { dont draw a title string.    }
    If ( Length ( Title ) > ( X2 - X1 - 3 ) ) Then   { If string larger than }
      Title [0] := Chr ( X2 - X1 - 3 );              { window, shorten it.   }
    Insert ( BArr [ Border ].BT, Title, 1 ); { Add start Title character }
    Title := Title + BArr [ Border ].ET;   { Add end Title character   }
    i := X1 + ((X2 - X1 + 1) div 2 ) - ( Length (Title) Div 2);
    GotoXY ( X1 + ( ( X2 - X1 + 1 ) Div 2 ) - ( Length ( Title ) Div 2 ), Y1 );
    Write ( Title );                       { Write the title to the window }
  End;

  Window ( X1 + 1, Y1 + 1, X2 - 1, Y2 - 1 ); { Make Turbo aware of window }
  TextAttr := tmp;                         { Restore orig. screen colors }
  ClrScr;
End;

Procedure DefineBorder;
{ Define a border for the DoBorder procedure }
```

```
Begin
  With BArr [ Num ] Do
  Begin
    UL := UpLeft;
    UR := UpRight;
    BL := BtmLeft;
    BR := BtmRight;
    HL := HorizLine;
    VL := VertLine;
    BT := BegTitle;
    ET := EndTitle;
  End;
End;

Procedure WindowSound;
{ Based on value of the SoundOn boolean variable, make a sound for }
{ opening or closing a window.                                     }
Begin
  If ( SoundOn ) Then
  Begin
    If Open Then
    Begin
      Sound ( 100 );   { Open a window sound }
      Delay ( 50 );
      Sound ( 200 );
      Delay ( 50 );
      Sound ( 300 );
      Delay ( 50 );
      NoSound;
    End
    Else
    Begin
      Sound ( 300 );   { Close a window sound }
      Delay ( 50 );
      Sound ( 200 );
      Delay ( 50 );
      Sound ( 100 );
      Delay ( 50 );
      NoSound;
    End;
  End;
End;

Procedure GetVideoAddress;
{ Based on the current video mode, set the width of the screen and }
{ the base address of the video screen.                           }
Var
  reg : Registers;
```

Listing 9.7 continues

Listing 9.7 continued

```pascal
Begin
  reg.AH := $0F;
  Intr ( $10, reg );  { BIOS interrupt to get current video mode }
  VidWidth := reg.AH;
  Case ( reg.AL ) Of
      0..3 : BaseAddr := $B800;  { Color display }
      7    : BaseAddr := $B000;  { Monochrome display }
      Else
      Begin            { Must be in a graphics mode, halt program }
        ReportError ( 'Not in a text mode!' );
      End;
  End;
End;

Procedure OpenWindow;
{ Perform all the work required to open a window on the screen, draw the }
{ border, make the sound, ...                                           }
Begin
  WindowSound ( TRUE );
  PushWindow ( X1, Y1, X2, Y2 );
  DoBorder ( X1, Y1, X2, Y2, Border, BorderColor, Title );
End;

Procedure CloseWindow;
{ Perform all the work required to close a window and make the sound. }
Begin
  WindowSound ( FALSE );
  PopWindow;
  With Stack [ StackPtr ] Do
  Begin
    If ( StackPtr = 0 ) Then
      Window ( sX1, sY1, sX2, sY2 )     { Main window }
    Else
      Window ( sX1 + 1, sY1 + 1, sX2 - 1, sY2 - 1 );
  End;
End;

Begin
  GetVideoAddress;                          { Get current video information  }
  FillChar ( Stack, SizeOf (Stack), 0 );  { Initialize window stack        }
  StackPtr := 0;                            { Initialize window stack pointer }
  SoundOn := TRUE;                          { Default sound to be on         }

  DefineBorder ( 1, ' ',' ',' ',' ',' ',' ',' ',' ' ); { Set predefined }

  DefineBorder ( 2, ' ',' ',' ',' ','-',' ',' ',' ' ); { border types.  }

  DefineBorder ( 3, ' ',' ',' ',' ','-',' ',' ',' ' );

  DefineBorder ( 4, ' ',' ',' ',' ',' ',' ',' ',' ' );
End.
```

Listing 9.8 calls the OpenWindow procedure with random values. This program is of no value other than demonstrating the use of the WindTool unit. It opens 100 windows, waits for you to press any key, then closes all the windows.

Listing 9.8. *WindDemo Program Code*

```pascal
Program WindDemo;

Uses
  Crt,
  WindTool;

Var
  ch : char;
  i,
  j : Integer;
  xSize,
  ySize,
  xStart,
  yStart : Byte;

Begin
  Randomize;
  ClrScr;
  For i := 1 to 100 Do
  Begin
    xSize  := Random ( 50 ) + 3;  { Size of window in X direction }
    ySize  := Random ( 20 ) + 3;  { Size of window in Y direction }
    xStart := Random ( 79 - xSize ) + 1; { Upper left X location of window }
    yStart := Random ( 25 - ySize ) + 1; { Upper left Y location of window }
    OpenWindow ( xStart, yStart, xStart + xSize, yStart + ySize,
                 Random ( 4 ) + 1, ( ( Random ( 8 ) ) shl 8 ) +
                 Random ( 16 ), 'Test window:test window' );
    For j := 1 to 10 do
      Writeln ( i, 'This is a test, this is only a test...' );
  End;
  ch := ReadKey;  { Wait until a key has been pressed }
  For i := 1 to 100 Do
    CloseWindow;
  ReadLn;
End.
```

Editing Tools

Many programmers are interested in building data entry screens to work with their windows. In this section, we build some simple tools for creating edit fields. We create another unit, EditTool, to hold these routines; this unit is independent of the WindTool unit (listing 9.7) we have been developing.

These routines put a reverse video field on the screen for data entry. To edit this field, several standard keys are supported: Home, End, Insert (Ins), Delete (Del), Left arrow, Right arrow, Backspace, Ctrl-Y, and Enter. The routine is easily modifiable to add or delete keystrokes.

Creating a Reverse Video Field

Many people prefer to do data entry in a reverse video field because questions are easily differentiated from input. By using GotoXY and Write/WriteLn, you can place your questions in the appropriate locations on the screen. To simulate where input will be done, a reverse video block the size of the input string should be added as well, as in listing 9.9

Listing 9.9. BlankXY

```
Procedure BlankLine;
{ This procedure will write a blank line to the screen at the input }
{ field location, for maxChars.                                     }
Begin
  blank [ 0 ] := Chr ( maxChars );
  GotoXY ( xPos, yPos );
  Write ( blank );
  GotoXY ( xPos, yPos );
End;

Procedure BlankXY ( x, y, max : Byte );
Var
  storeAttr : Word;
Begin
  storeAttr := TextAttr;
  TextColor ( Black );
  TextBackground ( LightGray );
  xPos := x;
  yPos := y;
  maxChars := max;
  BlankLine;
  TextAttr := storeAttr;
End;
```

The first thing listing 9.9 does is save the current screen attributes from the TextAttr variable from the Crt unit. Then the reverse video colors are set (black letters on a light gray background). Next, the global variables xPos and yPos are set to point where the input field is to start. MaxChars is set to the maximum number of characters to be allowed in the field. Now that everything is set up, the BlankLine routine is called. Finally, the TextAttr variable is restored.

The BlankLine routine is relatively simple. The routine simply modifies the zero element of the typed constant blank. Blank is set up as a string with a length of 80 characters filled with spaces. By modifying the zero element, we are specifying the number of characters in the string to be output. The cursor is moved to the appropriate location on the string, the string is output, and the cursor is moved to the start of this string. By writing a string of blanks, we are clearing this section of the screen and inserting the black-on-gray colors. This gives the effect of adding input fields.

Creating the Input Field

Because these tools are going to allow editing of the string with various keystrokes, the standard Read/ReadLn routines cannot be used. We must build the strings one character at a time, handling special characters (Backspace, Enter, etc.) differently.

Listing 9.10 adds a filter to these input tools to limit the characters that can be typed. Keys with characters not in the filter can be pressed, but they are ignored rather than added to the string. This allows you to program special fields, like one for phone numbers that can take only the following characters: ( ) - 0 1 2 3 4 5 6 7 8 9. The filter is essentially a set of characters. Set filter equal to the characters you want to be valid. By default, the filter is set to the printable ASCII character set (32-255).

Listing 9.10. *GetLine Procedure*

```
Procedure GetLine;
Var
  func,
  terminator : Boolean;      { loop control variable }
Begin
  cp := 1;                   { initialize the CP }
  terminator := FALSE;       { initialize the loop control variable }
  Repeat
    ch := Readkey;           { get keypress from user }
```

Listing 9.10 continues

Listing 9.10 *continued*

```
    func := FALSE;         { initialize function key variable }
    If ( ch = #0 ) Then    { check for an extended key press...}
    Begin
      ch := ReadKey;
      func := TRUE          { An extended key was pressed }
    End
    Else
    If ( ch in filter ) Then    { is it a valid character? }
    Begin
      inpSt [ cp ] := ch;                { insert character at CP }
      If ( cp > Ord ( inpSt [ 0 ] ) ) Then    { appending to end of string? }
        inpSt [ 0 ] := Chr ( Ord ( inpSt [ 0 ] ) + 1 ); { yes,increase length }
      Inc ( cp );                        { increase the CP }
      Write ( ch );                      { display the character }
      If ( cp > maxChars ) Then          { have we past the maximum # of chars? }
      Begin
        Dec ( cp );                      { Yes, decrease the CP }
        GotoXY ( cp + xPos - 1, yPos ); { move the cursor }
      End;
    End;
    terminator := ProcessChar ( func, ch ); { process the key press }
  Until terminator;
End;
```

Throughout the GetLine procedure (listing 9.10), the cp variable keeps track of the current cursor position. Because the user will input characters one at a time, and we are allowing restriction on the size of input and editing of the already-input characters, we need to track the cursor's current position.

The routine can be broken down as follows:

1. Initialize variables.

2. Get character input.

3. If the character is a member of the filter, insert it to the correct location in the string, and increment the cursor position.

4. Process the character that was read in.

This routine allows modification of the data with the arrow keys. This means there is no guarantee that the characters being input are being added to the end of the string, so we must develop code for special cases. Since cp is the cursor position, the character at that location is updated. Next, we check whether the cursor position indicates that we are appending to the end of the string. If so, we increment the length byte of the string.

Then we increment the cursor position and display the character just added. If the cursor position is beyond the maximum number of characters allowed for input, we decrement the cursor position to the last valid position.

Processing Characters

It is simple to add or delete a special character to this routine; listing 9.11 is a giant case statement.

Listing 9.11. *ProcessChar Procedure*

```
Function ProcessChar ( funcKey : Boolean; ch : Char ): Boolean;
{ This function will process the character passed in through CH and }
{ take appropriate actions. If the character determines the end of  }
{ input for that line, the function will return TRUE.              }
Var
  endInput : Boolean;
Begin
  endInput := FALSE;
  Case ch of
    BackSpace : Begin                             { Destructive backspace }
                  Delete ( inpSt, cp-1, 1 );      { -delete char before CP }
                  Dec ( cp );                     { -decrement the CP }
                  If ( cp < 1 ) Then
                    cp := 1;
                  DisplayString;                  { -display the new string }
                End;
    Enter     : Begin                             { End of line input }
                  endInput := TRUE;
                End;
    CTRL_Y    : Begin                             { Delete entire line }
                  BlankLine;                      { -draw blank line }
                  cp := 1;                        { -reset the CP }
                  inpSt := '';                    { -reset the input string }
                End;
    Ins       : If funcKey Then                   { Insert a blank space }
                Begin
                  Insert ( ' ', inpSt, cp );  { -insert the space char }
                  If ( Length ( inpSt ) > maxChars ) Then { dont insert past }
                    inpSt [ 0 ] := Chr ( maxChars );      { maxChars! }
                  DisplayString;                  { -display the new string }
                End;
    Del       : If funcKey Then                   { Delete character at CP }
```

Listing 9.11 continues

Listing 9.11 continued

```
                 Begin
                   Delete ( inpSt, cp, 1 );    { -delete char at CP }
                   DisplayString;              { -display the new string }
                 End;
     HomePos    : If funcKey Then              { Move to start of string }
                 Begin
                   cp := 1;                     { -reset the CP }
                   GotoXY ( cp + xPos -1, yPos ); { -reset the cursor }
                 End;
     EndPos     : If funcKey Then              { Move to the end of the string }
                 Begin
                    cp := Ord ( inpSt [ 0 ] ); { -set the CP to string length }
                    GotoXY ( cp + xPos, yPos ); { -move the cursor }
                 End;
     LeftArr    : If funcKey Then              { Move cursor left one char }
                 Begin
                   Dec ( cp );                  { -decrement the CP }
                   If cp < 1 Then               { -if at start of line, }
                     cp := 1;                   {  stay there          }
                   GotoXY ( cp + xPos - 1, yPos ); { -move the cursor }
                 End;
     RightArr   : If funcKey Then              { Move cursor right one char }
                 Begin
                   Inc ( cp );                     { -increase the CP }
                   If cp > Ord ( inpSt [ 0 ] ) Then { -if at end of string, }
                     cp := Ord ( inpSt [ 0 ] ) + 1; {  stay there          }
                   GotoXY ( cp + xPos - 1, yPos );  { -move the cursor }
                 End;
   End;
   ProcessChar := EndInput;
End;
```

For code readability, listing 9.11 uses constants instead of ASCII codes for the `case` selectors. Each selected key has its own block of code to be executed. What each block does is fairly obvious; the following are brief descriptions of what each does:

❏ **BackSpace:** This is a destructive backspace that deletes the character to the left of the current cursor position.

❏ **Enter:** This is the input terminator. The routine ends on this keystroke.

❏ **CTRL__Y:** This deletes the entire line.

❏ **Ins:** This inserts a space at the current cursor position and increments the string length accordingly.

❑ **Del:** This deletes the character at the current cursor position and decrements the string length accordingly.

❑ **HomePos:** This moves the cursor position to the start of the string.

❑ **EndPos:** This moves the cursor position to the end of the string.

❑ **LeftArr:** This moves the cursor position to the left by one position.

❑ **RightArr:** This moves the cursor position to the right by one position.

EditTool Unit

Listing 9.12 is the completed `EditTool` unit. Listing 9.13 is a simple demonstration program using both the `WindTool` unit and the `EditTool` unit. The program shows how you can use both of these units as tools to create a program that is well laid out.

Listing 9.12. EditTool Unit

```
Unit EditTool;

Interface

Uses
  Crt;

Type
  FilterType = Set of Char;

Var
  filter : FilterType;

Function ReadString ( x, y, max : Byte ) : String;

Procedure BlankXY ( x, y, max : Byte );

Procedure ResetFilter;

Implementation

Const
  Blank : String = '
  xe  BackSpace = #08; { Backspace  key }
  Enter     = #13; { Return/Enter key }
```

Listing 9.12 continues

Listing 9.12 continued

```
    CTRL_Y   = #25; { Control - Y }
    Ins      = #82; { Insert (INS) key }
    Del      = #83; { Delete (DEL) key }
    LeftArr  = #75; { Left arrow }
    RightArr = #77; { Right arrow }
    HomePos  = #71; { Home key }
    EndPos   = #79; { End key }

Var
  inpSt    : String; { Input string variable }
  ch       : Char;   { Dummy character variable }
  cp       : Byte;   { Current pointer inside input field }
  xPos,              { Global X position of input field }
  yPos,              { Global Y position of input field }
  maxChars : Byte;   { Maximum characters to be input }

Procedure BlankLine;
{ This procedure will write a blank line to the screen at the input }
{ field location, for maxChars.                                     }
Begin
  blank [ 0 ] := Chr ( maxChars );
  GotoXY ( xPos, yPos );
  Write ( blank );
  GotoXY ( xPos, yPos );
End;

Procedure BlankXY;
Var
  storeAttr : Word;
Begin
  storeAttr := TextAttr;
  TextColor ( Black );
  TextBackground ( LightGray );
  xPos := x;
  yPos := y;
  maxChars := max;
  BlankLine;
  TextAttr := storeAttr;
End;

Procedure DisplayString;
{ This procedure will write the input string to the screen at the }
{ field location, and preserve the cursor position.               }
Var
  xTmp,
  yTmp : Byte;
```

```
Begin
  xTmp := WhereX;
  yTmp := WhereY;
  BlankLine;
  Write ( inpSt );
  GotoXY ( cp + xPos - 1, yTmp );
End;

Procedure ResetFilter;
Begin
  filter := [#32..#255];
End;

Function ProcessChar ( funcKey : Boolean; ch : Char ): Boolean;
{ This function will process the character passed in through CH and }
{ take appropriate actions. If the character determines the end of  }
{ input for that line, the function will return TRUE.               }
Var
  endInput : Boolean;
Begin
  endInput := FALSE;
  Case ch of
    BackSpace : Begin                         { Destructive backspace }
                  Delete ( inpSt, cp-1, 1 );  { -delete char before CP }
                  Dec ( cp );                 { -decrement the CP }
                  If ( cp < 1 ) Then
                    cp := 1;
                  DisplayString;              { -display the new string }
                End;
    Enter     : Begin                         { End of line input }
                  endInput := TRUE;
                End;
    CTRL_Y    : Begin                         { Delete entire line }
                  BlankLine;                  { -draw blank line }
                  cp := 1;                    { -reset the CP }
                  inpSt := '';                { -reset the input string }
                End;
    Ins       : If funcKey Then               { Insert a blank space }
                Begin
                  Insert ( ' ', inpSt, cp );  { -insert the space char }
                  If ( Length ( inpSt ) > maxChars ) Then { dont insert past }
                    inpSt [ 0 ] := Chr ( maxChars );      { maxChars! }
                  DisplayString;              { -display the new string }
                End;
    Del       : If funcKey Then               { Delete character at CP }
                Begin
                  Delete ( inpSt, cp, 1 );    { -delete char at CP }
                  DisplayString;              { -display the new string }
                End;
```

Listing 9.12 continues

Listing 9.12 continued

```
    HomePos    : If funcKey Then                 { Move to start of string }
                 Begin
                   cp := 1;                       { -reset the CP }
                   GotoXY ( cp + xPos -1, yPos ); { -reset the cursor }
                 End;
    EndPos     : If funcKey Then                 { Move to the end of the string }
                 Begin
                   cp := Ord ( inpSt [ 0 ] );    { -set the CP to string length }
                   GotoXY ( cp + xPos, yPos );   { -move the cursor }
                 End;
    LeftArr    : If funcKey Then                 { Move cursor left one char }
                 Begin
                   Dec ( cp );                    { -decrement the CP }
                   If cp < 1 Then                 { -if at start of line, }
                     cp := 1;                     {  stay there          }
                   GotoXY ( cp + xPos - 1, yPos ); { -move the cursor }
                 End;
    RightArr   : If funcKey Then                 { Move cursor right one char }
                 Begin
                   Inc ( cp );                    { -increase the CP }
                   If cp > Ord ( inpSt [ 0 ] ) Then { -if at end of string, }
                     cp := Ord ( inpSt [ 0 ] ) + 1; {  stay there          }
                   GotoXY ( cp + xPos - 1, yPos );  { -move the cursor }
                 End;
  End;
  ProcessChar := EndInput;
End;

Procedure GetLine;
Var
  func,
  terminator : Boolean;    { loop control variable }
Begin
  cp := 1;                 { initialize the CP }
  terminator := FALSE;     { initialize the loop control variable }
  Repeat
    ch := Readkey;         { get keypress from user }
    func := FALSE;         { initialize function key variable }
    If ( ch = #0 ) Then    { check for an extended key press...}
    Begin
      ch := ReadKey;
      func := TRUE          { An extended key was pressed }
    End
    Else
    If ( ch in filter ) Then   { is it a valid character? }
```

```
    Begin
      inpSt [ cp ] := ch;              { insert character at CP }
      If ( cp > Ord ( inpSt [ 0 ] ) ) Then   { appending to end of string? }
        inpSt [ 0 ] := Chr ( Ord ( inpSt [ 0 ] ) + 1 ); { yes,increase length }
      Inc ( cp );                      { increase the CP }
      Write ( ch );                    { display the character }
      If ( cp > maxChars ) Then        { have we past the maximum # of chars? }
      Begin
        Dec ( cp );                    { Yes, decrease the CP }
        GotoXY ( cp + xPos - 1, yPos ); { move the cursor }
      End;
    End;
    terminator := ProcessChar ( func, ch ); { process the key press }
  Until terminator;
End;

Procedure EditLine;
{ This procedure sets up the input field and attributes }
Var
  storeAttr : Word;
Begin
  inpSt := '';
  storeAttr := TextAttr;
  TextColor ( Black );
  TextBackground ( White );
  BlankLine;
  GetLine;
  TextAttr := storeAttr;
End;

Function ReadString;
Begin
  xPos := x;
  yPos := y;
  maxChars := max;
  EditLine;
  ReadString := inpSt;
End;

Begin
  ResetFilter;
End.
```

Listing 9.13 demonstrates the basic layout one might use in writing a video-cassette rental program: first, you would need to get information about the customer and then information about the movies the customer wants to rent. This program does not provide a fully functional rental program; it shows how you can use what we have described in this chapter to create easy-to-use screens.

Listing 9.13. *Video Rental program*

```
Program Video;

Uses
  CRT,
  EditTool,
  WindTool;

Const
  MaxMovies = 5;  { Maximum movies a customer can check out }

Type
  MovieType = Array [1..MaxMovies] of Word;
  CustRec = Record
               Name : String [ 30 ];
               Address1,
               Address2 : String [ 50 ];
               City : String [ 20 ];
               Phone : String [ 14 ];
               Movies : MovieType;
            End;

Var
  cust : CustRec;

Procedure DisplayQuestions;
{ Display the questions about the customer on the screen and }
{ blank the fields for input.                                }
Begin
  GotoXY ( 2, 2 );
  Write ( 'Customer Name:' );
  GotoXY ( 2, 4 );
  Write ( 'Address (line1):' );
  GotoXY ( 2, 6 );
  Write ( 'Address (line2):' );
  GotoXY ( 2, 8 );
  Write ( 'City:' );
  GotoXY ( 2, 10 );
  Write ( 'Phone Number: ' );

  BlankXY ( 20,  2, 30 );
  BlankXY ( 20,  4, 50 );
  BlankXY ( 20,  6, 50 );
  BlankXY ( 20,  8, 20 );
  BlankXY ( 20, 10, 14 );
End;

Procedure GetCustInfo;
{ Get the information from the keyboard pertaining to the customer }
```

```
Begin
  cust.Name     := ReadString ( 20,  2, 30 );
  cust.Address1 := ReadString ( 20,  4, 50 );
  cust.Address2 := ReadString ( 20,  6, 50 );
  cust.City     := ReadString ( 20,  8, 20 );
  filter := ['(',')','-','0'..'9']; { set filter for phone type chars }
  cust.Phone    := ReadString ( 20, 10, 14 );
  ResetFilter;
End;

Procedure GetCustomer;
{ Procedure to control the window and inputting of information regarding }
{ the customer.                                                          }
Begin
  OpenWindow ( 1, 1, 80, 13, 3, (Cyan shl 8) + Blue, 'Customer Address' );
  DisplayQuestions;
  GetCustInfo;
  CloseWindow;
End;

Procedure DisplayMovieTitles;
{ Procedure to display the available movie selections }
Begin
  WriteLn ( '1. Movie Title', '11. Movie Title':30, '21. Movie Title':30 );
  WriteLn ( '2. Movie Title', '12. Movie Title':30, '22. Movie Title':30 );
  WriteLn ( '3. Movie Title', '13. Movie Title':30, '23. Movie Title':30 );
  WriteLn ( '4. Movie Title', '14. Movie Title':30, '24. Movie Title':30 );
  WriteLn ( '5. Movie Title', '15. Movie Title':30, '25. Movie Title':30 );
  WriteLn ( '6. Movie Title', '16. Movie Title':30, '26. Movie Title':30 );
  WriteLn ( '7. Movie Title', '17. Movie Title':30, '27. Movie Title':30 );
  WriteLn ( '8. Movie Title', '18. Movie Title':30, '28. Movie Title':30 );
  Write   ( '9. Movie Title', '19. Movie Title':30, '29. Movie Title':30 );
End;

Procedure DisplayMovieQuestions;
{ Procedure to display questions regarding movie choices and to }
{ blank the input fields.                                       }
Begin
  WriteLn ( 'Choice 1:' );
  WriteLn ( 'Choice 2:' );
  WriteLn ( 'Choice 3:' );
  WriteLn ( 'Choice 4:' );
  Write   ( 'Choice 5:' );

  BlankXY ( 11, 1, 5 );
  BlankXY ( 11, 2, 5 );
  BlankXY ( 11, 3, 5 );
  BlankXY ( 11, 4, 5 );
  BlankXY ( 11, 5, 5 );
End;
```

Listing 9.13 continues

Listing 9.13 continued

```
Procedure GetMovieQuestions;
{ Procedure to get the movie choices from the keyboard }
Var
  code,
  loop : Integer;
Begin
  filter := ['0'..'9'];  { filter only numeric characters }
  For loop := 1 to 5 Do
    Val ( ReadString ( 11, loop, 5 ), cust.Movies[ loop ], code );
  ResetFilter;
End;

Procedure GetMovie;
{ Procedure to manipulate the windows and control input for }
{ getting movie choices.                                    }
Var
  storeAttr : Word;  { variable to save screen colors }
Begin
  OpenWindow ( 1, 1, 80, 11, 2, (Blue shl 8) + Yellow, 'Movie Titles' );
  storeAttr := TextAttr;
  TextBackground ( Cyan );
  TextColor ( 6 );
  ClrScr;
  DisplayMovieTitles;

  OpenWindow ( 1, 13, 80, 19, 2, (Cyan shl 8) + Blue, 'Customer''s Movies' );
  DisplayMovieQuestions;
  GetMovieQuestions;
  CloseWindow;

  CloseWindow;
  TextAttr := storeAttr;
End;

Procedure CheckOut;
{ Report to screen the information received on the customer and }
{ movie selections.                                            }
Begin
  ClrScr;
  WriteLn ( cust.Name, ' who lives at:' );
  WriteLn ( '     ', cust.Address1 );
  WriteLn ( '     ', cust.Address2 );
  WriteLn ( '     ', cust.City );
  WriteLn ( 'has checked out the following movies numbers:' );
  WriteLn ( cust.Movies[1], ', ', cust.Movies[2], ', ', cust.Movies[3], ', ',
            cust.Movies[4], ', ',cust.Movies[5], '.' );
  WriteLn;
  WriteLn ( 'The customer''s phone number is ',cust.Phone, '.' );
End;
```

```
Begin
  TextColor ( LightGray );
  TextBackground ( Black );
  ClrScr;
  GetCustomer;
  GetMovie;
  CheckOut;
End.
```

CHAPTER 10

Graphics Routines

The Borland Graphics Interface (BGI) is a set of graphics routines provided by Borland International in all of its Professional Language Series packages. These routines provide a powerful interface between graphics hardware and an applications program. A programmer can manipulate the procedures and functions of the BGI to produce simple graphics images as well as stunning special effects. The BGI also allows for true device independence, freeing the programmer from the tedium of maintaining code for the various graphics standards supported by the IBM PC.

All of the code presented in this chapter will define a constant variable called PathToDrivers, which tells the program where to find the driver files and the font files. The drivers are those files contained in the BGI.ARC file with a .BGI extension. The font files will have a .CHR extension and are also contained in the BGI.ARC file.

This chapter presents the basics of the BGI and introduces methods of device-independent programming with Turbo Pascal. Also included are tips and tricks of programming each different graphics standard supported by the IBM PC and compatible computers, as well as the popular topic of transferring an image produced by the BGI to a hard copy device.

The BGI includes drivers for all of the graphics standards that are prevalent today on the IBM PC: Color Graphics Adapter (CGA), Enhanced Graphics Adapter (EGA), Multi-Color Graphics Array (MCGA), Video Graphics Array (VGA), Hercules Graphics Card (HGC), IBM 3270, AT&T 6300 modified-CGA card, and IBM 8514. Table 10.1 lists the drivers included with Turbo Pascal 5.0 and the features of each of these drivers.

301

Table 10.1. *Drivers and Their Capabilities*

Driver	Modes	Resolution	Colors
CGA	CGAHi	640 × 200	Black background, 1 drawing color
	CGAC0	320 × 200	Black, Lt. Green, Lt. Red, Yellow
	CGAC1	320 × 200	Black, Lt. Cyan, Lt. Magenta, White
	CGAC2	320 × 200	Black, Green, Red, Brown
	CGAC3	320 × 200	Black, Cyan, Magenta, Lt. Gray
CGA	MCGAHi	640 × 480	Black background, 1 drawing color
	MCGAMed	640 × 200	Black Background, 1 drawing color
	MCGAC0	320 × 200	Black, Lt. Green, Lt. Red, Yellow
	MCGAC1	320 × 200	Black, Lt. Cyan, Lt. Magenta, White
	MCGAC2	320 × 200	Black, Green, Red, Brown
	MCGAC3	320 × 200	Black, Cyan, Magenta, Lt. Gray
EGA	EGALo	640 × 200	16 Colors, 4 Video pages
	EGAHi	640 × 350	16 Colors, 2 Video pages
EGA64	EGA64Lo	640 × 200	16 Colors, 1 Video page
	EGA64Hi	640 × 350	4 Colors, 1 Video page
EGAMono	EGAMonoHi	640 × 350	2 Video pages 1 page with 64K)
IBM8514	IBM8514Lo	640 × 480	256 Colors
	IBM8514Hi	1024 × 768	256 Colors
HercMono	HercMonoHi	720 × 348	2 Video pages

Driver	Modes	Resolution	Colors
ATT400	ATT400Hi	640 × 400	Black background, 1 drawing color
	ATT400Med	640 × 200	Black background, 1 drawing color
	ATT400C0	320 × 200	Black, Lt. Green, Lt. Red, Yellow
	ATT400C1	320 × 200	Black, Lt. Cyan, Lt. Magenta, White
	ATT400C2	320 × 200	Black, Green, Red, Brown
	ATT400C3	320 × 200	Black, Cyan, Magenta, Lt. Gray
VGA	VGAHi	640 × 480	16 Colors 1 Video Page
	VGAMed	640 × 350	16 Colors 2 Video Pages
	VGALo	640 × 200	16 Colors 4 Video Pages
PC3270	IBM3270Hi	720 × 350	Black background, 1 drawing color

The BGI's most important routines are the InitGraph and CloseGraph procedures. The InitGraph procedure is used to initially place the computer into graphics mode; CloseGraph is used to completely shut down the graphics system. The InitGraph procedure is the key to the BGI's capability of creating programs that are truly device independent. The next section presents ways to get the most from this capability.

Upon calling InitGraph, the Graph unit allocates space from the program's heap memory for its variables. It is important for the programmer to know that each call to InitGraph will allocate this space, regardless of whether InitGraph has been previously called. This can be tricky, because calling InitGraph in conjunction with the procedure RestoreCrtMode to flip between text mode and graphics mode will quickly occupy heap memory, eventually causing an error to be returned by InitGraph. Only the CloseGraph procedure will deallocate heap memory reserved with a previous call to InitGraph. An example of how quickly this condition can occur is shown in the example program in listing 10.1.

Listing 10.1. *Heap Memory Test with InitGraph*

```
Program HeapMemoryUsage;
{$M $4000,0,$8000}       { Necessary to limit the amount of heap  }
{----------------------------------------------------------------}
{ This program is a demonstration of how quickly repetitive      }
{ calls to InitGraph will eat up heap memory, leaving very       }
{ little memory available for other dynamic operations.          }
{----------------------------------------------------------------}

Uses Graph, Crt;
               { Links in the necessary library units for this demo.}

Const
  PathForDrivers = '';      { Location of the BGI and CHR files. }
  ExitLoop : Boolean = False;   { Exiting condition for loop.    }

Var
  GraphDriver,          { Graph Driver to be passed to InitGraph  }
  GraphMode : Integer;{ Graph Mode to be passed to InitGraph      }
  Count : Word;         { Number of successful calls to InitGraph }
  GrErr : Integer;      { Error result from call to InitGraph     }

Begin
  GraphDriver := Detect; { Instruct Graph unit to Auto Detect     }
  Count := 0;            { Initialize counter to 0                }
  Repeat
    InitGraph( GraphDriver,GraphMode,PathFordrivers );
                         { Place computer into Graphics Mode       }
    GrErr := GraphResult;{ Store result of InitGraph call          }
    If( GrErr <> 0 ) Then
    Begin
      If( GrErr = -5 ) Then { -5 Indicates not enough memory      }
      Begin
        RestoreCrtMode;       { Make sure we are in a Text Mode    }
        Write( 'There is not sufficient memory on the Heap. ' );
        Writeln( 'InitGraph was called ', Count, ' times,' );
        Write( 'and there is now only ', MemAvail, ' bytes ' );
        Writeln( 'left in Heap Memory.' );
        ExitLoop := True; { Set condition to exit loop            }
      End
      Else
        Writeln( GraphErrorMsg( GrErr ) );
                         { Guard against other errors             }
    End
    Else
    Begin
      RestoreCrtMode;     { Flip from Graphics to Text Mode       }
      Inc( Count );       { Increment the loop counter variable  }
    End;
  Until ExitLoop;
  Readln;                 { Pause for output screen viewing.      }
End.
```

Fortunately, the BGI includes two routines that will allow switching between text mode and graphics mode, so it is not necessary to resort to drastic measures when flipping between video modes. These routines are the aforementioned `RestoreCrtMode` and `SetGraphMode`. `RestoreCrtMode` switches from graphics mode into the text mode that was active before `InitGraph` was called. The `SetGraphMode` procedure is then used to return the display to graphics mode.

This does not fully explain the capabilities of the `SetGraphMode` procedure. The `SetGraphMode` procedure will not only switch the display back into graphics mode, but it will also allow the programmer to choose any mode supported by the currently active graphics driver. The importance of this procedure is especially evident when the `Detect` feature of the BGI is used to initialize graphics mode.

For example, when using the predefined constant `Detect` to initialize graphics mode, the BGI queries the hardware to see what graphics standard it supports. Once this determination is made, the graphics mode `Detect` selects is the highest resolution that is supported by the chosen or detected driver. If you want to use `Detect` as your graphics driver and you happen to be running on a CGA or MCGA monitor, then to allow multiple colors on the screen at one time, you must use `SetGraphMode` to reset graphics mode. This concept is shown in listing 10.3.

The program example in listing 10.2 demonstrate the use of the BGI from within Turbo Pascal.

Listing 10.2. *Sample BGI Program*

```
Program BgiSampleOne;
{-------------------------------------------------------------------}
{ This is the first sample program using the BGI of Turbo           }
{ Pascal. It is intended as a general introduction to the          }
{ BGI's capabilities.                                              }
{-------------------------------------------------------------------}

Uses Crt, Graph;        { Link in the Crt and Graph units }

Const
  PathToDrivers = '';{ Used to tell InitGraph where to find its }
                     { necessary support files.                 }
  GraphModeMsg = 'System is now in GRAPHICS MODE!';
                     { Message to be output when in graph mode  }
  ExitProgramMsg = 'Press any key to exit program........';
                     { Message to be output to exit the program }
```

Listing 10.2 *continues*

Listing 10.2 continued

```
Var
  GraphDriver,
  GraphMode : Integer;    { Variables to pass to InitGraph    }
  GrErr : Integer;        { State of Graphics System.         }
  Ch : Char;              { Temporary variable for Readkey    }

Begin
  GraphDriver := Detect; { Request Auto Detection of driver   }
  InitGraph( GraphDriver, GraphMode, PathToDrivers );
                          { Initialize the Graphics Mode       }
  GrErr := GraphResult;   { See if an error occurred           }
  If( GrErr <> grOk ) Then
  Begin
    Writeln( 'An error has occurred: ', GraphErrorMsg( GrErr ) );
    Writeln( ExitProgramMsg );
    Ch := Readkey;
    Halt( 1 );
  End;
  Rectangle( 0,0,GetMaxX,GetMaxY );
                          { Places a border around the screen  }
  MoveTo( 5,5 );          { Update Current Pointer for border  }
  OutText( GraphModeMsg );{ Output the graphics message        }
  MoveTo( 5, 5 + TextHeight( GraphModeMsg) );
                          { Update Current Pointer for message }
  OutText( ExitProgramMsg );{ Output exiting message           }
  Ch := Readkey;          { Pause until a key is pressed       }
  CloseGraph;             { Shut down BGI and graphics mode    }
End.
```

Device Independence

The BGI provides ways for you to write device-independent graphics programs. The single most important procedure for accomplishing this independence is the InitGraph procedure, which takes three parameters. The first and second parameters of InitGraph instruct the BGI to query the hardware of the system running the program to determine its graphics capability. The third parameter tells the BGI where to find its necessary support files—the driver and font files with file extensions .BGI and .CHR contained in the BGI.ARC file and assumed to be in the current working directory.

Other considerations should also be made when creating a device-independent program:

❏ Make no assumptions on the resolution or screen locations of a given video mode. In other words, when placing something at the center of the screen on an EGA card at screen locations 319 on the x-axis and 174 on the y-axis, do not hard code these values. Instead, use the functions GetMaxX and GetMaxY to determine the maximum locations in each direction and divide this result by two. This way, the code is not specific to the resolution of one graphics adapter but can instead give the same results on all standards supported by the BGI.

❏ Consider what colors a particular card can produce in graphics mode. For instance, do not try to draw in both yellow and blue on a CGA or MCGA card when in its highest resolution mode; the hardware does not support this.

❏ Keep in mind what colors are available on an EGA card with only 64K of display memory.

❏ Be aware that text-based input and output (Read, Readln, Write, WriteLn) is only minimally supported by the BIOS of a color video adapter and not at all supported on a Monochrome Graphics Card.

Failure to keep these factors in the front of one's mind when creating a program that uses the BGI can result in a program that is incompatible with certain video modes and video hardware.

Listing 10.3 is an example of a device-independent program. It selects a mode that supports multiple colors (if possible on the active driver), makes no assumptions about the X and Y resolution of the screen, and outputs information to the graphics screen with the routines provided by the BGI—OutText and OutTextXY.

Listing 10.3. *Device-Independent Program*

```
Program ThirdBgiDemo;
{-----------------------------------------------------------------}
{ This is a sample program to introduce the user to a graphics   }
{ program using the Borland Graphics Interface. It also          }
{ introduces concepts of writing device-independent code.        }
{                                                                }
{ This program will first place a border around the edge of the  }
{ screen, and then proceed to use the SetAspectRatio procedure   }
{ to change the way a circle will appear on the screen. Note     }
{ the use of the Detect feature when initiating the graphics     }
```

Listing 10.3 *continues*

Listing 10.3 continued

```
{ mode.                                                             }
{-------------------------------------------------------------------}

Uses Crt, Graph;      { Link in the standard units Crt and Graph }

Const
   BorderColor : Byte = LightGreen;
                         { Color of the border that is drawn      }
   DrawingColor : Byte = Yellow;
                         { Main drawing color for images          }
   AltDrawingColor : Byte = LightCyan;
                         { Secondary drawing color                }
   EscString = 'Press any key to Exit';
                         { Message to be output when drawing image }
   Radius = 60;          { Default value for circle's radius       }
   AspectFactor = 2000;{ Multiplication factor for Aspect Ratio   }
   PathForDrivers = '';{ Location of the BGI's support files       }

Var
   GraphDriver,
   GraphMode     : Integer;{ Variables to be passed to InitGraph  }
   Ch            : Char    ;{ Temporary variable to pause program }
   GrErrorCode   : Integer;{ Used to store result of InitGraph    }
   CenterX,
   CenterY       : Integer;{ Value to store center of Screen      }
   Counter       : Integer;{ Loop control variable                }
   MaxX,
   MaxY,                    { Storage for Maximum X and Maximum Y  }
   XAsp,
   YAsp          : Word;   { Storage for current Aspect Ratios     }
   CGAColorSet,
   MonoColorSet : Boolean;{ Boolean to determine color choices    }

Procedure CreateColors( Mono : Boolean; CGASet : Boolean );
{-------------------------------------------------------------------}
{ This procedure will reset the constants defined above for        }
{ border color, drawing color, and alternate drawing color, if     }
{ mono card, a CGA card, or an MCGA card is detected at runtime    }
{-------------------------------------------------------------------}
Var
   MonoColorChoice : Word;{ We will assign the result of the       }
                           {  GetMaxColor procedure to this        }
                           { variable when an HGC is detected.     }
Begin
   If( Mono ) Then
   Begin
      MonoColorChoice := GetMaxColor;
      BorderColor := MonoColorChoice;
```

```
        DrawingColor := MonoColorChoice;
        AltDrawingColor := MonoColorChoice;
    End;
    If( CGASet ) Then
    Begin
      SetGraphMode( 1 ); { Select a CGA mode that allows Multiple }
                         { Colors on the screen                   }
      BorderColor := 1;  { Select first Palette entry             }
      DrawingColor := 2; { Select second Palette entry            }
      AltDrawingColor := 3;{ Select third Palette entry           }
    End;
  End;


Begin
  GraphDriver := Detect;{ Request BGI to use detect feature       }
  InitGraph( GraphDriver, GraphMode, PathForDrivers );
                       { Initialize the requested graphics mode   }
  GrErrorCode := GraphResult; { Check for error condition         }
  If( GrErrorCode <> grOK ) Then { If So, Act upon the error      }
  Begin
    Write( 'A graphics error has occurred: ' );
    Writeln( GraphErrorMsg( GrErrorCode ) );
    Writeln( 'Program Halted!' );
    Halt( 1 );
  End;
  MonoColorSet := False;{ Initialize variables before use         }
  CGAColorSet := False; {       "          "        "  "          }
  Case GraphDriver Of   { Take an action on the detected driver   }
    1..2 : CGAColorSet := True;   { CGA and MCGA }
    4    : SetGraphMode( 0 );{ Set 64K EGA card into mult color   }
    5    : MonoColorSet := True;  { EGA Mono       }
    7    : MonoColorSet := True;  { Herc Mono      }
    8    : CGAColorSet := True;   { ATT 400        }
    10   : MonoColorSet := True;  { PC 3270        }
  End;
  CreateColors( MonoColorSet, CGAColorSet );
  MaxX := GetMaxX;            { Determine the maximum X coordinate }
  MaxY := GetMaxY;           { Determine the maximum Y coordinate  }
  SetColor( BorderColor );{ Select the border color to be used    }
  Rectangle( 0,0,MaxX,MaxY );{ Draw the border                    }
  Counter := TextHeight( EscString ) + 2;
                        { Determine the height of the string to be }
                        { output and adjust line accordingly       }
  Line( 0,MaxY - Counter, MaxX, MaxY - Counter );
  SetTextJustify( LeftText, BottomText );
                        { Set the text justification to simplify   }
                        { output of the message                    }
```

Listing 10.3 continues

Listing 10.3 continued

```
Counter := TextWidth( EscString );
                    { Determine length of text to help in     }
                    { centering it                            }
OutTextXY( ( ( MaxX Div 2 ) - ( Counter Div 2 ) ),
          MaxY, EscString );
SetColor( DrawingColor );{ Select the main drawing color      }
CenterX := MaxX Div 2;   { Compute the coordinates of the     }
CenterY := MaxY Div 2;   { center of the graphics screen      }
GetAspectRatio( XAsp, YAsp );
Repeat
  For Counter := 1 to 5 Do
  Begin                 { Through each loop reset X Aspect ratio }
    SetAspectRatio( Counter * AspectFactor, YAsp );
    If( Odd( Counter ) ) Then
      SetColor( DrawingColor )
    Else
      SetColor( AltDrawingColor );
    Circle( CenterX, CenterY, Radius );
    SetColor( Black );
    Circle( CenterX, CenterY, Radius );
  End;
Until KeyPressed;       { Continue looping until a key is pressed }
Ch := Readkey;          { Remove the pressed key from the buffer  }
CloseGraph;             { Shut down the graphics system           }
End.
```

Data Input in Graphics Mode

We cannot use Read or ReadLn to get input into a program while it is in graphics mode because they are text-based routines. That leaves us with the only other input routine contained in any of the standard Turbo Pascal library units: the ReadKey function. This function reads a keystroke and assigns the keystroke to a character variable without echoing the input to the screen. The character can then be added to a temporary string that will eventually become the input variable, and you can handle the echoing of the inputted character with the appropriate technique based on the active video mode. By doing so, we can tailor these routines to be device independent, using the aforementioned concepts for writing such routines.

Since we will be working with string and character data in the input routine, one might wonder what the process is for inputting numerical data. An input string, which we will build with the routine, can be converted with Turbo Pascal's Val procedure into any numeric type.

In listing 10.4 we manipulate Turbo Pascal's internal storage for string variables into a routine to accomplish inputting of any type of data while in graphics mode. The following paragraphs describe some of the procedures and functions used in listing 10.4.

A general `ReadString` procedure is usable in both text mode and graphics mode; the only things that are modified for text use are how characters are echoed to the screen and how they are deleted when the Backspace key is pressed.

```
Procedure ReadString( Var S : String );
```

This procedure defines a local variable that will be the temporary working string and also a character variable to assign the result of the `ReadKey` function. The steps for building the string are these:

1. Initialize the temporary variables.

2. Loop until Enter is pressed.

3. Inside the loop, test the character just read to see whether it was a Backspace. If it was, delete the last character from the temporary working string and erase it from the current display; otherwise, add the character to your temporary input string.

The key to inputting, then, will not be the reading of the information, but the method of displaying the character entered.

To remove a character from the active display if Backspace is the input, use the `BlankIt` and `EchoIt` procedures:

```
Procedure BlankIt( Ch : Char );
```

```
Procedure EchoIt( Ch : Char );
```

The `EchoIt` procedure is the simpler of these routines; it prints the character for the currently active display type. The `BlankIt` procedure is more complex because the `OutText` routines in the BGI do not output the character in an XOR mode; whatever pixels are on in the current screen location remain on when the new character is written. This restricts us to writing the deleted character to the exact screen location it previously occupied, but doing so in the currently active background color. To do that, we have to reposition the current pointer (CP) to the beginning of the character to be erased, reset the text color, and redraw the character.

Repositioning the CP one character position is not difficult because the BGI includes the routines `TextHeight` and `TextWidth`, on which we can base our move. We make extensive use of these routines to reposition the CP and to create a cursor for use in graphics mode.

Listing 10.4 includes all three of the previously mentioned routines (ReadString, BlankIt, and EchoIt) written as a unit that you can include in your own programs. Listing 10.5 is a test program that works with the unit in listing 10.4.

Listings 10.4 and 10.5 use a few of the support routines provided by the BGI to help you write a device-independent program. Table 10.2 describes some other device-independent procedures and functions, their syntax and purpose.

Listing 10.4. Unit GrafRead

```
Unit GrafRead;
{----------------------------------------------------------------}
{ This unit provides users with a routine to input any type      }
{ of information regardless of the currently active video        }
{ display mode. This unit interfaces a typed constant that       }
{ must be set to indicate which mode is active.                  }
{----------------------------------------------------------------}

Interface

Uses Crt, Graph;         { Include the standard library units    }

Const
  GraphicsMode : Boolean = False;

Procedure ReadString( Var S : String );

Implementation

Procedure DrawCursor( On : Boolean );
{ This procedure will turn on and off a cursor for graphics      }
{ mode. The boolean parameter determines whether the cursor      }
{ will be drawn (TRUE) and when it will be deleted (FALSE).      }

Var
  CursorHeight,          { Value for the height of the cursor    }
  CursorWidth : Word;    { Value for the width of the cursor     }
  F : FillSettingsType;  { Variable to store the current fill    }
                         { settings, as we will modify them in   }
                         { this procedure.                       }
  XStart,                { Beginning X coordinate for cursor     }
  XEnd,                  { Ending X coordinate for the cursor    }
  YStart,                { Beginning Y coordinate for cursor     }
  YEnd : Word;           { Ending Y coordinate for the cursor    }

Begin
  CursorHeight := ( TextHeight( 'W' ) Div 8 );
                    { This calculation creates an underscore }
```

```
    CursorWidth := TextWidth( 'H' );
                      { Calculation to create width of cursor }
    XStart := GetX;    { Set Beginning as current X screen pos. }
    XEnd := XStart + CursorWidth;
                      { Define end location for cursor width   }
    YStart := GetY + TextHeight( 'W' );
                      { Define start location for cursor height}
    YEnd := YStart + CursorHeight;
                      { Define end location for cursor height  }
    GetFillSettings( F );{ Store current fill settings         }
    If( On ) Then
      SetFillStyle( SolidFill, GetColor )
                          { Set the fill style with drawing color }
    Else
      SetFillStyle( SolidFill, GetBKColor );
                          { Set fill style with background color }
    Bar( XStart, YStart, XEnd, YEnd );
                          { Draws the cursor using the bar proc }
    SetFillStyle( F.Pattern, F.Color );
                          { Restore the saved fill information  }
  End;

Procedure EchoIt( Ch : Char );
{ This procedure will echo the character CH to the currently  }
{ active screen type with either OutText or Write             }
Begin
  If( GraphicsMode ) Then
  Begin
    DrawCursor( False );{ Erase the cursor from current loc    }
    OutText( Ch );      { Draw the new character               }
    DrawCursor( True ); { Replace the cursor on current loc    }
  End
  Else
    Write( Ch );        { Simply write the char as its text    }
End;

Procedure BlankIt( Ch : Char );
{ This procedure will erase the last character in the input   }
{ string by redrawing the character in the current background }
{ color.                                                      }
Var
  XPos,                 { Value of current X screen position   }
  YPos : Word;          { Value of current Y screen position   }
  OrigDrawingColor : Byte;{ Temporary storage for active       }
                        { drawing color                        }
```

Listing 10.4 continues

Listing 10.4 *continued*

```
Begin
  If( GraphicsMode ) Then
  Begin
    DrawCursor( False );{ Erase the cursor                     }
    XPos := GetX;       { Store the current X position         }
    XPos := XPos - TextWidth( Ch );
                        { Calculate the previous characters     }
                        { starting X position                   }
    YPos := GetY;       { Store the current Y Position          }
    OrigDrawingColor := GetColor;
                        { Save the previous drawing color       }
    SetColor( GetBKColor );{ Set color to the background color }
    MoveTo( XPos,YPos );{ Update the current pointer            }
    OutText( Ch );      { Erase the character from the screen   }
    SetColor( OrigDrawingColor );
                        { Restore the drawing color             }
    MoveTo( XPos,YPos );{ Restore the current pointer           }
  End
  Else
  Begin
    XPos := WhereX;      { Store current X position             }
    XPos := XPos - 1;    { Backup position on character         }
    YPos := WhereY;      { Store current Y position             }
    GotoXY( XPos,Ypos );{ Update the current screen position    }
    Write( ' ' );        { Erase the character from the screen  }
    GotoXY( XPos,YPos );{ Update current screen position        }
  End;
End;


Procedure ReadChar( Var Ch : Char );
{ This procedure is necessary so we can place a cursor on the  }
{ screen if we are in graphics mode.                           }
Begin
  If( GraphicsMode ) Then
    DrawCursor( True ); { Place the cursor on the screen        }
  Ch := Readkey;        { Get a keypress from the user          }
End;


Procedure ReadString( Var S : String );
{ This is the driving procedure for this unit. If the enter    }
{ key is pressed in response to the prompt, or if the user     }
{ deletes all the inputted characters from the string, then    }
{ the procedure will not assign a value to this parameter.     }
Var
  Ch : Char;              { Inputted character from Readkey FN  }
  TempString : String;    { Input string that will be built     }
```

```
Begin
  FillChar( TempString, SizeOf( TempString ), #0 );
                        { Initialize the temporary string    }
  ReadChar( Ch );        { Get user input from the keyboard   }
  While( Ch <> #13 ) Do { Loop until the ENTER key is hit    }
  Begin
    If( Ch = #8 ) Then   { Was the delete key hit?            }
    Begin
      If( TempString[0] > #0 ) Then
                        { Check for char that can be deleted  }
      Begin
        Blankit( TempString[Length( TempString )] );
                        { Remove the char from the screen     }
        Dec( TempString[0] );
                        { Update the length of the string     }
      End
    End
    Else
    Begin
      EchoIt( Ch );        { Echo character to active display  }
      TempString := TempString + Ch;
                        { Add character to temporary string    }
    End;
    ReadChar( Ch );        { Get next input character          }
  End;
  If( Length( TempString) > 0 ) Then
                        { To determine if anything was entered }
    S := TempString;    { If so, return the result to caller   }
  If( GraphicsMode ) Then
    DrawCursor( False );{ Erase the graphics cursor.           }
End;

End.
```

Listing 10.5. *Program TestGrafRead Unit*

```
Program TestGrafReadUnit;
{----------------------------------------------------------------}
{ This program is a simple driver to test the GrafRead unit.    }
{ It will call the ReadString procedure while in both text      }
{ and graphics modes. It uses one of the stroked fonts while    }
{ in graphics mode.                                             }
{----------------------------------------------------------------}
```

Listing 10.5 continues

Listing 10.5 *continued*

```
Uses Crt, Graph, GrafRead; { Link the necessary units         }

Const
  PathToDrivers = '';       { Location of the support files    }

Var
  GraphDriver,
  GraphMode : Integer;      { Graph Driver and Mode            }
  Ch : Char;                { Pausing character                }
  InputString : String;     { String to be inputted            }
  C : Word;                 { Temporary calculation variable   }

Begin
  GraphDriver := Detect;
  FillChar( InputString, SizeOf( InputString ), #0 );
                            { Initialize string and driver vars }
  InitGraph( GraphDriver, GraphMode, PathToDrivers );
  SetTextStyle( TriplexFont, HorizDir, 2 );
  SetBKColor( Blue );       { Use other background than black  }
  GraphicsMode := True;     { Indicate we are in graphics mode }
  Rectangle( 0,0,GetMaxX,GetMaxY );
  MoveTo( 5,5 );            { Frame the screen, replace pointer }
  OutText( 'Enter a String: ' );
                            { Prompt user for input            }
  ReadString( InputString );
                            { Read the string                  }
  C := GetMaxY - TextHeight( 'W' ) - 5;
  OutTextXY( 5, C, InputString );
  Ch := Readkey;            { Echo the string to different loc }
  GraphicsMode := False;
  CloseGraph;               { Shut down the graphics mode      }
  Writeln( 'InputString = ', InputString );
                            { Echo the string in text mode     }
  ReadString( InputString );{ Read the string                 }
  Writeln( 'InputString now = ', InputString );
                            { Echo the string back to the screen}
  Readln;                   { Pause to view the output         }
End.
```

Table 10.2. *Device-Independent Procedures and Functions*

DetectGraph	Detects graphics hardware in the machine
GetGraphMode	Returns the currently selected graphics mode
GetMaxColor	Returns the highest color number supported by the active graphics mode
GetMaxMode	Returns the maximum value for a graphics mode supported by the current driver

GetMaxX	Returns the maximum resolution on the X axis
GetMaxY	Returns the maximum resolution on the Y axis
GetModeName	Returns a string that contains the name of the currently active graphics mode
GetModeRange	Returns the range of valid Graphics Mode values
GetPaletteSize	Returns the size of the active mode's palette
GetViewSettings	Returns the current XY coordinates and clip state
InitGraph	Initializes graphics mode
OutText	Outputs string information to the graphics screen at the current pointer
OutTextXY	Outputs string information to the graphics screen at an XY coordinate
SetGraphMode	Returns machine to a selected graphics mode
TextHeight	Returns the height in pixels for a string
TextWidth	Returns the width in pixels for a string

The DEMOS.ARC file on your Turbo Pascal Diskette 3 contains a good example of a large program written independent of any graphics standard. The program is called BGIDEMO.PAS and uses many of the procedures and functions discussed in this chapter. Examine BGIDEMO.PAS closely to see how to integrate these concepts into your programs. Specifically, examine the initialization routines as well as the way the routines calculate screen locations based on MaxX and MaxY instead of hard coding values.

Printing Graphics Images

With all the power the BGI gives a programmer, one feature is notably lacking: the ability to transfer a graphics screen of information to a parallel printer. This section presents two routines you can include in your programs to make such a transfer—one for an EPSON or EPSON-compatible printer and one for a Hewlett-Packard LaserJet.

The BGI does not provide a single, high-level routine for printing a graphics image, but it does provide several routines that can be used to build a powerful screen-dumping utility. We use the GetPixel function to accomplish this task; its syntax is as follows:

```
Function GetPixel( X, Y : Integer ) : Word;
```

This function will return the color at a specific location on the graphics screen. Since this routine produces only a black-and-white image, we are concerned only about a pixel being equal to the background color or some other drawing color. This corresponds to the pixel being on or off, indicating its inclusion in or exclusion from the graphics image being printed.

Listing 10.6 includes routines from the Turbo Pascal run-time library and a Text File Device Driver for the printer. The .LPT file in Turbo's standard Printer unit is opened as a text device, which means that an ASCII 26 (Ctrl-Z) character is not passed to the printer but is instead stripped by DOS from the output stream. An ASCII Z is essential to graphics output.

The first thing a graphics screen dump procedure needs to do is instruct the printer to place itself into a selected graphics mode. This mode is passed as a parameter to the procedure and transferred to the printer through an Esc code. The Esc code is printer dependent and is the first thing that needs to be changed if the routine is going to be sent to a different manufacturer's printer.

After the printer has been set to the correct mode, we use the GetViewSettings procedure contained in the BGI to determine the current viewport definition so that the printer prints only the contents of the active viewport rather than the entire video display. Once the viewport setting had been defined for the procedure, it can begin removing the pixel information from the screen and creating a byte of information to be sent to the printer.

The pixel information that will be placed into a byte variable is specific to the printer to which the image is being sent—an EPSON or EPSON-compatible in the case of listing 10.6. If you will be modifying listing 10.6 for use with some other manufacturer's printer, you will need to modify this section of the code.

For the byte-construction phase, think of each horizontal line as being made up of eight scan lines on the horizontal plane. The routine must examine each column of pixels within this line and determine which of the pixels has a color different from the background color, thus indicating that it is on. If the pixel is on, the routine turns on the corresponding bit in the data byte that will be sent to the printer. The routine progresses across the screen and down each line, repeatedly creating and sending these bytes until the entire active viewport is copied to the printer. Examine listing 10.6 to see how the routine to transfer an image to an EPSON or EPSON-compatible printer does these things. Listing 10.7 is a parallel routine for the Hewlett-Packard LaserJet printer.

Listing 10.6. EPSON Screen Dump

```
Unit GraphPRN;
{------------------------------------------------------------------}
{ This unit is designed to send graphics images to Epson-          }
{ compatible and late model IBM ProPrinter dot-matrix printers.    }
{ It takes the image from the currently active view port,          }
{ determined by a call to GetViewSettings, and transfers that      }
{ image to the printer.                                            }
{------------------------------------------------------------------}


Interface

Uses Dos, Graph;      { Link in the necessary standard units    }

Var
    LST : Text;            { New printer file variable          }

Procedure HardCopy (Gmode: Integer);
{ Procedure HardCopy prints the current Viewport to an IBM or     }
{ Epson-compatible graphics printer.                              }
{                                                                 }
{ Valid Gmode numbers are :                                       }
{     -4 to -1 for Epson and IBM Graphic Printers                 }
{      0 to 7  for Epson Printers                                 }


Implementation

Procedure HardCopy {Gmode: Integer};

Const
    Bits : Array [0..7] of Byte = (128,64,32,16,8,4,2,1);
                        { Values of each bit within byte variable }


Var
    X,Y,YOfs         : Integer;     { Screen  location variables  }
    BitData,MaxBits  : Byte;        { Number of bits to transfer  }
    Vport            : ViewPortType;{ Used to get view settings   }
    Height, Width    : Word;        { Size of image to transfer   }
    HiBit, LoBit     : Char;        {      Char size of image     }
    LineSpacing,                    { Additional  Info  for  dump }
    GraphixPrefix    : String[10];  {      "        "  "    "      }
    BKColor          : Byte;        { Value of current bk color   }
```

Listing 10.6 continues

Listing 10.6 *continued*

```
Begin
  LineSpacing   := #27+'3'+#24;  { 24/216 inch line spacing    }
  Case Gmode Of
    -1:   GraphixPrefix := #27+'K'; { Standard Density          }
    -2:   GraphixPrefix := #27+'L'; { Double Density            }
    -3:   GraphixPrefix := #27+'Y'; {  Dbl. Density Dbl. Speed  }
    -4:   GraphixPrefix := #27+'Z'; {  Quad. Density            }
    0..7: GraphixPrefix := #27+'*'+Chr( Gmode );{ 8-Pin Bit Img }
    Else
      Exit;                         { Invalid Mode Selection    }
  End;
  BKColor := GetBKColor;
  GetViewSettings( Vport );         { Get size of image to be   }
  Height := Vport.Y2 - Vport.Y1;    { printed                   }
  Width  := ( Vport.X2 + 1 ) - Vport.X1;
  HiBit := Chr( Hi( Width ) );      { Translate sizes to char   }
  LoBit := Chr( Lo( Width ) );      { for  output to printer    }
  Write( LST, LineSpacing );
  Y := 0;                           { First Y coordinate        }
  While Y < Height Do               { Do not go beyond viewport }
  Begin
    Write( LST,GraphixPrefix,LoBit,HiBit );
                                    { Tell printer graphics info}
    For X := 0 to Width-1 Do        { Go across screen lt to rt.}
    Begin
      BitData := 0;                 { Initialize to all off (0) }
      If y + 7 <= Height Then       { Make sure there are 8     }
        MaxBits := 7                { lines of info and set it  }
      Else                          { accordingly               }
        MaxBits := Height - Y;
      For YOfs := 0 to MaxBits do   { Go top to bottom on line  }
        If( GetPixel( X, YOfs+Y ) <> BKColor ) Then
            BitData := BitData or Bits[YOfs];
                                    { If pixel on, add to output}
      Write( LST, Chr( BitData ) );{ Byte is created, output it }
    End;
    WriteLn ( LST );
    Inc( Y,8 );                     { Inc by 8 as each line is 8}
                                    { actual scan line in height}
  End;
    Write( LST, #27 + 'a' );        { Send reset command        }
End;
{----------------------------------------------------------------}
{ What follows is the code for the text file device driver for  }
{ the .LST file variable defined above. This is necessary as    }
{ Turbo opens the LST device defined in the printer unit in a   }
{ "Cooked" mode.                                                }
{----------------------------------------------------------------}
```

```
{$F+}

Function LSTNoFunction( Var F: TextRec ): Integer;
{ This function performs a NUL operation on LST in case a Reset }
{ or a Rewrite is called.                                       }
Begin
  LSTNoFunction := 0;
End;

Function LSTOutputToPrinter( Var F: TextRec ): Integer;
{ This function sends the output to the printer port number    }
{ stored in the first byte of the UserData area of the Text    }
{ Record.                                                      }
Var
  Regs: Registers;
  P : word;
Begin
  With F do
  Begin
    P := 0;
    Regs.AH := 16;
    While( ( P < BufPos ) And ( ( Regs.AH and 16 ) = 16 ) Do
    Begin
      Regs.AL := Ord( BufPtr^[P] );
      Regs.AH := 0;
      Regs.DX := UserData[1];
      Intr( $17,Regs );
      Inc( P );
    end;
    BufPos := 0;
  End;
  If( Regs.AH and 16 ) = 16 Then
    LSTOutputToPrinter := 0                 { No error              }
  Else
    If( Regs.AH and 32 ) = 32 Then
      LSTOutputToPrinter := 159             { Out of Paper          }
    Else
      LSTOutputToPrinter := 160;            { Device write Fault }
End;

{$F-}

Procedure AssignLST( Port:Byte );
{ This procedure sets up the .LST text file record as would the }
{ Assign procedure, and initializes it as would a call to the   }
{ Reset procedure. It then stores the LPT port number in the    }
{ first byte of the UserData Area of the TextRec type.          }
```

Listing 10.6 continues

Listing 10.6 *continued*

```
 Begin
   With TextRec( LST ) do
 Begin
    Handle       := $FFF0;
    Mode         := fmOutput;
    BufSize      := SizeOf( Buffer );
    BufPtr       := @Buffer;
    BufPos       := 0;
    OpenFunc     := @LSTNoFunction;
    InOutFunc    := @LSTOutputToPrinter;
    FlushFunc    := @LSTOutputToPrinter;
    CloseFunc    := @LSTOutputToPrinter;
    UserData[1] := Port - 1;   { Sub 1 as DOS counts from zero    }
  End;
End;

Begin
  AssignLST( 1 );              { Sets output printer to LPT1 by }
                              { default. Change this value to  }
                              { select other LPT ports.        }
End.
```

Listing 10.7. *Hewlett-Packard LaserJet Screen Dump*

```
Unit HpCopy;
{ This unit is designed to dump graphics images produced by    }
{ Turbo Pascal's Graph Unit to a Hewlett-Packard LaserJet      }
{ printer.  You must be sure to set the aspect ratio with the  }
{ command SetAspectRatio( 3000,5000 ); before drawing a        }
{ circular object.                                             }
{ If the Aspect Ratio is NOT set, the image produced by this   }
{ routine will appear ellipsoid.                              }

Interface

Uses
  Crt, Dos, Graph;   { Link in the necessary support units    }

Var
   LST : Text;       { MUST Redefine because Turbo's Printer  }
                     { Unit does not open  LST with the File  }
                     { Mode as BINARY.                        }

Procedure HPHardCopy;

Implementation
```

```
Var
  Width, Height : Word;   { Variables used to store settings }
  Vport : ViewPortType;   { Used in the call GetViewSettings }

{$F+}
Function LSTNoFunction( Var F : TextRec ) : Integer;
{ This function performs a NUL operation for a Reset or     }
{ Rewrite on LST.                                           }

Begin
  LSTNoFunction := 0;
End;


Function LSTOutPutToPrinter( Var F : TextRec ) : Integer;
{ LSTOutPutToPrinter sends the output to the Printer port   }
{ number stored in the first byte of the UserData area of   }
{ the Text Record.                                          }

Var
  Regs : Registers;
  P : Word;

Begin
  With F Do
  Begin
    P := 0;
    Regs.AH := 16;
    While( P < BufPos ) and ( ( Regs.AH And 16 ) = 16 ) Do
    Begin
      Regs.AL := Ord( BufPtr^[P] );
      Regs.AH := 0;
      Regs.DX := UserData[1];
      Intr( $17, Regs );
      Inc( P );
    End;
    BufPos := 0;
  End;
  If( ( Regs.AH And 16 ) = 16 ) Then
    LstOutPutToPrinter := 0            { No Error              }
  Else
    If( ( Regs.AH And 32 ) = 32 ) Then
      LSTOutPutToPrinter := 159    { Out of Paper          }
    Else
      LSTOutPutToPrinter := 160;   { Device Write Fault }
End;
{$F-}


Procedure AssignLST( Port : Byte );
{ AssignLST both sets up the LST text file record as would }
```

Listing 10.*7 *continues

Listing 10.7 continued

```
{ ASSIGN, and initializes it as would a RESET.            }
{ The parameter  passed to this  procedure  corresponds to }
{ DOS's  LPT  number.  It is set  to 1 by default, but can }
{ easily be  changed to any  LPT  number by  changing  the }
{ parameter  passed  to  this  procedure  in  this unit's }
{ initialization code.                                     }

Begin
  With TextRec( Lst ) Do
  Begin
    Handle := $FFF0;
    Mode := fmOutput;
    BufSize := SizeOf( Buffer );
    BufPtr := @Buffer;
    BufPos := 0;
    OpenFunc := @LSTNoFunction;
    InOutFunc := @LSTOutPutToPrinter;
    FlushFunc := @LSTOutPutToPrinter;
    CloseFunc := @LSTOutPutToPrinter;
    UserData[1] := Port - 1;
  End;
End;


Procedure HPHardCopy;
{ Unlike Graphix Toolbox procedure HardCopy, this procedure }
{ has no parameters, though it could easily be rewritten to }
{ include  resolution in dots  per inch,  starting  column, }
{ inverse image, etc.                                       }
{                                                           }

Const
  DotsPerInch  = '100';
                    { 100 dots per inch  gives  full-screen }
                    { width of 7.2 inches for Hercules card }
                    { graphs, 6.4 inches for IBM color card }
                    { and 6.4  inches  for EGA card.  Other }
                    { allowable values are 75, 150, and 300.}
                    { 75 dots  per  inch  will  produce  a }
                    { larger full-screen graph which may be }
                    { too  large  to  fit  on an  8 1/2 inch }
                    { page; 150 and 300  dots per inch will }
                    { produce smaller graphs                }

  CursorPosition = '5';
                    { Column position of left side of graph }
  Esc            = #27;
                    { Escape character                      }
```

```
Var
  LineHeader     : String[6];
                      { Line  Header used for each  line sent }
                      { to the LaserJet printer.              }
  LineLength     : String[2];
                      { Length  in  bytes of  the  line to be }
                      { sent to the LaserJet.                 }
  Y              : Integer;
                      { Temporary loop Variable.              }

Procedure DrawLine( Y : Integer );
{ Draws a single line of dots.  No of Bytes sent to printer }
{ is Width + 1.  Argument of the procedure is the row no, Y }

Var
  GraphStr       : String[255]; { String   used for OutPut }
  Base           : Word;        { Starting   position of }
                                { output byte.           }
  BitNo,                        { Bit Number worked on   }
  ByteNo,                       { Byte number worked on  }
  DataByte       : Byte;        { Data Byte being built  }

Begin
  FillChar( GraphStr, SizeOf( GraphStr ), #0 );
  GraphStr := LineHeader;
  For ByteNo := 0 to Width  Do
  Begin
    DataByte := 0;
    Base := 8 * ByteNo;
    For BitNo := 0 to 7 Do
    Begin
      If( GetPixel( BitNo+Base, Y ) > 0 ) Then
        DataByte := DataByte + 128 Shr BitNo;
    End;
    GraphStr := GraphStr + Chr (DataByte)
  End;
  Write (Lst, GraphStr)
End; {Of Drawline}

Begin {Main procedure HPCopy}
  FillChar( LineLength, SizeOf( LineLength ), #0 );
  FillChar( LineHeader, SizeOf( LineHeader ), #0 );
  GetViewSettings( Vport );
  Width := ( Vport.X2 + 1 ) - Vport.X1;
  Width := ( ( Width - 7 ) Div 8 );
  Height := Vport.Y2 - Vport.Y1;
  Write (Lst, Esc + 'E');                        { Reset Printer   }
```

Listing 10.7 continues

Listing 10.7 continued

```
Write (Lst, Esc+'*t'+DotsPerInch+'R');   { Set density in  }
                                         { dots per inch   }
Write (Lst, Esc+'&a'+CursorPosition+'C');{ Move cursor to }
                                         { starting col    }
Write (Lst, Esc + '*r1A');          { Begin raster graphics }
Str (Width + 1, LineLength);
LineHeader := Esc + '*b' + LineLength + 'W';
For Y := 0 To Height + 1 Do
Begin
  DrawLine ( Y );
  DrawLine ( Y );
End;
Write (Lst, Esc + '*rB');                { End Raster graphics }
Write (Lst, Esc + 'E');                  { Reset  printer  and }
                                         { eject page          }
End;

Begin
  AssignLST( 2 );        { This is the parameter to change }
                         { if you  want  the output  to be }
                         { directed  to  a  different  LST }
                         { device.                         }
End.
```

BGI Tricks and Tips

In this section, we discuss several, less intuitive topics than those discussed so far, including how the palette is implemented on a variety of color cards and applying that to accomplish the simple task of drawing a black image on a color background. We also describe proper use of the SetRGBPalette procedure to program colors contained in the VGA color palette.

Understanding Palettes

The concept of a palette, as far as the BGI is concerned, is relevant only on EGA and VGA video adapters because HGC, CGA, and MCGA video adapters do not have as great a range of control on the colors that they can display. The HGC, for example, is a monochrome video card and therefore can display only black and white. The CGA card's palettes in the 320 × 200 resolution mode are hard coded and cannot be changed; however, you can control CGA and MCGA drawing color when it is in the high-resolution mode (CGAHi 640 × 200, MCGA Hi 640 × 400, MCGA Med 640 × 200) by calling the SetBKColor procedure and passing it the desired drawing color.

MCGA Palette

The MCGA card has some programmability over its displayable colors in its 320 × 200 four-color modes, but this capability is not implemented by the BGI in Turbo Pascal. As with the CGA high-resolution mode, you can control the drawing color used in the MCGAMed and MCGAHi mode by calling the SetBKColor procedure.

EGA Palette

The EGA palette contains 16 entries, numbered 0 through 15. Each of these entries can contain a value between 0 and 127 known as the palette entry's *raw color value*. This value is the one that actually controls the way the color appears on the screen. Even though the palette numbers are in contiguous order, the raw color values they contain are not. Figure 10.1 shows how the EGA's default palette and raw color values are configured.

Fig. 10.1. *Default EGA palette.*

Entry Number	0	1	2	3	4	5	6	7	8	9	10	11	12	13	14	15
Color Value	0	1	2	3	4	5	20	7	56	57	58	59	60	61	62	63

The BGI contains two procedures that modify the raw color value contained within each of the EGA's palette entries. The procedure that modifies these entries is the SetPalette procedure. The other BGI routine that modifies the palette is the SetBKColor procedure, which places the raw color value contained in the requested palette entry (the parameter that was passed to SetBKColor) into palette entry zero so that the background color comes from the zeroth entry of the palette. Figure 10.2 shows what the EGA's palette will look like after the statement SetBKColor(15); is executed.

Fig. 10.2. *EGA palette after using* `SetBKColor` *call.*

Entry Number	0	1	2	3	4	5	6	7	8	9	10	11	12	13	14	15
Color Value	63	1	2	3	4	5	20	7	56	57	58	59	60	61	62	63

`SetPalette`, on the other hand, places the raw color value that was passed to it—that is the second parameter—into the palette entry that was passed as the first parameter. For example, when the statement `SetPalette( 2,20 );` is executed, the resulting palette will resemble figure 10.3.

Fig. 10.3. *EGA palette after using SetPalette procedure.*

Entry Number	0	1	2	3	4	5	6	7	8	9	10	11	12	13	14	15
Color Value	0	1	20	3	4	5	20	7	56	57	58	59	60	61	62	63

Turbo Pascal's IDE supports several command-line parameters. One of these, the /P, instructs Turbo to save any changes made by the program to the palette. Be sure to specify this parameter when loading Turbo for this example; otherwise, this example will not behave correctly. To understand the EGA palette better, use the integrated debugger in Turbo Pascal 5.0 to single-step through listing 10.8 in this manner:

1. Set a watch on variable P by placing the cursor on the identifier P in the variable section; then press Ctrl-F7.

2. Single-step through the code by pressing F7.

Listing 10.8. *Ega Palette Demonstration*

```
Program EGAPaletteDemo;
{------------------------------------------------------------------}
{ This program is a demonstration of the EGA palette and how       }
{ the BGI implements it. To get full benefit from this             }
{ program, you should set a watch variable on the variable P       }
{ and then single-step through the code, paying attention to       }
{ what happens to that variable as each statement is executed.     }
{------------------------------------------------------------------}
```

```
Uses Crt, Graph;          { Link in necessary library units    }

Const
  PathToDrivers = '';     { Location of support file for BGI    }

Var
  GraphDriver,
  GraphMode : Integer;    { Variables for graphics mode         }
  P : PaletteType;        { Value to hold result of GetPalette  }

Begin
  GraphDriver := Detect;{ Initialize graphics mode with detect }
  InitGraph( GraphDriver, GraphMode, PathToDrivers );
  GetPalette( P );        { Get the default palette             }
  SetBKColor( 15 );   GetPalette( P );
                          { Set background color examine palette }
  SetPalette( 5,50 );  GetPalette( P );
                          { Set Palette entry 5, examine results }
  SetPalette( 6,0 );   GetPalette( P );
                          { Set Palette entry 6, examine results }
  CloseGraph;             { Shut down graphics system            }
End.
```

VGA Palette

Like the EGA palette, the VGA palette contains 16 entries numbered 0 through 15. The default palette of the VGA card is configured exactly like that of the EGA card (see figure 10.1), but instead of corresponding to a raw color value, each entry corresponds to the DAC (Digital to Analog Converter) register in the VGA hardware. The value within each palette location can be changed on the VGA card, as it can on the EGA card, with the SetPalette procedure. Additionally, the appearance of each color on the VGA palette can be changed by using the SetRGBPalette procedure, as discussed later in this chapter.

Drawing Black on Color

Examine listing 10.9 to see how to draw a black image on a color background. This may sound like a simple task, but it often stumps users because it is not as intuitive as one would expect. The basic steps are these:

1. Initialize the graphics mode.

2. Set the background color to something other than black. You can let the user decide what color to use.

3. Define some other palette entry as black because after executing the SetBKColor procedure, no palette entry has raw color value zero (black), as shown in listing 10.8. Because you no longer have a usable black color, use the SetPalette procedure to place black into the palette entry that has now become the background color.

4. Use the SetColor procedure to set the drawing color to the entry where black now resides.

5. Draw the desired figure.

Following these steps will give you a black figure on a color background.

Listing 10.9. *Black Figure on Color Background*

```
Program BlackImageDemo;
{-------------------------------------------------------------}
{ This program will draw a black image on a color background  }
{ by manipulating the EGA palette. This routine will also run }
{ unmodified on a VGA card.                                   }
{-------------------------------------------------------------}

Uses Crt, Graph;        { Link in necessary support routines   }

Const
  PathForDrivers = ''; { Location of BGI support files         }

Var
  GraphDriver,          { Variables for InitGraph procedure    }
  GraphMode : Integer;
  MaxX,
  MaxY : Word;          { Values to store maximum resolution   }
  Ch : Char;            { Character used to pause output screen }
  ColorNumber : Word;   { Input value that is the target color  }

Begin
  ClrScr;
  Repeat                { Loop until valid input is received  }
    GotoXY( 5,2 );
    Write( 'Enter color number for background: ' );
    Readln( ColorNumber );
  Until( ColorNumber > 0 ) and ( ColorNumber < 16 );
  GraphDriver := Detect;{ Request Autodetection for graphics  }
  InitGraph( GraphDriver, GraphMode, PathForDrivers );
                        { Place system into graphics mode     }
  MaxX := GetMaxX;      { Store maximum X resolution          }
  MaxY := GetMaxY;      { Store maximum Y resolution          }
  SetBKColor( ColorNumber );
                        { Reset BK Color to selected color    }
  SetPalette( ColorNumber,0 );
                        { Place Black into selected color loc. }
```

```
SetColor( ColorNumber );
                        { Choose "new" black as drawing color  }
                        { Now draw several images on screen     }
Rectangle( 5,5,MaxX - 5,MaxY - 5 );
Circle( MaxX Div 2, MaxY Div 2, 75 );
Line( MaxX Div 2,0,MaxX Div 2, MaxY );
Line( 0,MaxY Div 2, MaxX, MaxY Div 2 );
Ch := Readkey;          { Pause for screen viewing            }
CloseGraph;             { Shut down graphics system           }
End.
```

On MCGA, CGA, and monochrome systems, you can also draw with black on white by using the following commands:

```
SetFillStyle( SolidFill, GetMaxColor );
Bar( 0, 0, GetMaxX, GetMaxY );
SetColor( Black );
```

Then you can draw your image after the SetColor(Black) procedure call.

SetRGBPalette Procedure

The SetRGBPalette procedure is used to program the DACs of VGA and the 8514 graphics adapters. We describe the VGA adapter process, but the concepts are also applicable to the 8514. This procedure programs a specific DAC of the video adapter with a new Red, Green, and Blue value, modifying the appearance of the specified color.

Listing 10.10 uses the SetRGBPalette procedure to create 16 shades of gray. First the routine uses the SetPalette procedure to redefine the video adapter's palette to use DACs 0 through 15. Then the SetRGBPalette procedure reprograms each DAC to give a different shade of gray. This program displays a sequence of bars to show that we have created a sequence of increasing shades of gray.

One thing you can do to change the effect of this program is to change the value of the CValueIncrement constant. By placing different values in this constant, you can produce a new gray scale; try values like 4, 8, 16, and 32, and examine the way they affect the gray scale produced.

Listing 10.10. *Gray Scale Demonstration*

```
Program RGBPaletteGrayScale;
{-----------------------------------------------------------------}
{ This program is a demonstration of using the SetRGBPalette     }
{ procedure. It will reset the 16 palette entries to point to    }
{ DACs 0 through 15. These DACs will then be reprogrammed to     }
{ create 16 shades of gray.                                      }
{-----------------------------------------------------------------}

Uses Crt, Graph;          { Link in necessary library units     }

Const
  PathToDrivers = '';      { Location of support file for BGI    }
  CValueIncrement = 3;     { Increment for Red, Green, Blue gun  }

Var
  GraphDriver,
  GraphMode : Integer;    { Variables for graphics mode          }
  Ch : Char;              { Character to use for pausing          }
  P : PaletteType;        { Palette record for GetPalette proc    }
  I : Word;               { Loop counter variable.                }
  ColorValue : Word;      { Value used for Red, Green, Blue gun   }
  Y1, Y2,
  YInc,
  MaxX,
  MaxY : Word;            { Values used for creating bars         }

Begin
  GraphDriver := VGA;     { Initialize graphics driver for VGA   }
  GraphMode := VGAHi;     { Initialize mode to VGAHi res mode    }
  InitGraph( GraphDriver, GraphMode, PathToDrivers );
  ColorValue := 0;        { Start with true black                }
  For I := 0 to 15 Do     { Point each palette entry to DAC I    }
    SetPalette( I,I );
  For I := 0 to 15 Do     { Create the gray scales               }
  Begin
    SetRGBPalette( I,ColorValue,ColorValue,ColorValue );
    Inc( ColorValue, CValueIncrement );
  End;
  MaxY := GetMaxY;        { Store Maximum X resolution           }
  MaxX := GetMaxX;        { Store Maximum Y resolution           }
  YInc := MaxY Div 16;    { Create YInc as 1/16 of Y resolution  }
  Y1 := 0;
  Y2 := YInc;             { Initialize values for BAR procedure  }
  For I := 0 to 15 do     { Create 16 bars on screen with our    }
  Begin                   { new shades of gray                   }
    SetFillStyle( SolidFill, I );
    Bar( 0,Y1,MaxX,Y2 );
```

```
      Inc( Y1, YInc );
      Inc( Y2, YInc );
   End;
   Ch := Readkey;          { Pause for screen viewing     }
   CloseGraph;             { Shut down graphics system    }
End.
```

Saving and Restoring the BGI Image to Disk

Many people like to create images with the BGI and then save those images to disk for later recall, which is what listing 10.11 does with the following steps:

1. Create the image.

2. Use the GetImage procedure to save the image to heap memory.

3. Open an untyped file in which to save this image, using the BlockWrite procedure. With the power of the BlockWrite procedure, we need use only one call to this routine to save the image, and we can use the BlockRead procedure to read the saved image back in when we want to restore it.

Listing 10.11. *BGI Image Save and Restore*

```
Unit BGISave2;
{ This unit will save an image on the graphics screen to the  }
{ disk file passed as a parameter.  Because the size of an    }
{ image retrieved by the GetImage procedure can be larger than}
{ 64K, it is necessary to get the image and restore it in     }
{ several steps.  It is possible to save an EGA screen in two  }
{ steps, but the VGA screen in VGA Hi res mode is simply too   }
{ large to store in two steps.  Therefore, it is necessary to  }
{ store such a screen in four steps.  Why four?  Because if    }
{ I was to use 3 steps, it is much harder to arrive at an      }
{ exact size to make all 3 clips identical in size.           }
{ The first thing the routine will do is save the Y position  }
{ of each of the four sections as a word into the image file. }
{ This is then followed by the exact information stored by     }
{ Turbo Pascal's GetImage procedure.                          }
{ To restore the image from the disk file, the restore        }
{ routine will first read from the file the four Y positions   }
```

Listing 10.11 *continues*

Listing 10.11 continued

```
{ stored in the file, and then recalculate the image size      }
{ based on the values read.  Later versions will add to the     }
{ file the size of each of the four image chunks, thereby       }
{ removing the need to pass the X2 and Y2 parameters to the     }
{ RestoreImage procedure.                                       }

Interface

Uses Graph;

Procedure SaveImage( X1, Y1, X2, Y2 : Word; FileName : String );
{ This is the routine that is called to save an image to the    }
{ specified disk file.  It first determines if the image size   }
{ can be retrieved by one call to GetImage.  This is            }
{ determined by a call to the ImageSize function, and if what   }
{ is returned is less then what can be store in one block on    }
{ the heap, one call is made to GetImage and this info is       }
{ written to the file.                                          }

Procedure RestoreImage( X1,Y1,X2,Y2,PutPat : Word; FileName : String );
{ This routine is called to restore a previously stored image.}
{ It is currently necessary to pass the X2 and Y2 parameters    }
{ to the procedure, so it can recalculate the size of each      }
{ of the four image chunks.  Later version will be rewritten    }
{ so as to remove this requirement.                             }

Implementation

Uses Dos;      { Necessary to implement the Exist function.     }

Var
  ImSize : LongInt;

Function Exists( FName : String ) : Boolean;
{ Checks for the existence of the image file.                   }

Var
  Files : String;

Begin
  Files := FSearch( FName, '' );
  Exists := Files <> '';
End;

Procedure SaveBlock( X1,Y1,X2,Y2 : Word; Var F : File );
{ This procedure will save the block of the screen defined by }
{ X1 Y1 X2 Y2 into the file specified by F.                   }
```

```
Var
  P : Pointer;       { Location in heap to store the image     }
  ISize : Word;      { Size of Image to be stored on the heap  }

Begin
  ISize := ImageSize( X1,Y1,X2,Y2 );{ Determine size of Image }
  GetMem( P,ISize );                 { Get the Memory to store }
  GetImage( X1,Y1,X2,Y2,P^ );        { Get the image           }
  BlockWrite( F, P^, ISize );        { Write the Image to F    }
  FreeMem( P, ISize );               { Release the heap memory }
End;

Procedure StoreExtendedImage( X1,Y1,X2,Y2 : Word; FName : String );
{ This procedure will break the requested image block into    }
{ the four smaller blocks.  This is necessary because some     }
{ images are too large to store in one call to the GetImage    }
{ procedure.  In such cases, we will store the image in four    }
{ different blocks within the output file.                     }
Var
  F : File;          { Output file variable.                   }
  YPos : Array[0..4] of Word; { Location to store Y coords      }
  YRemain,           { Remainder of division for image size    }
  Y : Word;          { Size of each block along Y coords       }
  I : Byte;          { Loop control variable.                  }

Begin
  Y := ( Y2 - Y1 ) Div 4; { Calculate the Y increment.        }
  YRemain := ( Y2 - Y1 ) Mod 4; { Remainder of calculation    }
  YPos[0] := Y1 - 1; { Start at one less than what was passed }
  For I := 1 to 3 Do { Figure the other three starting Y vals }
    YPos[I] := YPos[I-1] + Y;
  YPos[4] := YPos[3] + Y + YRemain + 1;{ Tweak the last Y val }
  Assign( F, FName );    { Associate the File                  }
  Rewrite( F, 1 );       { Open it up for output               }
  BlockWrite( F, YPos, SizeOf( YPos ) ); { Write the setup     }
  For I := 0 to 3 Do     { Save each block into file           }
    SaveBlock( X1,( YPos[I] + 1 ),X2,YPos[I + 1], F );
  Close( F );            { Close it.                           }
End;

Procedure StoreImage( X1,Y1,X2,Y2 : Word; FName : String );
{ This procedure will save the image if it is small enough    }
{ to fit into one block of memory on the Heap.                }
Var
  P : Pointer;                   { Memory location to keep image }
  F : File;                      { Output file variable          }
```

Listing 10.11 continues

Listing 10.11 continued

```
Begin
  GetMem( P, ImSize );          { Reserve memory for image      }
  GetImage( X1,Y1,X2,Y2,P^ );   { Save image to Heap area        }
  Assign( F, FName );           { Open the disk file             }
  Rewrite( F, 1 );
  BlockWrite( F, P^, ImSize );  { Save the info into file        }
  Close( F );
End;

Procedure SaveImage( X1, Y1, X2, Y2 : Word; FileName : String );
Begin
  ImSize := ImageSize( X1, Y1, X2, Y2 );{ Check size of Image }
  If( ImSize <= 65520 ) Then            { Size OK?            }
    StoreImage( X1,Y1,X2,Y2,FileName )
  Else
    StoreExtendedImage( X1,Y1,X2,Y2,FileName );
End;

Procedure RetrieveImage( FName : String; P : Pointer );
{ This procedure will restore an image if it was small enough }
{ to be stored with one call to GetImage.                     }
Var
  F : File;                { Input File variable              }

Begin
  Assign( F, FName );      { Associate the filename with F    }
  Reset( F, ImSize );      { Open the file for input          }
  BlockRead( F, P^, 1 );   { Read in the image.               }
  Close( F );              { Close the File                   }
End;

Procedure PlaceImage( X1,Y1,X2,Y2,PutPat : Word; Var F : File );
{ This procedure calculates the size of each image block and }
{ reads the appropriate information from the file.           }
Var
  P : Pointer;             { Pointer to where the image is stored }
Begin
  ImSize := ImageSize( X1,Y1,X2,Y2 ); { Calculate the size     }
  GetMem( P, ImSize );       { Allocate the necessary memory    }
  BlockRead( F, P^, ImSize );{ Input the info from disk         }
  PutImage( X1,Y1,P^,PutPat );{ Place it onto the screen        }
  FreeMem( P, ImSize );      { Deallocate the heap memory       }
End;

Procedure RestoreExtendedImage( X1,Y1,X2,Y2,PutPat : Word;
                                FileName : String );
{ Driving procedure that will restore each of the four small }
{ images inside the file.                                    }
```

```
Var
  F : File;           { File that stores the image          }
  P : Pointer;        { Location to store each of the images }
  YPos : Array[0..4] of Word; { Holds each Y position        }
  I : Byte;           { Loop control variable               }

Begin
  Assign( F, FileName ); { Associate the filename with F     }
  Reset( F,1 );          { Open the file for Input           }
  BlockRead( F, YPos, SizeOf( YPos ) ); { Read the info      }
  For I := 0 to 3 Do     { Now restore each of the images    }
    PlaceImage( X1,( YPos[I] + 1 ),X2,YPos[I + 1],PutPat, F );
  Close( F );            { Close the file                    }
End;


Procedure RestoreImage( X1,Y1,X2,Y2,PutPat : Word;
                        FileName : String );
{ This is the procedure that will determine how the image was }
{ originally stored.  If it was done with one GetImage call,  }
{ then this procedure will restore that one image.  Otherwise }
{ it will call RestoreExtendedImage.                          }
Var
  F : File of Byte; { Open file as byte to determine its size }
  BufPtr : Pointer; { Buffer to store the image read          }

Begin
  Assign( F, FileName );
  Reset( F );          { Open the file for input              }
  ImSize := FileSize( F ); { Determine the files size         }
  Close( F );          { Close the file                       }
  If( ImSize <= 65520 ) Then
  Begin                { If it is small enough then restore it }
    GetMem( BufPtr, ImSize ); { Get the memory to store image }
    RetrieveImage( FileName, BufPtr ); { Read image from file }
    PutImage( X1,Y1,BufPtr^,PutPat );  { Restore it to screen }
  End
  Else                 { Otherwise, must restore in four steps }
    RestoreExtendedImage( X1,Y1,X2,Y2,PutPat,FileName );
End;

End.
```

BIOS Interface to the BGI

The BIOS contains some useful routines that are missing from the BGI routines supplied with Turbo Pascal. This section presents several routines that will interface BIOS to the BGI: a function that will return the current video mode; the GetRGBPalette procedure, which uses a BIOS function and can be used in conjunction with the BGI routine SetRGBPalette; and a procedure that uses a BIOS routine to create a gray scale.

Getting the Current Video Mode

There are two ways to determine what the currently active video mode is:

- ❏ Use BIOS interrupt $10, function $0F, which will return the active mode, the number of displayable columns, and the currently active video page.

- ❏ Look at the BIOS's video display data area where the current video mode is stored.

Listing 10.12 uses the second method, because we are only interested in the number of the current mode.

Table 10.3 shows the information in the BIOS's video display data area. At location $0040:$0049 is the value of the currently active video mode. All we have to do from inside Turbo Pascal is declare a byte variable at this memory location. Then, whenever we access this variable, we can determine the active mode. Listing 10.12 presents a function to do this; save this function under the file name GETMODE.INC because we use this routine in the sample program in listing 10.15.

Table 10.3. *Video Display Data Area (VDDA)*

Memory Location	Function
$0040:$0049	Current Crt mode
$0040:$004A	Number of Crt columns
$0040:$004C	Number of Crt rows
$0040:$004E	Start of video display
$0040:$0050	Current cursor position
$0040:$0060	Current cursor size
$0040:$0062	Active screen page

Listing 10.12. *Get Video Mode Function*

```
Function GetVideoMode : Byte;
{ This function will place a Turbo Pascal variable directly   }
{ into the video display data area where the current video    }
{ mode is stored.                                             }

Var
  Crt_Mode : Byte Absolute $40:$49;
                        { Location in VDDA where mode is kept }
```

```
Begin
  GetVideoMode := Crt_Mode;
                          { Assign this value to function name  }
End;
```

GetRGBPalette Procedure

The next BIOS routine we will interface to the BGI is one to read the RGB values from a specific DAC register. The routine produced is a companion routine to the SetRGBPalette routine in the BGI. The routine makes no check to see whether it is being used on a VGA or IBM 8514 video adapter.

The BIOS routine for this procedure is interrupt $10, function $10, subfunction $15. After loading the registers with the appropriate values and calling the interrupt, we can determine the red, green, and blue values of any of the DAC registers. Listing 10.13 contains the finished routine; save this file with the name GETRGBP.INC to use it with listing 10.15.

Listing 10.13. GetRGBPalette Procedure

```
Procedure GetRGBPalette( I : Word; Var R, G, B : Integer );
{ This procedure is a companion to the SetRGBPalette procedure }
{ within the BGI. It calls BIOS interrupt 10H function 10H      }
{ subfunction 15H to get the red, green, and blue values        }
{ within the specified DAC register.                            }

Var
  Regs : Registers;           { Variable used for INTR procedure }

Begin
  Regs.AH := $10;             { Select BIOS function 10H          }
  Regs.AL := $15;             { Select subfunction 15H            }
  Regs.BX := I;               { Select the DAC to query           }
  Intr( $10, Regs );          { Call the BIOS interrupt           }
  R := Regs.DH;               { Read the red value into R         }
  G := Regs.CH;               { Read the green value into G       }
  B := Regs.CL;               { Read the blue value into B        }
End;
```

Creating a Gray Scale

The last BIOS routine used in listing 10.15 is a routine to create a gray scale on a specified range of DACs. This routine is an alternative to the previously described method of creating a gray scale. The BIOS routine will take a beginning DAC register value and then the number of DACs to be part of the gray scale. It is possible to program all of the DACs, but since the BGI limits you to 16 colors on the screen while on a VGA card, it does not make much sense to do so.

In listing 10.14, Register AH gets the value $10 because this is the BIOS function that creates the gray scale used in this routine. Next, we load the AL register with the value $1B, which is the subfunction to create the gray scaling. The BX register is loaded with the number of the first DAC to be used in the gray scale, and the CX register is loaded with the number of DACs to be involved. Listing 10.14, which should be saved under the file name GRASCALE.INC, contains the interface to this BIOS procedure; it, too, does not check which driver is running it.

Listing 10.14. *BIOS Gray Scaling*

```
Procedure CreateGrayScale( FirstDAC,NumofDACs : Word );
{ This procedure will call BIOS Interrupt 10H Function 10H     }
{ subfunction 1BH to create a Gray Scale.  It will start with  }
{ the DAC specified by FirstDAC, for the number specified by   }
{ NumofDACs.  This is an alternate to using SetRGBPalette to   }
{ create a gray scale.                                         }

Var
  Regs : Registers;              { Variable used by INTR        }

Begin
  If( NumofDACs > 0 ) Then       { Check to see if input is valid }
  Begin
    Regs.AH := $10;              { Request Function 10H         }
    Regs.AL := $1B;              { Request Subfunction 1BH      }
    Regs.BX := FirstDAC;         { Beginning DAC for gray scale  }
    Regs.CX := NumofDACs;        { Number of DACs to include    }
    Intr( $10, Regs );           { Create the Gray Scale        }
  End;
End;
```

Using BIOS Interface

Listing 10.15 contains a sample program that ties the three routines just presented into one driving program. It calls the GetRGBPalette procedure and converts the results to string data for use with the OutText procedure. Then it calls the CreateGrayScale procedure and displays a sequence of bars in the newly created gray colors. The final test is on the GetVideoMode function, which is called once from graphics mode and then again from text mode.

Listing 10.15. *Test of GetRGBPalette, CreateGrayScale, GetVideoMode*

```
Program TestBIOSInterfaceRoutines;
{----------------------------------------------------------------}
{ This program tests the collection of routines presented         }
{ earlier that interface the BGI with the BIOS. The routines      }
{ can be found in listings 10.12, 10.13, and 10.14.               }
{----------------------------------------------------------------}

Uses Crt, Dos, Graph;      { Link in necessary library units    }

Const
  PathToDrivers = '';      { Location of support file for BGI    }
  DAC = 14;                { DAC to get the RGB values from      }

Var
  GraphDriver,
  GraphMode : Integer;     { Variables for graphics mode         }
  Ch : Char;               { Character to use for pausing        }
  RedVal,
  GreenVal,
  BlueVal : Integer;       { Values of each color in a DAC       }
  VideoMode : Byte;        { Value of active video mode          }
  OutString : String;      { String used to OutText Info         }

{$I GETMODE.INC}           { Include routine from list 10.11     }
{$I GETRGBP.INC}           { Include routine from list 10.12     }
{$I GRASCALE.INC}          { Include routine from list 10.13     }

Procedure ShowGrayScale;
{ This procedure will display a sequence of bars on the screen }
{ using the first 16 palette registers.                        }

Var
  MaxX, MaxY : Word;
  Y1,Y2,YInc : Word;       { Variables used to create bars       }
  I : Word;                { Loop counter variable               }
  P : PaletteType;         { Variable for original palette       }

Begin
  GetPalette( P );         { Save the original palette           }
  For I := 0 to 15 Do      { Reset palette to 1st 16 colors      }
    SetPalette( I,I );
  MaxY := GetMaxY;         { Create 16 bars on the screen        }
  MaxX := GetMaxX;
  YInc := MaxY Div 16;
  Y1 := 0;
```

Listing 10.15 *continues*

Listing 10.15 *continued*

```pascal
    Y2 := YInc;
    For I := 0 to 15 do
    Begin
      SetFillStyle( SolidFill, I );
      Bar( 0,Y1,MaxX,Y2 );
      Inc( Y1, YInc );
      Inc( Y2, YInc );
    End;
    Ch := Readkey;              { Pause for Screen viewing    }
    SetAllPalette( P );         { Restore original palette set }
End;


Begin
    GraphDriver := VGA;    { Initialize graphics mode to VGA  }
    GraphMode := VGAHi;
    InitGraph( GraphDriver, GraphMode, PathToDrivers );
    GetRGBPalette( DAC, RedVal, GreenVal, BlueVal );
    Str( RedVal, OutString );  { Convert result for displaying }
    MoveTo( 10,10 );           { Reposition Current Pointer    }
    OutText( 'Red = ' + OutString );
    Str( GreenVal, OutString );
    OutText( ' Green = ' + OutString );
    Str( BlueVal, OutString );
    OutText( ' Blue = ' + OutString );
    Ch := Readkey;             { Pause for screen viewing      }
    ClearViewPort;             { Clear the screen for next demo }
    CreateGrayScale( 0,16 );   { Create and display a gray scale }
    ShowGrayScale;
    ClearViewPort;             { Clear the screen for next demo }
    VideoMode := GetVideoMode;
    Str( VideoMode, OutString );
    OutTextXY( 10,10, OutString );
    Ch := Readkey;             { Pause for screen viewing      }
    CloseGraph;                { Shut down graphics system     }
    GotoXY( 10,10 );
    Write( GetVideoMode );
    Ch := Readkey;
End.
```

CHAPTER 11

Expanded Memory

Once upon a time, not so very long ago, people marveled at the vast amount of memory available on the IBM PC; 640 kilobytes of memory was a lot for a microcomputer. Most microcomputers before it supported only 64 kilobytes. Now, many people—not just power users—feel restricted by the amount of memory available.

Command shells, local area network shells, device drivers, and terminate-and-stay-resident (TSR) programs all take up that precious commodity of system memory. In your CONFIG.SYS file, any device drivers that you specify to load are taking some of your RAM. Network shells can take up to 70K of memory. All TSR programs take some memory to run. What can you do to reduce the amount of memory you use? Many programs on the market today use expanded memory (EMS) or extended memory or can swap to disk. For example, SideKick Plus from Borland is a huge program, but Borland's technology allows the TSR to only take up approximately 70K of RAM by allowing it to swap to expanded memory or to disk. Another program, SwapSp from Innovative Data Concepts, allows you to run SideKick Plus with only 9K of memory by swapping to disk, expanded memory, or extended memory.

In this chapter, we discuss the two types of memory available beyond the 640K barrier: extended memory and expanded memory. This chapter does not discuss swapping code, only loading data into EMS. (For information about swapping code to disk or EMS, see Chapter 8, "Overlays.")

343

Extended Memory

Extended memory is memory physically addressed beyond the first megabyte of memory and is only available on 80286 and 80386 computers. Computers that use 8086 or 8088 chips (like the original IBM PC) do not support extended memory because they can address only one megabyte of memory.

The major difficulty with using extended memory is that the CPU must be in a protected mode to access more than one megabyte of memory. The BIOS of 80286 and 80386 PCs provides two functions to allow access to extended memory, but these routines do not allow you to communicate with other programs that may be using extended memory. If you have a disk cache or a RAM disk that is using extended memory, and you write to the same address, information will be lost.

Following are descriptors of the two available BIOS calls for using extended memory. The first routine allows you to move data from conventional memory to extended memory and back. The second routine returns the size of the extended memory. Descriptors are used by 80286/386-based machines to define the physical address and length of a memory segment. A descriptor also contains information regarding memory attributes and rights, and whether a memory segment has been swapped to disk or is in RAM. For further information, please consult a 80286/386 programmer's guide.

Global Descriptor Table

    00h - 0Fh : Reserved, set to 0
    10h - 11h : Segment length in bytes (2*CX-1)
    12h - 14h : 24 bit source address
    15h   : Access rights byte, should always be 93h
    16h - 17h : Reserved, set to 0
    18h - 19h : Segment length in bytes (2*CX-1)
    1Ah - 1Ch : 24 bit destination address
    1Dh   : Access rights byte, should always be 93h
    1Eh - 2Fh : Reserved, set to 0

Interrupt 15h: Service 87h

    Pass in:
        AH = 87h
        CX = Size of block to move in Words
        ES = Segment of GDT (Global Descriptor Table)
        SI = Offset of GDT

Pass back:
    Carry flag is clear:
        AH = 0
    Carry flag is set:
        AH = 1 { if RAM parity error }
            2 { if exception interrupt error }
            3 { if gate address line 20 failed }

Interrupt 15h: Service 88h

Pass in:
    AH = 88h
Pass back:
    AX = kilobytes of Extended Memory

Expanded Memory

Expanded memory is the second method for accessing memory beyond the 640K barrier. In 1985, Lotus Development Corporation, Intel Corporation, and Microsoft Corporation created the Expanded Memory Specification (EMS) Version 3.0. Many programs, including Turbo Pascal, work with EMS V3.2 or later. In 1987, EMS V4.0 was released; it provided many significant enhancements.

Unlike extended memory, EMS will work with the 8086 and 8088 chips as well as the 80286 and 80386 chips. To use EMS, you must have a memory expansion card and software that support one of the various versions of EMS.

Communication with the EMS is done via interrupt 67h. The various registers contain the function/subfunction to call and the parameters of each. AH is the number of the function to call, and AL is the number of the subfunction (if any). BX usually contains the number of pages. The Expanded Memory Manager (EMM) driver uses a handle stored in DX to identify the allocated memory pages.

The contents of expanded memory is swapped from the EMS memory board through a process called *bank switching* into a 64K area in the conventional one-megabyte address space. This 64K area is called the *page frame*. The page frame address uses none of the conventional 640K; it sits in the high 384K of reserved memory, with its exact location determined through an interrupt call. EMS V3.0 was set up with page frames of 16K and allows access to only 8 megabytes of memory; EMS V4.0 allows pages to have sizes other than 16K and allows access to 32 megabytes.

Using EMS

To take advantage of EMS in programs you write with Turbo Pascal, you must follow these steps:

1. Determine whether an Expanded Memory Manager (EMM) has been loaded. You cannot use the EMM interrupt to see whether it is loaded because if the EMM driver is not loaded, the interrupt is not installed. The best way to determine whether the EMM driver is loaded is by checking a location in memory for a preset value. The segment that the interrupt vector points to with an offset of 10 should contain the string EMMXXXX0. You can use the GetIntVec procedure to get the address of the interrupt handler; the code will look like this:

```
Type
  ArType = Array [1..8] of Char;

Var
  p : ^ArType;

...
GetIntVec ( $67, Pointer (P) );
p := Ptr ( Seg ( p^ ), 10 );
If ( p^= 'EMMXXXX0' ) Then
  { The EMM driver is loaded. }
...
```

2. Make a call to the EMM service to check the status of the driver and hardware. Using the EMS32 unit (shown in listing 11.1), you can make a procedure call to GetStatus. If the call fails, the function EmmError returns true; you know something is wrong with the setup.

3. Check whether there is enough memory to meet your needs. You can do this by making another call to the EMS32 unit. The procedure GetNumberOfPages takes two variable parameters. The first parameter returns the total number of pages of EMS memory installed; the second returns the number of EMS pages available. In EMS V3.0, a page is 16K; from a simple calculation—pages available times 16384 (bytes/page)—you can tell how much memory is available. The initialization section of the EMS32 unit stores the maximum number of pages available at the start of the program in the variable EmmMaxAvail.

How the EMM works is relatively simple: all you have to do is allocate your memory. Move the memory into the page frame, access memory directly through the page frame, and swap more memory into the page frame as you need it.

> **Important:** Be sure your program releases the memory when it terminates. Unlike memory in normal heap operations, expanded memory that you allocate for your application remains allocated until the machine reboots. To release expanded memory for other programs, call the `ReleaseHandle` procedure as part of your exit procedure. This will ensure that if there is an error, Ctrl-C, or normal exit, the memory will be released.

Logical and Physical Pages

EMM uses two types of pages: the physical page and the logical page. The *physical page* is the physical page in the page frame. The page frame is 64K, and each page is 16K. Therefore, there can be up to 4 legal physical pages, numbered 0-3.

The *logical page* is the page on the EMS board. You cannot access logical pages directly; you must map a logical page onto a physical page before you can read from or write to it. The procedure `MapPage` will map your logical page into your physical page.

To access physical pages, a program must determine the address of the page frame. This address varies between computers so that the EMS board is compatible with other attached hardware. The procedure `GetPageFrame` will return the segment of the page frame and is automatically done in the initialization section of the EMS32 unit in listing 11.1.

EMS Access Unit

Listing 11.1. *EMS32.PAS*

```
Unit EMS32;

Interface

Uses
  DOS;
```

Listing 11.1 continues

Listing 11.1 continued

```
Type
  HandleRec = Record
                Handle,
                Pages : Word;
              End;
  HandleAr = Array [1..256] of HandleRec;

Var
  EmmInstalled : Boolean;
  EmmMaxAvail,
  EmmTotal     : Word;
  EmmSeg       : Word;
  EmmVer       : Byte;

Procedure ReportError;
Function EmmError : Boolean;

(********** LIM EMS 3.0 or later **********)
Procedure GetStatus;
Procedure GetPageFrame ( Var pageSeg : Word );
Procedure GetNumberOfPages ( Var total, unAlloc : Word );
Procedure AllocateHandleAndPages ( pages : Word; Var handle : Word );
Procedure MapPage ( physPage, logPage, handle : Word );
Procedure ReleaseHandle ( handle : Word );
Procedure GetVersion ( var version : Byte );
Procedure SavePageMap_30 ( handle : Word );
Procedure RestorePageMap_30 ( handle : Word );
Procedure GetHandleCount ( Var num : Word );
Procedure GetHandlePages ( handle : Word; Var pages : Word );
Procedure GetPagesForAllHandles ( Var size : Word; Var ar : HandleAr );

(********** LIM EMS 3.2 or later **********)
Procedure SavePageMap ( point : Pointer );
Procedure RestorePageMap ( point : Pointer );
Procedure Save_RestorePageMap ( srcPoint, destPoint : Pointer );
Procedure GetSizePageMap ( var size : Byte );

Implementation

Var
  reg   : Registers;
  error : Byte;

Function EmmError : Boolean;
Begin
  EmmError := ( error <> 0 );
End;
```

```
Procedure ReportError;
Begin
  error := reg.AH;
  If ( EMMError ) Then
    Case ( reg.AH ) Of
      $80 : WriteLn ( 'Internal EMM software error. Possible Memory Corruption' );
      $81 : WriteLn ( 'Problem in EMM hardware.' );
      $82 : WriteLn ( 'EMM busy.' );
      $83 : WriteLn ( 'Invalid handle.' );
      $84 : WriteLn ( 'No such function exists.' );
      $85 : WriteLn ( 'No more handles.' );
      $86 : WriteLn ( 'Error saving/restoring mapping context.' );
      $87 : WriteLn ( 'Physically not enough pages. No pages allocated.' );
      $88 : WriteLn ( 'Not enough available pages. No pages allocated.' );
      $89 : WriteLn ( 'Can not allocate 0 pages.' );
      $8A : WriteLn ( 'Logical page is outside range of pages assigned to
                       this handle.' );
      $8B : WriteLn ( 'Illegal physical page number (not [0..3]).' );
      $8C : WriteLn ( 'Page mapping save area full.' );
      $8D : WriteLn ( 'Save area already contains context with this handle.' );
      $8E : WriteLn ( 'Save area does not contain context with this handle.' );
      $8F : WriteLn ( 'No such subfunction exists.' );
    End;
End;

Procedure GetStatus;
{ Return a status code indicating whether EMS and hardware are }
{ present and functional.                                      }
Begin
  reg.AH := $40;
  Intr ( $67, reg );
  ReportError;
End;

Procedure GetPageFrame { Var pageSeg : Word };
{ This procedure will return the segment of the page frame in
  PAGESEG }
Begin
  reg.AH := $41;
  Intr ( $67, reg );
  PageSeg := reg.BX;
  ReportError;
End;

Procedure GetNumberOfPages { Var total, unAlloc : Word };
{ This procedure will place the total number of EM pages in TOTAL, }
{ and the total number of unallocated pages in UNALLOC.            }
```

Listing 11.1 continues

Listing 11.1 continued

```
Begin
  reg.AH := $42;
  Intr ( $67, reg );
  unAlloc := reg.BX;
  total := reg.DX;
  ReportError;
End;


Procedure AllocateHandleAndPages { pages : Word; Var handle : Word };
{ This procedure will return an EM handle in HANDLE pointing to }
{ PAGES number of logical pages.                                }
Begin
  reg.AH := $43;
  reg.BX := pages;
  Intr ( $67, reg );
  handle := reg.DX;
  ReportError;
End;


Procedure MapPage { physPage, logPage, handle : Word };
{ This will map the logical page LOGPAGE in HANDLE into physical }
{ page PHYSPAGE in the page frame.                              }
Begin
  reg.AH := $44;
  reg.AL := physPage;
  reg.BX := logPage;
  reg.DX := handle;
  Intr ( $67, reg );
  ReportError;
End;


Procedure ReleaseHandle { handle : Word };
{ This procedure will deallocate the EM pages assigned to HANDLE }
{ and release the handle.                                        }
Begin
  reg.AH := $45;
  reg.DX := handle;
  Intr ( $67, reg );
  ReportError;
End;


Procedure GetVersion { var version : Byte };
{ This procedure will return the EMS version in VERSION. }
Begin
  reg.AH := $46;
  Intr ( $67, reg );
  version := reg.AL;
  ReportError;
End;
```

```
Procedure SavePageMap_30 { handle : Word };
{ This procedure will save the page mapping registers of the EMM }
{ hardware and associate them with the EM handle HANDLE.         }
Begin
  reg.AH := $47;
  reg.DX := handle;
  Intr ( $67, reg );
  ReportError;
End;

Procedure RestorePageMap_30 { handle : Word };
{ This procedure will restore the page mapping registers of the EMM }
{ hardware that are associated with the EM handle HANDLE that was    }
{ saved by SavePageMap_30.                                           }
Begin
  reg.AH := $48;
  reg.DX := handle;
  Intr ( $67, reg );
  ReportError;
End;

Procedure GetHandleCount { Var num : Word };
{ This procedure will return the number of active EM handles in NUM. }
Begin
  reg.AH := $4B;
  Intr ( $67, reg );
  num := reg.BX;
  ReportError;
End;

Procedure GetHandlePages { handle : Word; Var pages : Word };
{ This procedure will return the number of EM pages allocated to HANDLE }
{ in PAGES.                                                             }
Begin
  reg.AH := $4C;
  reg.DX := handle;
  Intr ( $67, reg );
  pages := reg.BX;
  ReportError;
End;

Procedure GetPagesForAllHandles { Var size : Word; Var ar : HandleAr };
{ This procedure will load AR with all the active handles and the }
{ number of EM pages allocated to each. SIZE contains the number  }
{ of active handles.                                              }
Begin
  reg.AH := $4D;
  reg.ES := Seg ( ar );
```

Listing 11.1 continues

Listing 11.1 continued

```
    reg.DI := Ofs ( ar );
    Intr ( $67, reg );
    size := reg.BX;
    ReportError;
End;


Procedure SavePageMap { point : Pointer };
{ This procedure will save the page mapping information of the   }
{ EM hardware into the buffer pointed to by POINT. To determine  }
{ the size of POINT, use Procedure GetSizePageMap.               }
Begin
    reg.AH := $4E;
    reg.AL := $00;
    reg.ES := Seg ( point^ );
    reg.DI := Ofs ( point^ );
    Intr ( $67, reg );
    ReportError;
End;


Procedure RestorePageMap { point : Pointer };
{ This procedure will restore the page mapping information of the }
{ EM hardware that is pointed to by POINT. This information was   }
{ saved by the procedure SavePageMap.                            }
Begin
    reg.AH := $4E;
    reg.AL := $01;
    reg.DS := Seg ( point^ );
    reg.SI := Ofs ( point^ );
    Intr ( $67, reg );
    ReportError;
End;


Procedure Save_RestorePageMap { srcPoint, destPoint : Pointer };
{ This procedure will save the page mapping information of the   }
{ EM hardware into the buffer pointed to by DESTPOINT. Then it   }
{ will load the page mapping information into the hardware from   }
{ the buffer pointed to by SRCPOINT.                             }
Begin
    reg.AH := $4E;
    reg.AL := $02;
    reg.DS := Seg ( srcPoint^ );
    reg.SI := Ofs ( srcPoint^ );
    reg.ES := Seg ( destPoint^ );
    reg.DI := Ofs ( destPoint^ );
    Intr ( $67, reg );
    ReportError;
End;
```

```
Procedure GetSizePageMap { var size : Byte };
{ This procedure will return the size of the buffer that is used }
{ to store the page mapping information from the hardware.       }
Begin
  reg.AH := $4E;
  reg.AL := $03;
  Intr ( $67, reg );
  size := reg.AL;
  ReportError;
End;


Type
  arType = Array [1..8] of Char;


Var
  p : ^arType;


Begin
  EmmInstalled := FALSE;
  GetIntVec ( $67, Pointer ( p ) );
  p := ptr ( Seg ( p^ ), $0A );
  If ( p^ = 'EMMXXXX0' ) Then
  Begin
    GetStatus;
    If ( Not EmmError ) Then
      EmmInstalled := TRUE;

    GetNumberOfPages ( EmmTotal, EmmMaxAvail );
    If ( EmmError ) Then
      Halt;

    GetPageFrame ( EmmSeg );
    If ( EmmError ) Then
      Halt;

    GetVersion ( EmmVer );
    If ( EmmError ) Then
      Halt;
  End;
End.
```

To use the routines in the EMS32 unit in listing 11.1, you must understand how they are set up. Each of the routines automatically sets a flag denoting an error condition. It is up to the programmer using the routines to determine whether to ignore the errors. A call to the EmmError function returns a true if an error condition has occurred. Listing 11.1 sets the routines to display the error message to the screen but take no other action.

The initialization code of the EMS32 unit sets up several global variables. Using these variables, you can determine whether the EMM driver is loaded and working properly. You can also obtain the base address of the page frame, and several other facts. Table 11.1 show what each of the variables represents.

Table 11.1. *EMS32 Global Variables*

Variable	Type	Description
EmmInstalled	Boolean	This variable will contain a true if the EMM driver is in memory and the GetStatus procedure did not detect any problems.
EmmMaxAvail	word	This variable contains the maximum number of 16K pages that are available at the start of the program. This will not reflect any memory allocations done during the course of the program.
EmmTotal	word	This variable contains the maximum number of 16K pages that are installed in the hardware. This does not reflect what is available for use.
EmmSeg	word	This variable contains the segment of the page frame.
EmmVer	byte	This variable contains the version of the EMM driver that is loaded. It should be used before accessing any of the version specific procedures.

For the EmmVer variable, the method in which the version number is stored is special: the high four bits specify the main version number; the low four bits specify the fractional value of the version number. For example, the EmmVer for EMS V3.0 will be $30, V3.2 = $32, V4.0 = $40, etc.

Sample EMS Program

The sample program in listing 11.2 demonstrates how you can use the EMS32 unit in the following real-life situation:

Suppose that you are in the middle of a fairly extensive program. You are currently in graphics mode with a complex image on the screen, but you want to go into text mode to do some work that requires intense use of the heap. How can you save the graphics image for later restoration? Especially, how can you save the graphics image without chomping up your data segment or your heap space? The `GetImage` and `PutImage` routines are perfectly suited for the job; they take an untyped parameter and store the specified screen area into the buffer for later restoration.

The problem with screen images is the amount of memory that they occupy when you step into the higher resolutions and color modes. EGA and VGA screen images require more than 64K to store. If you are in a large application, this is a lot of memory to use. Your two big options are the heap or disk. Swapping the image to disk can be slow if you are working on a floppy system, and this looks unprofessional. Swapping to the heap, on the other hand, can consume large quantities of heap space. The optimal alternative is to swap it into EMS if the user has any available. Of course, you must provide an alternative so that you can swap to the heap in case the user does not have any EMS. To really flesh out this example, you would swap to disk if not enough heap space is left.

Listing 11.2. *ExmplEMS.Pas*

```
Program ExmplEMS;

Uses
  CRT,
  EMS32,
  Graph;

Type
  HandleRec = Record
                 H     : Word;
                 P     : Pointer;
              End;
  HandleArr = Array [1..10] of HandleRec;
```

Listing 11.2 continues

Listing 11.2 continued

```
Var
  gDriver,
  gMode   : Integer;
  loop1,
  loop2   : Integer;
  storage : HandleArr; { Used to store the screen data in }

Procedure DoDrawing;
{ This procedure will draw an image on the screen using all of the }
{ available colors. If the graphics display has no colors (i.e. HGC}
{ or CGA), then space out the lines that are being drawn so as to  }
{ make a pattern on the screen.                                    }
Var
  x1,y1    : Word;
  delta,
  maxColor : Byte;
Begin
  maxColor := GetMaxColor;  { Store the value to cut down on function calls }
  y1 := 0;  { First, draw the X coordinates lines }
  x1 := 0;
  If ( maxColor = 1 ) Then
    delta := 3              { So a pattern will be drawn on the screen }
  Else
    delta := 1;
  While ( x1 <= GetMaxX ) Do
  Begin
    If ( maxColor > 1 ) Then { Don't change colors if there are no others }
      SetColor ( x1 mod maxColor );
    Line ( x1, y1, GetMaxX - x1, GetMaxY );
    Inc ( x1, delta );
  End;
  x1 := 0;  { Now draw the Y coordinates lines }
  y1 := 0;
  While ( y1 <= GetmaxY ) Do
  Begin
    If ( maxColor > 1 ) Then { Don't change colors if there are no others }
      SetColor ( y1 mod maxColor );
    Line ( x1, GetMaxY - y1, GetMaxX, y1 );
    Inc ( y1, delta );
  End;
End;

Function LargestBlock : Word;
{ This function will return the largest size block that the }
{ GetImageSize will grab based on the current display type. }
Var
  y : Word;
```

```
Begin
  y := 0;
  While ( y < GetMaxY ) Do
  Begin
    If ( ImageSize ( 0, 0, GetMaxX, y ) = $FFFF ) Then
    Begin        { $FFFF indicates that the max size has been reached }
      LargestBlock := ( y - 1 );
      Exit;
    End;
    Inc ( y );
  End;
  LargestBlock := y;
End;


Procedure SwapGraph ( toMem : Boolean );
{ This procedure will allocate memory in EMS or the heap to  }
{ store the graphics screen in if TOMEM is set to TRUE. If   }
{ not, then the image in TOMEM is restored to the screen and }
{ the allocated memory is released.                          }
{ Nested procedures are used to do the actual gruntwork      }
{ to make the code more readable.                            }
Var
  blocks,
  size   : Word;


(*************************)
(*** NESTED PROCEDURE ***)
(*************************)
  Procedure SwapToEms;
  { This is a nested procedure that will allocate memory and }
  { copy the graphics image on the screen to this memory.    }
  Begin
    AllocateHandleAndPages ( ( blocks * 4 ), storage [1].H );
    If ( EmmError ) Then
      Halt;
    storage [1].P := Ptr ( EmmSeg, 0 );
    For loop1 := 1 to blocks Do
    Begin
      For loop2 := 0 to 3 do
      Begin
        MapPage ( loop2, ( ( loop1 - 1 ) * 4 ) + loop2, storage [1].H );
        If ( EmmError ) Then
          Halt;
      End;
      GetImage ( 0, ( loop1 - 1 ) * size, GetMaxX, loop1 * size, storage [1].p^ );
    End;
  End;
```

Listing 11.2 continues

Listing 11.2 continued

```
(************************)
(*** NESTED PROCEDURE ***)
(************************)
  Procedure SwapFromEms;
  { This nested procedure will undo what the SwapToEms procedure  }
  { has done. It will copy the information in the EMS handle back }
  { to the screen and deallocate the EMS handle.                  }
  Begin
    storage [1].P := Ptr ( EmmSeg, 0 );
    For loop1 := 1 to blocks Do
    Begin
      For loop2 := 0 to 3 do
      Begin
        MapPage ( loop2, ( ( loop1 - 1 ) * 4 ) + loop2, storage [1].H );
        If ( EmmError ) Then
          Halt;
      End;
      PutImage ( 0, ( loop1 - 1 ) * size, storage [1].p^, normalPut );
    End;
    ReleaseHandle ( storage [1].H );
    If ( EmmError ) Then
      Halt;
  End;


(************************)
(*** NESTED PROCEDURE ***)
(************************)
  Procedure SwapToRam;
  { This nested procedure will allocate memory on the heap and }
  { copy the information on the screen to this memory.         }
  Begin
    For loop1 := 1 to blocks Do
    Begin
      GetMem ( storage [loop1].P, $FFFF );
      storage [loop1].H := $FFFF; { to denote RAM usage, not EMS }
      If ( storage [loop1].P = NIL ) Then
        Halt;   {no heap space available}
      GetImage ( 0, ( loop1-1 )*size, GetMaxX, loop1*size, storage [loop1].P^ );
    End;
  End;


(************************)
(*** NESTED PROCEDURE ***)
(************************)
  Procedure SwapFromRam;
  { This nested procedure will undo what the SwapToRam procedure  }
  { did. It will copy the information in the various pointers back }
  { to the video display and deallocate the pointers from the heap. }
```

```
      Begin
        For loop1 := 1 to blocks Do
        Begin
          PutImage ( 0, ( loop1 - 1 ) * size, storage [loop1].P^, normalPut );
          FreeMem ( storage [loop1].P, $FFFF );
        End;
      End;


(*************************)
(** SwapGraph Procedure **)
(*************************)
Begin
  size := LargestBlock;
  blocks := GetMaxY div size;
  If ( ( GetMaxY mod size ) > 0 ) Then
    Inc ( blocks );

  If ( EmmInstalled ) and ( EmmMaxAvail >= ( blocks * 4 ) ) Then
    If ( toMem ) Then
      SwapToEms
    Else
      SwapFromEms
  Else
    If ( toMem ) Then
      SwapToRam
    Else
      SwapFromRam;
End;

Procedure DisplayEmmInfo;
{ This procedure is called after the swapping has been done  }
{ and displays how many EMS pages are available and how many }
{ EMS pages were used to store the graphics image.           }
Var
  tmpTotal,
  tmpUnAlloc : Word;
Begin
  GetNumberOfPages ( tmpTotal, tmpUnAlloc );
  WriteLn ( 'The graphics image has been swapped to memory.' );
  If ( EmmInstalled ) Then
    WriteLn ( 'There are ',tmpUnAlloc,' pages of EMS left.' );
  If ( storage [1].H <> $FFFF ) Then
  Begin
    GetHandlePages ( storage [1].H, tmpTotal );
    Write ( 'There were ', tmpTotal,' pages allocated to' );
    WriteLn ( 'store the screen with.' );
  End;
End;
```

Listing 11.2 continues

Listing 11.2 continued

```
Begin
  ClrScr;
  If ( EmmInstalled ) Then
  Begin
    WriteLn ( LongInt ( EmmTotal )*16,'k  of EMS total on this system.' );
    WriteLn ( EmmMaxAvail,' pages available. ( ',LongInt ( EmmMaxAvail )*16,'k ).' );
    ReadLn;
  End;

  gDriver := Detect;
a
  InitGraph ( gDriver, gMode, '' );
  If ( GraphResult <> grOk ) Then
    Halt;
  DoDrawing;
  SwapGraph ( TRUE );
  ReadLn;

  RestoreCrtMode;
  If ( EMMInstalled ) Then
    DisplayEmmInfo;
  ReadLn;

  SetGraphMode ( gMode );
  SwapGraph ( FALSE );
  ReadLn;

  CloseGraph;
End.
```

The program in listing 11.2 does the following:

❏ Sets up the EMS32 unit's global variables and checks the system to see whether the EMM driver is loaded.

❏ Displays some statistics about the state of the EMS memory: how much memory is installed and how much is available.

❏ Initializes the graphics system and does a simple drawing on the screen. Some special case code is provided for displays that support only one color (Hercules monochrome and CGA high).

❏ Calls the SwapGraph procedure with a Boolean variable. If the variable is true, the graphics image is swapped to memory. If the variable is false, the opposite is done and the memory that was allocated is freed.

❏ Computes the number of 64K blocks required to store the screen. The Y-coordinate position is also computed for these blocks. If the EMM driver is installed and there is enough available EMS memory, the EMS-swapping routines are called. If not, the standard heap-swapping routines are used.

❏ During the swapping, while in text mode, displays more statistics on the EMS; shows how many pages of EMS are still available.

The heap-swapping operations `SwapToRam` and `SwapFromRam` are straightforward; for each 64K block of the screen that is going to be saved, a separate pointer is allocated using `GetMem`. Then the portion of the screen that needs to be saved is copied in with the `GetImage` procedure (note that it passes a dereferenced pointer). To copy the information back, it loops through and does a `PutImage` on the stored information. Finally, it uses `FreeMem` for the variable that was allocated.

The EMS-swapping routine is more complicated. The first job of the routine is to allocate to one handle all of the pages required. This is different from the heap routines: you can have more than 64K allocated to one handle. However, you can access only 64K at a time through the page frame. After the error condition is checked, the routine sets the pointer to the base address of the page frame.

The next step involves two loops: the outer loop is once for each 64K block of data to be moved; the inner loop is for each page of memory that needs to be mapped to the page frame. The routine maps four pages at a time into the page frame; then the outer loop continues and uses `GetImage` to load the specified block of screen data into the page frame.

To swap from EMS back to the screen is essentially the same as swapping the other way. Again there are two loops: one to map and one to `PutImage`. After the loops are finished, the memory is deallocated from EMS. Do not forget to deallocate the memory! This cannot be stressed enough. If the memory is not deallocated, it will be unavailable to any other programs after this one terminates.

Special Considerations

When using EMS from a terminate-and-stay-resident (TSR) program or an interrupt service routine (ISR), you should not map pages in and out when a program that is running in the foreground is not expecting it. Determining when a safe time has come to map pages in and out can be tricky, but there are several routines that can help: `SavePageMap_30`,

RestorePageMap_30, SavePageMap, RestorePageMap, Save_RestorePageMap, and GetSizePageMap. The EMS V3.0 routines (SavePageMap_30 and RestorePageMap_30) require the handle of the memory you want to use; the EMS V3.2 version of the same routines (SavePageMap and RestorePageMap) do not. Instead, they require a buffer in which to store the information and from which to restore it. The size of the buffer can be determined dynamically by using the procedure GetSizePageMap. The routine Save_RestorePageMap will do two jobs in one: save the information in one buffer, and restore the information that is in another buffer.

CHAPTER 12

Networks

This chapter presents two methods of writing code for multiuser situations and discusses why this area of programming requires special planning and coding. It describes a method of communicating between two users with one file, providing an example game that demonstrates this communication, and discusses file locking with DOS calls.

Other than the simple routines that DOS provides, no real standard exists among the various network APIs (Application Program Interfaces). This chapter does not describe the requirements of any specific network's API. For information about a specific API, contact the network's manufacturer.

Multiuser Difficulties

Working on a network differs from working on a single-user PC in that networks allow many users to access a common storage area. The problems that can arise from this situation may not be immediately apparent to you, so consider the following simple example:

We have a simple network set up. This network consists of a file server and two users (Bob and Doug). Bob and Doug are working on a project together. They need to write a program that manipulates widgets. They both sit down at their machines and log onto the file server. On this server, they have placed a copy of Turbo Pascal. (Of course, they have purchased a site license that allows them to have more than one person using Turbo Pascal at a time, as Borland's No-Nonsense License Agreement requires.) Because both are working on a program to manipulate widgets, each comes up with an imaginative name for his source code: WIDGET.PAS.

363

Bob and Doug are both working on network drive F: in the same directory. The problem arises when it comes time to save their programs. Bob finishes his code first, he presses F2 from the Integrated Development Environment (IDE) and saves his program to disk; then he quits Turbo Pascal and goes to get a pizza. Doug, who is only a little slower, saves his program and joins Bob to help eat the pizza.

While Bob and Doug are eating the pizza, let's look at the directory where they were doing their work. Since both were working with a file called WIDGET.PAS, we type **DIR WIDGET.***. This shows us two files: `WIDGET.PAS` and `WIDGET.BAK`. Bob's magnificent code has been overwritten by Doug's. Since Turbo Pascal was not written to support networks, it had no way of knowing that two different users were working with the same file. Bob's code was saved to disk first, and Doug's code was saved on top of Bob's.

Assuming that Doug saved his code only once since Bob saved his, Bob's code is in the file WIDGET.BAK. But this really would be a stroke of luck because Doug saves his code frequently to avoid losing anything to a possible power outage.

There are two simple ways to get around this problem:

❏ Have Bob and Doug use different file names. That way, each would have his own unique file name. This is not a practical solution for systems that have many users at a time.

❏ Give each user a separate subdirectory in which to work. That way, no two users will be working in the same directory and chance overwriting one another's code.

There are several other, more complicated options that require more explanation and a bit of program rewriting as discussed in the following sections.

File Modes

DOS supports two methods of working with files:

❏ The File Control Block (FCB) structure works with DOS V1.0 and later.

❏ The file handles method works with DOS V2.0 and later.

When opening a file using a file handle, you can specify an access mode. The *access mode* allows you to open a file for read access, write access, or read/write access. DOS V3.0 and later supports some additional modes for sharing files, as shown in table 12.1.

Table 12.1. *Bit Fields for File Mode*

Bit	Description
0-2	Access Mode (000 : Read only access) (001 : Write only access) (010 : Read/Write access)
3	Reserved
4-6 *	Sharing Mode (000 : Compatibility mode) (001 : Deny All) (010 : Deny Write) (011 : Deny Read) (100 : Deny None)
7	Inheritance Flag

* Must have SHARE.EXE loaded or a Network BIOS that supports this.

The various access modes allow or deny access to a file on a network. The three different types of access modes are for the program that is opening the file. If a program needs only to read from a file, it can use the read-only access mode. The sharing mode is used to determine how other files can interact with the file. The sharing modes (except compatibility mode) are straightforward. The compatibility mode is the default and indicates that only the current program can access the file in question.

The FileMode variable affects only files opened with Reset. DOS will not allow a file opened with Rewrite to have a sharing method. The solution is to create the file with Rewrite, close the file, and immediately open the file with Reset and the correct FileMode value.

The deny all, deny write, deny read, and deny none responses of the sharing mode mean that other files cannot open the same file in that access method. For example, suppose file X is opened by a program in a certain access mode (it does not matter which) and a deny write. Any other program that wants to read the file must open the file with a read only access method. Tables 12.2 and 12.3 indicate what FileMode must be set to open a file after another program has set a specific sharing mode.

Table 12.2. *File Mode Values*

Access Method	Compatibility	Sharing Method		
		Deny Write	Deny Read	Deny None
Read Only	0	32	48	64
Write Only	1	33	49	65
Read/Write	2	34	50	66

Table 12.3. *Sharing Modes*

File mode for original process.	File mode for subsequent accesses.
0	0, 1, 2
1	0, 1, 2
2	0, 1, 2
32	32, 64
33	48, 64
34	64
48	33, 65
49	49, 65
50	50, 65
64	32, 33, 34, 64, 65, 66
65	48, 49, 50, 64, 65, 66
66	64, 65, 66

We can use the access modes to our advantage in a program. To avoid the collision Bob and Doug had earlier in this chapter, we could enable the first program to grab the file to keep the file open, preventing any programs from subsequently opening the file for use. As an alternative, we could allow another program to look at the information in the file but not to modify it, as the following simple setup demonstrates.

Listings 12.1 and 12.2 demonstrate how more than one program can peacefully share a file. The first program will be the "master" that creates the file and periodically updates it with new information. (This could be an example of a user doing input of the latest sales figures for your widgets.) The second program, the "servant," only reads this data file as it is updated; the program draws a pie chart on the screen and changes it dynamically as the data changes. (This is similar to the powerful program

Paradox. Paradox can draw graphics based on your data.) If the information in the data file changes, the user can press the appropriate keys to redraw the graphic with the changes.

Listing 12.1. *MASTER.PAS*

```
Program Master;

Uses
  CRT;
Const
  FileName = 'F:\DATA.DAT';              { Change name to reflect }
                                         { your specific network  }


Type
  arType = Array [1..5] of Word;

Var
  f : File Of arType;
  a : arType;
  ioErr : Word;

Begin
  FillChar ( a, SizeOf ( a ), 0 );  { Initialize the array to 0 }
  Assign ( f, FileName );
  Rewrite ( f );                         { Create a brand new file }
  Close ( f );
  FileMode := 34;                  { Access read/write - deny write }
  Reset ( f );                              { Open the file }
  Repeat
    Seek ( f, 0 );                        { Move to beginning of file }
    Inc ( a[1] );                           { Change the values }
    If ( a[1] mod 2 = 0 ) Then
      Inc ( a[2] );                                     { " }
    If ( a[1] mod 3 = 0 ) Then
      Inc ( a[3] );                                     { " }
    If ( a[1] mod 4 = 0 ) Then
      Inc ( a[4] );                                     { " }
    If ( a[1] mod 5 = 0 ) Then
      Inc ( a[5] );                                     { " }
    Write ( f, a );                             { Write to the file }
    WriteLn ( a[1]:4, a[2]:4, a[3]:4, a[4]:4, a[5]:4 );
    Delay ( 1000 );                  { Slow down the file updating }
  Until KeyPressed;                            { Stop if user input }
  Close ( f );                                  { Close the file }
End.
```

The program MASTER.PAS does several things. First, it creates the data file, opening it with Reset, as required for a file to be modified by FileMode. A file opened by Rewrite will be opened in the compatibility mode of the sharing method. Immediately after creating the file, MASTER.PAS closes it and opens it with Reset and the correct FileMode value. MASTER.PAS uses file mode 34, which corresponds to a read/write access method with a sharing mode of deny write (see table 12.2). Other programs can open but cannot write to the file. Therefore, the only program modifying the data file is MASTER.PAS.

Listing 12.2. SERVANT.PAS

```
Program Servant;

Uses
  CRT,
  Graph;

Const
  FileName = 'F:\DATA.DAT';              { Change name to reflect  }
                                         { your specific network   }

Type
  arType = Array [1..5] of Word;

Var
  f      : File Of arType;
  a      : arType;
  gd,                                         { For graphics }
  gm     : Integer;                                  { " }
  loop,                                   { General purpose variable }
  pieSeg,                            { Used to hold size of pie segment }
  sub,                               { Used to track total angle size }
  total  : Word;                     { Used to hold the sum of the array }

Begin
  gd := Detect;                                { Use Auto detect }
  InitGraph ( gd, gm, '' );              { Initialize the graphics }
  If ( GraphResult <> grOk ) Then
  Begin                                    { If graphics error, halt }
    WriteLn ( GraphResult );
    Halt;
  End;
  Assign ( f, FileName );
  FileMode := 64;                      { Access Read Only - Deny None }
  Repeat
    {$I-}
    Reset ( f );              { Loop until the file exists, this   }
    loop := IOResult;         { will make Servant wait until Master }
    {$I+}                     { has started running.                }
  Until ( loop = 0 );
  Repeat
    Seek ( f, 0 );                        { Move to start of the file }
    Read ( f, a );                          { Read the information }
```

```
      sub := 0;                                  { Initialize values }
      total := 0;                                            { " }
      For loop := 1 to 5 Do
        total := total + a[loop];                { Calculate total }
      For loop := 1 to 5 Do
      Begin
        SetFillStyle ( SolidFill, loop );    { Set a unique color }
        pieSeg := Round ( ( a[loop] / total ) * 360 );
        If ( pieSeg + sub > 360 ) Then   { Make sure we do not go over }
          pieSeg := 360 - sub;              { 360 degrees.            }
        PieSlice ( GetMaxX div 2, GetMaxY div 2, sub, sub + pieSeg,
                   GetMaxY div 2 - 20 );           { Draw pie slice }
        sub := sub + pieSeg;
      End;
  Until KeyPressed;                              { Stop on user input }
  Close ( f );                                    { Close the file }
  CloseGraph;
End.
```

SERVANT.PAS starts by setting the FileMode variable to 64, which indicates the file is to be read only, deny none (see table 12.2). Table 12.3 shows that this is a legitimate value for use in conjunction with 34. Next the program loops until the IOResult function returns a value of 0. This needs to be done because we want MASTER.PAS to create the file and start running before we load SERVANT.PAS. The only case that this does not protect against is the file already existing. (We leave that up to you to work around.)

Once in graphics mode with the file open, the program can start reading and interpreting the information. After reading in the array, the program computes the sum of all entries in the array. This will be used to determine what percentage of the total each element represents. This percentage is multiplied by 360 degrees to determine the angle size. Next, by totaling the previous angles, the program obtains the start and end angle required by PieSlice for each segment. Figure 12.1 shows a finished pie chart and the associated values.

Using Files as Semaphores

A semaphore is like a flag that can contain various values. As these values change, a process may execute or have to wait for the flag to change again. Some networks support semaphores, but such support is hardware-dependent. A crude sort of semaphore can be implemented with the information that we have already discussed.

Fig. 12.1. Determining start and end angle.

50	40	30	20	10	Array Values
33	27	20	13	07	% of Total Sum
120	96	72	48	24	% * 360° =
0/120	120/216	216/288	288/336	336/360	Start/End Angle

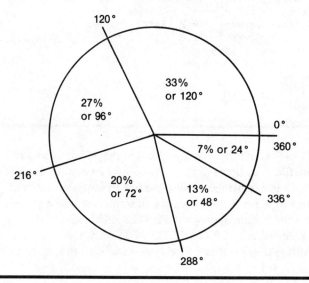

Using straightforward file access within Turbo Pascal, ignoring the sharing method, puts us into compatibility mode. This will allow only the process that opened the file to access it. All other processes will get a message that the file access is denied. If each process that needs to access the file only keeps it open briefly, all processes that need access to a file should get it.

To use a file as a semaphore, you need to implement some sort of status field within the file. You could base the semaphore on whether the file was unavailable or available. If you need more than one specific status, you can use more complex requirements. For example, listing 12.3 has several different points at which it wants other programs to be also. So a specific value is placed in the file. The program then waits for all the special status areas to contain the correct value.

Network Tic-Tac-Toe

Writing a program that will be run by more than one person at a time takes some special thinking. Not only do you have to write the program to watch for a special signal to come down the line, but you also have to send signals to the other programs to give them a chance to process.

As an example, consider a simple program that plays tic-tac-toe. The object of the game is to get three of your pieces in a row on a board that is three by three. One player uses X, and the other uses 0. Each player takes turns at placing a mark on the board to build three pieces in a row or to block an opponent.

This program could be written two ways:

1. Have one program running on one machine with both people playing on that machine.

2. Have two people playing on their own terminals that are connected through a network.

The signals that will need to be sent back and forth with the two identical programs are these:

1. The square that one player has chosen must be sent to the other player's program.

2. The first person to start the game signals that a game is ready to be started.

3. The second player signals that he or she is ready to play a game.

4. A signal indicates that a play has been made.

5. A signal indicates that a play is waiting to be made.

6. A signal indicates that the game is finished.

As we think this through, we realize that a separate status field must exist for each player. This way, both players can signal their current status and query their opponents' status. Both programs are setting their own status and checking the other status.

Additionally, you may have noticed that items 1 and 4 in your list of required signals are similar. You need to signal that a play has been made, and you have to send the position of that play. To do these things, you can define a data field in addition to the status field, which will enable you to send whatever data you need from one program to another with a file.

The first person to run the program will have to set up the data file. To determine whether the program is the first one, listing 12.3 checks whether the data file exists. If it does not, the program immediately creates the file with the `Rewrite` procedure and then writes the status information to the file and waits for the second player to start the program. If the file already exists, the program checks to see whether a game is in progress, by checking the status field for a legal starting value. If the data file indicates no game is in progress, then it sets its own status to indicate the intent to play a game.

You may wonder why we need an end-of-game signal. Both programs can independently determine whether the game is over by checking the playing field for a win/tie solution after each piece is placed. If we want the programs to behave properly, however, they should clean up after themselves. For example, suppose that the programs both end with no end-of-game signal. The data file is still on the network, containing legitimate status fields, which means that the next person who runs the program gets a message that a game is already in progress and waits for an indication that that game is finished. Therefore, when the program that was started first receives an end-of-game signal, it knows that the data file is safe to be erased.

To demonstrate why the EOG signal is important, consider a specific situation. We have two players, Player A and Player B. Player A started the game. Player A is the next person to make a move. The signal and move are sent to the data file. Player A's program realizes that the game was just won by Player A and erases the file. But Player B's program was not quick enough to read the data file between the time it was written with the new move and the time it was erased. Therefore, it goes on waiting for Player A to make its move. The solution is to have Player A make the move, realize that it won the game and wait for a EOG signal from Player B. This gives Player B time to read the file, note that Player A won the game, and signal to Player A that the game is over. Both programs are then aware that the game is over and neither needs to read the file again, so Player A can safely erase the data file.

Listing 12.3. TICTAC.PAS

```
Program TicTac;

Uses
  CRT;

Const
  PLAY = 1;        { Semaphore values }
  MOVE = 2;
```

```
    GOAHEAD = 3;
    WAITING = 4;
    GAMEOVER = 5;

Type
  PlayerRec   = Record
                    Status : Byte;   { semaphore status field }
                    Pos    : Byte;   { player's move field    }
                End;
  PlayerArray = Array [1..2] of PlayerRec;
  PlayerFile  = File of PlayerArray;

Var
  loop : Byte;
  first : boolean;       { TRUE = first program to start the game }
  FileName : String;     { Name of the data file }
  pa : PlayerArray;
  pf : PlayerFile;
  slot,                  { Holds the position of player in the playerarray }
  other : Byte;          { Holds the opponent position in the playerarray }
  pPos : Byte;
  board : Array [1..9] of Byte;      { Play field }
  solution : Byte;                   { Who won the game? }

Procedure Terminate; Forward;

Function PlayFileExists : Boolean;
{ This function will check to see if the play file that is specified }
{ in the global FileName variable exists in the current directory.   }
{ TRUE = File exists     }
{ FALSE = No file found }
Var
  ioErr : Word;
Begin
  Assign ( pf, FileName );
  {$I-}
  Reset ( pf );
  {$I+}
  ioErr := IOResult;
  If ( ioErr = 2 ) Then    { This is the first program to run }
  Begin
    PlayFileExists := FALSE;
    slot := 1;
    other := 2;
  End
  Else
  Begin                         { Somebody else already set the game up }
    If ( ioErr = 0 ) Then
      Close ( pf );
```

Listing 12.3 continues

Listing 12.3 *continued*

```
      slot := 2;
      other := 1;
   End;
End;


Procedure GameInProgress;
{ Not too elegant, but you may tailor this to your own needs }
Begin
   WriteLn ( 'Game already in progress.' );
   Halt;
End;


Function CheckSolution : Byte;
{ This function returns a one or two if there is a Win        }
{ Solution to the game. With a tic tac toe set up as follows: }
{   7   8   9                                                 }
{   4   5   6                                                 }
{   1   2   3                                                 }
{ The combinations checked will be:                          }
{        1.)  1 2 3                                           }
{        2.)  1 4 7                                           }
{        3.)  1 5 9                                           }
{        4.)  7 8 9                                           }
{        5.)  7 5 3                                           }
{        6.)  2 5 8                                           }
{        7.)  3 6 9                                           }
{        8.)  4 5 6                                           }
{ A 3 returned indicates a draw, and a 0 is returned          }
{ if the game is not over yet.                                }
Var
   Check : Array [1..2] of Boolean;
Begin
   For loop := 1 to 2 do
   Begin
      Check [loop] := FALSE;
      If ( board [1] = loop ) AND
         ( ( ( board [2] = loop ) AND ( board [3] = loop ) ) OR
           ( ( board [4] = loop ) AND ( board [7] = loop ) ) OR
           ( ( board [5] = loop ) AND ( board [9] = loop ) ) ) Then
         Check [loop] := TRUE
      Else
      If ( board [7] = loop ) AND
         ( ( ( board [8] = loop ) AND ( board [9] = loop ) ) OR
           ( ( board [5] = loop ) AND ( board [3] = loop ) ) ) Then
         Check [loop] := TRUE
      Else
      If ( (board [2] = loop) AND (board [5] = loop) AND (board [8] = loop) ) OR
         ( (board [3] = loop) AND (board [6] = loop) AND (board [9] = loop) ) OR
         ( (board [4] = loop) AND (board [5] = loop) AND (board [6] = loop) ) Then
         Check [loop] := TRUE;
   End;
```

```
        If ( Check [1] ) Then
          CheckSolution := 1
        Else
        If ( Check [2] ) Then
          CheckSolution := 2
        Else
        Begin
          Check [1] := TRUE;
          For loop := 1 to 9 Do
            Check [1] := Check [1] AND ( board [loop] in [1..2] );
          If ( Check [1] ) Then
            CheckSolution := 3  { Cat's game, no winner }
          Else
            CheckSolution := 0;
        End;
End;


Procedure Signal ( sig : Byte );
{ This procedure will set the appropriate status flag in the file }
{ specified by FileName to the value in SIG. SPECIAL CASE: If the }
{ flag SIG = PLAY, this procedure will determine if a game is     }
{ already in progress and will terminate the program if so.       }
Begin
  Assign ( pf, FileName );
  {$I-}
  Repeat                       { Repeat until the file is not    }
    Reset ( pf );              { locked. File is locked when     }
  Until ( IOResult = 0 );      { the other program is accessing. }
  {$I+}
  Read ( pf, pa );             { Read the player information }

  Case ( sig ) Of
      Move: Begin
              pa [ slot ].Pos := pPos;
              pa [ slot ].Status := MOVE;
              pa [ other ].Status := GOAHEAD;
            End;
      Play: Begin
              If ( pa [ slot ].Status <> WAITING ) Then
                GameInProgress;
              pa [ slot ].Status := PLAY;
            End;
      GameOver : pa [ slot ].Status := GAMEOVER;
  End;
  Seek ( pf, 0 );                    { Move to the start of the file }
  Write ( pf, pa );                  { Write the new information out }
  Close ( pf );                      { Close the file }
End;
```

Listing 12.3 continues

Listing 12.3 *continued*

```
Procedure WaitFor ( position, sig : Byte );
{ This procedure will wait for the appropriate status flag in the }
{ file specified by FileName to be set to the value in SIG.        }
Begin
  Assign ( pf, FileName );
  Repeat
    {$I-}
    Repeat
      Reset ( pf );              { Repeat until the file is not locked }
    Until ( IOResult = 0 );
    {$I+}
    Read ( pf, pa );             { Read the player information in }
    Close ( pf );                { Close the file }
    Delay ( 500 );      { Delay to give the other program a chance  }
                        { to change the status.                     }
  Until ( pa [ position ].Status = sig );
  If ( pa [ other ].Status in [Move,GameOver] ) Then
    board [ pa [ other ].Pos ] := other;
End;

Procedure Terminate;
{ This procedure will be called when the current program has }
{ determined that the game is over. It will either set the   }
{ EOG ( End of Game ) signal and end, or will wait for the   }
{ other program to signal end of game, then erase the file   }
{ and end.                                                   }
Begin
  If ( solution = 3 ) Then
    WriteLn ( 'Sorry, no winner in this game.' )
  Else
  If ( solution = slot ) Then
    WriteLn ( 'Congratulations! You won the game!' )
  Else
    WriteLn ( 'I am sorry, you lost the game.' );
  Signal ( GameOver );
  If ( slot = 1 ) Then
  Begin
    WaitFor ( other, GameOver );
    Assign ( pf, FileName );
    {$I-}
    Erase ( pf );
    {$I+}
  End;
End;

Procedure CreatePlayFile;
{ This procedure will create a new Play File, the name of this }
{ file is specified by the variable FileName.                  }
```

```
Begin
  Assign ( pf, FileName );
  Rewrite ( pf );
  pa [ slot ].Status := Play;
  pa [ other ].Status := Waiting;
  Write ( pf, pa );
  Close ( pf );
End;

Function XXorOO ( b : Byte ) : String;
Begin
  If ( board [ b ] = 1 ) Then
    XXorOO := 'XX'
  Else
  If ( board [ b ] = 2 ) Then
    XXorOO := 'OO'
  Else
    XXorOO := '  ';
End;

Procedure ShowBoard;
Var
  oldWindMin,
  oldWindMax : Word;
Begin
  oldWindMin := WindMin;
  oldWindMax := WindMax;
  Window ( 1,1,20,8 );
  ClrScr;
  WriteLn ( XXorOO ( 7 ):4, ' |', XXorOO ( 8 ):4, ' |', XXorOO ( 9 ):3 );
  WriteLn ( ' ----+-----+----' );
  WriteLn ( XXorOO ( 4 ):4, ' |', XXorOO ( 5 ):4, ' |', XXorOO ( 6 ):3 );
  WriteLn ( ' ----+-----+----' );
  WriteLn ( XXorOO ( 1 ):4, ' |', XXorOO ( 2 ):4, ' |', XXorOO ( 3 ):3 );
  WindMin := oldWindMin;
  WindMax := oldWindMax;
End;

Procedure GetMove;
{ This procedure will get the move of the player and make sure }
{ that it is a valid move.                                     }
Var
  x, y : Byte;
Begin
  ShowBoard;
  Repeat
    Window ( 1, 20, 80, 25 );
    ClrScr;
```

Listing 12.3 continues

Listing 12.3 *continued*

```
    Write ( 'What is your move? ' );
    ReadLn ( pPos );
  Until ( pPos in [1..9] ) AND ( board [ pPos ] = 0 );
  board [ pPos ] := Slot;
  ShowBoard;
End;

Begin
  ClrScr;
  CheckBreak := FALSE;              { Initialize the variables }
  For loop := 1 to 9 Do                     { " }
    board [ loop ] := 0;                    { " }
  FileName := 'F:\tictac.dat';              { " }   { Change name to reflect }
                                                    { your specific network  }

  If PlayFileExists Then
  Begin
    Signal ( Play ); { signal will abort if another game is in progress }
    First := FALSE;
    ShowBoard;        { display the empty playing field }
  End
  Else
  Begin
    CreatePlayFile;
    First := TRUE;
    WriteLn ( 'Waiting for other player to join game.' );
    WaitFor ( other, Play );
    ClrScr;
    GetMove;
    Signal ( Move );
  End;
  Repeat
    WaitFor ( slot, GoAhead );
    solution := CheckSolution;
    if ( Solution = 0 ) Then
    Begin
      GetMove;
      Signal ( Move );
    End;
    solution := CheckSolution;
  Until ( solution in [1..3] );
  ShowBoard;
  Terminate;
End.
```

TICTAC.PAS is mainly based on two procedures: WaitFor and Signal. These routines are how the programs communicate with each other. WaitFor waits until the status field of the player specified is set to a certain value. Signal sets the current player's status field to the value specified.

By examining the main code of the program, you can get a feel for how the semaphores work. One program will get to a certain point and wait for the other program to catch up. Then the first program proceeds to the next waiting point. The two programs are working side by side and using the data file to communicate with one another.

Record Locking

DOS V3.0 and later supports an interrupt to do record locking. *Record locking* is an alternative to preventing other programs from accessing any part of a file or allowing other programs to read only. With this interrupt (interrupt $21, function $5C), you can allow other programs to access the same file and only lock them out of portions of the file. The reason for locking only a portion of a file is so that it can be updated.

For example, a customer service department takes calls all day from customers making orders, doing inquiries, or getting returned materials authorization (RMA) numbers. Suppose all of the customer service representatives are connected on a network. One data file contains the information for all of the customers. With 20 people in the department, the data entry program would be slow if the entire file was locked each time it was accessed. By contrast, if the only record locked were the record of the particular customer being serviced, there would not be much of a slowdown. Since a customer can only be talking to one representative at a time, the other representatives do not have to worry about the record they want to look up being locked. There may be some collisions of two people looking at the same record, but that was taken into account when this interrupt was written.

To lock or unlock an entry in a file, you have to know two things about the file: the entry's length and its position in the file. If you are going to be locking only one record at a time, this can be easy to determine; the entry's length is the size of the record entry. You can get this value by using the SizeOf function to return the size of the object with which you are working. The offset is relatively simple to find: determine the number of entries previous to this entry and multiply that times the SizeOf the record. The following lines of code define a sample record structure.

```
Var
  Rec : Record
          i : Integer;
          s : String;
        End;
```

The size of `Rec` (as determined by `SizeOf`) is 258 bytes; an integer is 2 bytes, and a string is 256 bytes. When the size of the entry has been determined, you want to find the offset. The offset of the first entry would be 0 because entries precede it. To find the offset, multiply the number of entries preceding an entry times the size of the entry ($0 \times 258 = 0$). The third entry has an offset of 516 (two previous entries times size: $2 \times 258 = 516$).

Here are three things to remember when creating a program that uses record locking:

❏ The file on which you are performing record locking must have been opened in a specific shared mode. You can use record locking on files that were opened with `deny read` or `deny none` and on files opened for `write only` access or `read/write` access with `deny write`.

❏ You must never close a file that contains a locked record; this includes closing the file with the `Close` procedure, as well as closing it by terminating the program. Therefore, it is a good idea to use an exit procedure that goes through and tries to unlock all records (errors will occur when the exit procedure tries to unlock a record that is already unlocked, but such errors can be ignored).

❏ To prevent collisions, try to lock a record before you write to it. By doing this, if the attempt to lock fails, then you know not to write. We used this information to create the two routines in listing 12.4 to lock and unlock a record.

Listing 12.4. _FILELOCK.PAS_

```
Unit FileLock;

INTERFACE

Uses
  DOS;

Function Lock ( Var Untyped; pos, size : LongInt ) : Boolean;
Function UnLock ( Var Untyped; pos, size : LongInt ) : Boolean;

IMPLEMENTATION
```

```
Function Lock ( Var Untyped; pos, size : LongInt ) : Boolean;
Var
  reg : Registers;
  f : File absolute Untyped;
Begin
  pos := pos * FileRec ( f ).RecSize;
  size := size * FileRec ( f ).RecSize;
  reg.AH := $5C;
  reg.AL := $00;
  reg.BX := FileRec ( f ).Handle;
  reg.CX := Hi ( pos );
  reg.DX := Lo ( pos );
  reg.SI := Hi ( size );
  reg.DI := Lo ( size );
  Intr ( $21, reg );
  If ( ( reg.Flags AND FCarry ) <> 0 ) Then
    Lock := FALSE
  Else
    Lock := TRUE;
End;

Function UnLock ( Var Untyped; pos, size : LongInt ) : Boolean;
Var
  reg : Registers;
  f : File absolute Untyped;
Begin
  pos := pos * FileRec ( f ).RecSize;
  size := size * FileRec ( f ).RecSize;
  reg.AH := $5C;
  reg.AL := $01;
  reg.BX := FileRec ( f ).Handle;
  reg.CX := Hi ( pos );
  reg.DX := Lo ( pos );
  reg.SI := Hi ( size );
  reg.DI := Lo ( size );
  Intr ( $21, reg );
  If ( ( reg.Flags AND FCarry ) <> 0 ) Then
    UnLock := FALSE
  Else
    UnLock := TRUE;
End;

End.
```

Listing 12.4 uses a sly way of passing the file variable into the two functions. It defines an untyped variable parameter and then defines a variable of type file to be at the absolute address of the untyped parameter. This allows the program to pass files of different types to the same routine. Otherwise, it would need a different procedure for each different file type.

Turbo Pascal defines all random-access file variables with one structure. The Standard Units section of the *Turbo Pascal Reference Guide* shows the definition of a type in the Dos unit called `FileRec`. This is the type definition used by the compiler when working with file variables. To access the individual components of the `FileRec`, you must do two things: place the Dos unit in your uses statement, and typecast your file variable into a `FileRec`. To do the latter, place your file variable in parentheses preceded by the type `FileRec`. For example, if you wanted to get the actual DOS file handle from a variable that was defined as `File of Integer`, you would use this:

```
FileRec ( yourFileVar ).Handle.
```

In addition to returning the file handle, the `FileRec` also provides access to the size of the record. Unless the file variable was defined as "Var f : File;", this should reflect the correct size of the record with which you are dealing. If not, rewrite the procedures to take a size parameter. Then, pass the `SizeOf` for the record variable to the routine.

Listings 12.5 and 12.6 demonstrate how record locking works. Listing 12.5 alternates between locking a record for four seconds and having no records locked for four seconds. Listing 12.6 continually reads the data file and reports what records are locked.

Listing 12.5. LOCKIT.PAS

```
Program LockIt;

Uses
  CRT,
  DOS,
  FileLock;

Var
  f       : File of Integer;
  i       : integer;
  oldExit : Pointer;

{$F+}
Procedure MyExit;
{$F-}
Begin
{$I-}
  ExitProc := oldExit;
  Seek ( f, 0 );
  While not EOF ( f ) Do
```

```
Begin
  if Unlock ( f, FilePos ( f ), 1 ) Then ;
  Read ( f, i );
End;
Close ( f );
i := IOResult;
{$I+}
End;

Begin
  oldExit := ExitProc;
  ExitProc := @MyExit;

  Assign ( f, '...'F\data.dat' );       { Change name to reflect  }
                                        { your specific network   }

  Rewrite ( f );
  For i := 1 to 10 do
    Write ( f, i );
  Close ( f );
  FileMode := 66;
  Reset ( f );
  Repeat
    For i := 1 to 10 do
    Begin
      Repeat Until Lock ( f, i, 1 );
      Write ( 'Lock: ',i );
      Delay ( 4000 );

      Repeat Until Unlock ( f, i, 1 );
      WriteLn ( '  Unlocked' );
      Delay ( 4000 );
    End;
  Until KeyPressed;
End.
```

Listing 12.6. CheckIt.Pas

```
Program CheckIt;

Uses
  CRT,
  DOS,
  FileLock;
```

Listing 12.6 continues

Listing 12.6 continued

```
Var
   f : File of Integer;
   i : integer;
   oldExit : Pointer;

{$F+}
Procedure MyExit;
{$F-}
Begin
  ExitProc := oldExit;
  Seek ( f, 0 );
  While not EOF ( f ) Do
  Begin
    if Unlock ( f, FilePos ( f ), 1 ) Then ;
    Read ( f, i );
  End;
  Close ( f );
End;

Begin
  oldExit := ExitProc;
  ExitProc := @MyExit;

  Assign ( f, '...'F\data.dat' );      { Change name to reflect  }
                                       { your specific network   }
  FileMode := 66;
  Reset ( f );
  Repeat
    For i := 1 to 10 do
    Begin
      If ( not Lock ( f, i, 1 ) ) Then
      Begin
        GotoXY ( 1, i );
        WriteLn ( i, ' is locked.' )
      End
      Else
      Begin
        GotoXY ( 1, i );
        WriteLn ( '                      ' );
        Repeat Until Unlock ( f, i, 1 );
      End
    End;
  Until KeyPressed;
End.
```

To implement record locking in your program, you will probably want to follow these general guidelines:

1. Open with one of the specified shared modes the file on which you want to perform locking.

2. Attempt to lock the record in the file before updating it.

3. Unlock the record position.

Listing 12.7 is a pseudoprogram that demonstrates what a simple program would look like.

Listing 12.7. Pseudo File-Locking Program

```
Program Pseudo;

Uses
  FileLock;

Type
  RecType = ...
  FileType = File of RecType;

Var
  r       : RecType;
  f       : FileType;
  rn      : LongInt;
  oldExit : Pointer

{$F+}
Procedure MyExit;
{$F-}
Begin
  ExitProc := oldExit;
  Seek ( f, 0 );
  While not EOF ( f ) Do
  Begin
    if Unlock ( f, FilePos ( f ) ) Then ;
    Read ( f, r );
  End;
  Close ( f );
End;

Begin
  oldExit := ExitProc;
  ExitProc := @MyExit;
```

Listing 12.7 continues

Listing 12.7 continued

```
   Assign ( f, 'filename' );
   FileMode := 66;
   Reset ( f );
   Repeat
     rn := GetRecordNumber;
     Repeat Until Lock ( f, rn );
     Seek ( f, rn-1 );
     Read ( f, r );
     EditRecord ( r );
     Write ( f, r );
     Repeat Until UnLock ( f, rn );
   Until Done;          { Done is defined in pseudo unit FileLock }
   Close ( f );
End.
```

Listing 12.7 opens the pseudofile in a read/write access mode with a deny none shared mode. After determining what record number is going to be locked, it enters a loop that will repeat until that specific record is available to be locked. Then the program seeks that position, reads the record, and allows the user to edit it. Next, the record gets written out to disk and unlocked. The only pitfall with something like this is that the EditRecord routine may take a long time, which would lock other users out and prevent them from accessing this particular record. Some fancy coding may be done that times how long the EditRecord procedure takes. Another alternative is to lock the record, read it, and unlock it; then lock it, write to it, and unlock it. The only problem with this is that you could overwrite a record that someone just updated. The method used in listing 12.7 is safest in that way.

Conclusion

You can choose from several methods to deal with files in a network situation. If you are going to be tailoring a program to a specific type of network system, you may want to read its specific Application Program Interface (API). If you want to write programs for networks in general, you can choose one of two methods: opening a file in the compatibility shared mode, which will lock all other users out of the file, and record locking.

If you choose record locking, be sure to follow these rules:

☐ Always unlock any records that have been locked.

☐ Open files in a shared mode.

☐ Do not try writing to the record first; try locking it first.

☐ Never close a file or end a program that is using a file with locked records in it.

13

Object-Oriented
Programming

Turbo Pascal Version 5.5 introduces object-oriented programming (OOP), which adds power to an already powerful language. The main feature of object-oriented programming is extensibility; it lets you easily add to existing program features.

To benefit fully from reading this chapter, you should already have studied *Turbo Pascal Object-Oriented Programming Guide*, included with Turbo Pascal V5.5. This chapter pursues some ideas mentioned in that guide, as well as some ideas that are provided on the V5.5 distribution diskettes. This chapter does not teach you what object-oriented programming is or how to program in it. If any of the terms in this chapter or *Turbo Pascal Object-Oriented Programming Guide* confuse you, refer to the glossary at the end of this chapter.

In this chapter, we discuss the use of constructors and destructors in detail. We also discuss the Fail procedure and how it fits in with the dynamic allocation of objects. Finally, we discuss saving objects to disk, using the Streams example program provided on the Turbo Pascal diskettes, and we share a few tips about using objects in programs.

Constructors

When the compiler sees a call to an object's method that is not virtual (thereby making it *static*), it codes a call directly to that location at compile time. When the compiler sees a call to an object's virtual method, it codes a call to look up the location of that procedure in the object's Virtual Method Table (VMT). Any object that has a virtual method in it, or an ancestor, must have a constructor. The constructor loads the VMT into the instance of an object.

Each object type has a VMT that is placed in the data segment. There is no need to worry about VMTs taking up memory. Turbo Pascal compiles the code in such a way that there is only one VMT for each object, not for each instance of that object. Therefore, if you have 3 objects and 15 instances of those objects, you will have only 3 VMTs.

To let each instance of an object know where its VMT is located in memory, you must call the object's constructor. The primary purpose of the constructor is to set up the instance with the location of the VMT. This needs to be done at run time so that you can create dynamic objects. When you create a pointer to an object, all that pointer is pointing to is a location in memory that is to be treated in a specific format. A pointer knows where its methods are located because after the pointer is allocated by calling a special static method called a constructor, the address of the VMT is copied into the pointer location.

Constructors are primarily for objects that contain a virtual method, but there is no harm in having a constructor for a purely static object. The most harm it will do is to define a variable that is two bytes larger than it would be otherwise; the two bytes are for the address of the VMT. Even though there is no VMT, the constructor tries to place a value into that variable.

Because constructors are used with allocating memory for instances of objects, the New procedure has been enhanced into several different forms. New may take one or two parameters, the second parameter being a constructor. In this case, the first parameter must be a pointer to an object. The code executes through the following steps:

1. Memory is allocated for the pointer.

2. The constructor is called to insert the VMT address into the newly allocated memory location.

The Fail Procedure

Since the constructor is similar to a procedure, and since this procedure commonly does the setup work for the object, it may run out of memory. Suppose, for example, that we define an object that represents a window. We want to store the information that is within the window inside the object. The following lines show a definition of such an object:

```
Type
  WindObj = Object
                X1, Y1, X2, Y2 : Byte;
                Storage : Pointer;
                Constructor Init ( startX, startY, endX, endY : Byte );
            End;
Constructor WindObj.Init ( startX, startY, endX, endY : Byte );
Begin
  GetMem ( Storage, CalcSize ( startX, startY, endX, endY ) );
  X1 := startX;
  Y1 := startY;
  X2 := endX;
  Y2 := endY;
End;
```

The object WindObj contains the X and Y coordinates of the window and a pointer for storing the window. When we look at the constructor for this object, we notice that memory is allocated for the pointer to store the window information. CalcSize is a procedure that calculates the storage size of the window in bytes. The problem may arise that an instance has been defined as a pointer to WindObj (let's call it wPtr). Suppose that we use the New procedure to allocate memory for a window and call the constructor:

```
New ( wPtr, Init ( 1, 1, 79, 24 ) );
```

The program will allocate memory for the wPtr variable and then call the object's constructor. In the constructor a call is made to allocate memory for the storage of the window.

Suppose that there is enough memory for the instance of the object to be allocated but not for the storage. The object will be relatively useless. We will not be able to store window information in it or use it for anything. We may as well signal that we do not want to use it. This is the reason for the Fail procedure.

What Fail does is abort the constructor routine (the way the Exit procedure does), deallocate the memory that was allocated for the instance, and return nil in the instance. The remaining necessary action is for the line following the call to New to check the instance for a value other than nil.

Listing 13.1 is a sample section of code that illustrates what `Fail` can be used for. This program will loop, allocating a linked list of object instances. Each instance will also allocate memory within the constructor.

Listing 13.1. *Fail Demonstration Program*

```
Program FailHeap;
Type
  ListPtr = ^ListObj;
  ListObj = Object
              ptr : Pointer;
              ptrSize : Word;
              Constructor Init ( newSize : Word );
            End;
Constructor Init ( newSize : Word );
Begin
  GetMem ( ptr, newSize );
  If ( ptr = NIL ) Then
    Fail;
  ptrSize := newSize;
  next := NIL;
End;
Var
  i    : Integer;
  list : Array [1..200] of ListPtr;
Begin
  Repeat
    New ( list [ i ], Init ( 32767 ) );
    Inc ( i );
  Until ( list = NIL );
End.
```

Listing 13.1 serves no purpose other than demonstrating `Fail`. The program loops until a `nil` pointer is returned through the call to `New`. This can happen in one of two ways:

☐ Conventionally, no memory was left to allocate a pointer to the element of the array.

☐ In this case, there was enough memory to allocate a pointer to the element in the array, but not enough memory to allocate the pointer within the object.

A `nil` pointer is returned within the constructor at the call to `GetMem`, and the constructor is written to call `Fail` when this happens. `Fail` releases the memory to the array element and returns a `nil` pointer.

Destructors

The destructor's purpose is the opposite of that of the constructor; its job is to help remove the object. A destructor is not necessary for either static or virtual objects, but use of a destructor lets you deallocate a dynamic object at the same time that you call the shut-down code for the object.

You need to use a destructor for many reasons. Consider this example: suppose that you have an object that is part of a linked list. The object itself contains a pointer to the next object and a pointer to the previous object. A destructor can be used in the Dispose procedure similar to the way a constructor is used in the New procedure call. The program will first call the destructor and then deallocate the dynamic instance of the object. In our example of the linked list, the destructor could remove itself from the linked list.

The following lines of code describe the object about which we are talking:

```
Type
  List = Object
           next : ListPtr;
           last : ListPtr;
           Constructor Init ( before, after : ListPtr );
           Destructor Done;
           Procedure SetBeforeLink ( before : ListPtr );
           Procedure SetAfterLink ( after : ListPtr );
           Function GetBeforeLink : ListPtr;
           Function GetAfterLink : ListPtr;
         End;
```

Our linked list is a doubly linked list. We have a pointer to the node in front and a pointer to the node in back. This makes deletion from the list much easier. We define a constructor, a destructor, and a couple of procedures and functions as our methods. There is no place to store any data, which leads to another potential problem that we will discuss later. The constructor will set up our linked list by establishing the previous and following links in the list. Our other methods are used for setting the links and getting the links' values.

Listing 13.2 shows the code we used to create a linked list unit. Listing 13.3 is a sample program that shows how the unit can be used.

Listing 13.2. *Linked List Unit (Destructors)*

```
Unit ListUnit;
Interface
Type
  ListPtr = ^List;
  List = Object
           next : ListPtr;
           last : ListPtr;
           Constructor Init ( before, after : ListPtr );
           Destructor Done; Virtual
           Procedure SetBeforeLink ( before : ListPtr );
           Procedure SetAfterLink ( after : ListPtr );
           Function GetBeforeLink : ListPtr;
           Function GetAfterLink : ListPtr;
         End;
Implementation
Constructor List.Init ( before, after : ListPtr );
Var
  tmp : ListPtr;
Begin
  SetBeforeLink ( before );
  SetAfterLink ( after );
  If ( before <> NIL ) Then
    before^.SetAfterLink ( @Self );
  If ( after <> NIL ) Then
    after^.SetBeforeLink ( @Self );
End;
Destructor List.Done;
Var
  tmp : ListPtr;
Begin
  tmp := GetBeforeLink;
  tmp^.SetAfterLink ( GetAfterLink );
  tmp := GetAfterLink;
  tmp^.SetBeforeLink ( GetBeforeLink );
End;
Procedure List.SetBeforeLink ( before : ListPtr );
Begin
  last := before;
End;
Procedure List.SetAfterLink ( after : ListPtr );
Begin
  next := after;
End;
Function List.GetBeforeLink : ListPtr;
Begin
  GetBeforeLink := last;
```

```
End;
Function List.GetAfterLink : ListPtr;
Begin
  GetAfterLink := next;
End;
End.
```

Listing 13.3. Linked List Program

```
Program MyList;
Uses
  Crt,
  ListUnit;
Type
  MyObjPtr = ^MyObj;
  MyObj = Object ( list )
            Data : LongInt;
            Constructor Init ( newData : LongInt; before, after : ListPtr );
            Procedure SetData ( newData : LongInt ); Virtual;
            Function GetData : LongInt; Virtual;
            Function GetAfterLink : MyObjPtr;
            Function GetBeforeLink : MyObjPtr;
          End;
Constructor MyObj.Init ( newData : LongInt; before, after : ListPtr );
Begin
  List.Init ( before, after );
  data := newData;
End;
Procedure MyObj.SetData ( newData : LongInt );
Begin
  data := newData;
End;
Function MyObj.GetData : LongInt;
Begin
  GetData := data;
End;
Function MyObj.GetAfterLink : MyObjPtr;
Begin
  GetAfterLink := MyObjPtr ( List.GetAfterLink );
End;
Function MyObj.GetBeforeLink : MyObjPtr;
Begin
  GetBeforeLink := MyObjPtr ( List.GetBeforeLink );
End;
Procedure Display ( l : MyObjPtr );
```

Listing 13.3 continues

Listing 13.3 continued

```
Var
  ch  : Char;
  tmp : MyObjPtr;
Begin
  tmp := l;
  If ( l <> NIL ) Then
    Repeat
      WriteLn ( tmp^.GetData );
      tmp := tmp^.GetAfterLink;
    Until ( tmp = NIL );
  WriteLn;
  ch := ReadKey;
End;
Var
  head,
  l1,
  l2,
  l3 : MyObjPtr;
Begin
  New ( head, init ( 613, NIL, NIL ) ); { Initialize Head pointer }
  l1 := head;
  New ( l2, init ( 314159, l1, NIL ) ); { Add item to end of list }
  l1 := l2;
  New ( l2, init ( 1111, l1, NIL ) );      { Add item to end of list }
  New ( l3, init ( 1234, l1, l2 ) );     { Insert between l1 & l2 }
  ClrScr;
  Display ( head );
  l1 := head;
  While ( l1 <> NIL ) AND ( l1^.GetData <> 1234 ) Do
    l1 := l1^.GetAfterLink;
  If ( l1 <> NIL ) Then
    Dispose ( l1, Done );
  Display ( head );
  l1 := head;
  While ( l1 <> NIL ) AND ( l1^.GetData <> 1111 ) Do
    l1 := l1^.GetAfterLink;
  If ( l1 <> NIL ) Then
    Dispose ( l1, Done );
  Display ( head );
  l1 := head;
  While ( l1 <> NIL ) AND ( l1^.GetData <> 0 ) Do
    l1 := l1^.GetAfterLink;
  If ( l1 <> NIL ) Then
    Dispose ( l1, Done );
  Display ( head );
  l1 := head;
  head := head^.GetAfterLink; { Needed because you are deleting the Head }
```

```
While ( l1 <> NIL ) AND ( l1^.GetData <> 613 ) Do
  l1 := l1^.GetAfterLink;
If ( l1 <> NIL ) Then
  Dispose ( l1, Done );
Display ( head );
l1 := head;
head := NIL;          { Needed because the list is now empty }
While ( l1 <> NIL ) AND ( l1^.GetData <> 314159 ) Do
  l1 := l1^.GetAfterLink;
If ( l1 <> NIL ) Then
  Dispose ( l1, Done );
Display ( head );
l1 := head;
While ( l1 <> NIL ) AND ( l1^.GetData <> 0 ) Do
  l1 := l1^.GetAfterLink;
If ( l1 <> NIL ) Then
  Dispose ( l1, Done );
Display ( head );
End.
```

We make special use of the constructor and the destructor in the calls to the New and Dispose procedures. If you step through the program with the debugger, you can follow the steps the program goes through. Set a watch variable on MemAvail, and step into the New and Dispose calls. Do you see when the memory is allocated? For the call to New, the memory is allocated before the constructor is called. In the call to Dispose, the memory is released after the destructor is called.

Causes of Lockups

There is a problem with the code in listings 13.2 and 13.3 that lies in the fact that we are having to typecast the object pointers. This is a dangerous thing to do. With this demonstration program, there is no real hazard. But if you were to make some changes to it—for example, inserting an item into the list that is a List object, not a MyObj object—your program might lock up. This happens because when we go through the list in our Display procedure, we are counting on only MyObj objects. We call a function that is only used in the object MyObj. The List object does not have this method defined in its virtual method table, so some bogus address will be used as a procedure address. Usually, when this happens, the machine will lock up or dump garbage to the screen. The safest way to fix this problem is to merge the base object type with the List object.

There are other cases in which working with objects can lead to a lockup. Listing 13.4 is a sample program that will definitely cause problems.

***Listing 13.4.** VMT Mixup*

```
Type
  L1 = Object
          Constructor Init;
          Procedure First; Virtual;
        End;
  L2 = Object ( L1 )
          Constructor Init;
          Procedure Second; Virtual;
        End;
Constructor L1.Init;
Begin
End;
Procedure L1.First;
Begin
  Init;
End;
Constructor L2.Init;
Begin
End;
Procedure L2.Second;
Begin
  Init;
End;
Var
  L : L2;
Begin
  L.Init;
  L.First;
  L.Second;
End.
```

Can you see where the problem will arise? To find what is wrong and why, step through the program as the computer would:

1. Define an instance L of type L2.

2. Call the constructor for L2, Init.

3. Place the address of L2's VMT into variable L, and the constructor call is finished.

4. Call First.

5. Look up in the VMT and realize that First is something L2 has inherited.

6. Pass the Self parameter into First.

7. First will see this Self parameter as a parameter of type L1 because it knows nothing about L2. Because of this fact, L1.Init is called (not L2.Init). This is the important point: when the L1.Init constructor is called, the address of the L1 VMT is loaded into the instance, overwriting the previous VMT address.

8. When the main program goes to call L.Second, the program thinks that the VMT that is loaded is L2's, so it looks up the address of the Second procedure and calls it. This is where it locks up. It does so because the VMT that the look-up was just performed on is L1's not L2's, and the method address for Second has not yet been defined.

The moral of this story is that you should never call a constructor from within a method. This also pertains to any polymorphic procedures. Following is an example of the problem with a polymorphic procedure:

```
Procedure Init ( Var x:L1 );
Begin
  x.Init;
End;
```

Constructors should be called only from nonobject-related procedures or the main program. Make a habit of always calling the constructors at the start of a program.

Sample Object Program

Since one of the easier ways of learning a new concept is to visualize it, we have developed a short program that demonstrates object-oriented programming. Listing 13.5 is a game that pits you against monsters. Your object is to fight the monster and collect treasure and experience. The code is in a raw form and is very limited. (The monsters do not move or fight back, there is only one room, and there is no treasure.) However, the program does demonstrate the power of object-oriented programming. You can add treasure as an object and make the monsters move or fight back without too much difficulty. Additionally, you can add rooms.

The base object that we define is Location. It contains the X and Y coordinates of the object and a symbol to display on the screen that represents that object. From the object, we define two types of descendants: Thing and Being. Thing is the object that is a thing (it is not alive). Some of the objects that descend from Thing are Weapon and Armor. Being is the object that is living and can move and fight. Objects that descend from Being are the Player object and the Monster object.

We left out any movements of Monster because our purpose is to provide an object example more than a game example. It would complicate the readability of the code to add the strategy of moving the monsters in a smart way and to attack any Player objects that came within a certain range. The program does allow you to move around the screen and attack the monster.

Listing 13.5. Object Adventure

```
Program ObjAdv;
Uses
  CRT;
Const
  Blank : Char = ' ';
Type
  Location = Object
                X,
                Y : Byte;
                Symbol : Char;
                Constructor Init ( newChar : Char; newX, newY : Byte );
                Function GetX : Byte;
                Function GetY : Byte;
                Procedure Move ( newX, newY : Byte );
                Procedure Show; Virtual;
                Procedure Hide; Virtual;
             End;
  ThingPtr = ^Thing;
  Thing    = Object ( Location )
                Name : String;
                Data : ShortInt;
                Constructor Init ( newName : String; newChar : Char; newX,
                                   newY : Byte );
                Procedure Get;
                Procedure Put ( newX, newY : Byte );
                Function Swing : Byte; Virtual;
                Function GetAC : ShortInt; Virtual;
                Procedure SetAC ( newAC : ShortInt ); Virtual;
             End;
  Weapon   = Object ( Thing )
                Constructor Init ( newName : String; newX, newY : Byte;
                                   newDamage : ShortInt );
                Function Swing : Byte; Virtual;
             End;
  Armor    = Object ( Thing )
                Constructor Init ( newName : String; newX, newY : Byte;
                                   newAC : ShortInt );
                Function GetAC : ShortInt; Virtual;
                Procedure SetAC ( newAC : ShortInt ); Virtual;
             End;
```

```
BeingPtr = ^Being;
Being    = Object ( Location )
              Name : String;
              BaseDamage,
              Health,
              Wielding,
              Wearing : Byte;
              Inventory : Array [1..20] of ThingPtr;
              Constructor Init ( newName : String; newX, newY : Byte;
                                 newDamage, newHealth, newWeapon,
                                 newArmor : Byte );
              Procedure TakeHit ( toHit, damage : Byte );
              Function Swing : Byte;
              Procedure Wield ( obj : ThingPtr );
              Procedure Wear ( obj : ThingPtr );
           End;
Player   = Object ( Being )
              Constructor Init ( newName : String; newX, newY : Byte;
                                 newDamage, newHealth, newWeapon,
                                 newArmor : Byte );
           End;
Monster  = Object ( Being )
              Constructor Init ( newName : String; newX, newY : Byte;
                                 newDamage, newHealth, newWeapon,
                                 newArmor : Byte );
           End;
Area     = Object
              x1, y1,
              x2, y2 : Byte;
              ObjBeing : Array [1..20] of BeingPtr;
              Constructor Init ( newX1, newY1, newX2, newY2 : Byte );
              Procedure AddBeingToRoom ( bPtr : BeingPtr );
              Procedure MoveBeing ( Var creature : Being; posX,
                                    posY : Byte );
              Function Position ( locX, locY : Byte ) : BeingPtr;
           End;
Var
  mw,
  pw : Weapon;
  ma,
  pa : Armor;
  pp : Player;
  mm : Monster;
  a  : Area;
  ch : Char;
  status : Boolean;
  windY  : Byte;
Procedure SwitchWindow;
{ This procedure allows the program to switch between the status }
```

Listing 13.5 continues

Listing 13.5 continued

```
{ window and the playing window. The global variable STATUS is   }
{ used to indicate which is the current window. When switching    }
{ back to the playing window, WINDY is updated to contain the     }
{ current Y position in the status window.                        }
Begin
  status := Not status;
  If status Then
  Begin
    Window ( 61, 1, 80, 25 );           { Activate the status window }
    TextColor ( Black );
    TextBackground ( LightGray );
    GotoXY ( 1, windY );
  End
  Else
  Begin
    windY := WhereY;                    { Store the status Window Y }
    Window ( 1, 1, 60, 25 );            { Activate the player window }
    TextColor ( LightGray );
    TextBackground ( Black );
  End;
End;
{ ///////////////////////////////////////////////////////////////// }
{ ////////////////////////// Location's Methods ////////////////////// }
{ ///////////////////////////////////////////////////////////////// }
{
 X,
 Y : Byte;
 Symbol : Char;
}
Constructor Location.Init ( newChar : Char; newX, newY : Byte );
{ Initialize the instance of Location }
Begin
  X := NewX;
  Y := NewY;
  Symbol := NewChar;
End;
Procedure Location.Move ( newX, newY : Byte );
{ Move the X,Y position of the instance. There is a special case    }
{ involved with an instance of location. If the X and Y values are }
{ 0, then the instance is not to be drawn. The reason for this is   }
{ that the instance has been destroyed or is in possession of the  }
{ player.                                                          }
Begin
  Hide;
  X := NewX;
  Y := NewY;
  If NOT ( ( X = 0 ) AND ( Y = 0 ) ) Then
    Show;
End;
```

```
Function Location.GetX : Byte;
{ Return the value of the X field }
Begin
  GetX := X;
End;
Function Location.GetY : Byte;
{ Return the value of the Y field }
Begin
  GetY := Y;
End;
Procedure Location.Show;
{ Write the symbol of the instance on the screen at the location }
{ stored in fields X and Y.                                      }
Begin
  GotoXY ( X, Y );
  Write ( Symbol );
End;
Procedure Location.Hide;
{ Remove the symbol of the instance from the screen at the location }
{ stored in fields X and Y.                                         }
Begin
  GotoXY ( X, Y );
  Write ( Blank );
End;
{ ///////////////////////////////////////////////////////////////// }
{ ///////////////////////// Thing's Methods ///////////////////////// }
{ ///////////////////////////////////////////////////////////////// }
{
 X,
 Y : Byte;
 Symbol : Char;
 Name : String;
 Data : ShortInt;
}
Constructor Thing.Init ( newName : String; newChar : Char; newX,
                         newY : Byte );
{ Initialize the instance of Thing. Also, call Thing's immediate }
{ ancestor to initialize it's fields.                           }
Begin
  Location.Init ( newChar, newX, newY );
  Name := NewName;
  Data := ShortInt ( $FF );
End;
Procedure Thing.Get;
{ Unused in this program, but can be used later for picking up }
{ things that are in an Area.                                  }
Begin
  Location.Move ( 0, 0 );
End;
```

Listing 13.5 continues

Listing 13.5 continued

```
Procedure Thing.Put ( newX, newY : Byte );
{ Unused in this program, but can be used later for dropping }
{ things in an Area.                                         }
Begin
  Location.Move ( newX, newY );
End;
Function Thing.Swing : Byte;
{ Defined as a base value for all things. Default value of a }
{ swing is set to 0. If a descendant object is to be usable  }
{ as a weapon, this method should be replaced.               }
Begin
  Swing := 0;
End;
Function Thing.GetAC : ShortInt;
{ Defined as a base value for all things. Default value of AC }
{ is set to 0. If a descendant object is to be usable as Armor }
{ then this method should be replaced.                        }
Begin
  GetAC := 0;
End;
Procedure Thing.SetAC ( newAC : ShortInt );
{ Unused in this program. This method is a base for all things. }
{ If a descendant object is to be usable as Armor, then this    }
{ method should be replaced.                                    }
Begin
End;
{ ///////////////////////////////////////////////////////////////// }
{ /////////////////////////// Weapon's Methods ////////////////////// }
{ ///////////////////////////////////////////////////////////////// }
{
 X,
 Y : Byte;
 Symbol : Char;
 Name : String;
 Data : ShortInt;
}
Constructor Weapon.Init ( NewName : String; NewX, NewY : Byte;
                          NewDamage : ShortInt );
{ Initialize the instance of Weapon. Then call Weapon's immediate }
{ ancestor to initialize it's values.                             }
Begin
  Thing.Init ( NewName, '|', NewX, NewY );
  Data := NewDamage;
End;
Function Weapon.Swing : Byte;
{ This is the replacement procedure for Thing. This will compute }
{ a random amount of damage that the swinging of the weapon will }
{ produce. The random value is based on the DATA field of the    }
{ object.                                                        }
```

```
Begin
  Swing := Random ( data ) + 1;
End;
{ //////////////////////////////////////////////////////////////////// }
{ ///////////////////////// Armor's Methods ////////////////////////// }
{ //////////////////////////////////////////////////////////////////// }
{
 X,
 Y : Byte;
 Symbol : Char;
 Name : String;
 Data : ShortInt;
}
Constructor Armor.Init ( NewName : String; NewX, NewY : Byte;
                         NewAC : ShortInt );
{ Initialize the instance of Armor. Then call Armor's immediate }
{ ancestor to initialize it's values.                           }
Begin
  Thing.Init ( NewName, '#', NewX, NewY );
  Data := NewAC;
End;
Function Armor.GetAC : ShortInt;
{ This is the replacement procedure for Thing. This will return }
{ the Armor Class of the instance. The AC is stored in the DATA }
{ field of the object.                                          }
Begin
  GetAC := Data;
End;
Procedure Armor.SetAC ( newAC : ShortInt );
{ Unused in this program. This is the replacement procedure for }
{ Thing. This could be used to modify the Armor Class of the    }
{ instance. The AC is stored in the DATA field of the object.   }
Begin
  Data := newAC;
End;
{ //////////////////////////////////////////////////////////////////// }
{ ///////////////////////// Being's Methods ////////////////////////// }
{ //////////////////////////////////////////////////////////////////// }
{
 X,
 Y : Byte;
 Symbol : Char;
 Name : String;
 BaseDamage,
 Health,
 Wielding,
 Wearing : Byte;
 Inventory : Array [1..20] of ThingPtr;
}
```

Listing 13.5 continues

Listing 13.5 continued

```
Constructor Being.Init ( NewName : String; NewX, NewY : Byte; NewDamage,
                         NewHealth, NewWeapon, NewArmor : Byte );
{ Initialize the instance of Being. Also, call Being's immediate }
{ ancestor to initialize it's fields.                            }
Begin
  Location.Init ( Symbol, NewX, NewY );
  Name := NewName;
  BaseDamage := NewDamage;
  Health := NewHealth;
  Wielding := NewWeapon;
  Wearing := NewArmor;
  FillChar ( Inventory, SizeOf ( Inventory ), 0 );
End;
Procedure Being.TakeHit ( ToHit, Damage : Byte );
{ This procedure takes two parameters. The first parameter is }
{ a number from 1-100 that indicates whether this instance of }
{ being will be hit. The second parameter determines how much }
{ damage the instance will take for the hit.                  }
Var
  tmp : Byte;
Begin
  If ( Wearing = 0 ) Then
    tmp := 10
  Else
    tmp := Inventory [Wearing]^.GetAC;
  tmp := 10 * ( 10 - tmp );       { Compute the Armor class of the instance }
  SwitchWindow;
  If ( ToHit <= tmp ) Then
  Begin
    WriteLn ( 'A hit! For ',Damage,' points of damage!' );
    If ( ( health - damage ) <= 0 ) Then
    Begin
      health := 0;
      SwitchWindow;
      hide;
      SwitchWindow;
      WriteLn ( 'You killed the monster.' );
    End
    Else
      health := health - damage;
  End
  Else
    WriteLn ( 'A miss.' );
  SwitchWindow;
End;
Function Being.Swing : Byte;
{ Return how much damage the instance will give for an attack }
{ with the current weapon of the instance.                    }
```

```
Var
  tmp : Byte;
Begin
  tmp := Inventory [Wielding]^.Swing;
  If ( tmp = 0 ) Then
    tmp := Random ( 4 ) + 1;
  Swing := tmp;
End;
Procedure Being.Wield ( obj : ThingPtr );
{ Set the weapon that the instance is going to wield }
Var
  tmp : Byte;
Begin
  tmp := 1;
  While ( tmp <= 20 ) AND ( Inventory [tmp] <> NIL ) Do
    Inc ( tmp );
  If ( tmp > 20 ) Then
    WriteLn ( 'Overloaded, cannot wield that item' )
  Else
  Begin
    Inventory [ tmp ] := obj;
    Wielding := tmp;
  End;
End;
Procedure Being.Wear ( obj : ThingPtr );
{ Set the armor class that the instance will wear }
Var
  tmp : Byte;
Begin
  tmp := 1;
  While ( tmp <= 20 ) AND ( Inventory [tmp] <> NIL ) Do
    Inc ( tmp );
  If ( tmp > 20 ) Then
    WriteLn ( 'Overloaded, can not wear that item' )
  Else
  Begin
    Inventory [ tmp ] := obj;
    Wearing := tmp;
  End;
End;
{ ///////////////////////////////////////////////////////////////// }
{ /////////////////////// Player's Methods ///////////////////////// }
{ ///////////////////////////////////////////////////////////////// }
{
  X,
  Y : Byte;
  Symbol : Char;
  Name : String;
  BaseDamage,
```

Listing 13.5 continues

Listing 13.5 continued

```
   Health,
   Wielding,
   Wearing : Byte;
   Inventory : Array [1..20] of ThingPtr;
   }
Constructor Player.Init ( newName : String; newX, newY : Byte; newDamage,
                          newHealth, newWeapon, newArmor : Byte );
{ Initialize the instance of Player. Also, call Player's immediate }
{ ancestor to initialize its fields.                               }
Begin
   Symbol := '@';  { This is the symbol that the player is represented by }
   Being.Init ( newName, newX, newY, newDamage, newHealth, newWeapon,
                newArmor );
End;
{ //////////////////////////////////////////////////////////////////// }
{ //////////////////////// Monster's Methods ///////////////////////// }
{ //////////////////////////////////////////////////////////////////// }
{
   X,
   Y : Byte;
   Symbol : Char;
   Name : String;
   BaseDamage,
   Health,
   Wielding,
   Wearing : Byte;
   Inventory : Array [1..20] of ThingPtr;
   }
Constructor Monster.Init ( newName : String; newX, newY : Byte; newDamage,
                           newHealth, newWeapon, newArmor : Byte );
{ Initialize the instance of Monster. Also, call Monster's immediate }
{ ancestor to initialize its fields.                                 }
Begin
   Symbol := '*';  { This is the symbol that the monster is represented by }
   Being.Init ( newName, newX, newY, newDamage, newHealth, newWeapon,
                newArmor );
End;
{ //////////////////////////////////////////////////////////////////// }
{ //////////////////////// Area's Methods //////////////////////////// }
{ //////////////////////////////////////////////////////////////////// }
{
   ObjBeing : Array [1..20] of BeingPtr;
   }
Constructor Area.Init ( newX1, newY1, newX2, newY2 : Byte );
{ Initialize the instance of Area. Area represents a room. }
{ The parameters determine the boundaries of the room.     }
```

```
Begin
  FillChar ( ObjBeing, SizeOf ( ObjBeing ), 0 );
  x1 := newX1;
  y1 := newY1;
  x2 := newX2;
  y2 := newY2;
End;
Procedure Area.AddBeingToRoom ( bPtr : BeingPtr );
{ Add an instance of Being to the Area. }
Var
  tmp : Byte;
Begin
  tmp := 1;
  While ( tmp <= 20 ) AND ( ObjBeing [tmp] <> NIL ) Do
    Inc ( tmp );
  If ( tmp <= 20 ) Then
    ObjBeing [ tmp ] := bPtr;
End;
Function Area.Position ( locX, locY : Byte ) : BeingPtr;
{ Return an instance of Being (if any) at the X,Y position }
{ specified. NIL will be returned if no instance exists at }
{ the specified location.                                  }
Var
  tmp : Byte;
Begin
  tmp := 1;
  While ( tmp <= 20 ) AND NOT ( ( ObjBeing [tmp]^.X = locX ) AND
         ( ObjBeing [tmp]^.Y = locY ) ) AND ( ObjBeing [tmp] <> NIL ) Do
    Inc ( tmp );
  If ( tmp <= 20 ) AND ( ObjBeing [tmp] <> NIL ) AND
     ( ObjBeing [tmp]^.Health > 0 ) Then
    Position := ObjBeing [tmp]
  Else
    Position := NIL;
End;
Procedure Area.MoveBeing ( Var creature : Being; posX, posY : Byte );
{ Move an instance of Being to a new X,Y location if no other   }
{ instance is at that location. If a being is at that location, }
{ then attack it.                                               }
Var
  tmpNum : Byte;
  tmpObj : BeingPtr;
Begin
  tmpNum := 1;
  While ( tmpNum <= 20 ) AND ( @creature <> ObjBeing [tmpNum] ) Do
    Inc ( tmpNum );
  If ( tmpNum <= 20 ) Then
```

Listing 13.5 continues

Listing 13.5 continued

```
Begin
  If ( posX >= x1 ) AND ( posX <= x2 ) AND
     ( posY >= y1 ) AND ( posY <= y2 ) Then
  Begin
    tmpObj := position ( posX, posY );
    If ( tmpObj = NIL ) Then
      creature.Move ( posX, posY )
    Else
      tmpObj^.TakeHit ( Random ( 100 ), creature.Swing );
  End;
End;
End;
Begin
  mw.Init ( 'Long Sword', 0, 0, 8 );
  ma.Init ( 'Leather', 0, 0, 8 );
  mm.Init ( 'Orc', 10, 10, 4, 8, 0, 0 );
  mm.Wear ( @ma );
  mm.Wield ( @mw );
  pw.Init ( 'Long Sword', 0, 0, 8 );
  pa.Init ( 'Chain', 0, 0, 6 );
  pp.Init ( 'Elf', 14, 14, 4, 8, 0, 0 );
  pp.Wear ( @pa );
  pp.Wield ( @pw );
  a.Init ( 1, 1, 60, 24 );
  a.AddBeingToRoom ( @mm );
  a.AddBeingToRoom ( @pp );
  Randomize;
  status := TRUE;
  SwitchWindow;    { Initialize the playing window }
  ClrScr;
  SwitchWindow;    { Initialize the status window  }
  ClrScr;
  SwitchWindow;    { Activate the playing window    }
  pp.Show;
  mm.Show;
  Repeat
    ch := ReadKey;
    Case ch of
      #0 : Begin
             ch := ReadKey;
             Case ch of
               #72 : Begin { Up }
                       a.MoveBeing ( pp, pp.GetX, pp.GetY-1 );
                     End;
               #75 : Begin { Left }
                       a.MoveBeing ( pp, pp.GetX-1, pp.GetY );
                     End;
```

```
            #77 : Begin { Right }
                    a.MoveBeing ( pp, pp.GetX+1, pp.GetY );
                  End;
            #80 : Begin { Down }
                    a.MoveBeing ( pp, pp.GetX, pp.GetY+1 );
                  End;
          End;
        End;
    End;
  Until ( ch = #27 )
End.
```

Object-Oriented Points To Ponder

In this section, we point out styles we have used in this chapter and some other tidbits about using object-oriented programming in Turbo Pascal:

☐ We choose the names Init and Done for our constructors and destructors. It is a good idea to define these methods with names like these; by doing so, you enable anybody looking at your code to understand immediately that these are calls to a constructor and a destructor. Several of the programs in *Turbo Pascal Object-Oriented Programming Guide* follow this guideline.

☐ A descendant constructor should always call its immediate ancestor's constructor. This is not a requirement, but it is a good idea. It reduces the amount of repetitive code in your program. Why write all the initialization code if a previous constructor has already done it?

☐ It is acceptable to call constructors of descendants from within the current constructor. However, it is not safe to do this within other methods (for the reasons discussed in the "Causes of Lockups" section of this chapter).

☐ You must always call a constructor if you are working with an object with virtual methods, even if the virtual method is inherited, or the constructor is inherited—or both. The VMT address needs to get loaded into the instance of the object before any virtual methods are called.

☐ Because of the nature of virtual methods, you cannot override one virtual method to have a previous one loaded. This would defeat the purpose of virtual methods.

❑ Objects are similar to records, but there are significant differences: you cannot define a variant object, and you cannot have absolutes within an object. As an alternative, you can define a variant record type and a field of that type within your object, which should suffice in almost all cases.

❑ Because virtual methods are linked in the formal method at compile time, the smart linker cannot strip out unused methods. Therefore, all your virtual methods will get linked into your program. Static methods can be removed by the smart linker in the compiler.

Saving Objects to Disk

The Turbo Pascal diskettes from Borland provide a sample program that demonstrates how to save objects to disk.

You cannot define a variable to be a file of some object type, primarily because of polymorphism. If the file is a file of some base object A, by the definition of polymorphism it is also a file of any descendant of A. Most of the time, descendants add data to the object. If you allow this to happen, the file is not a file of some fixed record length. If the file is of varying lengths, to associate the information in the file with the objects in the program, you have to use the tricky way around it as shown in the demonstration program (Stream) from Borland.

The idea behind the Stream is that you register your object with a Stream object. When you request to write your object out using this Stream, a special number is written at the start of the object's data. This number is associated with the order in which the objects were registered. Any program that defines these objects and registers them in the exact same order should be able to read the objects in from the Stream.

Glossary of Object-Oriented Programming Terms

Abstract object: The primary purpose of an abstract object is to provide a base object type for other objects to inherit. It is not designed to have instance of its type occur, only to generate descendant objects.

Ancestor object: Object from which the current object was derived directly, or indirectly through inheritance. The object from which the current object is immediately derived is the *immediate ancestor*. In figure 13.1, object D has an immediate ancestor object B and other ancestors A and Base.

***Fig. 13.1.** Object hierarchy.*

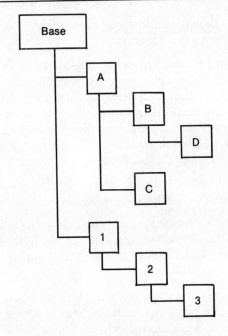

Constructor: A special procedure with several purposes. The first and foremost purpose is to load the address of virtual method table (VMT) into the instance of the calling object. The next purpose is to aid in the process of allocating memory for the current object. Finally, any initialization that needs to be done for the current object can be done within this routine. This routine can be used in conjunction with New.

Descendant objects: Objects derived from the current object. An *immediate descendant* is an object that is derived directly from the current object. In figure 13.1, object Base has two immediate descendants, A and 1. All of the objects in the figure are descendants of Base.

Destructor: A special procedure that helps deallocate the current object. If an object has any special jobs that need to be done before being removed, that code can be placed here. This special procedure can be called from within a call to Dispose.

Early binding: When the procedure and the call to the procedure are connected at the compilation stage. This is the opposite of *late binding.*

Encapsulation: Combining a record type with procedures and functions (the type's methods) to create a new data type, an object.

Extensibility: Being able to add easily to existing code without making major modifications to the programs.

Inheritance: Things received from an ancestor. Objects that are derived from previous objects inherit the predecessor's object fields and methods. This carries as many levels deep as there can be objects. The deepest nested object inherits all information from its immediate ancestor back to the original base object. Figure 13.1 shows that object 3 inherits all of the fields and methods defined in objects 2, 1, and Base. All objects in figure 13.1 inherit from Base; B, C, and D all inherit from A.

Instance: A variable. If we have the statement Var A : MyObject;, we can say that A is an instance of the type MyObject.

Late binding: When a procedure and the call to the procedure are not connected until the last possible moment—at run time. This is achieved through use of the virtual method table. Late binding applies only to virtual methods.

Method: A procedure or function defined within an object. It is inheritable from one object to any of its descendants. In fact, a method is so closely knit to an object that it is automatically defined with a With statement around it referring to the current object.

Object: A data structure similar to a record. It has data fields and also methods (procedures and functions). Additionally, objects can inherit fields and methods from ancestor objects.

Polymorphism: Allows objects whose type is unknown to be processed at compile time. This is performed with the help of objects and inheritance. An example would be a procedure that takes a parameter of object Base. Any object of type Base or descendant of Base can be passed into this routine. The routine treats the parameter as a variable of type Base.

Self: An invisible parameter passed to each method, containing all of the data fields and the VMT table of the object that is being called.

Static methods: Methods the compiler allocates and resolves at compile time. These are methods that are called directly through an address coded into the program.

Virtual methods: Methods linked at run time. When a call is made to the virtual method, the address of the correct method to call is looked up in the virtual method table. These are indirect calls to methods.

Virtual method table (VMT): A table stored in the data segment. This table contains all of the virtual methods that are defined for each object type. (One VMT is allocated for each type of object, not each instance.) When a call is made to a virtual method, the address of the method is looked up in this table and then called. The address of this table is loaded into each object's instance when the object's constructor is called.

Summary

By way of sample programs, we have shown how constructors work and what their purpose is. We have shown how to use the `fail` procedure when a constructor needs to be aborted. We have also looked at how constructors and destructors are used in conjunction with `New` and `Dispose`.

This chapter also discussed a couple of the "traps" of object-oriented programming. In the section "Causes of Lockups," some common misunderstandings are straightened out. Finally, we provide a brief glossary of OOP terminology.

CHAPTER 14

Miscellaneous Tricks

This chapter is a collection of tricks and useful hints for programming with Turbo Pascal. Some of them are ideas we have developed in dealing with customers when they call for support, and some are ideas the customers have come up with. The general topics discusses in this chapter include the following:

❏ Self-modifying code

❏ Comparison of complex data types

❏ Case statements with strings

❏ Math functions

❏ Special locations in memory

❏ Direct address computation

❏ Absolute disk read/write

❏ Patches

❏ Technical support

Self-Modifying Code

With self-modifying code, the program can change its own parameters as it runs. For example, you could use self-modifying code to count the number of times a program has been loaded and run. Programs can be

417

written to store information within themselves, and this stored information can be used as a counter.

To store information within a program's code, you must use *typed constants*. This is a form of having preinitialized variables; the variable is loaded into the data segment when the program is started. To create a typed constant, do the following:

1. Use the CONST descriptor to indicate that you are about to change a block of constants.

2. Define the label you want to use to identify the variable.

3. Follow the label with the type of the variable (i.e. Integer, Real, String, etc.).

4. Define the constant value you want the variable to contain at the start of the program.

Unlike normal constants, a typed constant can be changed during the course of the program. Unfortunately, when the program is terminated, the new value is lost. The next time the program is loaded, the variable will be initialized to its original value. There are some conditions where this is desired, and there are some cases in which you would like to retain the new value.

The value the variable will start up with is stored in the .EXE file in standard format. To retain the new value, you need to find the location of the variable and modify that value in the .EXE file. Then, each time the program is loaded from disk, it will contain the new value.

To find where the variable is stored in the .EXE file, you must search for what the variable contains. This is because the symbolic name you specified as a label is not stored in the program. If you have a string that contains the characters *blue*, you could open the .EXE file as a text file and search for that character combination. The unfortunate situation may arise in which the value for which you are searching is duplicated elsewhere in the program. For example, if your variable is a Byte variable that contains 13, the odds are good that there will be two occurrences of it at the very least. To ensure that the variable for which you are searching is unique, you must define the variable to be unique.

To make the typed constant unique, define it as a record that contains an ID string as well as the information you want to change. For example, if the information that you want to be able to change is a real, you could define the record as follows:

```
Type
  BurnType = Record
               ID    : String [10];
               MyVal : Real;
             End;
```

It is important that you set the ID string in your record to be the exact length of the literal string you will use as the unique value because a string is actually an array from 0 to the length specified (255 if no length is specified). The zeroth element contains the number of legitimate characters stored in the array. Suppose that the string is 10 characters in length and you assign a string of 5 characters (ABCDE) to it. The remaining 5 characters are undefined. Since you will be searching for an exact match, you must set the entire array with legitimate values.

To set the typed constant, you follow the construct mentioned earlier, except that you use parentheses to surround the information in the record and insert the record field label before the data. The following code fragment provides an example:

```
Const
  MyBurnIn : BurnType = ( ID:'MyUniqueID'; MyVal:3.1415926 );
```

This assignment creates a variable of type BurnType and assigns the literal string MyUniqueID to the ID portion of the record and 3.1415926 to the MyVal portion. For further information about defining a record typed constant, refer to *Turbo Pascal Reference Guide*.

Once you have defined the typed constant, you can use it as a regular variable. It is a variable that is preset to a value. To change the value of the typed constant for future execution of the program, you need to open the program as a file from disk and search for the unique ID string. In the .EXE file format, the data segment information is stored near the end, so the fastest way to search for the ID string is to start at the end and then work toward the beginning. Listing 14.1 demonstrates how to do the backward search. All this program does is print out its current value and modify it on disk for the next execution of the program. This will work only if you compile the program to disk and run the program from DOS; it will not run from the integrated development environment.

Listing 14.1. *BURNIN.PAS*

```pascal
Program BurnIn;
Type
  String10 = String [10];
  BurnType = Record
               ID    : String10;
               MyVal : Real;
             End;
Const
  MyBurnIn : BurnType = ( ID:'MyUniqueID'; MyVal:3.1415926 );
Var
  c : LongInt;
  f : File;
  s : String10;
Begin
  WriteLn ( 'ID is currently     = ',MyBurnIn.ID );
  WriteLn ( 'MyVal is currently = ',MyBurnIn.MyVal );
  MyBurnIn.MyVal := MyBurnIn.MyVal + 1;
  WriteLn ( 'Next time, MyVal    = ',MyBurnIn.MyVal );
  Assign ( f, ParamStr ( 0 ) );  { Set file variable = to program that is }
  Reset ( f, 1 );                { currently running. Set buffer size = 1 }
  c := FileSize ( f );           { Get current size of the file           }
  c := c - SizeOf ( s );         { Set size to  size - string length      }
  s := '';                       { Initialize the search string           }
  While ( c > 0 ) and ( s <> MyBurnIn.ID ) Do
  Begin            { Loop until we reach the start of the file, or a match is }
                   { found.                                                   }
    Seek ( f, c );                       { Move file pointer to new location  }
    BlockRead ( f, s, SizeOf ( s ) );  { Block read into the search string  }
    Dec ( c );                           { Decrement the counter by 1 position }
  End;
  If ( c > 0 ) Then              { If we did find the string, do the following }
  Begin
    Seek ( f, c + 1 );           { Seek to the offset of the found string      }
    BlockWrite ( f, MyBurnIn, SizeOf ( MyBurnIn ) ); { Write the new record }
  End;
  Close ( f );                   { Close the file }
End.
```

Listing 14.1 reveals the basic steps for updating the .EXE file:

1. Assign the name of the program, which is obtained by calling `ParamStr` with a parameter of zero.

2. Do a `Reset` of the file with a parameter of one for the buffer size.

3. Calculate the length of the file minus the size of the string for which we are searching.

4. Enter a loop.

5. Within the loop, seek a counter position, read the specified number of bytes into the string variable, and compare the string with the unique ID string. This loop will continue until the string is found, or the counter reaches zero. If the counter reaches zero, the string is not in the file. (Listing 14.1 ignores that possibility because it is a simple case, and the string will always be there.)

6. After exiting that loop, seek the counter position minus one. (You have to subtract one because you added one to the counter before exiting the loop.)

7. Write the updated record information to the file and close the file.

Every time you run this program from DOS, you should see the number increase by one. This will happen until you recompile the program. Recompiling the program resets the value to what the source code specifies.

Comparison of Complex Data Types

People often want to be able to compare records or arrays. For example, you might want to see whether record number one is the same as record number two. Perhaps, you read an array from disk, and you want to compare the array with one already in memory to determine whether they are the same.

Turbo Pascal does not provide the facility to do this, so programmers have had to use For loops and some logic to determine whether two complex variables are equal. You can use listing 14.2 to compare any two variable types. It takes three parameters and makes use of untyped parameters. The first two parameters should be of the same type, and the third parameter is the size of first parameter.

Listing 14.2. *Comparison of Any Two Variables*

```
Function Equal ( Var one, two; Size : Word ) : Boolean;
Type
  MaxArray = Array [1..65535] of Byte;
Var
  a : MaxArray absolute one;
  b : MaxArray absolute two;
  c : Word;
  d : Boolean;
```

Listing 14.2 continues

Listing 14.2 continued

```
Begin
  d := TRUE;
  c := 1;
  While ( c <= Size ) AND ( d ) Do
  Begin
    d := d AND ( a[c] = b[c] );
    Inc ( c );
  End;
  Equal := d;
End;
```

Listing 14.2 is a quick-and-dirty routine that does the following:

1. Defines a structure as large as any one variable can be.

2. Defines two variables of this type to be stored at the same location as the two untyped parameters that were passed in.

3. Initializes a Boolean variable to `true` and enters a loop.

4. Continues the loop to the specified size of the structure and sets the Boolean variable to `true` or `false` depending on whether the two arrays are comparing correctly.

5. Assigns the Boolean value to the function result.

This trick does not work with structures that contain strings. If the string is defined to be 10 characters in length, but contains only 3 legal characters ("Cow"), the rest of the storage space is undefined. Therefore, unless the string in the record fills the entire storage space, or the storage space is initialized, two records may not compare correctly. (As discussed in the following section, strings are a special case to compare.)

Using untyped variables can get you into some sticky situations. You should not assign anything to the variables that are passed in—to avoid overwriting memory to which you have no right. Suppose that a `Byte` variable is passed in, and the size that is passed states that it is 30 bytes large. The parameter that was passed in is a pointer to the actual storage place of the `Byte` variable and is allocated only for one byte of storage.

Listing 14.3 uses this new function. This routine can be useful, but it can also deceive you.

Listing 14.3. Sample Compare Program

```pascal
Program Compare;
Function Equal ( Var one, two; Size : Word ) : Boolean;
Type
  MaxArray = Array [1..65535] of Byte;
Var
  a : MaxArray absolute one;
  b : MaxArray absolute two;
  c : Word;
  d : Boolean;
Begin
  d := TRUE;
  c := 1;
  While ( c <= Size ) AND ( d ) Do
  Begin
    d := d AND ( a[c] = b[c] );
    Inc ( c );
  End;
  Equal := d;
End;
Type
  Rec1 = Record
             l : LongInt;
             r : Real;
             c : Char;
         End;
  Rec2 = Record
             w : LongInt;
             x : Real;
             y : Char;
             z : Integer;
         End;
Var
  a, b : Rec1;
  c, d : Rec2;
Begin
  a.l := 500;
  a.r := 3.141;
  a.c := 'C';
  b.l := 501;
  b.r := 3.141;
  b.c := 'C';
  WriteLn ( Equal ( a, b, SizeOf ( a ) ) );
  b.l := 500;
  WriteLn ( Equal ( a, b, SizeOf ( b ) ) );
  c.w := 500;
  c.x := 3.141;
```

Listing 14.3 continues

Listing 14.3 continued

```
  c.y := 'C';
  c.z := -1000;
  d.w := 500;
  d.x := 3.141;
  d.y := 'C';
  d.z := 1000;
  WriteLn ( Equal ( c, d, SizeOf ( c ) ) );
  d.z := -1000;
  WriteLn ( Equal ( c, d, SizeOf ( c ) ) );
  WriteLn ( Equal ( a, c, SizeOf ( a ) ) );
End.
```

Listing 14.3 has four variables defined as two different record structures. A and B are the same, as are C and D. During the testing, this routine inadvertently tests A and C. The test shows that they are equal. In a sense, they are equal. C is a superset of what is contained in A. Those two sets contain the same information, but C contains additional information. If you are not aware of this situation, your program's logic could be thrown off. On the other hand, this adds more power to the Compare function. If the first portion of a record is the same, you can compare those portions.

Case Statements With Strings

The case statement works only with ordinal data types. You cannot use it with string variables. For a rather simple way around this problem, define a constant string variable that contains all the possible strings you want to test, separated with unique separators. If you want to check only for single words, spaces make a good separator. For the case selector, you use the string Pos function. The case constants are simply the position of the substring within the constant string. Listing 14.4 shows how this works.

Listing 14.4. String Case Example

```
Program CaseStr;
Const
  StrConst = 'DOG CAT COW PIG SNAKE SEAL FROG DONE';
Var
  i : Integer;
  s : String;
```

```
Begin
  Repeat
    WriteLn ( 'Which animal do you want to hear? ');
    ReadLn ( s );
    For i := 1 to Length ( s ) Do
      s [i] := UpCase ( s [i] );
    If ( Length ( s ) > 0 ) Then
      Case ( Pos ( s, StrConst ) ) Of
         1 : WriteLn ( 'Bark Bark' );
         5 : WriteLn ( 'Meow' );
         9 : WriteLn ( 'Moooo' );
        13 : WriteLn ( 'Oink oink' );
        17 : WriteLn ( 'Hsssss' );
        23 : WriteLn ( 'Oorp orp' );
        28 : WriteLn ( 'Ribbet' );
        33 : ;
      Else
        WriteLn ( 'I do not know that animal. "Done" to quit.' );
      End;
  Until ( s = 'DONE' );
End.
```

The choice of a unique separator is important. Suppose that you add to the list at the end HORSE and FLY separated by a space. You specify that the HORSE (position 38) says "Neigh" and the FLY (position 44) says "Bzzzz". Suppose that somebody wants to know what a Horse Fly sounds like. The program should report that it does not know that animal, but instead it reports "Neigh" because the position of HORSE FLY is the same position as HORSE. A carriage return (ASCII 13) would be a better choice of separator.

Math Functions

Many times, people need to do a quick math calculation in their code, but the language does not directly support it. Rather than lugging your calculus and algebra books around, you can use the following formulas for common math functions.

The power function takes a number to a power and returns the result. Some programming languages have this capability built in, but Pascal does not. It is a simple formula to include. To raise X to the Y power, use the following:

$$X^Y = EXP (Y * LN (X));$$

Similarly, you can use the powers that Turbo Pascal has to get the logarithm of X with base Y. *Log X base Y* is natural log X/natural log Y.

$$LOG_{YX} = LN (X) / LN (Y)$$

The last two formulas are ArcSin and ArcCos, which are derived as follows:

$$ArcSin X = ArcTan (X / SQRT (1 - SQR (X)))$$

$$ArcCos X = ArcTan (SQRT (1 - SQR (X)) / X)$$

Memory Locations

The PC contains some useful addresses that you may be able to use in your programs. There is a location where different programs can communicate. Each time the clock ticks, a memory location is updated. You can determine whether an extended keyboard is attached to the machine. You also can clear the keyboard buffer.

Clock Ticks

In Chapter 7, we discussed the timer-tick interrupt. One of the jobs of this interrupt is to update a location in memory once every 58 milliseconds. This location can be used to do a quick comparison of how long one method takes over another. You can access this location with the MemW command. This command is accessed like an array but takes an address instead of an offset. To get the number of clock ticks, use the following:

```
MyVal := MemW [ $0040 : $006C ];
```

Inter Process Communication Area

Another location in memory that programmers may find of use is the Inter Process Communication area. This is a location 16 bytes in size and not used by DOS. You can place information in this address to communicate something to a child or parent process. You can use the Mem or MemW command,

```
Mem [ $0000 : $04F0 ] through Mem [ $0000 : $04FF ]
```

or you can define a 16-byte array `Absolute` to this address:

```
Type
   ArType = Array [1..16] of Byte;
Var
   IPCA = ArType Absolute $0000:$04F0;
```

Extended Keyboard Address

Another useful address is required for determining whether an extended keyboard is attached to the machine on which the program is running. An extended keyboard usually has its function keys across the top of the keyboard instead of up the left side. It also has two additional keys: F11 and F12. To determine whether this keyboard is attached, check location $0000:$0496:

```
Var
   ExtendedKey : Byte Absolute $0000:$0496;
```

If this location is not equal to zero, an extended keyboard is attached.

Keyboard Buffer

You can clear any keys in the keyboard buffer by using the following loop:

```
While KeyPressed Do
        ch := ReadKey;
```

Ch is a dummy variable.

Another way to clear the keyboard buffer is to set the keyboard head equal to the keyboard tail and the keyboard buffer as a circular buffer. You can set the tail equal to the head this way:

```
MemW [ $0000 : $041C ] := MemW [ $0000 : $041A ];
```

PrintScreen

There is a location in memory that DOS uses to determine whether a print screen is in progress. If it is in progress, any subsequent calls to print the screen are ignored. Therefore, to disable PrtSc, you can trick DOS by setting this flag to indicate that the screen is being printed.

```
Mem [ $0050 : $0000 ] := 1;
```

From that point on, the print screen will be disabled.

You can reenable the print screen by setting the flag to indicate that a print screen is not occurring. The following line lets DOS toggle the `PrintScreen` function.

```
Mem [ $0050 : $0000 ] := 0;
```

Time-Out Length for Printers

There is a location that the BIOS uses for time-out information. This location determines how many tries the BIOS will make before reporting a time out. There is a separate byte for each printer. The bytes each contain the number of retries and default to $14, which is 20 retries. You can set this to a fairly small number, like one or two. Do not set it to zero, or it will loop forever.

```
Type
  ArType = Array [1..4] Byte;
Var
  PrnTimeOut : ArType absolute $0040:$0078;
```

Files and Debugging

A useful tip that was not mentioned Chapter 2 can help you determine why you are running out of file handles. If you get the error message that too many files are open, somehow you are probably not closing all of the files that you are opening. You can easily watch the table DOS uses for keeping track of the file handles by adding a watch variable (Ctrl-F7) in Turbo Debugger or the IDE debugger. The watch variable to add is

```
PTR ( PREFIXSEG, $18 )^,20m
```

What this does is define a pointer to a location in the prefix segment at offset 18. The `20m` indicates that 20 bytes are to be displayed. Wherever you see `$FF`, there is an unused file handle. DOS defaults to eight handles per program; you can change that number with the files statement in your CONFIG.SYS file. (Read your DOS manual for more information on changing your CONFIG.SYS file.) DOS will recognize at most 20 files without making any modifications. It is possible to get DOS to accept more, but the process is complicated. Every program that is loaded will take five handles. The five handles are Standard Input, Standard Output, Standard Error, Standard Auxiliary, and Standard List.

Computing a Direct Address

To compute an address, you need a segment and an offset. Each segment can contain up to 64K of data. The offset helps to address this 64K data area. It can range from $0000 to $FFFF. The computer takes these addresses and converts them to a direct address that the machine understands. You can compute this direct address by doing the following:

```
Address := Segment * 16 + Offset
```

This shifts the segment left four bits and adds the offset to it. Two different segment/offset combinations may point to the same address, so the Turbo Pascal heap does what is called *normalizing*. It computes the address and then reverses the process to give you the smallest possible offset combination. The granularity of this conversion will give you an offset of 15 at most. Every 16 bytes is a segment boundary.

Absolute Disk Read/Write

In Chapter 7, we mentioned that this chapter would discuss how to use interrupts $25 and $26. These interrupts are special cases that cannot be called with the Intr procedure call because they leave extra information on the stack that must be removed. The flags parameter of the Registers record will be left on the stack after the call. To remove the parameter, you must use inline code to make the call.

Interrupt $25 call takes several parameters. AL should be set to the drive number: 0 corresponds to drive A:, 1 to drive B:, and so on. CX should be set to the number of sectors to read. DX should be set to the logical sector number. Finally, DS:BX should be set to the segment and offset of the disk transfer area (DTA).

In listing 14.5 are procedures that will make the Int 25 and 26 calls via inline code.

Listing 14.5. *Absolute Disk Read/Write (Interrupts 25 and 26)*

```
Procedure AbsRead ( var buf; drive, number, logical : Word );
var
  result : integer;
begin
  inline (
    $55/                 { PUSH BP        ; Interrupt 25 trashes all registers    }
```

Listing 14.5 continues

Listing 14.5 continued

```
    $1E/               { PUSH DS        ; Store DS                              }
    $33/$C0/           { XOR  AX,AX     ; set AX to zero                        }
    $89/$86/Result/    { MOV  Result, AX ; Move AX to Result                    }
    $8A/$86/Drive/     { MOV  AL, Drive  ; Move Drive to AL                      }
    $8B/$8E/Number/    { MOV  CX, Number ; Move Number to CX                     }
    $8B/$96/Logical/   { MOV  DX, Logical; Move Logical to DX                    }
    $C5/$9e/Buf/       { LDS  BX, Buf    ; Move Buf to DS:BX                     }
    $CD/$25/           { INT  25h        ; Call interrupt $25                    }
    $5B/               { POP  BX         ; Remove the flags value from the stack }
    $1F/               { POP  DS         ; Restore DS                            }
    $5D/               { POP  BP         ; Restore BP                            }
    $73/$04/           { JNB  Done       ; Jump ...                             }
    $89/$86/Result );  { MOV  Result, AX ; move error code to AX                 }
                       { Done:                                                  }
  If ( Result <> 0 ) Then
    { Error condition... };
End;
Procedure AbsWrite ( var buf; drive, number, logical : Word );
var
  result : Word;
begin
  inline (
    $55/               { PUSH BP         ; Interrupt 25 trashes all registers    }
    $1E/               { PUSH DS         ; Store DS                              }
    $33/$C0/           { XOR  AX,AX      ; set AX to zero                        }
    $89/$86/Result/    { MOV  Result, AX ; Move AX to Result                    }
    $8A/$86/Drive/     { MOV  AL, Drive  ; Move Drive to AL                      }
    $8B/$8E/Number/    { MOV  CX, Number ; Move Number to CX                     }
    $8B/$96/Logical/   { MOV  DX, Logical; Move Logical to DX                    }
    $C5/$9E/Buf/       { LDS  BX, Buf    ; Move Buf to DS:BX                     }
    $CD/$26/           { INT  25h        ; Call interrupt $25                    }
    $5B/               { POP  BX         ; Remove the flags value from the stack }
    $1F/               { POP  DS         ; Restore DS                            }
    $5D/               { POP  BP         ; Restore BP                            }
    $73/$04/           { JNB  Done       ; Jump ...                             }
    $89/$86/Result );  { MOV  Result, AX ; move error code to AX                 }
                       { Done:                                                  }
  If ( Result <> 0 ) Then
    { Error condition... };
End;
```

The routines in listing 14.5 do the following:

1. Store the DS and BP registers. The BP register must be stored
   because we use BP relative addressing to determine where variables
   are located on the stack, and interrupts $25 and $26 destroy all[1]

registers except segment registers. The DS register must be saved because we overwrite its value for one of the parameters to the interrupt call.

2. Initialize the `Result` variable to zero.

3. Start loading the parameters into the specified registers.

4. Move the drive number into AL, the number of bytes to read/write into CX, the number of the logical sector to start reading from into DX, and the buffer address into DS and BX.

5. Do the actual interrupt call.

6. Pop the flag's value that is still on the stack into the BX register. We do not need to consult this value; we ignore it.

7. Restore the BP and DS registers. If an error condition has occurred, load the value in AX (the error code) into the `Result` variable.

The read and write routines have been written separately, but they are virtually identical. It would not be too difficult to make them into one routine to which you can pass a flag to determine which you wish to use. Because these are powerful and potentially dangerous routines (you could overwrite your boot sector and lose lots of information), we recommend that you keep them separate. This will ensure that you do not accidentally forget what state to set the flag to for reading or writing.

Do not use the `AbsWrite` routine unless you definitely know what you are doing. Even if you do know what you are doing, you may want to back up any valuable data that is on your machine before experimenting with these routines.

Patches

As clean a product as Turbo Pascal V5.0 is, a few patches are necessary to fix minor problems in it. The patches follow and require the use of DEBUG that comes with most versions of DOS.

> Warning!!! These patches are only for Turbo Pascal V5.0. Do not attempt to use these patches on any other version of the compiler. Turbo Pascal V5.5 does not need these corrections.

Turbo Debugger Include Files Patches

The following patch fixes a minor problem that prevented Turbo Debugger from knowing the name of an `include` file.

Patch for TPC.EXE

1. Rename TPC.EXE to TPC.BIN.

2. Debug TPC.BIN.

3. Type the following:

   A A5D3 <Enter>

   CMP SI,DX <Enter>

   <Enter>

4. Save the changes to disk.

5. Quit.

6. Rename TPC.BIN back to TPC.EXE.

Patch for TURBO.EXE

1. Rename TURBO.EXE to TURBO.BIN.

2. Debug TURBO.BIN.

3. Dump the register values.

4. Calculate the value of the CS register + 1000h.

5. Type the following:

   A above__value:A41E <Enter>

   CMP SI,DX <Enter>

   <Enter>

6. Save the changes to disk.

7. Quit.

8. Rename TURBO.BIN back to TURBO.EXE.

VGA Mode Patch

When on a VGA in graphics mode 13h, the graphics image will not get saved completely, this patch corrects the problem.

1. Rename TURBO.EXE to TURBO.BIN.

2. Debug TURBO.BIN.

3. Type the following:

   E A62A

4. At the prompt ????:A62A 12._, type the following:

   13 <Enter>

5. Save the changes to disk.

6. Quit.

7. Rename TURBO.BIN back to TURBO.EXE.

Interrupt 60h Overwritten Patch

When in the Turbo IDE, interrupt 60h may get overwritten. This patch corrects this problem.

1. Rename TURBO.EXE to TURBO.BIN.

2. Debug TURBO.BIN.

3. Type the following:

   E 1576

4. At the prompt ????:1576 04._, type the following:

   02 <Enter>

5. Save the changes to disk.

6. Quit.

7. Rename TURBO.BIN back to TURBO.EXE.

EGA Graphics Mode Patch

This will patch a problem that occurs when you are working within the IDE with a program that uses an EGA graphics page other than page 0.

1. Rename TURBO.EXE to TURBO.BIN.

2. Debug TURBO.BIN.

3. Type the following:

   E A02D 90 90 90 90 90 90 90 90 90 90 90 90 90 90 90 90

4. Type the following:

   E A03D 90 90 90 90 90 90 90

5. Save the changes to disk.

6. Quit.

7. Rename TURBO.BIN back to TURBO.EXE.

Technical Support

Borland International has an excellent team of support representatives, and you can obtain support for any of your Borland products through various means: using the CompuServe Information Service (GO BORLAND), letters, and phone.

CompuServe Support

The CompuServe Information Service is the best place to get technical support. Not only will you get help from Borland representatives, but you may even get help from other users who have encountered the same difficulties you have. The people on the Borland forums are helpful and knowledgeable. Someone on the forum will be able to answer your question, whether it is basic (How do I install my product?) or advanced (How do I write a terminate-and-stay-resident program?). The best things about using CompuServe to get support are the number of users out there who can help you and the data libraries to which you have access. Literally hundreds of programs are available that show how to do many different things: serial communications, windowing packages, TSR libraries, keyboard handlers, EMS handlers. The list goes on.

The CompuServe service is easy to learn to use. It is menu-driven, and people are more than willing to help you. An example of a useful and well-written library is the Tesseract library. This is a shareware library of routines that make writing a terminate-and-stay-resident program almost trivial in Turbo Pascal, Turbo C, or Turbo Assembler. These routines take the headaches out of writing a TSR. Support for the library is provided to users on the Computer Language Magazine Forum (GO CLMFOR) on CompuServe.

Mail Support

If you do not have access to a modem, the best way to obtain technical support is through the mail. Borland requires that you send the serial number of the product(s) about which you are writing with questions. If you need to send a program to demonstrate the problem, they also require that the program be placed onto a diskette and that it be fewer than 100 lines in length. The technical support department receives many letters every day and cannot spend the time required to examine larger programs. Every problem we have encountered can be reproduced in well under 100 lines. (If you have a problem that you cannot reproduce in under 100 lines, the problem probably lies in something as simple as an uninitialized pointer.)

Phone Support

If the problem is important, and you cannot wait to send a letter, your last resort is to call for technical support. You must have your serial number when you call, or you will be denied support. When you call, it is extremely important that you be near your computer and have all of the information ready in front of you. Try to be as brief as possible when describing the problem. Calling for support should be a last resort, after you have tried CompuServe and sending a letter.

Borland does not provide technical support to teach people how to program. It is expected that you have learned or are learning the language on your own. Borland has an excellent product that helps teach Turbo Pascal, the *Turbo Pascal Tutor*. This product is recommended for anybody who is learning to program in Pascal, or Turbo Pascal specifically.

Technical support is not provided to help you write your programs. If you are encountering a problem that appears to be the fault of the compiler, narrow the problem as far as possible before contacting Borland. If the problem disappears as you narrow your code, the code you eliminated is probably the cause of the problem.

Another important thing to do before contacting Technical Support is to read the README file on your original program diskette. Last-minute changes or manual corrections may be provided on the diskette. For example, the Install program that is provided with Turbo Pascal V5.0 and later is not mentioned in the V5.0 manual. It is mentioned only in the README file for that version. The Install program is important because it will automatically copy the files into the correct directories for you and unpack several files that are compressed to fit onto the distribution diskettes.

Turbo Users Group

Turbo Users Group (TUG) is a good source of public domain and shareware programs. TUG has libraries of public domain and shareware programs that it sends out for nominal fees. It also has a newsletter that discusses a large range of different topics dealing with Turbo programming. The TUG deals with more than just Turbo Pascal; its members also use Turbo Assembler, Turbo Debugger, Turbo Basic, Turbo C, and Turbo Prolog. To contact this organization, use the following information:

The Turbo Users Group
PO Box 1510
Poulsbo, WA 98370
(206) 779-9508

Common Problems

During the development stages of your program, you should always have range checking on {$R+}; the code does not default to {R+}. Range checking ensures all the arrays and strings you are accessing are within the defined bounds of the variable. For example, suppose that you define a variable as an array from 1 to 10. With range checking off, you can access the eleventh element of this array, even though its legal limit is 10. Having range checking enabled will catch this problem at run time. Otherwise, you may overwrite your program or data.

Another common mistake occurs with pointers. If you fail to allocate memory for your pointers with New or GetMem, you should not access them because the pointer will not contain a legal value until one of these calls is made. Programs commonly lock up, or cause DOS errors (Cannot load COMMAND.COM. System halted.) because a pointer variable was not allocated memory before a value was assigned to it. After the variable has been disposed of, make sure you do not access it again, unless you use New or GetMem. You can use the debugger to step through your program and watch the variables you are accessing to make sure memory is getting allocated for them. Many people are under the false impression that nil is an illegal address for a pointer and the compiler will not allow assignments to it. This is wrong; if you assign a pointer to nil, you are making a pointer that points to the beginning of memory segment 0, offset 0. DOS stores the interrupt vector table at this location. Therefore, if you assign a pointer to nil and then assign a value to the pointer, you have overwritten the interrupt vector table, and the machine will probably hang.

Conclusion

The tips in this chapter will help you in your programming needs and save you a little time. If you have not encountered any of the problems that the patches in this chapter fix, we recommend that you do not apply the patches to the program. Instead, apply them as necessary if the problems arise. If you are upgrading to Turbo Pascal V5.5, you will not need them at all.

If you discover special tricks of the trade, feel free to tell other people about them. The best place to share these kinds of resources is on an electronic service like CompuServe, on a bulletin board system in your area, or in a magazine or users' group like TUG. Everybody likes to hear about simple ways to do things. Maybe your idea will provoke others to post theirs.

Index

#219 character, 195
80386 debugging, 61-62
@ symbol identifiers, 102
{$F+} compiler directive, 201-202
{$F-} compiler directive, 201-202
{$V-} compiler directive, 41

A

Absolute Disk Read/Write (Interrupts 25 and 26) listing, 429-430
Abstract object, 412
access mode, 364
Accessing a Global Variable listing, 69-70
active call, 233
Add Watch window, 40
Alt-F (File Menu) key, 12
Alt-F6 key, 11
Ancestor object, 412
Append procedure, 178
Application Program Interface (API), 386-387
ARC file extension, 8
ARG directive, 80-81
assembly language mnemonic, 142
assembly language, vs inline code, 142
Assembly Mnemonics listing, 143
Assign procedure, 174

B

BGI Image Save and Restore listing, 333-337
BGI Program listing, 305-306
BGI.ARC file, 301, 306
BINOBJ utility, 245-246
BIOS Crt unit, 178
BIOS Crt Unit listing, 186-195
BIOS device, 175
BIOS Gray Scaling listing, 340
BIOS interface, with graphics, 340-342
BiosBkWrite procedure, 195
Black Figure on Color Background listing, 330-331
black images, drawing on color background, 329-331
BlankIt procedure, 311
BlankXY listing, 286
Block cursor patch listing, 13
Boolean variable, 206-208
borders
  window, 263
    drawing, 274-276
Borland Graphics Interface (BGI), 3, 301
BP relative addressing, 72-73
braces, comment, 11
Break/watch menu, 44-45

BreakOut.Pas listing, 213-214
Breakpoint Program listing, 55
Breakpoint window, 53-54
breakpoints, 46
    complex, 53-57
buffer files, flushing, 170-171
buffers, 175, 179
    overlay, 232-234
BURNIN.PAS listing, 420
BYTE-aligned, 68

C

C-intrinsic functions, 102
CALL FAR function, 152
CALL function, 152
Call Stack function listing, 47
Call Stack option, 46-48
Call Stack window, 46-47
calling conventions, 152
calls
    active, 233
    FAR, 80-81, 175, 201-202
    inline, 145-148
    NEAR, 80-81, 155
    to external routine, 98-100
Cannot find run-time error location message,
    16
case statements, 424-425
CGA display character, 195
characters, #219, 195
    CGA display, 195
    in windows, 289-291
CheckIt.PAS listing, 383-385
circular queue, 234
CLD Turbo Assembler command, 85, 88
clock ticks, 426
Close function, 175, 179

CloseGraph procedure, 303
code segment, CSEG, 92
code
    changing indentation of, 10
    entry, 67
    exit, 67
    inline, 141-172
    self-modifying, 417-421
    Turbo C Runtime Library (RTL), 103-105
commands
    DOS, DEBUG, 142-148
    Turbo Assembler
        CLD, 85, 88
        LODSB, 85, 88
        STOSB, 85, 88
comment braces, 11
Comparison of Any Two Variables listing,
    421-422
compiler directives, 16-18
    Force Far Calls off {$F-}, 201-202
    Force Far Calls on {$F+}, 201-202
    Var-String Checking off {$V-}, 41
    Debug Information off {$D-}, 43
    Debug Information on {$D+}, 36
    Input/Output off {$I-}, 42
    Local Symbol Generation off {SL-}, 43
    Local Symbol Information on {$L+}, 36
    Overlay Code Generation {$O}, 234-235
    Range Checking off {$R-}, 42
    Stack-Overflow Checking {$S-}, 42
    viewing environment-set, 12
compilers, Turbo C (TCC), parameters for,
    92-93
complex
    breakpoints, 53-57
    data types, comparing, 421-424
CompuServe support, 434-435
conditional defines, 223

Config auto save option, 15
CONFIG.SYS file, 343, 428
configuration file, 9
constants
    CValueIncrement, 331
    typed, 418-419
constructors, 390, 413
    descendant, 411
context-sensitive help, 30
CPASDEMO.OBJ file, 138
current pointer, repositioning, 311
Cursor Manipulation Routines listing,
    166-168
cursor
    enlarging, 12-13
    manipulation routines, 166-168
CValueIncrement constant, 331

D

Data Segment, 76-77
    DSEG, 92
data
    input in graphics mode, 310-317
    items, modifying, 48-51
    overlaying, 250-254
    structure, defining, 272
    types, comparing complex, 421-424
DEBUG DOS command, 142-148
Debug Include File listing, 52
Debug Information off {$D-} compiler
    directive, 43
Debug Information on {$D+} compiler
    directive, 16, 36
Debug menu, 36
debugger example listing, 39-41
debugger IDE parameters, 36
debugger memory constraints, 41-42

debugging
    80386, 61-62
    adding watch variables, 43-45
    files, 428
    integrated, 35
    keystrokes, list of, 37-38
    large programs, 43
    remote, 59-61
    small programs, 42
DefineBorder procedure, 263
Delete watch option, 45
DEMOS.ARC file, 317
descendant constructor, 411
descendant object, 413
Destination Index (DI), 85
destructors, 393-397, 413
Determining Unit Order in OVR file listing,
    256-259
device dependent programs, 3
device drivers
    examples, 180-195
    listings, 176-178
    TD386, 61-62
Device-Independent
    functions, list of, 316-317
    graphics programs, 306-310
    procedures, list of, 316-317
Device-Independent Program listing, 307-310
direct address, computing, 429
directives
    ARG, 80-81
    compiler, 16-18
    Debug Information {$D+}, 16, 36, 43
    Emulation {$E+}, 16
    environment-set compiler, 12
    Force Far Calls {$F+/-}, 16
    Input/Output Checking {$I+}, 16-17
    LOCAL, 82
    Local Symbol Information {$L+}, 17

Memory Allocation Size {$M}, 17
MODEL, 83
Range Checking {$R-}, 17
Stack-Overflow Checking {$S+}, 17
Var-String Checking {$V+}, 18
directories
EXE, 14
include, 14
object, 14
separating with semicolons, 14
TPU, 14
unit, 14
directory options, setting, 13-14
DoBorder listing, 275-276
DoBorder routine, 262
Driving Program for 8.15 listing, 256
Driving Program for EchoDev Unit listing, 185
Driving Program listing, 178

E

early binding, 413
EchoIt procedure, 311
Edit auto save option, 15
Edit watch option, 45
EditTool Unit listing, 291-295
EGA
graphics mode patch, 433-434
palette, 327
Ega Palette Demonstration listing, 328-329
EmmError function, 353
EmmMaxAvail variable, 346
EMS32.PAS listing, 347-353
Emulation {$E+} directive, 16
encapsulation, 414
entry code, 67
environment-set compiler directives, 12

EPSON Screen Dump listing, 319-322
equates, 73
error help, 32
errors, I/O, 175
Evaluate listing, 50
Evaluate option, 49, 58
Evaluate window, 48-51
event-driven programming, 223
Example TFDD listing, 176-177
EXE directory, 14
exit code, 67
Exit procedure, 203
ExmplEMS.Pas listing, 355-360
expanded memory, 3
explained, 343-345
Expanded Memory Manager (EMM), 346-347
Expanded Memory Specification (EMS), 346-347
expanded memory steps (EMS), 3
EXPTABS.ASM listing, 117
extended
keyboard address, 427
memory, explained, 343-345
extensibility, 414
external
method, 80
routine, calls to, 98-100

F

F1 (Help) key, 31
Fail Demonstration program listing, 392
Fail procedure, 391-392
FAR call, 80-81, 175, 201-202
fields, Mode, 178-180
File Control Block (FCB), 364
file editor help, 31
file extensions, ARC, 8

File menu, 12
file modes, 364-369
    bit fields, list of, 365
    values, list of, 366
FILELOCK.PAS listing, 380-382
FileMode variable, 365
files
    alternating between multiple, 11
    as semaphores, 369-371
    BGI.ARC, 301, 306
    CONFIG.SYS, 343, 428
    configuration, 9
    CPASDEMO.OBJ, 138
    debugging, 428
    DEMOS.ARC, 317
    flushing buffer, 170-171
    global changing, 15
    graphics, 8
    include, 14
    linking object (OBJ), 91-105
    MAP, 14
    OBJ, 14, 245-246
    OVR, 239-245
    printing, 12
    random access 179
    restrictions of linked object, 92
    saving options to, 14-15
    TCCONFIG.TC, 92
    TDH386.SYS, 61
    TDREMOTE.EXE, 60
    TOOLS.PAS, 116-117
    TPC.CFG, 9
    TPU, 14
    TURBO.EXE, 15
    TURBO.PCK, 18-30
    TURBO.TP, 15
    TURBOC.CFC, 93
    unlinkable object, 103
    UNPACK.COM, 8

WINDTOOL.OBJ, 278
Final Turbo Pascal Program listing, 144-145
flags, INDOS, 200
floppy diskette installation, 8
Flush File Buffer listing, 170-171
Flush function, 179
fonts, user loaded, 195
Force Far Calls {$F+/-} directive, 16
function result registers, 75
function results, 74-75
    returning, 152-153
functions
    C-intrinsic, 102
    CALL, 152
    CALL FAR, 152
    Close, 175, 179
    EmmError, 353
    Flush, 179
    GetPixel, 317-318
    GetVideoMode, 340
    HiWord, 169-170
    ignore, 175
    inline, 152-153
    inline macros for, 164-166
    InOut, 180
    IOResult, 17
    LoWord, 169-170
    math, 425-426
    Open, 175, 178-179
    power, 425-426
    ReadKey, 310
    SizeOf, 379
    with inline code, 151

G

Game.Pas listing, 216-222
GameInt9.Pas listing, 215-216

Generic Initialization Procedure listing, 174
Get Video Address listing, 264-265
Get Video Mode Function listings, 338-339
GetIntVec procedure, 202, 346
GetLine Procedure listing, 287-288
GetPageFrame procedure, 347
GetPixel function, 317-318
GetRGBPalette procedure, 339
GetRGBPalette procedure listing, 339
GetVideoMode function, 340
GetViewSettings procedure, 318
GetWindowSize listing, 265
global variables, 67-70
    with EMS, 354
    with inline code, 157
Gprint.Pas listing, 208-211
graphics
    drivers, list of, 302-303
    files, 8
    images
        printing, 317-326
        saving to disk, 333-337
    mode, 180
        data input, 310-317
    programs, device-independent, 306-310
    screen, 174
Gray Scale Demonstration listing, 332-333
gray scale, creating, 339-340

H

hard disk installation, 8-9
hardware interrupts, 198-199
Heap Memory Test with InitGaph listing, 304
help
    context-sensitive, 30
    error, 32
    file editor, 31
    programming, 31-32
    resident, 33
    THELP, 33-34
Hewlett-Packard LaserJet Screen Dump
    listing, 322-326

I

I/O error, 175
IDE menu, 31
identifiers, variable, 156-157
ignore function, 175
include
    directories, 14
    files, 14
INDOS flag, 200
inheritance, 414
InitGraph procedure, 303, 306
INKEY.ASM listing, 118-119
inline calls, 145-148
inline code
    creating, 142-145
    explained, 141
    function results, 152-153
    global variables, 157
    jumps from, 149-151
    macros with, 158-164
    oversized parameters, 155-156
    parameter location, 151
    parameters, 153-155
    referencing pointer variables, 157-158
    variable identifiers, 156-157
    variables, 155-156
    vs assembly language, 142
    with functions, 151
    with procedures, 151
Inline Function listing, 154
inline functions, 152-153

Inline Jump Instructions listing, 150
inline keyword, 141
Inline Macro and Parameter Types listing,
    161-163
Inline Macro Returning Function Result
    listing, 164-165
inline macros, 144, 158-164
    functions as, 164-166
    parameters for, 160-164
inline procedure, 144
inline statement, 141-142
InOut function, 180
InOut routines, 180
input field, window, 287-289
Input/Output Checking off {$I-} compiler
    directive, 42
Input/Output Checking on {$I+} compiler
    directive, 16-17
Inspect item option, 58
Inspect window, 57-59
Inspect Window listing, 58-59
Install Turbo Pascal
    Floppy Drive option, 8
    Hard Drive option, 8-9
installation, possible problems, 9
instance, 414
instructions
    jump, 149-151
    RET, 80-81
Int05.Pas listing, 207-208
Int1C.Pas listing, 225
integrated debugging, 35
Integrated debugging option, 36
Integrated Development Environment (IDE)
    2
    debugger parameters, 36
    explained, 7
Inter Process Communication Area, 426-427
interface routines, 2

Interrupt 60h Overwritten patch, 433
interrupt keyword, 200-201
Interrupt service routines, (ISR), 3
    restoration process, 203-204
    restrictions, 199-200
interrupt vectors
    saving, 202
    setting new, 202-203
interrupts
    explained, 197-198
    hardware, 198-199
    logical, 198
    print screen, 206-208
    software, 199
    timer, 224-227
IOResult function, 17

J

jump instructions, from inline code, 149-151

K

keyboard buffer, 427
keyboard shortcuts
    Alt-F (File Menu), 12
    Alt-F6, 11
    Ctrl-K, 10
    Ctrl-KB, 10
    Ctrl-KI, 10
    Ctrl-KK, 10
    Ctrl-KP, 12
    Ctrl-KR (Block Read), 24
    Ctrl-KU, 10
    Ctrl-KW (Block Write), 24
    Ctrl-Q, 11
    Ctrl-QA (Search and Replace), 24

Ctrl-QF (Search), 24
Ctrl-QW, 10-11
debugger, 37-38
keys, F1 (Help), 31
keywords
inline, 141
interrupt, 200-201
RETURNS, 81-82

L

last error position, finding, 10-11
late binding, 413-414
linked language assembly, restrictions, 66
Linked List Program listing, 395-397
Linked List Unit (Destructors) listing, 394-395
linking object (OBJ) files, 91-105
linking utilities, 105-138
LISTER.PAS program, 12
listings
Absolute Disk Read/Write (Interrupts 25 and 26), 429-430
Accessing a Global Variable, 69-70
Assembly Mnemonics, 143
BGI Image Save and Restore, 333-337
BGI Program, 305-306
BIOS Crt Unit, 186-195
BIOS Gray Scaling, 340
Black Figure on Color Background, 330-331
BlankXY, 286
Block cursor patch, 13
BreakOut.Pas, 213-214
Breakpoint Program, 55
BURNIN.PAS, 420
Call Stack function, 47
CheckIt.PAS, 383-385

Comparison of Any Two Variables, 421-422
Cursor Manipulation Routines, 166-168
Debug Include File, 52
debugger example, 39-41
Determining Unit Order in OVR file, 256-259
Device-Independent Program, 307-310
DoBorder, 275-276
Driving Program for 8.15, 256
Driving Program for EchoDev Unit, 185
Driving Programs, 177-178
EditTool Unit, 291-295
EGA Palette Demonstration, 328-329
EMS32.PAS, 347-353
EPSON Screen Dump, 319-322
Evaluate, 50
Example TFDD, 176-177
ExmplEMS.Pas, 355-360
EXPTABS.ASM, 117
Fail Demonstration program, 392
FILELOCK.PAS, 380-382
Final Turbo Pascal Program, 144-145
Flush File Buffer, 170-171
Game.Pas, 216-222
GameInt9.Pas, 215-216
Generic Initialization Procedure, 174
Get Video Address, 264-265
Get Video Mode Function, 338-339
GetLine Procedure, 287-288
GetRGBPalette Procedure, 339
GetWindowSize, 265
Gprint.Pas, 208-211
Gray Scale Demonstration, 332-333
Heap Memory Test with InitGraph, 304
Hewlett-Packard LaserJet Screen Dump, 322-326
INKEY.ASM, 118-119
Inline Function, 154

Inline Jump Instructions, 150

Inline Macro and Parameter Types, 161-163

Inline Macro Returning Function Result, 164-165

Inspect Window, 58-59

Int05.Pas, 207-208

Int1C.Pas, 225

Linked List Program, 395-397

Linked List Unit (Destructors), 394-395

LOCKIT.PAS, 382-383

LoWord and HiWord Functions, 169-170

MACROS.ASM, 119-122

Main Driving Program, 252-253

Main Program, 241-242

MASTER.PAS, 367

MEMCOMP.ASM, 122-123

Modified C Module, 97

Modified Pascal Code, 97-98

MyGraph.Pas, 212

Object Adventure, 400-411

Overlay Initializing Unit, 247-249

Overlay Program, 237-238

Overlay Unit 1, 235-236

Overlay Unit 2, 236

Overlay Unit 3, 236-237

PARSE.ASM, 123-127

PickEdit Program, 26-29

ProcessChar Procedure, 289-290

Program C2P, 110-116

Program TC2TP, 106-109

Program TestGrafRead Unit, 315-316

Program To Create Data File, 253

Pseudo File-Locking Program, 385-386

PushWindow and PopWindow, 273-274

Replacement Printer Unit, 181-183

RIGHTSTR.ASM, 127-129

Sample Compare Program, 423-424

Sample Unit for Procedure Order in .OVR File, 240

SEARCH.ASM, 129-131

SERVANT.PAS, 368-369

SI and DI Save Routine, 97

Signature Routine and Surrounding Unit, 255

Skeleton.Pas, 205-206

String Case Example, 424-425

Strip Character Pascal Code, 87

Strip Character Turbo Assembler Code, 86-87

Swap Procedure Pascal Code, 84-85

Swap Procedure Turbo Assembler Code, 84

Test of Get RGB Palette, Create Gray Scale, Get Video Mode 341-342

TICTAC.PAS, 372-379

TimeIt.Pas, 226-227

TOOLS.PAS, 135-138

TPC Debugging Batch File, 52

Translated Inline Statement, 144

TRIM.ASM, 131-134

Turbo C Calling C RTL, 104

Turbo C Character Conversion Module, 93-94

Turbo C Module, 99

Turbo C Module (Call to Turbo Pascal), 95

Turbo C Variable Modification Module, 101

Turbo Pascal Character Conversion Program, 94-95

Turbo Pascal Driving Program, 95-96

Turbo Pascal Driving Routine for Call to CRTL Function, 104-105

Turbo Pascal Program, 99-100

Turbo Pascal Variable Modification
Program, 101-102
UCASE.ASM, 134-135
Unit A, 243-244
Unit GrafRead, 312-315
Unit One, 242
Unit Three, 243
Unit to Access OBJ Data, 251-252
Unit to Echo Screen and Printer, 183-185
Unit Two, 242-243
Using NOPs, 145-146
Variable Parameter Access with Inline
Code, 156-157
Variable Versus Pointer Parameters, 158
Video Rental program, 296-299
VMT Mixup, 398
WindTool Assembler Code, 267-270
WindTool Unit Code, 279-285
LOCAL directive, 82
Local Symbol Generation off {SL-} compiler
directive, 43
Local Symbol Information on {$L+} compiler
directive, 17, 36
local variables, 72-74
LOCKIT.PAS listing, 382-383
LODSB Turbo Assembler command, 85, 88
logical interrupts, 198
logical page, 347
LoWord and HiWord Function listing,
169-170

M

MACROS.ASM listing, 119-122
macros
C, defining registers, 96
inline, 158-164
mail support, 435

Main Driving Program listing, 252-253
Main Program listing, 241-242
MAP file, 14
markers, 10
MASTER.PAS listing, 367
math functions, 425-426
MCGA palette, 327
MEMCOMP.ASM listing, 122-123
Memory Allocation Size {$M} directive, 17
memory
constraints, debugger, 41-42
expanded, 3, 343-345
extended, 343-345
locations, 426
overlays in, 254
video, 264-271
menus
Break/watch, 44-45
Debug, 36
File, 12
IDE, 31
Options/Compiler, 36-37
messages
Cannot find run-time error location, 16
Symbol not found, 44
Unknown identifier, 44
methods, 414
calling, 79
writing in assembler, 80
Mode field, 178-180
MODEL directive, 83
modes
access, 364
file, 364-369
graphics, 180
data input, 310-317
sharing, 366
video, 264-265
Modified C Module listing, 97

Modified Pascal Code listing, 97-98
modules, linking with Turbo C Runtime
    Library, 103-105
MovWindow routine, 262
multiuser
    difficulties, 363-364
    programs, 371-379
MyGraph.Pas listing, 212

N

NEAR call, 80-81, 155
networks, multiuser difficulties, 363-364
New procedure, 390
New value option, 49
null modem cable, 60

O

OBJ files, 14, 245-246
Object Adventure listing, 400-411
object
    directories, 14
    files
        linking restrictions, 92
        unlinkable, 103
object-oriented programming, 1
    explained, 389
objects
    Abstract, 412
    Ancestor, 412
    Descendant, 413
    saving to disk, 412
    static, 75-76
    Stream, 412
offsets, pick list, 18-23
Open function, 175, 178-179

OpenWindow routine, 262
operators, override, 148-149
options
    Call stack, 46-48
    Config auto save, 15
    Delete watch, 45
    directory, 13-14
    Edit auto save, 15
    Edit watch, 45
    Evaluate, 49, 58
    Inspect item, 58
    Install Turbo Pascal on a floppy drive, 8
    Install Turbo Pascal on a hard drive, 8
    Integrated debugging, 36
    New value, 49
    Range, 58
    Result, 49
    Save Options, 15
    saving to a file, 14-15
    Unpack Example & Utility Archives:, 9
    Update Turbo Pascal V4.0 to V5.0, 8-9
Options/Compiler menu, 36-37
Options/Environment window, 15
overlay buffer, 232-234
Overlay Code Generation compiler directive
    {$O}, 234-235
Overlay Initializing Unit listing, 247-249
overlay manager
    errors in, 246-250
    requirements, 234-235
Overlay Program listing, 237-238
overlay stubs, 246
Overlay Unit 1 listing, 235-236
Overlay Unit 2 listing, 236
Overlay Unit 3 listing, 236-237
overlay utilities, 255-259
overlayed programs, execution, 245-246
overlaying data, 250-254

overlays
    explained, 213-232
    keeping in memory, 254
override operators, 148-149
oversized parameters, with inline code,
    155-156
OVR file, 239-245
    order of units procedures, 241
OvrGetRetry procedure, 234
OvrSetRetry procedure, 234

P

page
    logical, 347
    physical, 347
palettes
    EGA, 327
    MCGA, 327
    understanding, 326-327
    VGA, 329
parameter location, with inline code, 152
parameters
    accessing, 153-155
    oversized, 155-156
    reference, 152
    value, 152
PARSE.ASM listing, 123-127
patches, 431-434
    EGA graphics mode, 433-434
    Interrupt 60h Overwritten, 433
    Turbo Debugger Include Files (TPC.EXE),
      432
    TURBO.EXE, 432
    VGA mode, 433
PathToDrivers constant variable, 301
phone support, 435-436
physical page, 347

pick list, 18
pick list offsets, 18-23
PickEdit program listing, 26-29
place markers, 10
pointer variables, referencing, 157-158
polymorphism, 414
power function, 425-426
print screen interrupts, 206-208
printers, time-out length for, 428
printing
    files, 12
    graphics images, 317-326
    program listings, 12
PrintScreen, disabling, 427-428
procedures
    Append, 178
    Assign, 174
    BiosBkWrite, 195
    BlankIt, 311
    CloseGraph, 303
    DefineBorder, 263
    EchoIt, 311
    Exit, 203
    Fail, 391-392
    GetIntVec, 202, 346
    GetPageFrame, 347
    GetRGBPalette, 339
    GetViewSettings, 318
    InitGraph, 303, 306
    New, 390
    OvrGetRetry, 234
    OvrSetRetry, 234
    ReadString, 311
    Reset, 178
    RestoreCrtMode, 305
    Rewrite, 178
    SetBKColor, 327
    SetGraphMode, 305
    SetIntVec, 202-203

SetRGBPalette, 327, 331-333
window, 261-262
with inline code, 151
ProcessChar Procedure listing, 289-290
profiler program, 224
Program C2P listing, 110-116
program listings, printing, 12
program lockups, 397-399
Program TC2TP listing, 106-109
Program TestGrafRead Unit listing, 315-316
Program To Create Data File listing, 253
program utilities, 3-4
programming
event-driven, 223
help, 31-32
object-oriented, 1, 389-416
programs
adding sound, 264
advantages of Turbo C, 91
debugging large, 43
debugging small, 42
debugging with Turbo Debugger, 51-62
LISTER.PAS, 12
profiler, 224
TINST, 15
troubleshooting, 436-437
writing multiuser, 371-379
Pseudo File-Locking Program listing, 385-386
PushWindow and PopWindow listing,
273-274

R

random access files, 179
Range Checking off {$R-} compiler directive,
17, 42
Range option, 58
raw color value, 327

ReadKey function, 310
ReadString procedure, 311
record locking, 379-386
reference parameter, with inline code, 152
registers
defining C macro for, 96
function result, 75
remote debugging, 59-61
replace string, 24
Replacement Printer Unit listing, 181-183
Reset procedure, 178
resident help, 33
RestoreCrtMode procedure, 305
Result option, 49
RET instruction, 80-81
RETURNS keyword, 81-82
reverse video field, window, 286-287
Rewrite procedure, 178
RIGHTSTR.ASM listing, 127-129
routines
DoBorder, 262
InOut, 180
interfacing, 2
MovWindow, 262
OpenWindow, 262
WindowSound, 262

S

Sample Compare Program listing, 423-424
Sample Unit for Procedure Order in .OVR
File listing, 240
Save Options option, 15
saving
graphics images, 333-337
interrupt vectors, 202
objects to disk, 412
screens, graphics, 174

self-modifying code, 4, 417-421

semaphores, using files as, 369-371

semicolons, separating directories, 14

SEARCH.ASM listing, 129-131

serial devices, 174

SERVANT.PAS listing, 368-369

SetBKColor procedure, 327

SetGraphMode procedure, 305

SetIntVec procedure, 202-203

SetRGBPalette procedure, 327, 331-333

sharing modes, list of, 366

SI and DI Save Routine listing, 97

Signature Routine and Surrounding Unit
listing, 255

SizeOf function, 379

Skeleton.pas listing, 205-206

software interrupts, 199

sound
  adding to programs, 264
  adding to windows tools, 277-278

source code, Turbo C Runtime Library
  (RTL), 103-105

Source Index (SI), 85

stack, window, 271

Stack-Overflow Checking off {$S-} compiler
  directive, 42

Stack-Overflow Checking on {$S+} compiler
  directive, 17

statements
  case, 424-425
  inline, 141-142
  Write, 178, 180
  Writeln, 178

static methods, 79, 414

static objects, 75-76

STOSB Turbo Assembler command, 85, 88

Stream object, 412

String Case Example listing, 424-425

strings, with case statements, 424-425

Strip Character Pascal Code listing, 87

Strip Character Turbo Assembler Code
  listings, 86-87

structure, text file, 178

support
  CompuServe, 434-435
  mail, 435
  phone, 435-436
  technical, 434
  Turbo Users Group (TUG), 436

swap procedure, 83-86

Swap Procedure Pascal Code listing, 84-85

Swap Procedure Turbo Assembler Code
  listing, 84

Symbol not found message, 44

symbols, @, 102

T

TCCONFIG.TC file, 92

TD386 device driver, 61-62

TDH386.SYS file, 61

TDREMOTE command line parameters, 60

TDREMOTE.EXE file, 60

terminate and stay resident programs (TSR),
  4
  with EMS, 361-362

Test of Get RGB Palette, Create Gray Scale,
  Get Video Mode
  listing, 341-342

text file, 174
  handling routines, 173
  structure, 178

text file device drivers (TFDD) 173-195
  implementing, 173

text, storing under windows, 262-263

THELP, 33-34

TICTAC.PAS listing, 372-379

TimeIt.Pas listing, 226-227
timer interrupt, 224-227
TINST program, 15
titles, on windows, 277
TOOLS.PAS file, 116-117
TPC Debugging Batch File listing, 52
TPC.CFG file, 9
TPU directory, 14
TPU files, 14
Translated Inline Statement listing, 144
TRIM.ASM listing, 131-134
troubleshooting programs, 436-437
Turbo C
    Calling C RTL listing, 104
    Character Conversion Module listing,
      93-94
    compiler (TCC), parameters for, 92-93 ·
    Module listing, 99
    Module (Call to Turbo Pascal) listing, 99
    Runtime Library (RTL) source code,
      103-105
    Variable Modification Module listing, 101
Turbo Debugger, 51-62
Turbo Debugger Include Files (TPC.EXE),
    patch, 432
Turbo Pascal
    Character Conversion Program listing,
      94-95
    Driving Program listing, 95-96
    Program listing, 99-100
    Variable Modification Program listing,
      101-102
Turbo Users Group (TUG) support, 436
Turbo Pascal Driving Routine for Call to
    CRTL Function
    listing 104-105
TURBO.EXE file, 15
TURBO.EXE patch, 432
TURBO.PCK file, 18-30

editing, 25-30
TURBO.TP file, 15
TURBOC.CFG file, 93
typed constants, 418-419

U

UCASE.ASM listing, 134-135
Unit A listing, 243-244
unit directories, 14
Unit GrafRead listing, 312-315
Unit One listing, 242
Unit Three listing, 243
Unit to Access OBJ Data listing, 251-252
Unit to Echo Screen and Printer listing,
    183-185
Unit Two listing, 242-243
Unknown identifier message, 44
Unpack Example & Utility Archives: option, 9
UNPACK.COM file, 8
Update Turbo Pascal V4.0 to V 5.0 option,
    8-9
user-loaded fonts, 195
Using NOPs listing, 145-146
utilities
    BINOBJ, 245-246
    linking, 105-138
    overlay, 255-259
    program, 3

V

value parameters, 70-71
    with inline code, 152
Var-String Checking {$V+} directive, 18
variable identifiers, with inline code, 156-157

Variable Parameter Access with Inline Code
    listing, 156-157
Variable Versus Pointer Parameters listing,
    158
variables
    accessing, 155-156
    Boolean, 206-208
    EmmMaxAvail, 346
    EMS global, 354
    FileMode, 365
    global, 67-70
    inline, 157
    local, 72-74
    modifying, 101-102
    PathToDrivers, 301
    pointer, 157-158
    watch, 43-45
    watch formatting parameters, 45
    with inline code, 155-156
VGA
    mode patch, 433
    palette, 329
video attribute byte, 266
video display data area
    functions, 338
    memory locations, 338
video memory
    using, 265-271
    writing to, 264
video mode
    determining, 264-265
        current, 338-339
Video Rental program listing, 296-299
Virtual Method Table (VMT), 76-78, 390,
    415
virtual
    methods, 79, 414
    objects, 76-77
VMT Mixup listing, 398

W

watch expressions, 44
watch variables, 43-45
    deleting, 45
    editing, 45
    formatting parameters, 45
    values for, 44
Watch window, 57-59
window borders, 263
    drawing, 274-276
window procedure, 261-262
window stack, 271
window stack operations, 272-274
windows tools, adding sound to, 277-278
windows
    Add Watch, 40
    Breakpoint, 53-54
    Call Stack, 46-47
    editing tools, 285-286
    Evaluate, 48-51
    input field, 287-289
    Inspect, 57-59
    Options/Environment, 15
    processing characters, 289-291
    requirements, 261-262
    reverse video field, 286-287
    storing text under, 262-263
    titles on, 277
    Watch, 57-59
WindowSound routine, 262
WindTool Assembler Code listing, 267-270
WindTool Unit Code listing, 279-285
WINDTOOL.OBJ file, 278
WORD-aligned, 68
Write statement, 178, 180
Writeln statement, 178

More Computer Knowledge from Que

Using Turbo Pascal

by Michael Yester

Excellent in-depth coverage of Turbo Pascal through Version 5.5! This exciting combination of step-by-step tutorial and lasting reference teaches you the Pascal language and protocol. Also included are disciplined programming techniques for the most effective programming results.

Order #883
$21.95 USA
0-88022-396-0, 724 pp.

Turbo Pascal Programmer's Toolkit

by Tom Rugg and Phil Feldman

Programming experts Rugg and Feldman provide you with dozens of Turbo Pascal programs and subprograms in this book/disk set with ready-to-run applications. Includes routines for input/output, sorting and searching, and data manipulation. Covers Turbo Pascal through Version 5.5.

Order #978
$39.95 USA
0-88022-447-9, 650 pp.

Using Assembly Language

by Allen Wyatt

This practical text provides thorough coverage of all assembly language concepts! You'll learn how to develop, manage and debug routines, plus how to access BIOS and DOS services. In addition the book explains step-by-step how you can interface assembly language with other programming languages—including Pascal, C, and BASIC. An outstanding resource!

Order #107
$24.95 USA
0-88022-297-2, 746 pp.

DOS Programmer's Reference, 2nd Edition

by Terry Dettmann

A nuts-and-bolts guide for applications programmers! This valuable text covers DOS Version 4, and presents a useful combination of tutorial and reference information. Includes coverage of DOS functions, BIOS functions, and using DOS with other programming languages. A must for experienced applications programmers!

Order #1006
$27.95 USA
0-88022-458-4, 850 pp.

Free Catalog!

Mail us this registration form today, and we'll send you a free catalog featuring Que's complete line of best-selling books.

Name of Book _____

Name _____

Title _____

Phone ( ) _____

Company _____

Address _____

City _____

State _____ ZIP _____

Please check the appropriate answers:

1. Where did you buy your Que book?
   - ☐ Bookstore (name: _____)
   - ☐ Computer store (name: _____)
   - ☐ Catalog (name: _____)
   - ☐ Direct from Que
   - ☐ Other: _____

2. How many computer books do you buy a year?
   - ☐ 1 or less
   - ☐ 2-5
   - ☐ 6-10
   - ☐ More than 10

3. How many Que books do you own?
   - ☐ 1
   - ☐ 2-5
   - ☐ 6-10
   - ☐ More than 10

4. How long have you been using this software?
   - ☐ Less than 6 months
   - ☐ 6 months to 1 year
   - ☐ 1-3 years
   - ☐ More than 3 years

5. What influenced your purchase of this Que book?
   - ☐ Personal recommendation
   - ☐ Advertisement
   - ☐ In-store display
   - ☐ Price
   - ☐ Que catalog
   - ☐ Que mailing
   - ☐ Que's reputation
   - ☐ Other: _____

6. How would you rate the overall content of the book?
   - ☐ Very good
   - ☐ Good
   - ☐ Satisfactory
   - ☐ Poor

7. What do you like *best* about this Que book?
   _____
   _____

8. What do you like *least* about this Que book?
   _____
   _____

9. Did you buy this book with your personal funds?
   - ☐ Yes   ☐ No

10. Please feel free to list any other comments you may have about this Que book.
    _____
    _____
    _____

Que

Order Your Que Books Today!

Name _____

Title _____

Company _____

City _____

State _____ ZIP _____

Phone No. ( ) _____

Method of Payment:

Check ☐ (Please enclose in envelope.)

Charge My: VISA ☐   MasterCard ☐

American Express ☐

Charge # _____

Expiration Date _____

Order No.	Title	Qty.	Price	Total

You can **FAX** your order to **1-317-573-2583**. Or call **1-800-428-5331, ext. ORDR** to order direct.
Please add $2.50 per title for shipping and handling.

Subtotal _____

Shipping & Handling _____

Total _____

Que

NO POSTAGE
NECESSARY
IF MAILED
IN THE
UNITED STATES

BUSINESS REPLY MAIL
First Class Permit No. 9918   Indianapolis, IN

Postage will be paid by addressee

11711 N. College
Carmel, IN 46032